Introduction to Probability and Statistics Using R

G. Jay Kerns

FIRST EDITION

IPSUR: Introduction to Probability and Statistics Using R

ISBN: 978-0-557-24979-4

Date: July 28, 2010

Contents

Preface

This book was expanded from lecture materials I use in a one semester upper-division undergraduate course entitled *Probability and Statistics* at Youngstown State University. Those lecture materials, in turn, were based on notes that I transcribed as a graduate student at Bowling Green State University. The course for which the materials were written is 50-50 Probability and Statistics, and the attendees include mathematics, engineering, and computer science majors (among others). The catalog prerequisites for the course are a full year of calculus.

The book can be subdivided into three basic parts. The first part includes the introductions and elementary *descriptive statistics*; I want the students to be knee-deep in data right out of the gate. The second part is the study of *probability*, which begins at the basics of sets and the equally likely model, journeys past discrete/continuous random variables, and continues through to multivariate distributions. The chapter on sampling distributions paves the way to the third part, which is *inferential statistics*. This last part includes point and interval estimation, hypothesis testing, and finishes with introductions to selected topics in applied statistics.

I usually only have time in one semester to cover a small subset of this book. I cover the material in Chapter 2 in a class period that is supplemented by a take-home assignment for the students. I spend a lot of time on Data Description, Probability, Discrete, and Continuous Distributions. I mention selected facts from Multivariate Distributions in passing, and discuss the meaty parts of Sampling Distributions before moving right along to Estimation (which is another chapter I dwell on considerably). Hypothesis Testing goes faster after all of the previous work, and by that time the end of the semester is in sight. I normally choose one or two final chapters (sometimes three) from the remaining to survey, and regret at the end that I did not have the chance to cover more.

In an attempt to be correct I have included material in this book which I would normally not mention during the course of a standard lecture. For instance, I normally do not highlight the intricacies of measure theory or integrability conditions when speaking to the class. Moreover, I often stray from the matrix approach to multiple linear regression because many of my students have not yet been formally trained in linear algebra. That being said, it is important to me for the students to hold something in their hands which acknowledges the world of mathematics and statistics beyond the classroom, and which may be useful to them for many semesters to come. It also mirrors my own experience as a student.

The vision for this document is a more or less self contained, essentially complete, correct, introductory textbook. There should be plenty of exercises for the student, with full solutions for some, and no solutions for others (so that the instructor may assign them for grading). By `Sweave`'s dynamic nature it is possible to write randomly generated exercises and I had planned to implement this idea already throughout the book. Alas, there are only 24 hours in a day. Look for more in future editions.

Seasoned readers will be able to detect my origins: *Probability and Statistical Inference* by Hogg and Tanis [44], *Statistical Inference* by Casella and Berger [13], and *Theory of Point Estimation/Testing Statistical Hypotheses* by Lehmann [59, 58]. I highly recommend each of those books to every reader of this one. Some R books with "introductory" in the title that I recommend are *Introductory Statistics with R* by Dalgaard [19] and *Using R for Introductory Statistics* by Verzani [87]. Surely there are many, many other good introductory books about R, but frankly, I have tried to steer clear of them for the past year or so to avoid any undue influence on my own writing.

I would like to make special mention of two other books: *Introduction to Statistical Thought* by Michael Lavine [56] and *Introduction to Probability* by Grinstead and Snell [37]. Both of these books are *free* and are what ultimately convinced me to release IPSUR under a free license, too.

Please bear in mind that the title of this book is "Introduction to Probability and Statistics Using R", and not "Introduction to R Using Probability and Statistics", nor even "Introduction to Probability and Statistics and R Using Words". The people at the party are Probability and Statistics; the handshake is R. There are several important topics about R which some individuals will feel are underdeveloped, glossed over, or wantonly omitted. Some will feel the same way about the probabilistic and/or statistical content. Still others will just want to learn R and skip all of the mathematics.

Despite any misgivings: here it is, warts and all. I humbly invite said individuals to take this book, with the GNU Free Documentation License (GNU-FDL) in hand, and make it better. In that spirit there are at least a few ways in my view in which this book could be improved.

Better data. The data analyzed in this book are almost entirely from the `datasets` package in base R, and here is why:

1. I made a conscious effort to minimize dependence on contributed packages,
2. The data are instantly available, already in the correct format, so we need not take time to manage them, and
3. The data are *real*.

I made no attempt to choose data sets that would be interesting to the students; rather, data were chosen for their potential to convey a statistical point. Many of the data sets are decades old or more (for instance, the data used to introduce simple linear regression are the speeds and stopping distances of cars in the 1920's).

In a perfect world with infinite time I would research and contribute recent, *real* data in a context crafted to engage the students in *every* example. One day I hope to stumble over said time. In the meantime, I will add new data sets incrementally as time permits.

More proofs. I would like to include more proofs for the sake of completeness (I understand that some people would not consider more proofs to be improvement). Many proofs have been skipped entirely, and I am not aware of any rhyme or reason to the current omissions. I will add more when I get a chance.

More and better graphics: I have not used the `ggplot2` package [90] because I do not know how to use it yet. It is on my to-do list.

More and better exercises: There are only a few exercises in the first edition simply because I have not had time to write more. I have toyed with the `exams` package [38] and I believe that it is a right way to move forward. As I learn more about what the package can do I would like to incorporate it into later editions of this book.

About This Document

IPSUR contains many interrelated parts: the ***Document***, the ***Program***, the ***Package***, and the ***Ancillaries***. In short, the *Document* is what you are reading right now. The *Program* provides an efficient means to modify the Document. The *Package* is an R package that houses the Program and the Document. Finally, the *Ancillaries* are extra materials that reside in the Package and were produced by the Program to supplement use of the Document. We briefly describe each of them in turn.

The Document

The *Document* is that which you are reading right now – IPSUR's *raison d'être*. There are transparent copies (nonproprietary text files) and opaque copies (everything else). See the GNU-FDL in Appendix B for more precise language and details.

`IPSUR.tex` is a transparent copy of the Document to be typeset with a LaTeX distribution such as MikTeX or TeX Live. Any reader is free to modify the Document and release the modified version in accordance with the provisions of the GNU-FDL. Note that this file cannot be used to generate a randomized copy of the Document. Indeed, in its released form it is only capable of typesetting the exact version of IPSUR which you are currently reading. Furthermore, the `.tex` file is unable to generate any of the ancillary materials.

`IPSUR-xxx.eps`, `IPSUR-xxx.pdf` are the image files for every graph in the Document. These are needed when typesetting with LaTeX.

`IPSUR.pdf` is an opaque copy of the Document. This is the file that instructors would likely want to distribute to students.

`IPSUR.dvi` is another opaque copy of the Document in a different file format.

The Program

The *Program* includes `IPSUR.lyx` and its nephew `IPSUR.Rnw`; the purpose of each is to give individuals a way to quickly customize the Document for their particular purpose(s).

`IPSUR.lyx` is the source LyX file for the Program, released under the GNU General Public License (GNU GPL) Version 3. This file is opened, modified, and compiled with LyX, a sophisticated open-source document processor, and may be used (together with `Sweave`) to generate a randomized, modified copy of the Document with brand new data sets for some of the exercises and the solution manuals (in the Second Edition). Additionally, LyX can easily activate/deactivate entire blocks of the document, *e.g.* the proofs of the theorems, the student solutions to the exercises, or the instructor answers to the problems, so that the new author may choose which sections (s)he would like to include in the final Document (again, Second Edition). The `IPSUR.lyx` file is all that a person needs (in addition to a properly configured system – see Appendix G) to generate/compile/export to all of the other formats described above and below, which includes the ancillary materials `IPSUR.Rdata` and `IPSUR.R`.

`IPSUR.Rnw` is another form of the source code for the Program, also released under the GNU GPL Version 3. It was produced by exporting `IPSUR.lyx` into R/Sweave format (`.Rnw`).

This file may be processed with Sweave to generate a randomized copy of `IPSUR.tex` – a transparent copy of the Document – together with the ancillary materials `IPSUR.Rdata` and `IPSUR.R`. Please note, however, that `IPSUR.Rnw` is just a simple text file which does not support many of the extra features that LyX offers such as WYSIWYM editing, instantly (de)activating branches of the manuscript, and more.

The Package

There is a contributed package on `CRAN`, called `IPSUR`. The package affords many advantages, one being that it houses the Document in an easy-to-access medium. Indeed, a student can have the Document at his/her fingertips with only three commands:

```
> install.packages("IPSUR")
> library(IPSUR)
> read(IPSUR)
```

Another advantage goes hand in hand with the Program's license; since IPSUR is free, the source code must be freely available to anyone that wants it. A package hosted on `CRAN` allows the author to obey the license by default.

A much more important advantage is that the excellent facilities at R-Forge are building and checking the package daily against patched and development versions of the absolute latest pre-release of R. If any problems surface then I will know about it within 24 hours.

And finally, suppose there is some sort of problem. The package structure makes it *incredibly* easy for me to distribute bug-fixes and corrected typographical errors. As an author I can make my corrections, upload them to the repository at R-Forge, and they will be reflected *worldwide* within hours. We aren't in Kansas anymore, Dorothy.

Ancillary Materials

These are extra materials that accompany IPSUR. They reside in the `/etc` subdirectory of the package source.

`IPSUR.RData` is a saved image of the R workspace at the completion of the Sweave processing of IPSUR. It can be loaded into memory with File ▹ Load Workspace or with the command `load("/path/to/IPSUR.Rdata")`. Either method will make every single object in the file immediately available and in memory. In particular, the data BLANK from Exercise BLANK in Chapter BLANK on page BLANK will be loaded. Type BLANK at the command line (after loading `IPSUR.RData`) to see for yourself.

`IPSUR.R` is the exported R code from `IPSUR.Rnw`. With this script, literally every R command from the entirety of IPSUR can be resubmitted at the command line.

Notation

We use the notation `x` or `stem.leaf` notation to denote objects, functions, *etc.*. The sequence "Statistics ▹ Summaries ▹ Active Dataset" means to click the Statistics menu item, next click the Summaries submenu item, and finally click Active Dataset.

Acknowledgements

This book would not have been possible without the firm mathematical and statistical foundation provided by the professors at Bowling Green State University, including Drs. Gábor Székely, Craig Zirbel, Arjun K. Gupta, Hanfeng Chen, Truc Nguyen, and James Albert. I would also like to thank Drs. Neal Carothers and Kit Chan.

I would also like to thank my colleagues at Youngstown State University for their support. In particular, I would like to thank Dr. G. Andy Chang for showing me what it means to be a statistician.

I would like to thank Richard Heiberger for his insightful comments and improvements to several points and displays in the manuscript.

Finally, and most importantly, I would like to thank my wife for her patience and understanding while I worked hours, days, months, and years on a *free book*. In retrospect, I can't believe I ever got away with it.

List of Figures

List of Tables

Chapter 1

An Introduction to Probability and Statistics

This chapter has proved to be the hardest to write, by far. The trouble is that there is so much to say – and so many people have already said it so much better than I could. When I get something I like I will release it here.

In the meantime, there is a lot of information already available to a person with an Internet connection. I recommend to start at Wikipedia, which is not a flawless resource but it has the main ideas with links to reputable sources.

In my lectures I usually tell stories about Fisher, Galton, Gauss, Laplace, Quetelet, and the Chevalier de Mere.

1.1 Probability

The common folklore is that probability has been around for millennia but did not gain the attention of mathematicians until approximately 1654 when the Chevalier de Mere had a question regarding the fair division of a game's payoff to the two players, if the game had to end prematurely.

1.2 Statistics

Statistics concerns data; their collection, analysis, and interpretation. In this book we distinguish between two types of statistics: descriptive and inferential.

Descriptive statistics concerns the summarization of data. We have a data set and we would like to describe the data set in multiple ways. Usually this entails calculating numbers from the data, called descriptive measures, such as percentages, sums, averages, and so forth.

Inferential statistics does more. There is an inference associated with the data set, a conclusion drawn about the population from which the data originated.

I would like to mention that there are two schools of thought of statistics: frequentist and bayesian. The difference between the schools is related to how the two groups interpret the underlying probability (see Section 4.3). The frequentist school gained a lot of ground among statisticians due in large part to the work of Fisher, Neyman, and Pearson in the early twentieth century. That dominance lasted until inexpensive computing power became widely available; nowadays the bayesian school is garnering more attention and at an increasing rate.

This book is devoted mostly to the frequentist viewpoint because that is how I was trained, with the conspicuous exception of Sections 4.8 and 7.3. I plan to add more bayesian material in later editions of this book.

Chapter Exercises

Chapter 2

An Introduction to R

2.1 Downloading and Installing R

The instructions for obtaining R largely depend on the user's hardware and operating system. The R Project has written an R Installation and Administration manual with complete, precise instructions about what to do, together with all sorts of additional information. The following is just a primer to get a person started.

2.1.1 Installing R

Visit one of the links below to download the latest version of R for your operating system:

Microsoft Windows: `http://cran.r-project.org/bin/windows/base/`

MacOS: `http://cran.r-project.org/bin/macosx/`

Linux: `http://cran.r-project.org/bin/linux/`

On Microsoft Windows, click the `R-x.y.z.exe` installer to start installation. When it asks for "Customized startup options", specify Yes. In the next window, be sure to select the SDI (single document interface) option; this is useful later when we discuss three dimensional plots with the `rgl` package [1].

Installing R on a USB drive (Windows) With this option you can use R portably and without administrative privileges. There is an entry in the R for Windows FAQ about this. Here is the procedure I use:

1. Download the Windows installer above and start installation as usual. When it asks *where* to install, navigate to the top-level directory of the USB drive instead of the default `C` drive.
2. When it asks whether to modify the Windows registry, uncheck the box; we do NOT want to tamper with the registry.
3. After installation, change the name of the folder from `R-x.y.z` to just plain `R`. (Even quicker: do this in step 1.)
4. Download the following shortcut to the top-level directory of the USB drive, right beside the `R` folder, not inside the folder.

http://ipsur.r-forge.r-project.org/book/download/R.exe

Use the downloaded shortcut to run R.

Steps 3 and 4 are not required but save you the trouble of navigating to the `R-x.y.z/bin` directory to double-click `Rgui.exe` every time you want to run the program. It is useless to create your own shortcut to `Rgui.exe`. Windows does not allow shortcuts to have relative paths; they always have a drive letter associated with them. So if you make your own shortcut and plug your USB drive into some *other* machine that happens to assign your drive a different letter, then your shortcut will no longer be pointing to the right place.

2.1.2 Installing and Loading Add-on Packages

There are *base* packages (which come with R automatically), and *contributed* packages (which must be downloaded for installation). For example, on the version of R being used for this document the default base packages loaded at startup are

```
> getOption("defaultPackages")
[1] "datasets"  "utils"     "grDevices" "graphics"  "stats"     "methods"
```

The base packages are maintained by a select group of volunteers, called "R Core". In addition to the base packages, there are literally thousands of additional contributed packages written by individuals all over the world. These are stored worldwide on mirrors of the Comprehensive R Archive Network, or `CRAN` for short. Given an active Internet connection, anybody is free to download and install these packages and even inspect the source code.

To install a package named `foo`, open up R and type `install.packages("foo")`. To install `foo` and additionally install all of the other packages on which `foo` depends, instead type `install.packages("foo", depends = TRUE)`.

The general command `install.packages()` will (on most operating systems) open a window containing a huge list of available packages; simply choose one or more to install.

No matter how many packages are installed onto the system, each one must first be loaded for use with the `library` function. For instance, the `foreign` package [18] contains all sorts of functions needed to import data sets into R from other software such as SPSS, SAS, *etc.*. But none of those functions will be available until the command `library(foreign)` is issued.

Type `library()` at the command prompt (described below) to see a list of all available packages in your library.

For complete, precise information regarding installation of R and add-on packages, see the R Installation and Administration manual, `http://cran.r-project.org/manuals.html`.

2.2 Communicating with R

One line at a time This is the most basic method and is the first one that beginners will use.

RGui (Microsoft® Windows)

Terminal

Emacs/ESS, XEmacs

JGR

Multiple lines at a time For longer programs (called *scripts*) there is too much code to write all at once at the command prompt. Furthermore, for longer scripts it is convenient to be able to only modify a certain piece of the script and run it again in R. Programs called *script editors* are specially designed to aid the communication and code writing process. They have all sorts of helpful features including R syntax highlighting, automatic code completion, delimiter matching, and dynamic help on the R functions as they are being written. Even more, they often have all of the text editing features of programs like Microsoft® Word. Lastly, most script editors are fully customizable in the sense that the user can customize the appearance of the interface to choose what colors to display, when to display them, and how to display them.

R Editor (Windows): In Microsoft® Windows, RGui has its own built-in script editor, called R Editor. From the console window, select File ▹ New Script. A script window opens, and the lines of code can be written in the window. When satisfied with the code, the user highlights all of the commands and presses Ctrl+R. The commands are automatically run at once in R and the output is shown. To save the script for later, click File ▹ Save as... in R Editor. The script can be reopened later with File ▹ Open Script... in RGui. Note that R Editor does not have the fancy syntax highlighting that the others do.

RWinEdt: This option is coordinated with WinEdt for LaTeX and has additional features such as code highlighting, remote sourcing, and a ton of other things. However, one first needs to download and install a shareware version of another program, WinEdt, which is only free for a while – pop-up windows will eventually appear that ask for a registration code. RWinEdt is nevertheless a very fine choice if you already own WinEdt or are planning to purchase it in the near future.

Tinn-R/Sciviews-K: This one is completely free and has all of the above mentioned options and more. It is simple enough to use that the user can virtually begin working with it immediately after installation. But Tinn-R proper is only available for Microsoft® Windows operating systems. If you are on MacOS or Linux, a comparable alternative is Sci-Views - Komodo Edit.

Emacs/ESS: Emacs is an all purpose text editor. It can do absolutely anything with respect to modifying, searching, editing, and manipulating, text. And if Emacs can't do it, then you can write a program that extends Emacs to do it. Once such extension is called *ESS*, which stands for *E*macs *S*peaks *S*tatistics. With ESS a person can speak to R, do all of the tricks that the other script editors offer, and much, much, more. Please see the following for installation details, documentation, reference cards, and a whole lot more:

`http://ess.r-project.org`

Fair warning: if you want to try Emacs and if you grew up with Microsoft® Windows or Macintosh, then you are going to need to relearn everything you thought you knew about computers your whole life. (Or, since Emacs is completely customizable, you can reconfigure Emacs to behave the way you want.) I have personally experienced this transformation and I will never go back.

JGR (read "Jaguar"): This one has the bells and whistles of RGui plus it is based on Java, so it works on multiple operating systems. It has its own script editor like R Editor but with additional features such as syntax highlighting and code-completion. If you do not use Microsoft® Windows (or even if you do) you definitely want to check out this one.

Kate, Bluefish, *etc.* There are literally dozens of other text editors available, many of them free, and each has its own (dis)advantages. I only have mentioned the ones with which I have had substantial personal experience and have enjoyed at some point. Play around, and let me know what you find.

Graphical User Interfaces (GUIs) By the word "GUI" I mean an interface in which the user communicates with R by way of points-and-clicks in a menu of some sort. Again, there are many, many options and I only mention ones that I have used and enjoyed. Some of the other more popular script editors can be downloaded from the R-Project website at `http://www.sciviews.org`. On the left side of the screen (under **Projects**) there are several choices available.

R Commander provides a point-and-click interface to many basic statistical tasks. It is called the "Commander" because every time one makes a selection from the menus, the code corresponding to the task is listed in the output window. One can take this code, copy-and-paste it to a text file, then re-run it again at a later time without the R Commander's assistance. It is well suited for the introductory level. `Rcmdr` also allows for user-contributed "Plugins" which are separate packages on `CRAN` that add extra functionality to the `Rcmdr` package. The plugins are typically named with the prefix `RcmdrPlugin` to make them easy to identify in the `CRAN` package list. One such plugin is the `RcmdrPlugin.IPSUR` package which accompanies this text.

Poor Man's GUI is an alternative to the `Rcmdr` which is based on GTk instead of Tcl/Tk. It has been a while since I used it but I remember liking it very much when I did. One thing that stood out was that the user could drag-and-drop data sets for plots. See here for more information: `http://wiener.math.csi.cuny.edu/pmg/`.

Rattle is a data mining toolkit which was designed to manage/analyze very large data sets, but it provides enough other general functionality to merit mention here. See [91] for more information.

Deducer is relatively new and shows promise from what I have seen, but I have not actually used it in the classroom yet.

2.3 Basic R Operations and Concepts

The R developers have written an introductory document entitled "An Introduction to R". There is a sample session included which shows what basic interaction with R looks like. I recommend that all new users of R read that document, but bear in mind that there are concepts mentioned which will be unfamiliar to the beginner.

Below are some of the most basic operations that can be done with R. Almost every book about R begins with a section like the one below; look around to see all sorts of things that can be done at this most basic level.

2.3.1 Arithmetic

```
> 2 + 3          # add
[1] 5
```

```
> 4 * 5 / 6    # multiply and divide
[1] 3.333333
> 7^8          # 7 to the 8th power
[1] 5764801
```

Notice the comment character #. Anything typed after a # symbol is ignored by R. We know that 20/6 is a repeating decimal, but the above example shows only 7 digits. We can change the number of digits displayed with `options`:

```
> options(digits = 16)
> 10/3                 # see more digits
[1] 3.333333333333333
> sqrt(2)              # square root
[1] 1.414213562373095
> exp(1)               # Euler's constant, e
[1] 2.718281828459045
> pi
[1] 3.141592653589793
> options(digits = 7)  # back to default
```

Note that it is possible to set `digits` up to 22, but setting them over 16 is not recommended (the extra significant digits are not necessarily reliable). Above notice the `sqrt` function for square roots and the `exp` function for powers of e, Euler's number.

2.3.2 Assignment, Object names, and Data types

It is often convenient to assign numbers and values to variables (objects) to be used later. The proper way to assign values to a variable is with the <- operator (with a space on either side). The = symbol works too, but it is recommended by the R masters to reserve = for specifying arguments to functions (discussed later). In this book we will follow their advice and use <- for assignment. Once a variable is assigned, its value can be printed by simply entering the variable name by itself.

```
> x <- 7*41/pi    # don't see the calculated value
> x               # take a look
[1] 91.35494
```

When choosing a variable name you can use letters, numbers, dots "`.`", or underscore "`_`" characters. You cannot use mathematical operators, and a leading dot may not be followed by a number. Examples of valid names are: `x`, `x1`, `y.value`, and `y_hat`. (More precisely, the set of allowable characters in object names depends on one's particular system and locale; see An Introduction to R for more discussion on this.)

Objects can be of many *types*, *modes*, and *classes*. At this level, it is not necessary to investigate all of the intricacies of the respective types, but there are some with which you need to become familiar:

integer: the values 0, ±1, ±2, ...; these are represented exactly by R.

double: real numbers (rational and irrational); these numbers are not represented exactly (save integers or fractions with a denominator that is a multiple of 2, see [85]).

character: elements that are wrapped with pairs of " or ';

logical: includes `TRUE`, `FALSE`, and `NA` (which are reserved words); the `NA` stands for "not available", *i.e.*, a missing value.

You can determine an object's type with the `typeof` function. In addition to the above, there is the `complex` data type:

```
> sqrt(-1)                # isn't defined
[1] NaN
> sqrt(-1+0i)             # is defined
[1] 0+1i
> sqrt(as.complex(-1))  # same thing
[1] 0+1i
> (0 + 1i)^2              # should be -1
[1] -1+0i
> typeof((0 + 1i)^2)
[1] "complex"
```

Note that you can just type `(1i)^2` to get the same answer. The `NaN` stands for "not a number"; it is represented internally as `double`.

2.3.3 Vectors

All of this time we have been manipulating vectors of length 1. Now let us move to vectors with multiple entries.

Entering data vectors

1. `c`: If you would like to enter the data `74,31,95,61,76,34,23,54,96` into R, you may create a data vector with the `c` function (which is short for *concatenate*).

   ```
   > x <- c(74, 31, 95, 61, 76, 34, 23, 54, 96)
   > x

   [1] 74 31 95 61 76 34 23 54 96
   ```

   The elements of a vector are usually coerced by R to the the most general type of any of the elements, so if you do `c(1, "2")` then the result will be `c("1", "2")`.

2. scan: This method is useful when the data are stored somewhere else. For instance, you may type `x <- scan()` at the command prompt and R will display `1:` to indicate that it is waiting for the first data value. Type a value and press Enter, at which point R will display `2:`, and so forth. Note that entering an empty line stops the scan. This method is especially handy when you have a column of values, say, stored in a text file or spreadsheet. You may copy and paste them all at the `1:` prompt, and R will store all of the values instantly in the vector `x`.

3. repeated data; regular patterns: the `seq` function will generate all sorts of sequences of numbers. It has the arguments `from`, `to`, `by`, and `length.out` which can be set in concert with one another. We will do a couple of examples to show you how it works.

```
> seq(from = 1, to = 5)

[1] 1 2 3 4 5

> seq(from = 2, by = -0.1, length.out = 4)

[1] 2.0 1.9 1.8 1.7
```

   Note that we can get the first line much quicker with the colon operator `:`

```
> 1:5

[1] 1 2 3 4 5
```

   The vector LETTERS has the 26 letters of the English alphabet in uppercase and `letters` has all of them in lowercase.

Indexing data vectors Sometimes we do not want the whole vector, but just a piece of it. We can access the intermediate parts with the `[]` operator. Observe (with `x` defined above)

```
> x[1]
[1] 74
> x[2:4]
[1] 31 95 61
> x[c(1, 3, 4, 8)]
[1] 74 95 61 54
> x[-c(1, 3, 4, 8)]
[1] 31 76 34 23 96
```

Notice that we used the minus sign to specify those elements that we do *not* want.

```
> LETTERS[1:5]
[1] "A" "B" "C" "D" "E"
> letters[-(6:24)]
[1] "a" "b" "c" "d" "e" "y" "z"
```

2.3.4 Functions and Expressions

A function takes arguments as input and returns an object as output. There are functions to do all sorts of things. We show some examples below.

```
> x <- 1:5
> sum(x)

[1] 15

> length(x)

[1] 5

> min(x)

[1] 1

> mean(x)        # sample mean

[1] 3

> sd(x)          # sample standard deviation

[1] 1.581139
```

It will not be long before the user starts to wonder how a particular function is doing its job, and since R is open-source, anybody is free to look under the hood of a function to see how things are calculated. For detailed instructions see the article "Accessing the Sources" by Uwe Ligges [60]. In short:

1. Type the name of the function without any parentheses or arguments. If you are lucky then the code for the entire function will be printed, right there looking at you. For instance, suppose that we would like to see how the `intersect` function works:

```
> intersect

function (x, y)
{
    y <- as.vector(y)
    unique(y[match(as.vector(x), y, 0L)])
}
<environment: namespace:base>
```

2. If instead it shows `UseMethod("`*something*`")` then you will need to choose the *class* of the object to be inputted and next look at the *method* that will be *dispatched* to the object. For instance, typing `rev` says

```
> rev

function (x)
UseMethod("rev")
<environment: namespace:base>
```

The output is telling us that there are multiple methods associated with the `rev` function. To see what these are, type

```
> methods(rev)

[1] rev.default      rev.dendrogram*

   Non-visible functions are asterisked
```

Now we learn that there are two different `rev(x)` functions, only one of which being chosen at each call depending on what `x` is. There is one for `dendrogram` objects and a `default` method for everything else. Simply type the name to see what each method does. For example, the `default` method can be viewed with

```
> rev.default

function (x)
if (length(x)) x[length(x):1L] else x
<environment: namespace:base>
```

3. Some functions are hidden by a *namespace* (see An Introduction to R [85]), and are not visible on the first try. For example, if we try to look at the code for `wilcox.test` (see Chapter 15) we get the following:

```
> wilcox.test

function (x, ...)
UseMethod("wilcox.test")
<environment: namespace:stats>

> methods(wilcox.test)

[1] wilcox.test.default* wilcox.test.formula*

   Non-visible functions are asterisked
```

If we were to try `wilcox.test.default` we would get a "not found" error, because it is hidden behind the namespace for the package `stats` (shown in the last line when we tried `wilcox.test`). In cases like these we prefix the package name to the front of the function name with three colons; the command `stats:::wilcox.test.default` will show the source code, omitted here for brevity.

4. If it shows `.Internal(`*something*`)` or `.Primitive("`*something*`")`, then it will be necessary to download the source code of R (which is *not* a binary version with an `.exe` extension) and search inside the code there. See Ligges [60] for more discussion on this. An example is `exp`:

```
> exp

function (x)  .Primitive("exp")
```

Be warned that most of the `.Internal` functions are written in other computer languages which the beginner may not understand, at least initially.

2.4 Getting Help

When you are using R, it will not take long before you find yourself needing help. Fortunately, R has extensive help resources and you should immediately become familiar with them. Begin by clicking Help on Rgui. The following options are available.

- **Console**: gives useful shortcuts, for instance, Ctrl+L, to clear the R console screen.
- **FAQ on R**: frequently asked questions concerning general R operation.
- **FAQ on R for Windows**: frequently asked questions about R, tailored to the Microsoft Windows operating system.
- **Manuals**: technical manuals about all features of the R system including installation, the complete language definition, and add-on packages.
- **R functions (text)...**: use this if you know the *exact* name of the function you want to know more about, for example, `mean` or `plot`. Typing `mean` in the window is equivalent to typing `help("mean")` at the command line, or more simply, `?mean`. Note that this method only works if the function of interest is contained in a package that is already loaded into the search path with `library`.
- **HTML Help**: use this to browse the manuals with point-and-click links. It also has a Search Engine & Keywords for searching the help page titles, with point-and-click links for the search results. This is possibly the best help method for beginners. It can be started from the command line with the command `help.start()`.
- **Search help...**: use this if you do not know the exact name of the function of interest, or if the function is in a package that has not been loaded yet. For example, you may enter `plo` and a text window will return listing all the help files with an alias, concept, or title matching '`plo`' using regular expression matching; it is equivalent to typing `help.search("plo")` at the command line. The advantage is that you do not need to know the exact name of the function; the disadvantage is that you cannot point-and-click the results. Therefore, one may wish to use the HTML Help search engine instead. An equivalent way is `??plo` at the command line.
- **search.r-project.org...**: this will search for words in help lists and email archives of the R Project. It can be very useful for finding other questions that other users have asked.
- **Apropos...**: use this for more sophisticated partial name matching of functions. See `?apropos` for details.

On the help pages for a function there are sometimes "Examples" listed at the bottom of the page, which will work if copy-pasted at the command line (unless marked otherwise). The `example` function will run the code automatically, skipping the intermediate step. For instance, we may try `example(mean)` to see a few examples of how the `mean` function works.

2.4.1 R Help Mailing Lists

There are several mailing lists associated with R, and there is a huge community of people that read and answer questions related to R. See here `http://www.r-project.org/mail.html`

for an idea of what is available. Particularly pay attention to the bottom of the page which lists several special interest groups (SIGs) related to R.

Bear in mind that R is free software, which means that it was written by volunteers, and the people that frequent the mailing lists are also volunteers who are not paid by customer support fees. Consequently, if you want to use the mailing lists for free advice then you must adhere to some basic etiquette, or else you may not get a reply, or even worse, you may receive a reply which is a bit less cordial than you are used to. Below are a few considerations:

1. Read the FAQ (`http://cran.r-project.org/faqs.html`). Note that there are different FAQs for different operating systems. You should read these now, even without a question at the moment, to learn a lot about the idiosyncrasies of R.

2. Search the archives. Even if your question is not a FAQ, there is a very high likelihood that your question has been asked before on the mailing list. If you want to know about topic `foo`, then you can do `RSiteSearch("foo")` to search the mailing list archives (and the online help) for it.

3. Do a Google search and an `RSeek.org` search.

If your question is not a FAQ, has not been asked on R-help before, and does not yield to a Google (or alternative) search, then, and only then, should you even consider writing to R-help. Below are a few additional considerations.

1. **Read the posting guide (`http://www.r-project.org/posting-guide.html`) before posting.** This will save you a lot of trouble and pain.

2. Get rid of the command prompts (>) from output. Readers of your message will take the text from your mail and copy-paste into an R session. If you make the readers' job easier then it will increase the likelihood of a response.

3. Questions are often related to a specific data set, and the best way to communicate the data is with a `dump` command. For instance, if your question involves data stored in a vector `x`, you can type `dump("x","")` at the command prompt and copy-paste the output into the body of your email message. Then the reader may easily copy-paste the message from your email into R and `x` will be available to him/her.

4. Sometimes the answer the question is related to the operating system used, the attached packages, or the exact version of R being used. The `sessionInfo()` command collects all of this information to be copy-pasted into an email (and the Posting Guide requests this information). See Appendix A for an example.

2.5 External Resources

There is a mountain of information on the Internet about R. Below are a few of the important ones.

The R Project for Statistical Computing: (`http://www.r-project.org/`) Go here first.

The Comprehensive R Archive Network: (`http://cran.r-project.org/`) This is where R is stored along with thousands of contributed packages. There are also loads of contributed information (books, tutorials, *etc.*). There are mirrors all over the world with duplicate information.

R-Forge: (http://r-forge.r-project.org/) This is another location where R packages are stored. Here you can find development code which has not yet been released to CRAN.

R Wiki: (http://wiki.r-project.org/rwiki/doku.php) There are many tips and tricks listed here. If you find a trick of your own, login and share it with the world.

Other: the R Graph Gallery (http://addictedtor.free.fr/graphiques/) and R Graphical Manual (http://bm2.genes.nig.ac.jp/RGM2/index.php) have literally thousands of graphs to peruse. RSeek (http://www.rseek.org) is a search engine based on Google specifically tailored for R queries.

2.6 Other Tips

It is unnecessary to retype commands repeatedly, since R remembers what you have recently entered on the command line. On the Microsoft® Windows RGui, to cycle through the previous commands just push the ↑ (up arrow) key. On Emacs/ESS the command is `M-p` (which means hold down the Alt button and press "p"). More generally, the command `history()` will show a whole list of recently entered commands.

- To find out what all variables are in the current work environment, use the commands `objects()` or `ls()`. These list all available objects in the workspace. If you wish to remove one or more variables, use `remove(var1, var2, var3)`, or more simply use `rm(var1, var2, var3)`, and to remove all objects use `rm(list = ls())`.

- Another use of `scan` is when you have a long list of numbers (separated by spaces or on different lines) already typed somewhere else, say in a text file. To enter all the data in one fell swoop, first highlight and copy the list of numbers to the Clipboard with Edit ▹ Copy (or by right-clicking and selecting Copy). Next type the `x <- scan()` command in the R console, and paste the numbers at the `1:` prompt with Edit ▹ Paste. All of the numbers will automatically be entered into the vector `x`.

- The command `Ctrl+l` clears the screen in the Microsoft® Windows RGui. The comparable command for Emacs/ESS is

- Once you use R for awhile there may be some commands that you wish to run automatically whenever R starts. These commands may be saved in a file called `Rprofile.site` which is usually in the `etc` folder, which lives in the R home directory (which on Microsoft® Windows usually is `C:\Program Files\R`). Alternatively, you can make a file `.Rprofile` to be stored in the user's home directory, or anywhere R is invoked. This allows for multiple configurations for different projects or users. See "Customizing the Environment" of *An Introduction to R* for more details.

- When exiting R the user is given the option to "save the workspace". I recommend that beginners DO NOT save the workspace when quitting. If Yes is selected, then all of the objects and data currently in R's memory is saved in a file located in the working directory called `.RData`. This file is then automatically loaded the next time R starts (in which case R will say `[previously saved workspace restored]`). This is a valuable feature for experienced users of R, but I find that it causes more trouble than it saves with beginners.

Chapter Exercises

Chapter 3

Data Description

In this chapter we introduce the different types of data that a statistician is likely to encounter, and in each subsection we give some examples of how to display the data of that particular type. Once we see how to display data distributions, we next introduce the basic properties of data distributions. We qualitatively explore several data sets. Once that we have intuitive properties of data sets, we next discuss how we may numerically measure and describe those properties with descriptive statistics.

What do I want them to know?

- different data types, such as quantitative versus qualitative, nominal versus ordinal, and discrete versus continuous
- basic graphical displays for assorted data types, and some of their (dis)advantages
- fundamental properties of data distributions, including center, spread, shape, and crazy observations
- methods to describe data (visually/numerically) with respect to the properties, and how the methods differ depending on the data type
- all of the above in the context of grouped data, and in particular, the concept of a factor

3.1 Types of Data

Loosely speaking, a datum is any piece of collected information, and a data set is a collection of data related to each other in some way. We will categorize data into five types and describe each in turn:

Quantitative data associated with a measurement of some quantity on an observational unit,

Qualitative data associated with some quality or property of the observational unit,

Logical data to represent true or false and which play an important role later,

Missing data that should be there but are not, and

Other types everything else under the sun.

In each subsection we look at some examples of the type in question and introduce methods to display them.

3.1.1 Quantitative data

Quantitative data are any data that measure or are associated with a measurement of the quantity of something. They invariably assume numerical values. Quantitative data can be further subdivided into two categories.

- *Discrete data* take values in a finite or countably infinite set of numbers, that is, all possible values could (at least in principle) be written down in an ordered list. Examples include: counts, number of arrivals, or number of successes. They are often represented by integers, say, 0, 1, 2, *etc.*.

- *Continuous data* take values in an interval of numbers. These are also known as scale data, interval data, or measurement data. Examples include: height, weight, length, time, *etc.* Continuous data are often characterized by fractions or decimals: 3.82, 7.0001, 4 $\frac{5}{8}$, *etc.*.

Note that the distinction between discrete and continuous data is not always clear-cut. Sometimes it is convenient to treat data as if they were continuous, even though strictly speaking they are not continuous. See the examples.

Example 3.1. Annual Precipitation in US Cities. The vector `precip` contains average amount of rainfall (in inches) for each of 70 cities in the United States and Puerto Rico. Let us take a look at the data:

```
> str(precip)

 Named num [1:70] 67 54.7 7 48.5 14 17.2 20.7 13 43.4 40.2 ...
 - attr(*, "names")= chr [1:70] "Mobile" "Juneau" "Phoenix" "Little Rock" ...

> precip[1:4]

     Mobile      Juneau     Phoenix Little Rock
       67.0        54.7         7.0        48.5
```

The output shows that `precip` is a numeric vector which has been *named*, that is, each value has a name associated with it (which can be set with the `names` function). These are quantitative continuous data.

Example 3.2. Lengths of Major North American Rivers. The U.S. Geological Survey recorded the lengths (in miles) of several rivers in North America. They are stored in the vector `rivers` in the `datasets` package (which ships with base R). See `?rivers`. Let us take a look at the data with the `str` function.

```
> str(rivers)

 num [1:141] 735 320 325 392 524 ...
```

The output says that `rivers` is a numeric vector of length 141, and the first few values are 735, 320, 325, *etc.* These data are definitely quantitative and it appears that the measurements have been rounded to the nearest mile. Thus, strictly speaking, these are discrete data. But we will find it convenient later to take data like these to be continuous for some of our statistical procedures.

Example 3.3. Yearly Numbers of Important Discoveries. The vector `discoveries` contains numbers of "great" inventions/discoveries in each year from 1860 to 1959, as reported by the 1975 World Almanac. Let us take a look at the data:

```
> str(discoveries)
 Time-Series [1:100] from 1860 to 1959: 5 3 0 2 0 3 2 3 6 1 ...
> discoveries[1:4]
[1] 5 3 0 2
```

The output is telling us that `discoveries` is a *time series* (see Section 3.1.5 for more) of length 100. The entries are integers, and since they represent counts this is a good example of discrete quantitative data. We will take a closer look in the following sections.

Displaying Quantitative Data

One of the first things to do when confronted by quantitative data (or any data, for that matter) is to make some sort of visual display to gain some insight into the data's structure. There are almost as many display types from which to choose as there are data sets to plot. We describe some of the more popular alternatives.

Strip charts (also known as Dot plots) These can be used for discrete or continuous data, and usually look best when the data set is not too large. Along the horizontal axis is a numerical scale above which the data values are plotted. We can do it in R with a call to the `stripchart` function. There are three available methods.

overplot plots ties covering each other. This method is good to display only the distinct values assumed by the data set.

jitter adds some noise to the data in the y direction in which case the data values are not covered up by ties.

stack plots repeated values stacked on top of one another. This method is best used for discrete data with a lot of ties; if there are no repeats then this method is identical to overplot.

See Figure 3.1.1, which is produced by the following code.

```
> stripchart(precip, xlab = "rainfall")
> stripchart(rivers, method = "jitter", xlab = "length")
> stripchart(discoveries, method = "stack", xlab = "number")
```

The leftmost graph is a strip chart of the `precip` data. The graph shows tightly clustered values in the middle with some others falling balanced on either side, with perhaps slightly more falling to the left. Later we will call this a symmetric distribution, see Section 3.2.3. The middle graph is of the `rivers` data, a vector of length 141. There are several repeated values in the rivers data, and if we were to use the overplot method we would lose some of them in the display. This plot shows a what we will later call a right-skewed shape with perhaps some extreme values on the far right of the display. The third graph strip charts `discoveries` data which are literally a textbook example of a right skewed distribution.

The `DOTplot` function in the `UsingR` package [86] is another alternative.

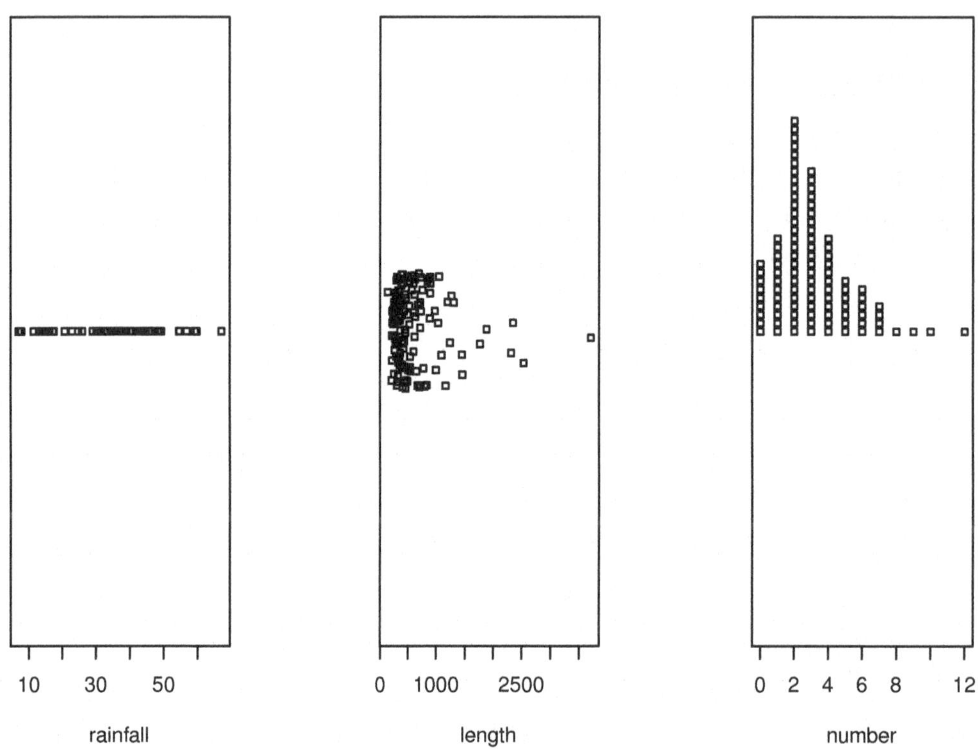

Figure 3.1.1: Strip charts of the `precip`, `rivers`, and `discoveries` data

The first graph uses the `overplot` method, the second the `jitter` method, and the third the `stack` method.

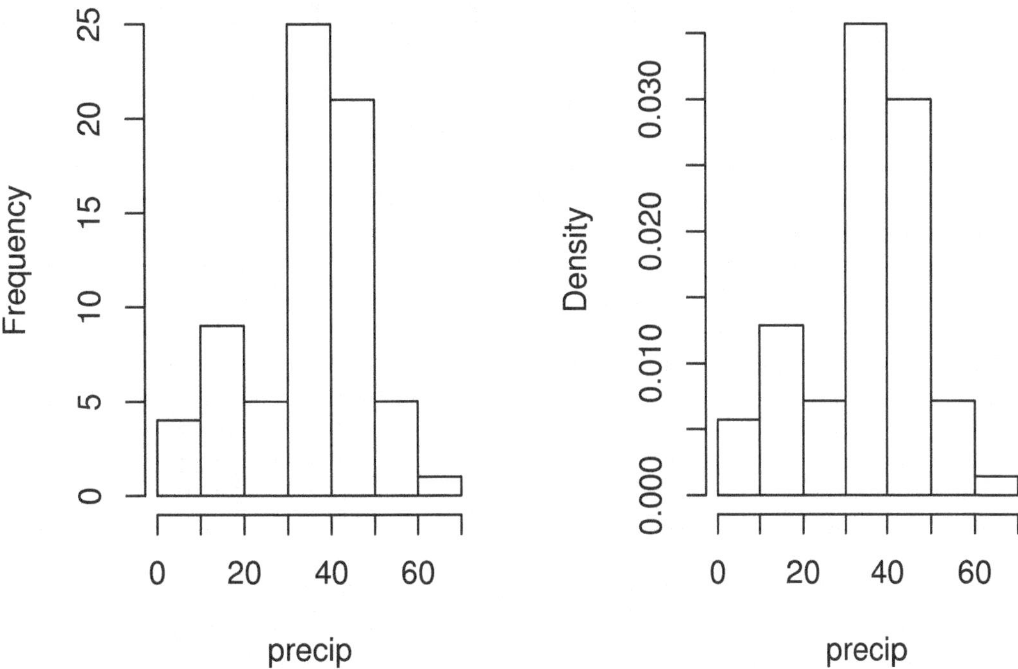

Figure 3.1.2: (Relative) frequency histograms of the `precip` data

Histogram These are typically used for continuous data. A histogram is constructed by first deciding on a set of classes, or bins, which partition the real line into a set of boxes into which the data values fall. Then vertical bars are drawn over the bins with height proportional to the number of observations that fell into the bin.

These are one of the most common summary displays, and they are often misidentified as "Bar Graphs" (see below.) The scale on the y axis can be frequency, percentage, or density (relative frequency). The term histogram was coined by Karl Pearson in 1891, see [66].

Example 3.4. Annual Precipitation in US Cities. We are going to take another look at the `precip` data that we investigated earlier. The strip chart in Figure 3.1.1 suggested a loosely balanced distribution; let us now look to see what a histogram says.

There are many ways to plot histograms in R, and one of the easiest is with the `hist` function. The following code produces the plots in Figure 3.1.2.

```
> hist(precip, main = "")
> hist(precip, freq = FALSE, main = "")
```

Notice the argument `main = ""`, which suppresses the main title from being displayed – it would have said "Histogram of `precip`" otherwise. The plot on the left is a frequency histogram (the default), and the plot on the right is a relative frequency histogram (`freq = FALSE`).

Please be careful regarding the biggest weakness of histograms: the graph obtained strongly depends on the bins chosen. Choose another set of bins, and you will get a different histogram.

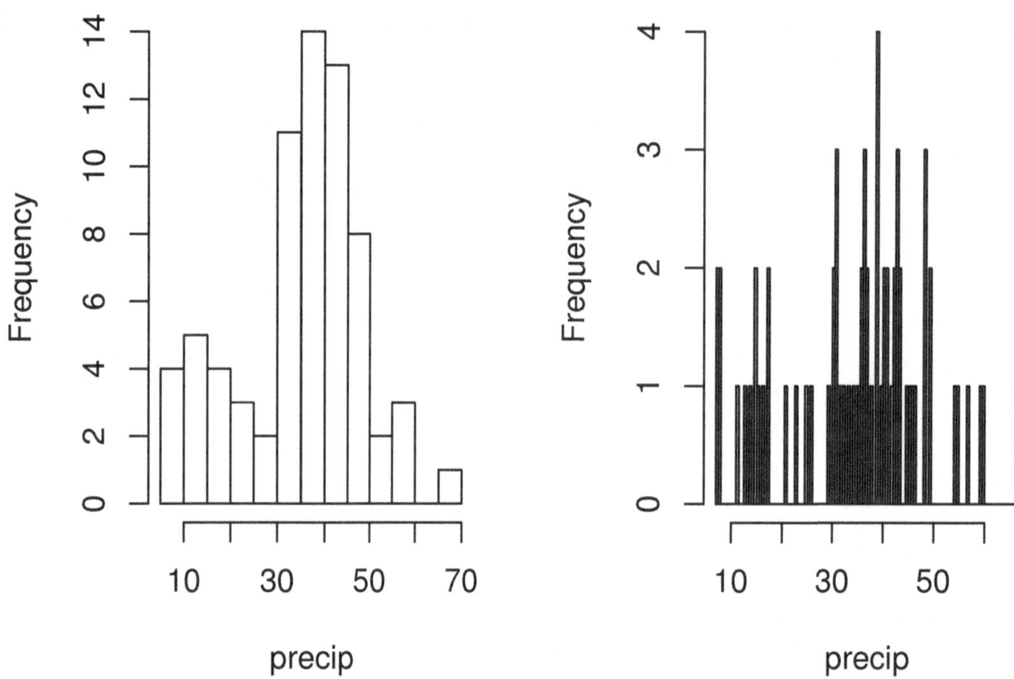

Figure 3.1.3: More histograms of the `precip` data

Moreover, there are not any definitive criteria by which bins should be defined; the best choice for a given data set is the one which illuminates the data set's underlying structure (if any). Luckily for us there are algorithms to automatically choose bins that are likely to display well, and more often than not the default bins do a good job. This is not always the case, however, and a responsible statistician will investigate many bin choices to test the stability of the display.

Example 3.5. Recall that the strip chart in Figure 3.1.1 suggested a relatively balanced shape to the `precip` data distribution. Watch what happens when we change the bins slightly (with the `breaks` argument to `hist`). See Figure 3.1.3 which was produced by the following code.

```
> hist(precip, breaks = 10, main = "")
> hist(precip, breaks = 200, main = "")
```

The leftmost graph (with `breaks = 10`) shows that the distribution is not balanced at all. There are two humps: a big one in the middle and a smaller one to the left. Graphs like this often indicate some underlying group structure to the data; we could now investigate whether the cities for which rainfall was measured were similar in some way, with respect to geographic region, for example.

The rightmost graph in Figure 3.1.3 shows what happens when the number of bins is too large: the histogram is too grainy and hides the rounded appearance of the earlier histograms. If we were to continue increasing the number of bins we would eventually get all observed bins to have exactly one element, which is nothing more than a glorified strip chart.

Stemplots (more to be said in Section 3.4) Stemplots have two basic parts: *stems* and *leaves*. The final digit of the data values is taken to be a *leaf*, and the leading digit(s) is (are) taken to be *stems*. We draw a vertical line, and to the left of the line we list the stems. To the right of the line, we list the leaves beside their corresponding stem. There will typically be several leaves for each stem, in which case the leaves accumulate to the right. It is sometimes necessary to round the data values, especially for larger data sets.

Example 3.6. `UKDriverDeaths` is a time series that contains the total car drivers killed or seriously injured in Great Britain monthly from Jan 1969 to Dec 1984. See `?UKDriverDeaths`. Compulsory seat belt use was introduced on January 31, 1983. We construct a stem and leaf diagram in R with the `stem.leaf` function from the `aplpack` package [92].

```
> library(aplpack)
> stem.leaf(UKDriverDeaths, depth = FALSE)
```

```
1 | 2: represents 120
 leaf unit: 10
            n: 192
   10 | 57
   11 | 136678
   12 | 123889
   13 | 0255666888899
   14 | 00001222344444555556667788889
   15 | 0000111112222223444455555566677779
   16 | 01222333444445555555678888889
   17 | 11233344566667799
   18 | 00011235568
   19 | 01234455667799
   20 | 0000113557788899
   21 | 145599
   22 | 013467
   23 | 9
   24 | 7
HI: 2654
```

The display shows a more or less balanced mound-shaped distribution, with one or maybe two humps, a big one and a smaller one just to its right. Note that the data have been rounded to the tens place so that each datum gets only one leaf to the right of the dividing line.

Notice that the `depths` have been suppressed. To learn more about this option and many others, see Section 3.4. Unlike a histogram, the original data values may be recovered from the stemplot display – modulo the rounding – that is, starting from the top and working down we can read off the data values 1050, 1070, 1110, 1130, *etc.*

Index plot Done with the `plot` function. These are good for plotting data which are ordered, for example, when the data are measured over time. That is, the first observation was measured at time 1, the second at time 2, *etc.* It is a two dimensional plot, in which the index (or time) is the x variable and the measured value is the y variable. There are several plotting methods for index plots, and we discuss two of them:

spikes: draws a vertical line from the x-axis to the observation height (`type = "h"`).

points: plots a simple point at the observation height (`type = "p"`).

Example 3.7. Level of Lake Huron 1875-1972. Brockwell and Davis [11] give the annual measurements of the level (in feet) of Lake Huron from 1875–1972. The data are stored in the time series `LakeHuron`. See `?LakeHuron`. Figure 3.1.4 was produced with the following code:

```
> plot(LakeHuron, type = "h")
> plot(LakeHuron, type = "p")
```

The plots show an overall decreasing trend to the observations, and there appears to be some seasonal variation that increases over time.

3.1.2 Qualitative Data, Categorical Data, and Factors

Qualitative data are simply any type of data that are not numerical, or do not represent numerical quantities. Examples of qualitative variables include a subject's name, gender, race/ethnicity, political party, socioeconomic status, class rank, driver's license number, and social security number (SSN).

Please bear in mind that some data *look* to be quantitative but are *not*, because they do not represent numerical quantities and do not obey mathematical rules. For example, a person's shoe size is typically written with numbers: 8, or 9, or 12, or $12\,\frac{1}{2}$. Shoe size is not quantitative, however, because if we take a size 8 and combine with a size 9 we do not get a size 17.

Some qualitative data serve merely to *identify* the observation (such a subject's name, driver's license number, or SSN). This type of data does not usually play much of a role in statistics. But other qualitative variables serve to *subdivide* the data set into categories; we call these *factors*. In the above examples, gender, race, political party, and socioeconomic status would be considered factors (shoe size would be another one). The possible values of a factor are called its *levels*. For instance, the factor *gender* would have two levels, namely, male and female. Socioeconomic status typically has three levels: high, middle, and low.

Factors may be of two types: *nominal* and *ordinal*. Nominal factors have levels that correspond to names of the categories, with no implied ordering. Examples of nominal factors would be hair color, gender, race, or political party. There is no natural ordering to "Democrat" and "Republican"; the categories are just names associated with different groups of people.

In contrast, ordinal factors have some sort of ordered structure to the underlying factor levels. For instance, socioeconomic status would be an ordinal categorical variable because the levels correspond to ranks associated with income, education, and occupation. Another example of ordinal categorical data would be class rank.

Factors have special status in R. They are represented internally by numbers, but even when they are written numerically their values do not convey any numeric meaning or obey any mathematical rules (that is, Stage III cancer is not Stage I cancer + Stage II cancer).

Example 3.8. The `state.abb` vector gives the two letter postal abbreviations for all 50 states.

```
> str(state.abb)

 chr [1:50] "AL" "AK" "AZ" "AR" "CA" "CO" "CT" "DE" ...
```

These would be ID data. The `state.name` vector lists all of the complete names and those data would also be ID.

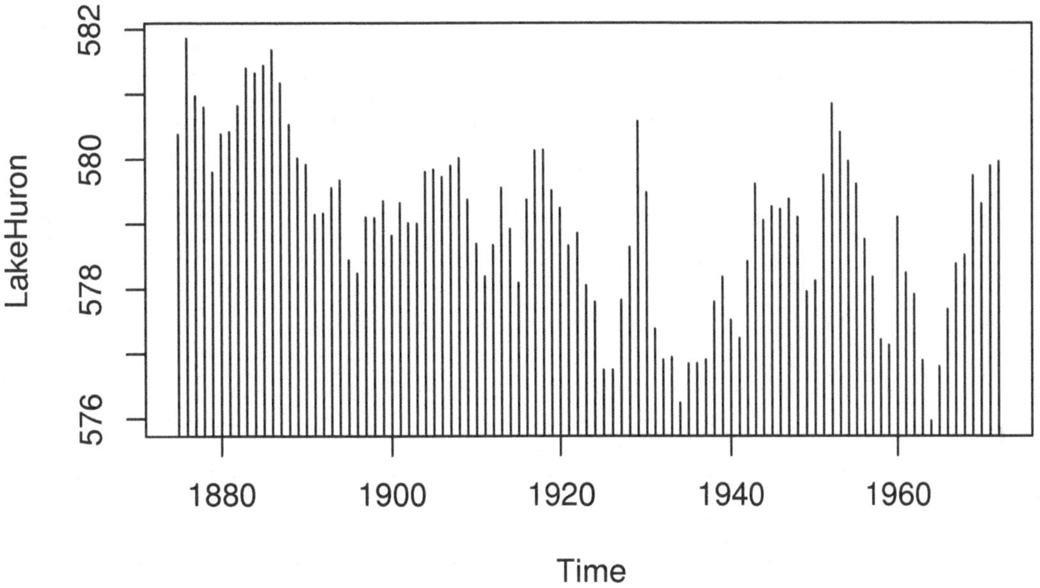

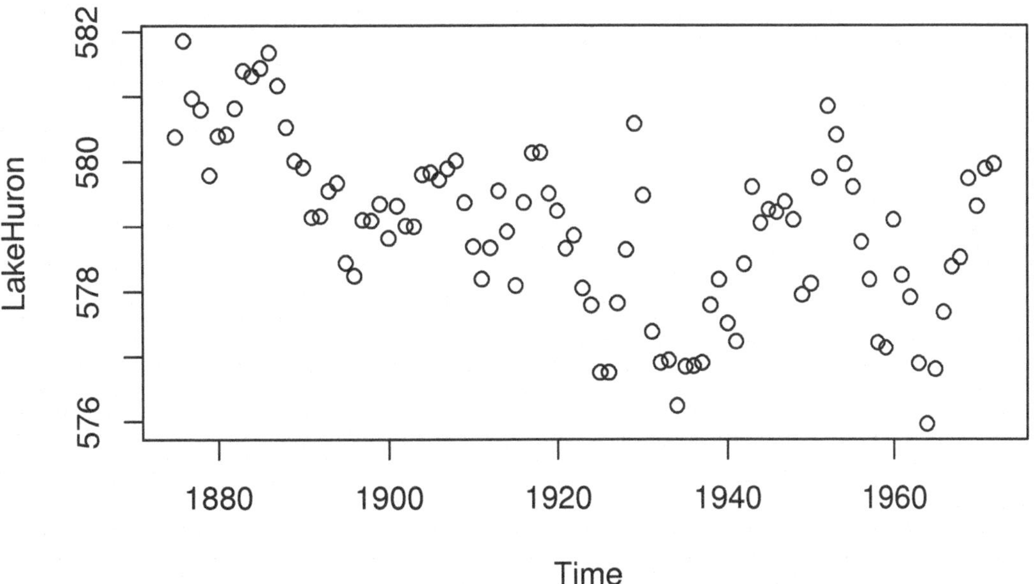

Figure 3.1.4: Index plots of the LakeHuron data

Example 3.9. U.S. State Facts and Features. The U.S. Department of Commerce of the U.S. Census Bureau releases all sorts of information in the *Statistical Abstract of the United States*, and the `state.region` data lists each of the 50 states and the region to which it belongs, be it Northeast, South, North Central, or West. See `?state.region`.

```
> str(state.region)
 Factor w/ 4 levels "Northeast","South",..: 2 4 4 2 4 4 1 2 2 2 ...
> state.region[1:5]
[1] South West  West  South West
Levels: Northeast South North Central West
```

The `str` output shows that `state.region` is already stored internally as a factor and it lists a couple of the factor levels. To see all of the levels we printed the first five entries of the vector in the second line.need to print a piece of the from

Displaying Qualitative Data

Tables One of the best ways to summarize qualitative data is with a table of the data values. We may count frequencies with the `table` function or list proportions with the `prop.table` function (whose input is a frequency table). In the R Commander you can do it with Statistics ▹ Frequency Distribution.... Alternatively, to look at tables for all factors in the `Active data set` you can do Statistics ▹ Summaries ▹ Active Dataset.

```
> Tbl <- table(state.division)
> Tbl                   # frequencies
state.division
       New England    Middle Atlantic     South Atlantic
                 6                  3                  8
East South Central West South Central East North Central
                 4                  4                  5
West North Central           Mountain            Pacific
                 7                  8                  5
> Tbl/sum(Tbl)          # relative frequencies
state.division
       New England    Middle Atlantic     South Atlantic
              0.12               0.06               0.16
East South Central West South Central East North Central
              0.08               0.08               0.10
West North Central           Mountain            Pacific
              0.14               0.16               0.10
> prop.table(Tbl)     # same thing
state.division
       New England    Middle Atlantic     South Atlantic
              0.12               0.06               0.16
East South Central West South Central East North Central
              0.08               0.08               0.10
West North Central           Mountain            Pacific
              0.14               0.16               0.10
```

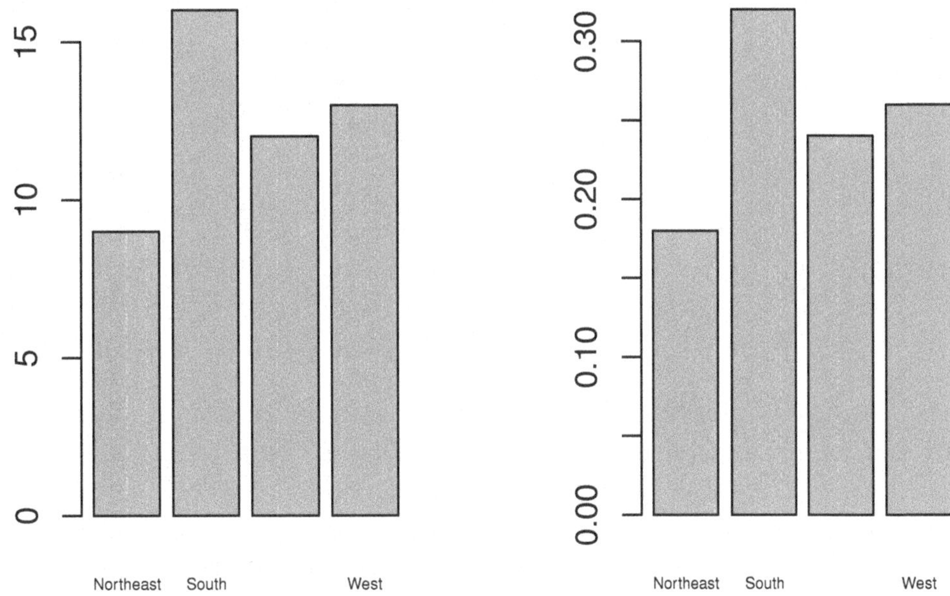

Figure 3.1.5: Bar graphs of the `state.region` data

The left graph is a frequency barplot made with `table` and the right is a relative frequency barplot made with `prop.table`.

Bar Graphs A bar graph is the analogue of a histogram for categorical data. A bar is displayed for each level of a factor, with the heights of the bars proportional to the frequencies of observations falling in the respective categories. A disadvantage of bar graphs is that the levels are ordered alphabetically (by default), which may sometimes obscure patterns in the display.

Example 3.10. U.S. State Facts and Features. The `state.region` data lists each of the 50 states and the region to which it belongs, be it Northeast, South, North Central, or West. See `?state.region`. It is already stored internally as a factor. We make a bar graph with the `barplot` function:

```
> barplot(table(state.region), cex.names = 0.5)
> barplot(prop.table(table(state.region)), cex.names = 0.5)
```

See Figure 3.1.5. The display on the left is a frequency bar graph because the y axis shows counts, while the display on the left is a relative frequency bar graph. The only difference between the two is the scale. Looking at the graph we see that the majority of the fifty states are in the South, followed by West, North Central, and finally Northeast. Over 30% of the states are in the South.

Notice the `cex.names` argument that we used, above. It shrinks the names on the x axis by 50% which makes them easier to read. See `?par` for a detailed list of additional plot parameters.

Pareto Diagrams A pareto diagram is a lot like a bar graph except the bars are rearranged such that they decrease in height going from left to right. The rearrangement is handy because it can visually reveal structure (if any) in how fast the bars decrease – this is much more difficult when the bars are jumbled.

Example 3.11. U.S. State Facts and Features. The `state.division` data record the division (New England, Middle Atlantic, South Atlantic, East South Central, West South Central, East North Central, West North Central, Mountain, and Pacific) of the fifty states. We can make a pareto diagram with either the `RcmdrPlugin.IPSUR` package or with the `pareto.chart` function from the `qcc` package [77]. See Figure 3.1.6. The code follows.

```
> library(qcc)
> pareto.chart(table(state.division), ylab = "Frequency")
```

Dot Charts These are a lot like a bar graph that has been turned on its side with the bars replaced by dots on horizontal lines. They do not convey any more (or less) information than the associated bar graph, but the strength lies in the economy of the display. Dot charts are so compact that it is easy to graph very complicated multi-variable interactions together in one graph. See Section 3.6. We will give an example here using the same data as above for comparison. The graph was produced by the following code.

```
> x <- table(state.region)
> dotchart(as.vector(x), labels = names(x))
```

See Figure 3.1.7. Compare it to Figure 3.1.5.

Pie Graphs These can be done with R and the R Commander, but they fallen out of favor in recent years because researchers have determined that while the human eye is good at judging linear measures, it is notoriously bad at judging relative areas (such as those displayed by a pie graph). Pie charts are consequently a very bad way of displaying information. A bar chart or dot chart is a preferable way of displaying qualitative data. See `?pie` for more information.

We are not going to do any examples of a pie graph and discourage their use elsewhere.

3.1.3 Logical Data

There is another type of information recognized by R which does not fall into the above categories. The value is either `TRUE` or `FALSE` (note that equivalently you can use `1 = TRUE`, `0 = FALSE`). Here is an example of a logical vector:

```
> x <- 5:9
> y <- (x < 7.3)
> y
[1]  TRUE  TRUE  TRUE FALSE FALSE
```

Many functions in R have options that the user may or may not want to activate in the function call. For example, the `stem.leaf` function has the `depths` argument which is `TRUE` by default. We saw in Section 3.1.1 how to turn the option off, simply enter `stem.leaf(x, depths = FALSE)` and they will not be shown on the display.

We can swap `TRUE` with `FALSE` with the exclamation point `!`.

```
Package 'qcc', version 2.0.1
Type 'citation("qcc")' for citing this R package in publications.

Pareto chart analysis for table(state.division)
                     Frequency Cum.Freq. Percentage Cum.Percent.
  Mountain                   8         8         16           16
  South Atlantic             8        16         16           32
  West North Central         7        23         14           46
  New England                6        29         12           58
  Pacific                    5        34         10           68
  East North Central         5        39         10           78
  West South Central         4        43          8           86
  East South Central         4        47          8           94
  Middle Atlantic            3        50          6          100
```

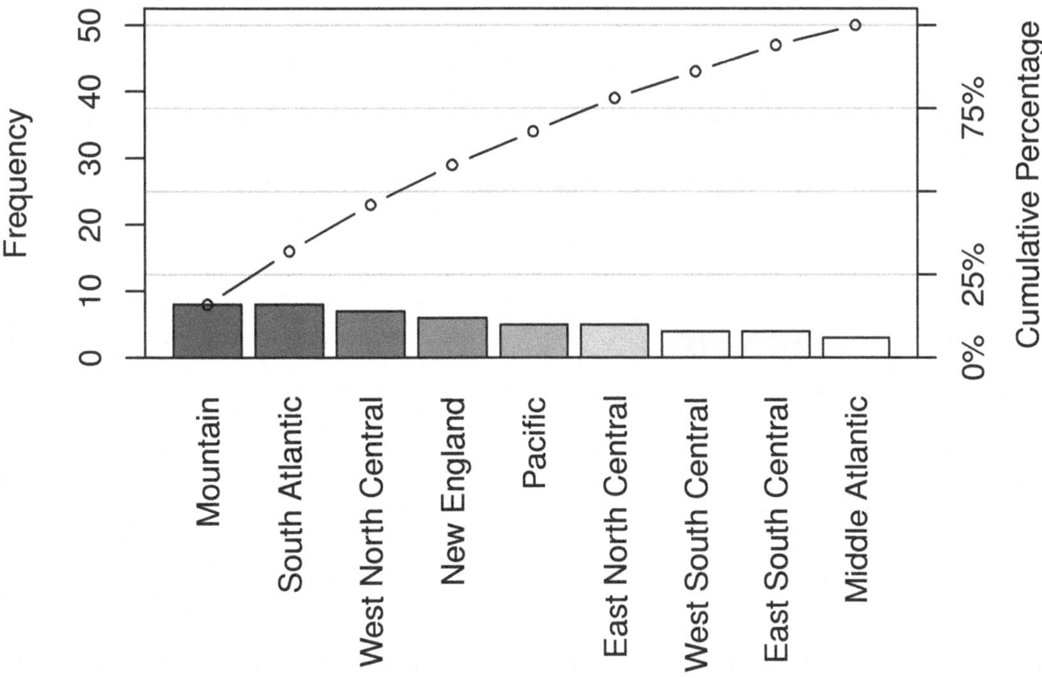

Figure 3.1.6: Pareto chart of the `state.division` data

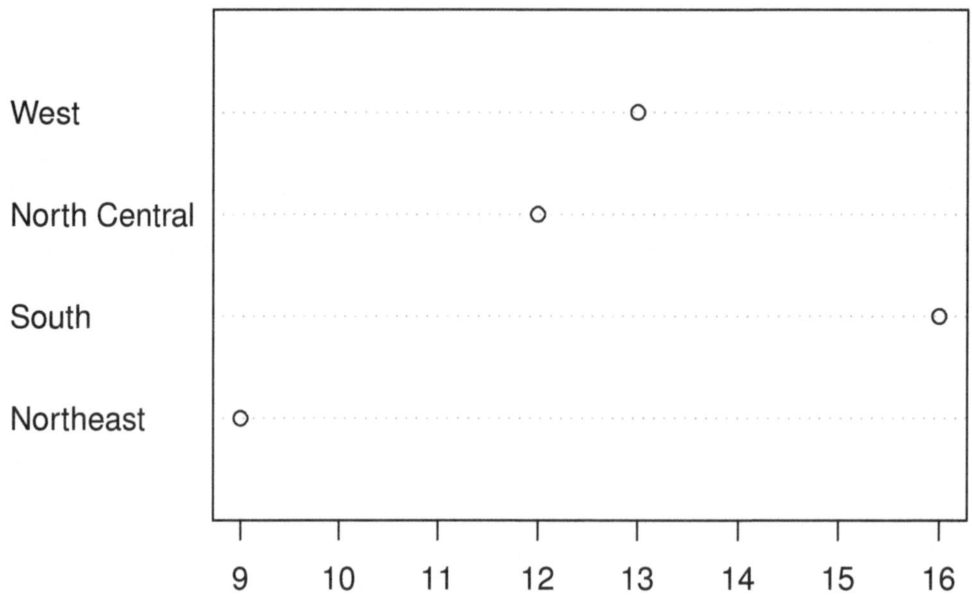

Figure 3.1.7: Dot chart of the `state.region` data

```
> !y
[1] FALSE FALSE FALSE  TRUE  TRUE
```

3.1.4 Missing Data

Missing data are a persistent and prevalent problem in many statistical analyses, especially those associated with the social sciences. R reserves the special symbol `NA` to representing missing data.

Ordinary arithmetic with `NA` values give `NA`'s (addition, subtraction, *etc.*) and applying a function to a vector that has an `NA` in it will usually give an `NA`.

```
> x <- c(3, 7, NA, 4, 7)
> y <- c(5, NA, 1, 2, 2)
> x + y
[1]  8 NA NA  6  9
```

Some functions have a `na.rm` argument which when `TRUE` will ignore missing data as if it were not there (such as `mean`, `var`, `sd`, `IQR`, `mad`, ...).

```
> sum(x)
[1] NA
```

```
> sum(x, na.rm = TRUE)
```

```
[1] 21
```

Other functions do not have a `na.rm` argument and will return `NA` or an error if the argument has `NA`s. In those cases we can find the locations of any `NA`s with the `is.na` function and remove those cases with the `[]` operator.

```
> is.na(x)
```

```
[1] FALSE FALSE  TRUE FALSE FALSE
```

```
> z <- x[!is.na(x)]
> sum(z)
```

```
[1] 21
```

The analogue of `is.na` for rectangular data sets (or data frames) is the `complete.cases` function. See Appendix D.4.

3.1.5 Other Data Types

3.2 Features of Data Distributions

Given that the data have been appropriately displayed, the next step is to try to identify salient features represented in the graph. The acronym to remember is *C*enter, *U*nusual features, *S*pread, and *S*hape. (CUSS).

3.2.1 Center

One of the most basic features of a data set is its center. Loosely speaking, the center of a data set is associated with a number that represents a middle or general tendency of the data. Of course, there are usually several values that would serve as a center, and our later tasks will be focused on choosing an appropriate one for the data at hand. Judging from the histogram that we saw in Figure 3.1.3, a measure of center would be about 35.

3.2.2 Spread

The spread of a data set is associated with its variability; data sets with a large spread tend to cover a large interval of values, while data sets with small spread tend to cluster tightly around a central value.

3.2.3 Shape

When we speak of the *shape* of a data set, we are usually referring to the shape exhibited by an associated graphical display, such as a histogram. The shape can tell us a lot about any underlying structure to the data, and can help us decide which statistical procedure we should use to analyze them.

Symmetry and Skewness A distribution is said to be *right-skewed* (or *positively skewed*) if the right tail seems to be stretched from the center. A *left-skewed* (or *negatively skewed*) distribution is stretched to the left side. A symmetric distribution has a graph that is balanced about its center, in the sense that half of the graph may be reflected about a central line of symmetry to match the other half.

We have already encountered skewed distributions: both the discoveries data in Figure 3.1.1 and the precip data in Figure 3.1.3 appear right-skewed. The `UKDriverDeaths` data in Example 3.6 is relatively symmetric (but note the one extreme value 2654 identified at the bottom of the stemplot).

Kurtosis Another component to the shape of a distribution is how "peaked" it is. Some distributions tend to have a flat shape with thin tails. These are called *platykurtic*, and an example of a platykurtic distribution is the uniform distribution; see Section 6.2. On the other end of the spectrum are distributions with a steep peak, or spike, accompanied by heavy tails; these are called *leptokurtic*. Examples of leptokurtic distributions are the Laplace distribution and the logistic distribution. See Section 6.5. In between are distributions (called *mesokurtic*) with a rounded peak and moderately sized tails. The standard example of a mesokurtic distribution is the famous bell-shaped curve, also known as the Gaussian, or normal, distribution, and the binomial distribution can be mesokurtic for specific choices of p. See Sections 5.3 and 6.3.

3.2.4 Clusters and Gaps

Clusters or gaps are sometimes observed in quantitative data distributions. They indicate clumping of the data about distinct values, and gaps may exist between clusters. Clusters often suggest an underlying grouping to the data. For example, take a look at the `faithful` data which contains the duration of `eruptions` and the `waiting` time between eruptions of the Old Faithful geyser in Yellowstone National Park. (Do not be frightened by the complicated information at the left of the display for now; we will learn how to interpret it in Section 3.4).

```
> library(aplpack)
> stem.leaf(faithful$eruptions)
```

```
1 | 2: represents 1.2
 leaf unit: 0.1
            n: 272
   12     s | 667777777777
   51    1. | 888888888888888888888888888899999999999
   71    2* | 00000000000011111111
   87     t | 2222222222333333
   92     f | 44444
   94     s | 66
   97    2. | 889
   98    3* | 0
  102     t | 3333
  108     f | 445555
  118     s | 6666677777
  (16)   3. | 8888888899999999
  138    4* | 0000000000000000111111111111111
  107     t | 22222222222233333333333333333
```

```
78      f | 44444444444445555555555555555555
43      s | 6666666666677777777777
21     4. | 8888888888899999
 4     5* | 0001
```

There are definitely two clusters of data here; an upper cluster and a lower cluster.

3.2.5 Extreme Observations and other Unusual Features

Extreme observations fall far from the rest of the data. Such observations are troublesome to many statistical procedures; they cause exaggerated estimates and instability. It is important to identify extreme observations and examine the source of the data more closely. There are many possible reasons underlying an extreme observation:

- **Maybe the value is a typographical error.** Especially with large data sets becoming more prevalent, many of which being recorded by hand, mistakes are a common problem. After closer scrutiny, these can often be fixed.
- **Maybe the observation was not meant for the study**, because it does not belong to the population of interest. For example, in medical research some subjects may have relevant complications in their genealogical history that would rule out their participation in the experiment. Or when a manufacturing company investigates the properties of one of its devices, perhaps a particular product is malfunctioning and is not representative of the majority of the items.
- **Maybe it indicates a deeper trend or phenomenon**. Many of the most influential scientific discoveries were made when the investigator noticed an unexpected result, a value that was not predicted by the classical theory. Albert Einstein, Louis Pasteur, and others built their careers on exactly this circumstance.

3.3 Descriptive Statistics

3.3.1 Frequencies and Relative Frequencies

These are used for categorical data. The idea is that there are a number of different categories, and we would like to get some idea about how the categories are represented in the population. For example, we may want to see how the

3.3.2 Measures of Center

The *sample mean* is denoted $\overline{x}$ (read "x-bar") and is simply the arithmetic average of the observations:

$$\overline{x} = \frac{x_1 + x_2 + \cdots + x_n}{n} = \frac{1}{n}\sum_{i=1}^{n} x_i. \tag{3.3.1}$$

- Good: natural, easy to compute, has nice mathematical properties
- Bad: sensitive to extreme values

It is appropriate for use with data sets that are not highly skewed without extreme observations.

The *sample median* is another popular measure of center and is denoted $\tilde{x}$. To calculate its value, first sort the data into an increasing sequence of numbers. If the data set has an odd number of observations then $\tilde{x}$ is the value of the middle observation, which lies in position $(n + 1)/2$; otherwise, there are two middle observations and $\tilde{x}$ is the average of those middle values.

- Good: resistant to extreme values, easy to describe
- Bad: not as mathematically tractable, need to sort the data to calculate

One desirable property of the sample median is that it is resistant to extreme observations, in the sense that the value of $\tilde{x}$ depends only the values of the middle observations, and is quite unaffected by the actual values of the outer observations in the ordered list. The same cannot be said for the sample mean. Any significant changes in the magnitude of an observation x_k results in a corresponding change in the value of the mean. Hence, the sample mean is said to be sensitive to extreme observations.

The *trimmed mean* is a measure designed to address the sensitivity of the sample mean to extreme observations. The idea is to "trim" a fraction (less than 1/2) of the observations off each end of the ordered list, and then calculate the sample mean of what remains. We will denote it by $\overline{x}_{t=0.05}$.

- Good: resistant to extreme values, shares nice statistical properties
- Bad: need to sort the data

3.3.3 How to do it with R

- You can calculate frequencies or relative frequencies with the `table` function, and relative frequencies with `prop.table(table())`.
- You can calculate the sample mean of a data vector `x` with the command `mean(x)`.
- You can calculate the sample median of `x` with the command `median(x)`.
- You can calculate the trimmed mean with the `trim` argument; `mean(x, trim = 0.05)`.

3.3.4 Order Statistics and the Sample Quantiles

A common first step in an analysis of a data set is to sort the values. Given a data set x_1, x_2, $\ldots$,x_n, we may sort the values to obtain an increasing sequence

$$x_{(1)} \leq x_{(2)} \leq x_{(3)} \leq \cdots \leq x_{(n)} \tag{3.3.2}$$

and the resulting values are called the *order statistics*. The kth entry in the list, $x_{(k)}$, is the kth order statistic, and approximately $100(k/n)\%$ of the observations fall below $x_{(k)}$. The order statistics give an indication of the shape of the data distribution, in the sense that a person can look at the order statistics and have an idea about where the data are concentrated, and where they are sparse.

The *sample quantiles* are related to the order statistics. Unfortunately, there is not a universally accepted definition of them. Indeed, R is equipped to calculate quantiles using nine distinct definitions! We will describe the default method (`type = 7`), but the interested reader can see the details for the other methods with `?quantile`.

Suppose the data set has n observations. Find the sample quantile of order p ($0 < p < 1$), denoted $\tilde{q}_p$, as follows:

First step: sort the data to obtain the order statistics $x_{(1)}, x_{(2)}, \ldots, x_{(n)}$.

Second step: calculate $(n - 1)p + 1$ and write it in the form $k.d$, where k is an integer and d is a decimal.

Third step: The sample quantile $\tilde{q}_p$ is

$$\tilde{q}_p = x_{(k)} + d(x_{(k+1)} - x_{(k)}). \tag{3.3.3}$$

The interpretation of $\tilde{q}_p$ is that approximately $100p\%$ of the data fall below the value $\tilde{q}_p$.

Keep in mind that there is not a unique definition of percentiles, quartiles, *etc.* Open a different book, and you'll find a different procedure. The difference is small and seldom plays a role except in small data sets with repeated values. In fact, most people do not even notice in common use.

Clearly, the most popular sample quantile is $\tilde{q}_{0.50}$, also known as the sample median, $\tilde{x}$. The closest runners-up are the *first quartile* $\tilde{q}_{0.25}$ and the *third quartile* $\tilde{q}_{0.75}$ (the *second quartile* is the median).

3.3.5 How to do it with R

At the command prompt We can find the order statistics of a data set stored in a vector `x` with the command `sort(x)`.

You can calculate the sample quantiles of any order p where $0 < p < 1$ for a data set stored in a data vector `x` with the `quantile` function, for instance, the command `quantile(x, probs = c(0, 0.25, 0.37))` will return the smallest observation, the first quartile, $\tilde{q}_{0.25}$, and the 37th sample quantile, $\tilde{q}_{0.37}$. For $\tilde{q}_p$ simply change the values in the `probs` argument to the value p.

With the R Commander In `Rcmdr` we can find the order statistics of a variable in the `Active data set` by doing Data ▹ Manage variables in Active data set... ▹ Compute new variable.... In the Expression to compute dialog simply type `sort(varname)`, where `varname` is the variable that it is desired to sort.

In `Rcmdr`, we can calculate the sample quantiles for a particular variable with the sequence Statistics ▹ Summaries ▹ Numerical Summaries.... We can automatically calculate the quartiles for all variables in the `Active data set` with the sequence Statistics ▹ Summaries ▹ Active Dataset.

3.3.6 Measures of Spread

Sample Variance and Standard Deviation The *sample variance* is denoted s^2 and is calculated with the formula

$$s^2 = \frac{1}{n-1} \sum_{i=1}^{n} (x_i - \overline{x})^2. \tag{3.3.4}$$

The *sample standard deviation* is $s = \sqrt{s^2}$. Intuitively, the sample variance is approximately the average squared distance of the observations from the sample mean. The sample standard deviation is used to scale the estimate back to the measurement units of the original data.

- Good: tractable, has nice mathematical/statistical properties
- Bad: sensitive to extreme values

We will spend a lot of time with the variance and standard deviation in the coming chapters. In the meantime, the following two rules give some meaning to the standard deviation, in that there are bounds on how much of the data can fall past a certain distance from the mean.

Fact 3.12. *Chebychev's Rule: The proportion of observations within k standard deviations of the mean is at least* $1 - 1/k^2$, i.e., *at least 75%, 89%, and 94% of the data are within 2, 3, and 4 standard deviations of the mean, respectively.*

Note that Chebychev's Rule does not say anything about when $k = 1$, because $1 - 1/1^2 = 0$, which states that at least 0% of the observations are within one standard deviation of the mean (which is not saying much).

Chebychev's Rule applies to any data distribution, *any* list of numbers, no matter where it came from or what the histogram looks like. The price for such generality is that the bounds are not very tight; if we know more about how the data are shaped then we can say more about how much of the data can fall a given distance from the mean.

Fact 3.13. *Empirical Rule: If data follow a bell-shaped curve, then approximately 68%, 95%, and 99.7% of the data are within 1, 2, and 3 standard deviations of the mean, respectively.*

Interquartile Range Just as the sample mean is sensitive to extreme values, so the associated measure of spread is similarly sensitive to extremes. Further, the problem is exacerbated by the fact that the extreme distances are squared. We know that the sample quartiles are resistant to extremes, and a measure of spread associated with them is the *interquartile range* (IQR) defined by $IQR = q_{0.75} - q_{0.25}$.

- Good: stable, resistant to outliers, robust to nonnormality, easy to explain
- Bad: not as tractable, need to sort the data, only involves the middle 50% of the data.

Median Absolute Deviation A measure even more robust than the IQR is the *median absolute deviation* (MAD). To calculate it we first get the median $\widetilde{x}$, next the *absolute deviations* $|x_1 - \tilde{x}|, |x_2 - \tilde{x}|, \ldots, |x_n - \tilde{x}|$, and the MAD is proportional to the median of those deviations:

$$MAD \propto \text{median}(|x_1 - \tilde{x}|,\ |x_2 - \tilde{x}|, \ldots, |x_n - \tilde{x}|). \tag{3.3.5}$$

That is, the $MAD = c \cdot \text{median}(|x_1 - \tilde{x}|,\ |x_2 - \tilde{x}|, \ldots, |x_n - \tilde{x}|)$, where c is a constant chosen so that the MAD has nice properties. The value of c in R is by default $c = 1.4286$. This value is chosen to ensure that the estimator of σ is correct, on the average, under suitable sampling assumptions (see Section 9.1).

- Good: stable, very robust, even more so than the IQR.
- Bad: not tractable, not well known and less easy to explain.

Comparing Apples to Apples

We have seen three different measures of spread which, for a given data set, will give three different answers. Which one should we use? It depends on the data set. If the data are well behaved, with an approximate bell-shaped distribution, then the sample mean and sample standard deviation are natural choices with nice mathematical properties. However, if the data have an unusual or skewed shape with several extreme values, perhaps the more resistant choices among the *IQR* or *MAD* would be more appropriate.

However, once we are looking at the three numbers it is important to understand that the estimators are not all measuring the same quantity, on the average. In particular, it can be shown that when the data follow an approximately bell-shaped distribution, then on the average, the sample standard deviation s and the *MAD* will be the approximately the same value, namely, σ, but the *IQR* will be on the average 1.349 times larger than s and the *MAD*. See 8 for more details.

3.3.7 How to do it with R

At the command prompt From the console we may compute the sample range with `range(x)` and the sample variance with `var(x)`, where `x` is a numeric vector. The sample standard deviation is `sqrt(var(x))` or just `sd(x)`. The *IQR* is `IQR(x)` and the median absolute deviation is `mad(x)`.

In R Commander In `Rcmdr` we can calculate the sample standard deviation with the Statistics ▹ Summaries ▹ Numerical Summaries... combination. R Commander does not calculate the *IQR* or *MAD* in any of the menu selections, by default.

3.3.8 Measures of Shape

Sample Skewness The *sample skewness*, denoted by g_1, is defined by the formula

$$g_1 = \frac{1}{n}\frac{\sum_{i=1}^{n}(x_i - \overline{x})^3}{s^3}. \tag{3.3.6}$$

The sample skewness can be any value $-\infty < g_1 < \infty$. The sign of g_1 indicates the direction of skewness of the distribution. Samples that have $g_1 > 0$ indicate right-skewed distributions (or positively skewed), and samples with $g_1 < 0$ indicate left-skewed distributions (or negatively skewed). Values of g_1 near zero indicate a symmetric distribution. These are not hard and fast rules, however. The value of g_1 is subject to sampling variability and thus only provides a suggestion to the skewness of the underlying distribution.

We still need to know how big is "big", that is, how do we judge whether an observed value of g_1 is far enough away from zero for the data set to be considered skewed to the right or left? A good rule of thumb is that data sets with skewness larger than $2\sqrt{6/n}$ in magnitude are substantially skewed, in the direction of the sign of g_1. See Tabachnick & Fidell [83] for details.

Sample Excess Kurtosis The *sample excess kurtosis*, denoted by g_2, is given by the formula

$$g_2 = \frac{1}{n}\frac{\sum_{i=1}^{n}(x_i - \overline{x})^4}{s^4} - 3. \tag{3.3.7}$$

The sample excess kurtosis takes values $-2 \leq g_2 < \infty$. The subtraction of 3 may seem mysterious but it is done so that mound shaped samples have values of g_2 near zero. Samples with $g_2 > 0$ are called *leptokurtic*, and samples with $g_2 < 0$ are called *platykurtic*. Samples with $g_2 \approx 0$ are called *mesokurtic*.

As a rule of thumb, if $|g_2| > 4\sqrt{6/n}$ then the sample excess kurtosis is substantially different from zero in the direction of the sign of g_2. See Tabachnick & Fidell [83] for details.

Notice that both the sample skewness and the sample kurtosis are invariant with respect to location and scale, that is, the values of g_1 and g_2 do not depend on the measurement units of the data.

3.3.9 How to do it with R

The `e1071` package [22] has the `skewness` function for the sample skewness and the `kurtosis` function for the sample excess kurtosis. Both functions have a `na.rm` argument which is `FALSE` by default.

Example 3.14. We said earlier that the `discoveries` data looked positively skewed; let's see what the statistics say:

```
> library(e1071)
> skewness(discoveries)

[1] 1.207600

> 2 * sqrt(6/length(discoveries))

[1] 0.4898979
```

The data are definitely skewed to the right. Let us check the sample excess kurtosis of the `UKDriverDeaths` data:

```
> kurtosis(UKDriverDeaths)

[1] 0.07133848

> 4 * sqrt(6/length(UKDriverDeaths))

[1] 0.7071068
```

so that the `UKDriverDeaths` data appear to be mesokurtic, or at least not substantially leptokurtic.

3.4 Exploratory Data Analysis

This field was founded (mostly) by John Tukey (1915-2000). Its tools are useful when not much is known regarding the underlying causes associated with the data set, and are often used for checking assumptions. For example, suppose we perform an experiment and collect some data... now what? We look at the data using exploratory visual tools.

3.4.1 More About Stemplots

There are many bells and whistles associated with stemplots, and the `stem.leaf` function can do many of them.

Trim Outliers: Some data sets have observations that fall far from the bulk of the other data (in a sense made more precise in Section 3.4.6). These extreme observations often obscure the underlying structure to the data and are best left out of the data display. The `trim.outliers` argument (which is `TRUE` by default) will separate the extreme observations from the others and graph the stemplot without them; they are listed at the bottom (respectively, top) of the stemplot with the label `HI` (respectively `LO`).

Split Stems: The standard stemplot has only one line per stem, which means that all observations with first digit 3 are plotted on the same line, regardless of the value of the second digit. But this gives some stemplots a "skyscraper" appearance, with too many observations stacked onto the same stem. We can often fix the display by increasing the number of lines available for a given stem. For example, we could make two lines per stem, say, `3*` and `3.`. Observations with second digit 0 through 4 would go on the upper line, while observations with second digit 5 through 9 would go on the lower line. (We could do a similar thing with five lines per stem, or even ten lines per stem.) The end result is a more spread out stemplot which often looks better. A good example of this was shown on page 34.

Depths: these are used to give insight into the balance of the observations as they accumulate toward the median. In a column beside the standard stemplot, the frequency of the stem containing the sample median is shown in parentheses. Next, frequencies are accumulated from the outside inward, including the outliers. Distributions that are more symmetric will have better balanced depths on either side of the sample median.

3.4.2 How to do it with R

At the command prompt The basic command is `stem(x)` or a more sophisticated version written by Peter Wolf called `stem.leaf(x)` in the R Commander. We will describe `stem.leaf` since that is the one used by R Commander.

With the R Commander WARNING: Sometimes when making a stem plot the result will not be what you expected. There are several reasons for this:

- Stemplots by default will trim extreme observations (defined in Section 3.4.6) from the display. This in some cases will result in stemplots that are not as wide as expected.
- The leafs digit is chosen automatically by `stem.leaf` according to an algorithm that the computer believes will represent the data well. Depending on the choice of the digit, `stem.leaf` may drop digits from the data or round the values in unexpected ways.

Let us take a look at the `rivers` data set.

```
> stem.leaf(rivers)
```

```
1 | 2: represents 120
 leaf unit: 10
            n: 141
    1     1 | 3
   29     2 | 0111133334555556666778888899
   64     3 | 00000111122223333455555666677888999
  (18)    4 | 011222233344566679
   59     5 | 000222234467
   47     6 | 0000112235789
   34     7 | 12233368
   26     8 | 04579
   21     9 | 0008
   17    10 | 035
   14    11 | 07
   12    12 | 047
    9    13 | 0
HI: 1450 1459 1770 1885 2315 2348 2533 3710
```

The stemplot shows a right-skewed shape to the `rivers` data distribution. Notice that the last digit of each of the data values were dropped from the display. Notice also that there were eight extreme observations identified by the computer, and their exact values are listed at the bottom of the stemplot. Look at the scale on the left of the stemplot and try to imagine how ridiculous the graph would have looked had we tried to include enough stems to include these other eight observations; the stemplot would have stretched over several pages. Notice finally that we can use the depths to approximate the sample median for these data. The median lies in the row identified by `(18)`, which means that the median is the average of the ninth and tenth observation on that row. Those two values correspond to `43` and `43`, so a good guess for the median would be 430. (For the record, the sample median is $\widetilde{x} = 425$. Recall that stemplots round the data to the nearest stem-leaf pair.)

Next let us see what the `precip` data look like.

```
> stem.leaf(precip)

1 | 2: represents 12
 leaf unit: 1
            n: 70
LO: 7 7.2 7.8 7.8
    8     1* | 1344
   13     1. | 55677
   16     2* | 024
   18     2. | 59
   28     3* | 0000111234
  (15)    3. | 555566677788899
   27     4* | 0000122222334
   14     4. | 56688899
    6     5* | 44
    4     5. | 699
HI: 67
```

Here is an example of split stems, with two lines per stem. The final digit of each datum has been dropped for the display. The data appear to be left skewed with four extreme values to the left and one extreme value to the right. The sample median is approximately 37 (it turns out to be 36.6).

3.4.3 Hinges and the Five Number Summary

Given a data set $x_1, x_2, \ldots, x_n$, the hinges are found by the following method:

- Find the order statistics $x_{(1)}, x_{(2)}, \ldots, x_{(n)}$.
- The *lower hinge* h_L is in position $L = \lfloor (n+3)/2 \rfloor /2$, where the symbol $\lfloor x \rfloor$ denotes the largest integer less than or equal to x. If the position L is not an integer, then the hinge h_L is the average of the adjacent order statistics.
- The *upper hinge* h_U is in position $n + 1 - L$.

Given the hinges, the *five number summary* ($5NS$) is

$$5NS = (x_{(1)},\ h_L,\ \tilde{x},\ h_U,\ x_{(n)}). \tag{3.4.1}$$

An advantage of the $5NS$ is that it reduces a potentially large data set to a shorter list of only five numbers, and further, these numbers give insight regarding the shape of the data distribution similar to the sample quantiles in Section 3.3.4.

3.4.4 How to do it with R

If the data are stored in a vector `x`, then you can compute the $5NS$ with the `fivenum` function.

3.4.5 Boxplots

A boxplot is essentially a graphical representation of the $5NS$. It can be a handy alternative to a stripchart when the sample size is large.

A boxplot is constructed by drawing a box alongside the data axis with sides located at the upper and lower hinges. A line is drawn parallel to the sides to denote the sample median. Lastly, whiskers are extended from the sides of the box to the maximum and minimum data values (more precisely, to the most extreme values that are not potential outliers, defined below).

Boxplots are good for quick visual summaries of data sets, and the relative positions of the values in the $5NS$ are good at indicating the underlying shape of the data distribution, although perhaps not as effectively as a histogram. Perhaps the greatest advantage of a boxplot is that it can help to objectively identify extreme observations in the data set as described in the next section.

Boxplots are also good because one can visually assess multiple features of the data set simultaneously:

Center can be estimated by the sample median, $\tilde{x}$.

Spread can be judged by the width of the box, $h_U - h_L$. We know that this will be close to the IQR, which can be compared to s and the MAD, perhaps after rescaling if appropriate.

Shape is indicated by the relative lengths of the whiskers, and the position of the median inside the box. Boxes with unbalanced whiskers indicate skewness in the direction of the long whisker. Skewed distributions often have the median tending in the opposite direction of skewness. Kurtosis can be assessed using the box and whiskers. A wide box with short whiskers will tend to be platykurtic, while a skinny box with wide whiskers indicates leptokurtic distributions.

Extreme observations are identified with open circles (see below).

3.4.6 Outliers

A *potential outlier* is any observation that falls beyond 1.5 times the width of the box on either side, that is, any observation less than $h_L - 1.5(h_U - h_L)$ or greater than $h_U + 1.5(h_U - h_L)$. A *suspected outlier* is any observation that falls beyond 3 times the width of the box on either side. In R, both potential and suspected outliers (if present) are denoted by open circles; there is no distinction between the two.

When potential outliers are present, the whiskers of the boxplot are then shortened to extend to the most extreme observation that is not a potential outlier. If an outlier is displayed in a boxplot, the index of the observation may be identified in a subsequent plot in `Rcmdr` by clicking the Identify outliers with mouse option in the Boxplot dialog.

What do we do about outliers? They merit further investigation. The primary goal is to determine why the observation is outlying, if possible. If the observation is a typographical error, then it should be corrected before continuing. If the observation is from a subject that does not belong to the population of interest, then perhaps the datum should be removed. Otherwise, perhaps the value is hinting at some hidden structure to the data.

3.4.7 How to do it with R

The quickest way to visually identify outliers is with a boxplot, described above. Another way is with the `boxplot.stats` function.

Example 3.15. The `rivers` data. We will look for potential outliers in the `rivers` data.

```
> boxplot.stats(rivers)$out
 [1] 1459 1450 1243 2348 3710 2315 2533 1306 1270 1885 1770
```

We may change the `coef` argument to 3 (it is 1.5 by default) to identify suspected outliers.

```
> boxplot.stats(rivers, coef = 3)$out
[1] 2348 3710 2315 2533 1885
```

3.4.8 Standardizing variables

It is sometimes useful to compare data sets with each other on a scale that is independent of the measurement units. Given a set of observed data $x_1, x_2, \ldots, x_n$ we get z scores, denoted $z_1, z_2, \ldots, z_n$, by means of the following formula

$$z_i = \frac{x_i - \overline{x}}{s}, \quad i = 1, 2, \ldots, n.$$

3.4.9 How to do it with R

The `scale` function will rescale a numeric vector (or data frame) by subtracting the sample mean from each value (column) and/or by dividing each observation by the sample standard deviation.

3.5 Multivariate Data and Data Frames

We have had experience with vectors of data, which are long lists of numbers. Typically, each entry in the vector is a single measurement on a subject or experimental unit in the study. We saw in Section 2.3.3 how to form vectors with the `c` function or the `scan` function.

However, statistical studies often involve experiments where there are two (or more) measurements associated with each subject. We display the measured information in a rectangular array in which each row corresponds to a subject, and the columns contain the measurements for each respective variable. For instance, if one were to measure the height and weight and hair color of each of 11 persons in a research study, the information could be represented with a rectangular array. There would be 11 rows. Each row would have the person's height in the first column and hair color in the second column.

The corresponding objects in R are called *data frames*, and they can be constructed with the `data.frame` function. Each row is an observation, and each column is a variable.

Example 3.16. Suppose we have two vectors `x` and `y` and we want to make a data frame out of them.

```
> x <- 5:8
> y <- letters[3:6]
> A <- data.frame(v1 = x, v2 = y)
```

Notice that `x` and `y` are the same length. This is *necessary*. Also notice that `x` is a numeric vector and `y` is a character vector. We may choose numeric and character vectors (or even factors) for the columns of the data frame, but each column must be of exactly one type. That is, we can have a column for `height` and a column for `gender`, but we will get an error if we try to mix function `height` (numeric) and `gender` (character or factor) information in the same column.

Indexing of data frames is similar to indexing of vectors. To get the entry in row i and column j do `A[i,j]`. We can get entire rows and columns by omitting the other index.

```
> A[3, ]

  v1 v2
3  7  e

> A[1, ]

  v1 v2
1  5  c

> A[, 2]

[1] c d e f
Levels: c d e f
```

There are several things happening above. Notice that `A[3,]` gave a data frame (with the same entries as the third row of `A`) yet `A[1, ]` is a numeric vector. `A[ ,2]` is a factor vector because the default setting for `data.frame` is `stringsAsFactors = TRUE`.

Data frames have a `names` attribute and the names may be extracted with the `names` function. Once we have the names we may extract given columns by way of the dollar sign.

```
> names(A)
[1] "v1" "v2"
> A$v1
[1] 5 6 7 8
```

The above is identical to `A[ ,1]`.

3.5.1 Bivariate Data

- Introduce the sample correlation coefficient.
- Two-Way Tables. Done with `table`, or in the R Commander by following Statistics ▹ Contingency Tables ▹ Two-way Tables. You can also enter and analyze a two-way table.
- Scatterplot: look for linear association and correlation.
  - carb ~ optden, data = Formaldehyde
  - conc ~ rate, data = Puromycin
  - xyplot(accel ~ dist, data = attenu) nonlinear association
  - xyplot(eruptions ~ waiting, data = faithful) (linear, two groups)
  - xyplot(Petal.Width ~ Petal.Length, data = iris)
  - xyplot(pressure ~ temperature, data = pressure) (exponential growth)
  - xyplot(weight ~ height, data = women) (strong positive linear)

3.5.2 Multivariate Data

Multivariate Data Display

- Multi-Way Tables. You can do this with `table`, or in R Commander by following Statistics ▹ Contingency Tables ▹ Multi-way Tables.
- Scatterplot matrix. used for displaying pairwise scatterplots simultaneously. Again, look for linear association and correlation.
- 3D Scatterplot. See Figure 270
- `plot(state.region, state.division)`
- `barplot(table(state.division,state.region), legend.text=TRUE)`

3.6 Comparing Populations

Sometimes we have data from two or more groups (or populations) and we would like to compare them and draw conclusions. What we should imagine is

Some issues that we would like to address:

- Comparing centers and spreads: variation within versus between groups
- Comparing clusters and gaps
- Comparing outliers and unusual features
- Comparing shapes.

3.6.1 Numerically

I am thinking here about the Statistics ▹ Numerical Summaries ▹ Summarize by groups option or the Statistics ▹ Summaries ▹Table of Statistics option.

3.6.2 Graphically

- Boxplots
    - Variable width: the width of the drawn boxplots are proportional to $\sqrt{n_i}$, where n_i is the size of the ith group. Why? Because many statistics have variability proportional to the reciprocal of the square root of the sample size.
    - Notches: extend to $1.58 \cdot (h_U - h_L)/\sqrt{n}$. The idea is to give roughly a 95% confidence interval for the difference in two medians. See Chapter 10.
- Stripcharts
- Bar Graphs
    - plot(xtabs(Freq ~ Admit + Gender, data = UCBAdmissions)) # rescaled barplot
    - barplot(xtabs(Freq ~ Admit + Gender, data = UCBAdmissions)) # stacked bar chart
    - barplot(xtabs(Freq ~ Admit, data = UCBAdmissions))
    - barplot(xtabs(Freq ~ Gender + Admit, data = UCBAdmissions), legend = TRUE, beside = TRUE) # oops, discrimination.
    - barplot(xtabs(Freq ~ Admit+Dept, data = UCBAdmissions), legend = TRUE, beside = TRUE) # different departments have different standards
    - barplot(xtabs(Freq ~ Gender+Dept, data = UCBAdmissions), legend = TRUE, beside = TRUE) # men mostly applied to easy departments, women mostly applied to difficult departments
    - barplot(xtabs(Freq ~ Gender+Dept, data = UCBAdmissions), legend = TRUE, beside = TRUE)
    - barchart(Admit ~ Freq, data = C)
    - barchart(Admit ~ Freq|Gender, data = C)

- barchart(Admit ~ Freq | Dept, groups = Gender, data = C)
- barchart(Admit ~ Freq | Dept, groups = Gender, data = C, auto.key = TRUE)

- Histograms
  - ~ breaks | wool*tension, data = warpbreaks
  - ~ weight | feed, data = chickwts
  - ~ weight | group, data = PlantGrowth
  - ~ count | spray, data = InsectSprays
  - ~ len | dose, data = ToothGrowth
  - ~ decrease | treatment, data = OrchardSprays (or rowpos or colpos)

- Scatterplots
  - xyplot(Petal.Width ~ Petal.Length, data = iris, group = Species)

```
> library(lattice)
> xyplot()
```

- Scatterplot matrices
  - splom(~ cbind(GNP.deflator,GNP,Unemployed,Armed.Forces,Population,Year,Employed), data = longley)
  - splom(~ cbind(pop15,pop75,dpi), data = LifeCycleSavings)
  - splom(~ cbind(Murder, Assault, Rape), data = USArrests)
  - splom(~ cbind(CONT, INTG, DMNR), data = USJudgeRatings)
  - splom(~ cbind(area,peri,shape,perm), data = rock)
  - splom(~ cbind(Air.Flow, Water.Temp, Acid.Conc., stack.loss), data = stackloss)
  - splom(~ cbind(Fertility,Agriculture,Examination,Education,Catholic,Infant.Mortality), data = swiss)
  - splom(~ cbind(Fertility,Agriculture,Examination), data = swiss) (positive and negative)

- Dot charts
  - dotchart(USPersonalExpenditure)
  - dotchart(t(USPersonalExpenditure))
  - dotchart(WorldPhones) (transpose is no good)
  - freeny.x is no good, neither is volcano
  - dotchart(UCBAdmissions[,,1])
  - dotplot(Survived ~ Freq | Class, groups = Sex, data = B)
  - dotplot(Admit ~ Freq | Dept, groups = Gender, data = C)

- Mosaic plot

  - mosaic(~ Survived + Class + Age + Sex, data = Titanic) (or just mosaic(Titanic))
  - mosaic(~ Admit + Dept + Gender, data = UCBAdmissions)

- Quantile-quantile plots: There are two ways to do this. One way is to compare two independent samples (of the same size). qqplot(x,y). Another way is to compare the sample quantiles of one variable to the theoretical quantiles of another distribution.

Given two samples $\{x_1, x_2, \ldots, x_n\}$ and $\{y_1, y_2, \ldots, y_n\}$, we may find the order statistics $x_{(1)} \leq x_{(2)} \leq \cdots \leq x_{(n)}$ and $y_{(1)} \leq y_{(2)} \leq \cdots \leq y_{(n)}$. Next, plot the n points $(x_{(1)}, y_{(1)})$, $(x_{(2)}, y_{(2)})$ $, \ldots, (x_{(n)}, y_{(n)})$.

It is clear that if $x_{(k)} = y_{(k)}$ for all $k = 1, 2, \ldots, n$, then we will have a straight line. It is also clear that in the real world, a straight line is NEVER observed, and instead we have a scatterplot that hopefully had a general linear trend. What do the rules tell us?

- If the y-intercept of the line is greater (less) than zero, then the center of the Y data is greater (less) than the center of the X data.

- If the slope of the line is greater (less) than one, then the spread of the Y data is greater (less) than the spread of the X data..

3.6.3 Lattice Graphics

The following types of plots are useful when there is one variable of interest and there is a factor in the data set by which the variable is categorized.

It is sometimes nice to set `lattice.options(default.theme = "col.whitebg")`

Side by side boxplots

```
> library(lattice)
> bwplot(~weight | feed, data = chickwts)
```

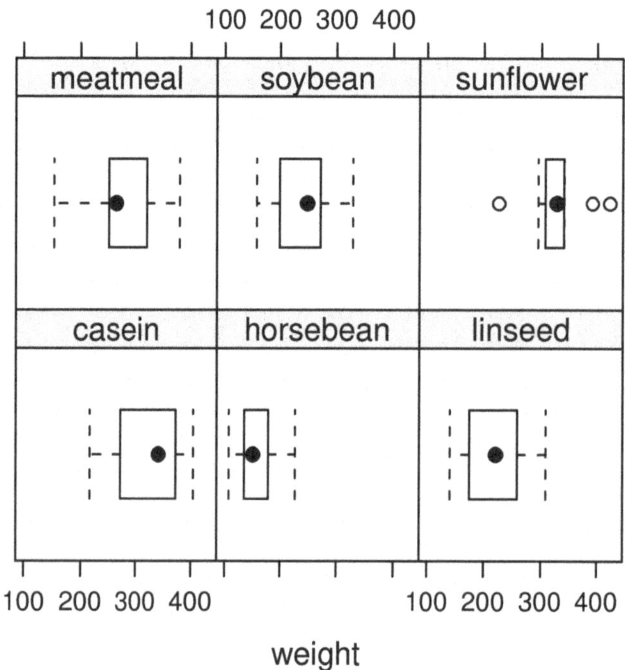

Figure 3.6.1: Boxplots of `weight` by `feed` type in the `chickwts` data

Histograms

```
> histogram(~age | education, data = infert)
```

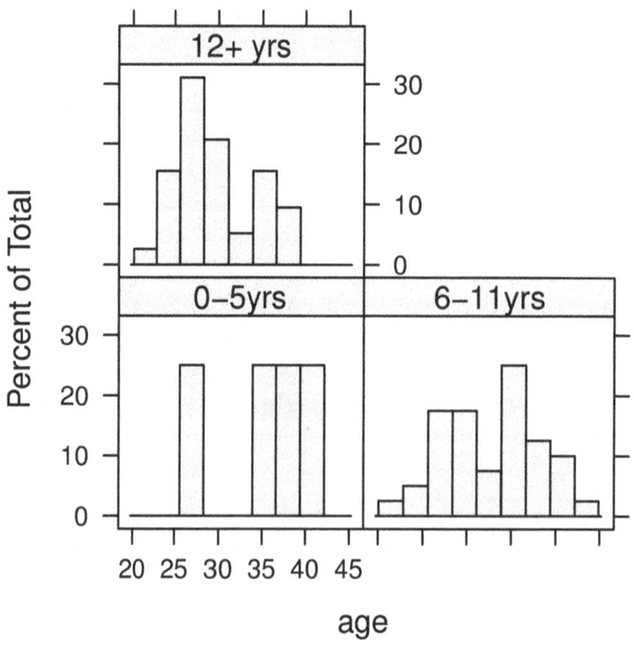

Figure 3.6.2: Histograms of `age` by `education` level from the `infert` data

Scatterplots

```
> xyplot(Petal.Length ~ Petal.Width | Species, data = iris)
```

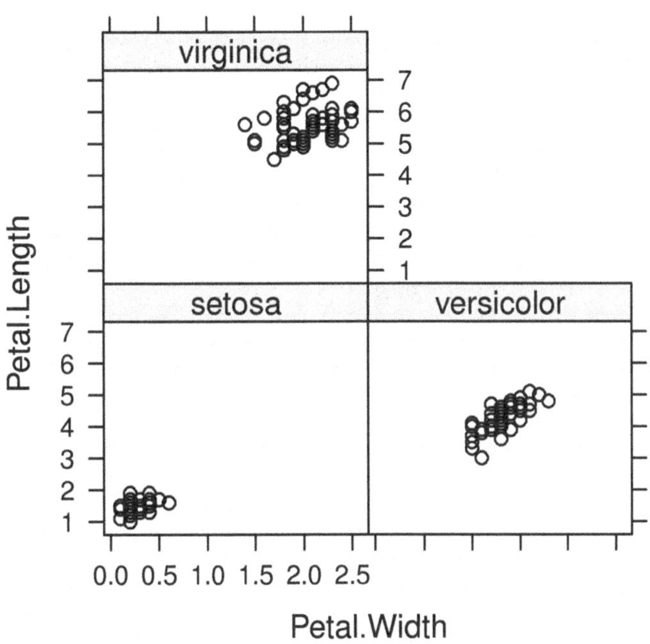

Figure 3.6.3: An `xyplot` of `Petal.Length` versus `Petal.Width` by `Species` in the `iris` data

Coplots

```
> coplot(conc ~ uptake | Type * Treatment, data = CO2)
```

```
NULL
```

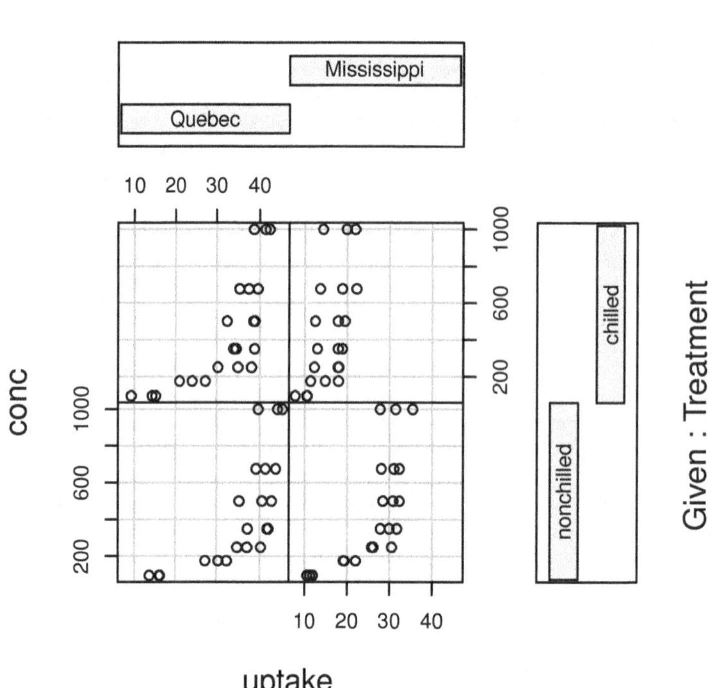

Figure 3.6.4: A `coplot` of `conc` versus `uptake` by `Type` and `Treatment` in the `CO2` data

Chapter Exercises

Directions: Open R and issue the following commands at the command line to get started. Note that you need to have the RcmdrPlugin.IPSUR package installed, and for some exercises you need the e1071 package.

```
library(RcmdrPlugin.IPSUR)
data(RcmdrTestDrive)
attach(RcmdrTestDrive)
names(RcmdrTestDrive)  # shows names of variables
```

To load the data in the R Commander (Rcmdr), click the Data Set button, and select RcmdrTestDrive as the active data set. To learn more about the data set and where it comes from, type ?RcmdrTestDrive at the command line.

Exercise 3.1. Perform a summary of all variables in RcmdrTestDrive. You can do this with the command

```
summary(RcmdrTestDrive)
```

Alternatively, you can do this in the Rcmdr with the sequence Statistics ▷ Summaries ▷ Active Data Set. Report the values of the summary statistics for each variable.

Answer:

```
> summary(RcmdrTestDrive)
     order            race      smoke        gender        salary     
 Min.   :  1.00   AfAmer: 18   No :134   Female:95   Min.   :11.62  
 1st Qu.: 42.75   Asian :  8   Yes: 34   Male  :73   1st Qu.:15.93  
 Median : 84.50   Other : 16                         Median :17.59  
 Mean   : 84.50   White :126                         Mean   :17.10  
 3rd Qu.:126.25                                      3rd Qu.:18.46  
 Max.   :168.00                                      Max.   :21.19  
   reduction          before          after          parking      
 Min.   :4.904   Min.   :51.17   Min.   :48.79   Min.   : 1.000  
 1st Qu.:5.195   1st Qu.:63.36   1st Qu.:62.80   1st Qu.: 1.000  
 Median :5.501   Median :67.62   Median :66.94   Median : 2.000  
 Mean   :5.609   Mean   :67.36   Mean   :66.85   Mean   : 2.524  
 3rd Qu.:5.989   3rd Qu.:71.28   3rd Qu.:70.88   3rd Qu.: 3.000  
 Max.   :6.830   Max.   :89.96   Max.   :89.89   Max.   :18.000  
```

Exercise 3.2. Make a table of the *race* variable. Do this with Statistics ▷ Summaries ▷ IPSUR - Frequency Distributions...

1. Which ethnicity has the highest frequency?

2. Which ethnicity has the lowest frequency?

3. Include a bar graph of *race*. Do this with Graphs ▷ IPSUR - Bar Graph...

Solution: First we will make a table of the *race* variable with the `table` function.

```
> table(race)
race
AfAmer  Asian  Other  White
    18      8     16    126
```

1. For these data, White has the highest frequency.

2. For these data, Asian has the lowest frequency.

3. The graph is shown below.

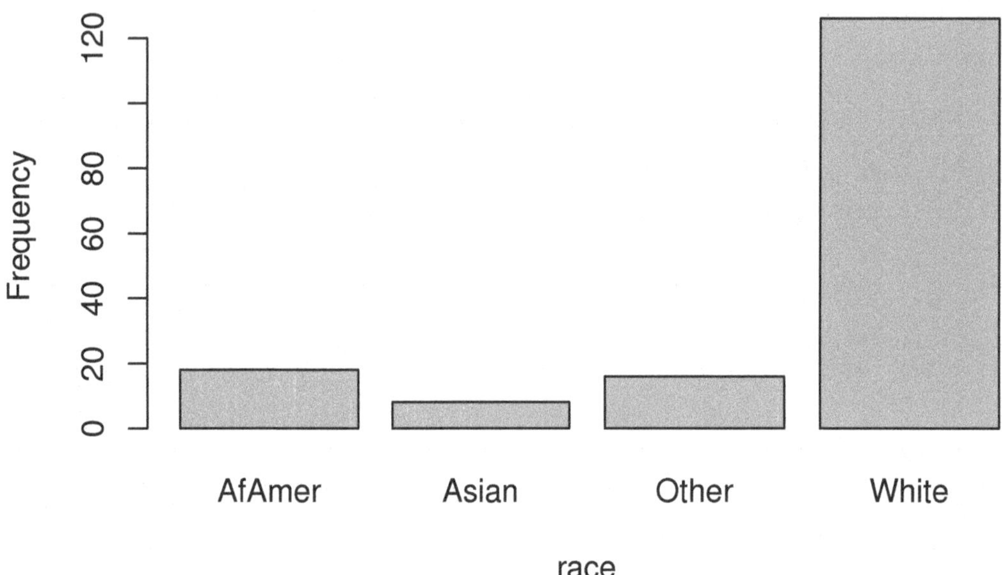

Exercise 3.3. Calculate the average *salary* by the factor *gender*. Do this with Statistics ▹ Summaries ▹ Table of Statistics...

1. Which *gender* has the highest mean *salary*?

2. Report the highest mean *salary*.

3. Compare the spreads for the genders by calculating the standard deviation of *salary* by *gender*. Which *gender* has the biggest standard deviation?

4. Make boxplots of *salary* by *gender* with the following method:

   On the `Rcmdr`, click Graphs ▹ IPSUR - Boxplot...
   In the Variable box, select *salary*.
   Click the Plot by groups... box and select *gender*. Click OK.
   Click OK to graph the boxplot.

   How does the boxplot compare to your answers to (1) and (3)?

Solution: We can generate a table listing the average salaries by gender with two methods. The first uses `tapply`:

```
> x <- tapply(salary, list(gender = gender), mean)
> x

gender
  Female     Male
16.46353 17.93035
```

The second method uses the by function:

```
> by(salary, gender, mean, na.rm = TRUE)

gender: Female
[1] 16.46353
--------------------------------------------------------
gender: Male
[1] 17.93035
```

Now to answer the questions:

1. Which gender has the highest mean salary?

   We can answer this by looking above. For these data, the gender with the highest mean salary is Male.

2. Report the highest mean salary.

   Depending on our answer above, we would do something like

   ```
   mean(salary[gender == Male])
   ```

   for example. For these data, the highest mean salary is

   ```
   > x[which(x == max(x))]

       Male
   17.93035
   ```

3. Compare the spreads for the genders by calculating the standard deviation of *salary* by *gender*. Which gender has the biggest standard deviation?

   ```
   > y <- tapply(salary, list(gender = gender), sd)
   > y

   gender
     Female     Male
   2.122113 1.077183
   ```

   For these data, the the largest standard deviation is approximately 2.12 which was attained by the Female gender.

4. Make boxplots of *salary* by *gender*. How does the boxplot compare to your answers to (1) and (3)?

   The graph is shown below.

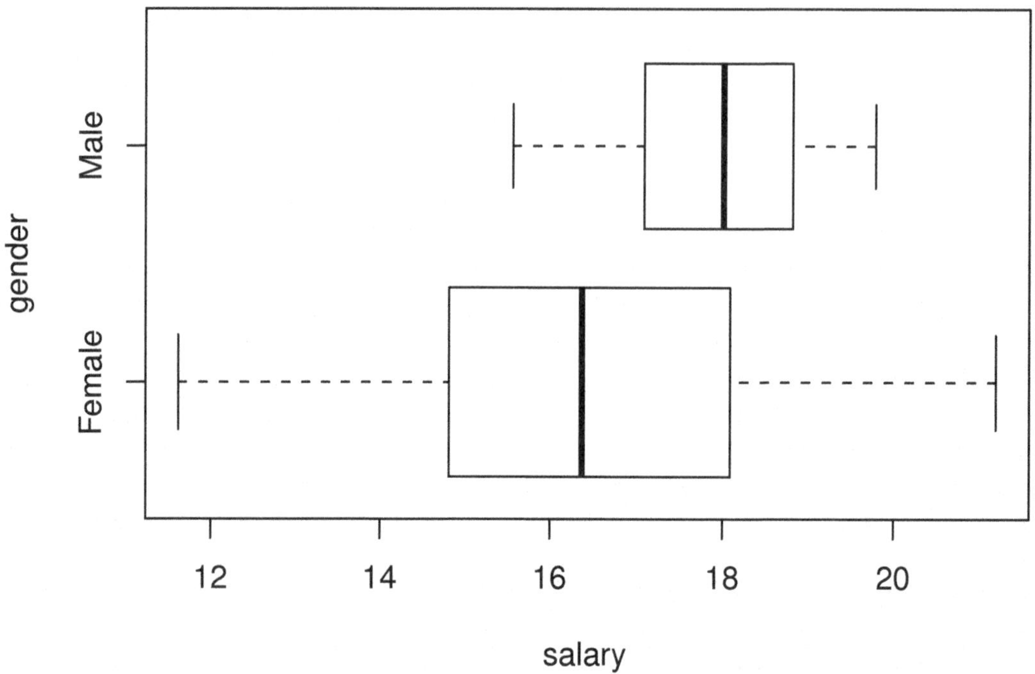

   Answers will vary. There should be some remarks that the center of the box is farther to the right for the Male gender, and some recognition that the box is wider for the Female gender.

Exercise 3.4. For this problem we will study the variable *reduction*.

1. Find the order statistics and store them in a vector `x`. *Hint:* `x <- sort(reduction)`
2. Find $x_{(137)}$, the 137th order statistic.
3. Find the IQR.
4. Find the Five Number Summary (5NS).
5. Use the 5NS to calculate what the width of a boxplot of *reduction* would be.
6. Compare your answers (3) and (5). Are they the same? If not, are they close?
7. Make a boxplot of *reduction*, and include the boxplot in your report. You can do this with the `boxplot` function, or in `Rcmdr` with Graphs ▹ IPSUR - Boxplot...
8. Are there any potential/suspected outliers? If so, list their values. *Hint:* use your answer to (a).

9. Using the rules discussed in the text, classify answers to (8), if any, as *potential* or *suspected* outliers.

Answers:

```
> x[137]
[1] 6.101618
> IQR(x)
[1] 0.7943932
> fivenum(x)
[1] 4.903922 5.193638 5.501241 5.989846 6.830096
> fivenum(x)[4] - fivenum(x)[2]
[1] 0.796208
```

Compare your answers (3) and (5). Are they the same? If not, are they close?
Yes, they are close, within 0.00181484542950905 of each other.
The boxplot of *reduction* is below.

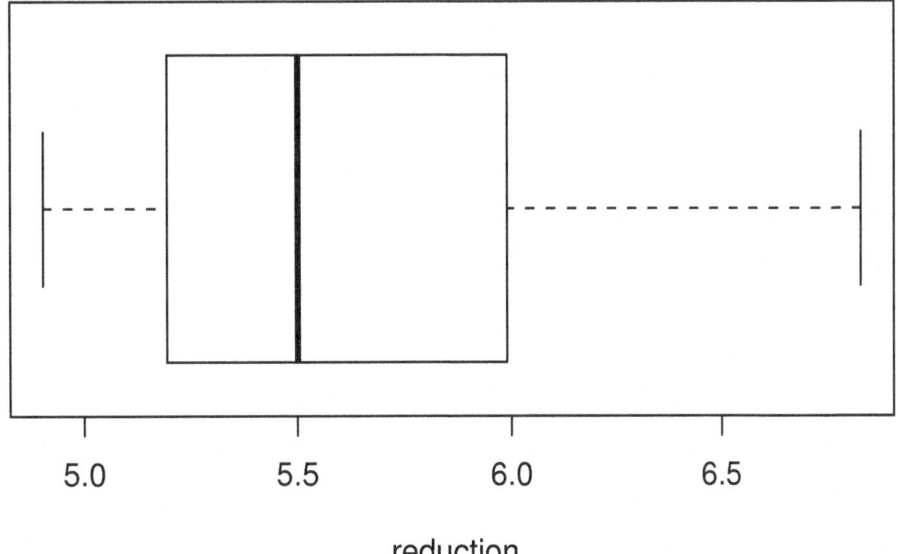


```
> temp <- fivenum(x)
> inF <- 1.5 * (temp[4] - temp[2]) + temp[4]
> outF <- 3 * (temp[4] - temp[2]) + temp[4]
> which(x > inF)
integer(0)
> which(x > outF)
```

```
integer(0)
```

Observations would be considered potential outliers, while observation(s) would be considered a suspected outlier.

Exercise 3.5. In this problem we will compare the variables *before* and *after*. Don't forget `library(e1071)`.

1. Examine the two measures of center for both variables. Judging from these measures, which variable has a higher center?

2. Which measure of center is more appropriate for *before*? (You may want to look at a boxplot.) Which measure of center is more appropriate for *after*?

3. Based on your answer to (2), choose an appropriate measure of spread for each variable, calculate it, and report its value. Which variable has the biggest spread? (Note that you need to make sure that your measures are on the same scale.)

4. Calculate and report the skewness and kurtosis for *before*. Based on these values, how would you describe the shape of *before*?

5. Calculate and report the skewness and kurtosis for *after*. Based on these values, how would you describe the shape of *after*?

6. Plot histograms of *before* and *after* and compare them to your answers to (4) and (5).

Solution:

1. Examine the two measures of center for both variables that you found in problem 1. Judging from these measures, which variable has a higher center?

   We may take a look at the `summary(RcmdrTestDrive)` output from Exercise 3.1. Here we will repeat the relevant summary statistics.

   ```
   > c(mean(before), median(before))

   [1] 67.36338 67.61824

   > c(mean(after), median(after))

   [1] 66.85215 66.93608
   ```

   The idea is to look at the two measures and compare them to make a decision. In a nice world, both the mean and median of one variable will be larger than the other which sends a nice message. If We get a mixed message, then we should look for other information, such as extreme values in one of the variables, which is one of the reasons for the next part of the problem.

2. Which measure of center is more appropriate for *before*? (You may want to look at a boxplot.) Which measure of center is more appropriate for *after*?

   The boxplot of *before* is shown below.

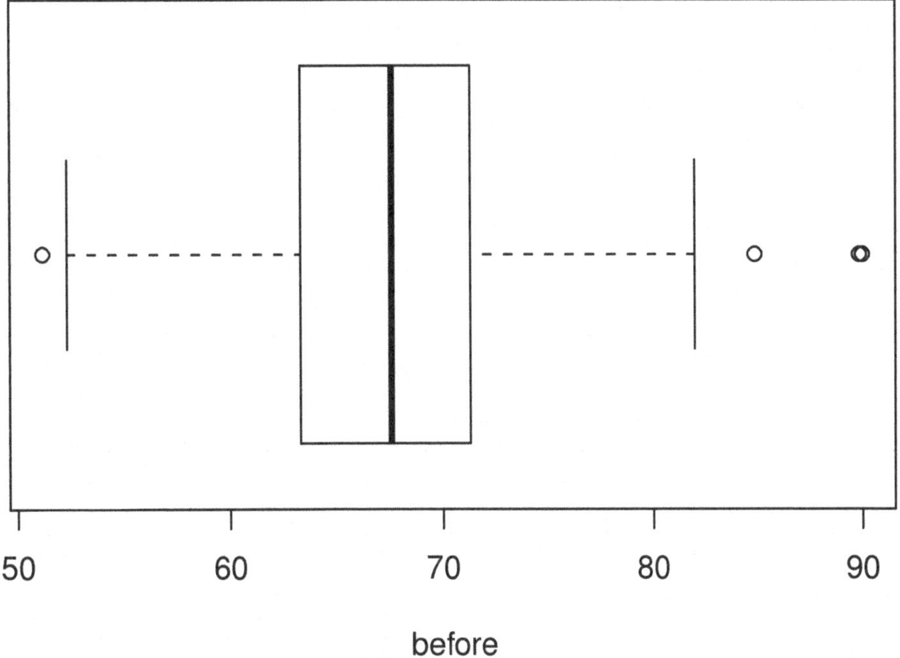

We want to watch out for extreme values (shown as circles separated from the box) or large departures from symmetry. If the distribution is fairly symmetric then the mean and median should be approximately the same. But if the distribution is highly skewed with extreme values then we should be skeptical of the sample mean, and fall back to the median which is resistant to extremes. By design, the before variable is set up to have a fairly symmetric distribution.

A boxplot of *after* is shown next.

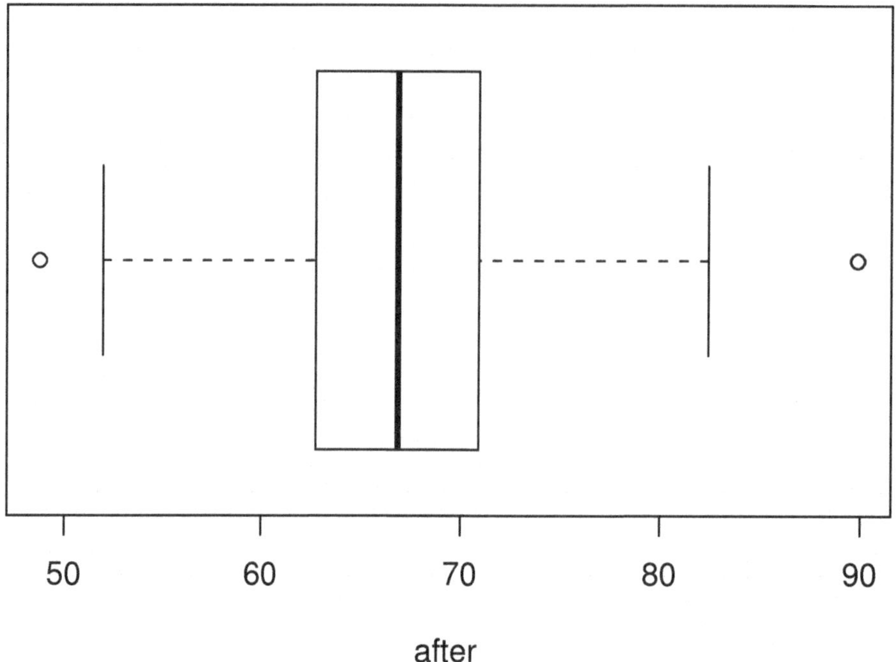

The same remarks apply to the *after* variable. The *after* variable has been designed to be left-skewed... thus, the median would likely be a good choice for this variable.

3. Based on your answer to (2), choose an appropriate measure of spread for each variable, calculate it, and report its value. Which variable has the biggest spread? (Note that you need to make sure that your measures are on the same scale.)

   Since *before* has a symmetric, mound shaped distribution, an excellent measure of center would be the sample standard deviation. And since *after* is left-skewed, we should use the median absolute deviation. It is also acceptable to use the IQR, but we should rescale it appropriately, namely, by dividing by 1.349. The exact values are shown below.

```
> sd(before)

[1] 6.201724

> mad(after)

[1] 6.095189

> IQR(after)/1.349

[1] 5.986954
```

   Judging from the values above, we would decide which variable has the higher spread. Look at how close the `mad` and the `IQR` (after suitable rescaling) are; it goes to show why the rescaling is important.

4. Calculate and report the skewness and kurtosis for *before*. Based on these values, how would you describe the shape of *before*?

   The values of these descriptive measures are shown below.

```
> library(e1071)
> skewness(before)

[1] 0.4016912

> kurtosis(before)

[1] 1.542225
```

   We should take the sample skewness value and compare it to $2\sqrt{6/n} \approx 0.378$ in absolute value to see if it is substantially different from zero. The direction of skewness is decided by the sign (positive or negative) of the skewness value.

   We should take the sample kurtosis value and compare it to $2 \cdot \sqrt{24/168} \approx 0.756$), in absolute value to see if the excess kurtosis is substantially different from zero. And take a look at the sign to see whether the distribution is platykurtic or leptokurtic.

5. Calculate and report the skewness and kurtosis for *after*. Based on these values, how would you describe the shape of *after*?

   The values of these descriptive measures are shown below.

```
> skewness(after)

[1] 0.3235134

> kurtosis(after)

[1] 1.452301
```

   We should do for this one just like we did previously. We would again compare the sample skewness and kurtosis values (in absolute value) to 0.378 and 0.756, respectively.

6. Plot histograms of *before* and *after* and compare them to your answers to (4) and (5).

   The graphs are shown below.

Histogram of before

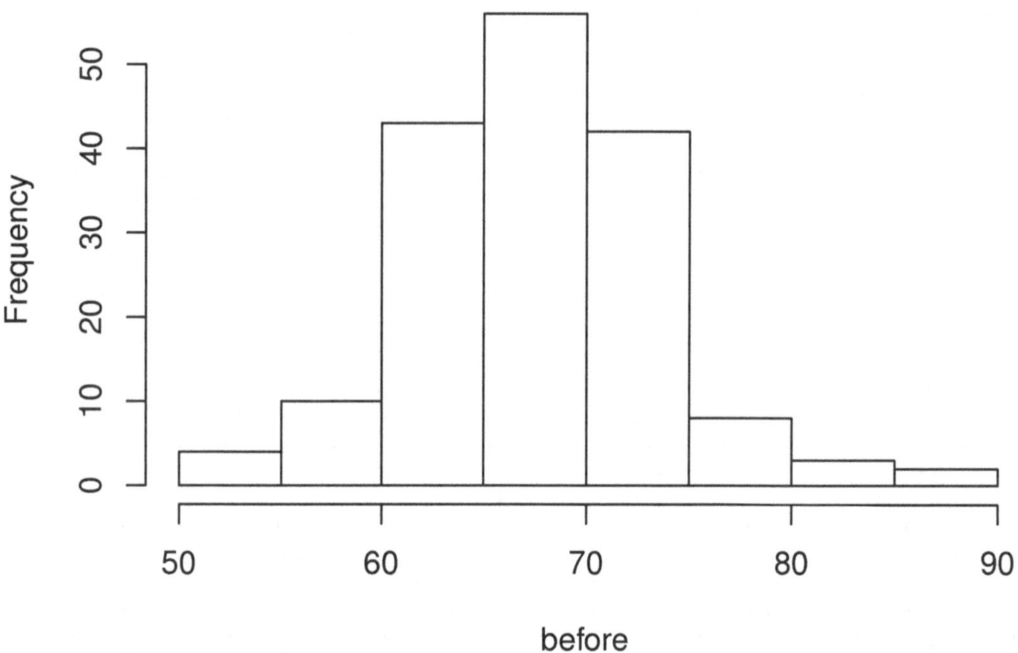

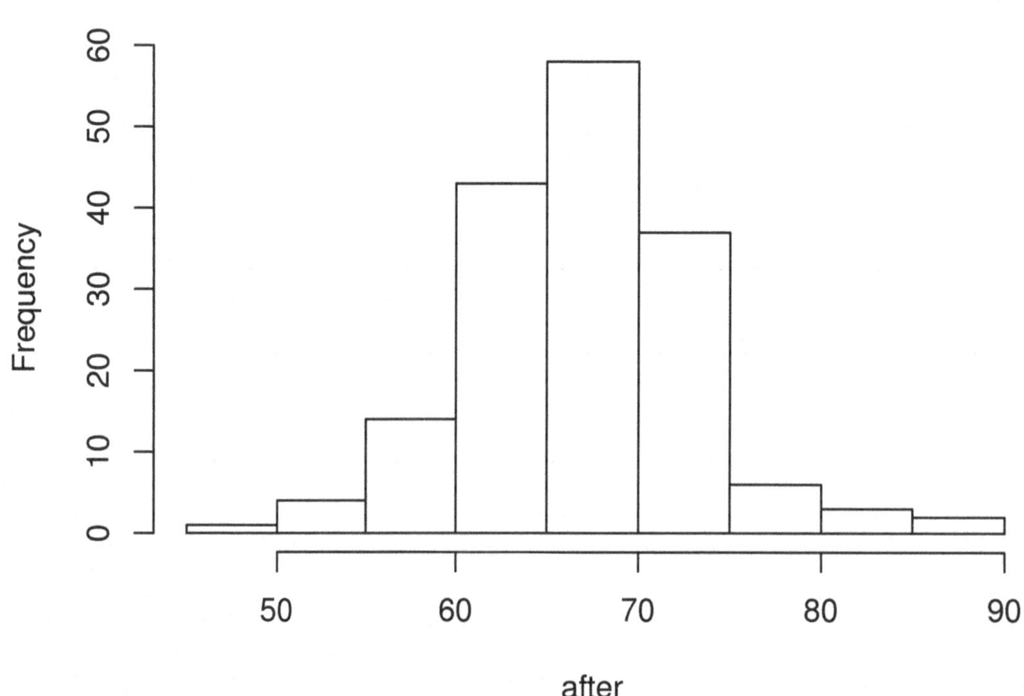

Answers will vary. We are looking for visual consistency in the histograms to our statements above.

Exercise 3.6. Describe the following data sets just as if you were communicating with an alien, but one who has had a statistics class. Mention the salient features (data type, important properties, anything special). Support your answers with the appropriate visual displays and descriptive statistics.

1. Conversion rates of Euro currencies stored in `euro`.
2. State abbreviations stored in `state.abb`.

Chapter 4

Probability

In this chapter we define the basic terminology associated with probability and derive some of its properties. We discuss three interpretations of probability. We discuss conditional probability and independent events, along with Bayes' Theorem. We finish the chapter with an introduction to random variables, which paves the way for the next two chapters.

In this book we distinguish between two types of experiments: *deterministic* and *random*. A *deterministic* experiment is one whose outcome may be predicted with certainty beforehand, such as combining Hydrogen and Oxygen, or adding two numbers such as $2 + 3$. A *random* experiment is one whose outcome is determined by chance. We posit that the outcome of a random experiment may not be predicted with certainty beforehand, even in principle. Examples of random experiments include tossing a coin, rolling a die, and throwing a dart on a board, how many red lights you encounter on the drive home, how many ants traverse a certain patch of sidewalk over a short period, *etc*.

What do I want them to know?

- that there are multiple interpretations of probability, and the methods used depend somewhat on the philosophy chosen
- nuts and bolts of basic probability jargon: sample spaces, events, probability functions, *etc.*
- how to count
- conditional probability and its relationship with independence
- Bayes' Rule and how it relates to the subjective view of probability
- what we mean by 'random variables', and where they come from

4.1 Sample Spaces

For a random experiment E, the set of all possible outcomes of E is called the *sample space* and is denoted by the letter S. For the coin-toss experiment, S would be the results "Head" and "Tail", which we may represent by $S = \{H, T\}$. Formally, the performance of a random experiment is the unpredictable selection of an outcome in S.

4.1.1 How to do it with R

Most of the probability work in this book is done with the `prob` package [52]. A sample space is (usually) represented by a *data frame*, that is, a rectangular collection of variables (see Section 3.5.2). Each row of the data frame corresponds to an outcome of the experiment. The data frame choice is convenient both for its simplicity and its compatibility with the R Commander. Data frames alone are, however, not sufficient to describe some of the more interesting probabilistic applications we will study later; to handle those we will need to consider a more general *list* data structure. See Section 4.6.3 for details.

Example 4.1. Consider the random experiment of dropping a Styrofoam cup onto the floor from a height of four feet. The cup hits the ground and eventually comes to rest. It could land upside down, right side up, or it could land on its side. We represent these possible outcomes of the random experiment by the following.

```
> S <- data.frame(lands = c("down", "up", "side"))
> S

  lands
1  down
2    up
3  side
```

The sample space S contains the column `lands` which stores the outcomes `"down"`, `"up"`, and `"side"`.

Some sample spaces are so common that convenience wrappers were written to set them up with minimal effort. The underlying machinery that does the work includes the `expand.grid` function in the `base` package, `combn` in the `combinat` package [14], and `permsn` in the `prob` package[1].

Consider the random experiment of tossing a coin. The outcomes are H and T. We can set up the sample space quickly with the `tosscoin` function:

```
> library(prob)
> tosscoin(1)

  toss1
1     H
2     T
```

The number 1 tells `tosscoin` that we only want to toss the coin once. We could toss it three times:

```
> tosscoin(3)

  toss1 toss2 toss3
1     H     H     H
2     T     H     H
3     H     T     H
```

[1]The seasoned R user can get the job done without the convenience wrappers. I encourage the beginner to use them to get started, but I also recommend that introductory students wean themselves as soon as possible. The wrappers were designed for ease and intuitive use, not for speed or efficiency.

```
4     T    T    H
5     H    H    T
6     T    H    T
7     H    T    T
8     T    T    T
```

Alternatively we could roll a fair die:

```
> rolldie(1)
  X1
1  1
2  2
3  3
4  4
5  5
6  6
```

The `rolldie` function defaults to a 6-sided die, but we can specify others with the `nsides` argument. The command `rolldie(3, nsides = 4)` would be used to roll a 4-sided die three times.

Perhaps we would like to draw one card from a standard set of playing cards (it is a long data frame):

```
> head(cards())
  rank suit
1    2 Club
2    3 Club
3    4 Club
4    5 Club
5    6 Club
6    7 Club
```

The `cards` function that we just used has optional arguments `jokers` (if you would like Jokers to be in the deck) and `makespace` which we will discuss later. There is also a `roulette` function which returns the sample space associated with one spin on a roulette wheel. There are EU and USA versions available. Interested readers may contribute any other game or sample spaces that may be of general interest.

4.1.2 Sampling from Urns

This is perhaps the most fundamental type of random experiment. We have an urn that contains a bunch of distinguishable objects (balls) inside. We shake up the urn, reach inside, grab a ball, and take a look. That's all.

But there are all sorts of variations on this theme. Maybe we would like to grab more than one ball – say, two balls. What are all of the possible outcomes of the experiment now? It depends on how we sample. We could select a ball, take a look, put it back, and sample again. Another way would be to select a ball, take a look – but do not put it back – and sample again (equivalently, just reach in and grab two balls). There are certainly more possible outcomes of the experiment in the former case than in the latter. In the first (second) case we say that sampling is done *with* (*without*) *replacement*.

There is more. Suppose we do not actually keep track of which ball came first. All we observe are the two balls, and we have no idea about the order in which they were selected. We call this *unordered sampling* (in contrast to *ordered*) because the order of the selections does not matter with respect to what we observe. We might as well have selected the balls and put them in a bag before looking.

Note that this one general class of random experiments contains as a special case all of the common elementary random experiments. Tossing a coin twice is equivalent to selecting two balls labeled H and T from an urn, with replacement. The die-roll experiment is equivalent to selecting a ball from an urn with six elements, labeled 1 through 6.

4.1.3 How to do it with R

The `prob` package accomplishes sampling from urns with the `urnsamples` function, which has arguments `x`, `size`, `replace`, and `ordered`. The argument `x` represents the urn from which sampling is to be done. The `size` argument tells how large the sample will be. The `ordered` and `replace` arguments are logical and specify how sampling will be performed. We will discuss each in turn.

Example 4.2. Let our urn simply contain three balls, labeled 1, 2, and 3, respectively. We are going to take a sample of size 2 from the urn.

Ordered, With Replacement

If sampling is with replacement, then we can get any outcome 1, 2, or 3 on any draw. Further, by "ordered" we mean that we shall keep track of the order of the draws that we observe. We can accomplish this in R with

```
> urnsamples(1:3, size = 2, replace = TRUE, ordered = TRUE)
```

```
  X1 X2
1  1  1
2  2  1
3  3  1
4  1  2
5  2  2
6  3  2
7  1  3
8  2  3
9  3  3
```

Notice that rows 2 and 4 are identical, save for the order in which the numbers are shown. Further, note that every possible pair of the numbers 1 through 3 are listed. This experiment is equivalent to rolling a 3-sided die twice, which we could have accomplished with `rolldie(2, nsides = 3)`.

Ordered, Without Replacement

Here sampling is without replacement, so we may not observe the same number twice in any row. Order is still important, however, so we expect to see the outcomes `1,2` and `2,1` somewhere in our data frame.

```
> urnsamples(1:3, size = 2, replace = FALSE, ordered = TRUE)

  X1 X2
1  1  2
2  2  1
3  1  3
4  3  1
5  2  3
6  3  2
```

This is just as we expected. Notice that there are less rows in this answer due to the more restrictive sampling procedure. If the numbers 1, 2, and 3 represented "Fred", "Mary", and "Sue", respectively, then this experiment would be equivalent to selecting two people of the three to serve as president and vice-president of a company, respectively, and the sample space shown above lists all possible ways that this could be done.

Unordered, Without Replacement

Again, we may not observe the same outcome twice, but in this case, we will only retain those outcomes which (when jumbled) would not duplicate earlier ones.

```
> urnsamples(1:3, size = 2, replace = FALSE, ordered = FALSE)

  X1 X2
1  1  2
2  1  3
3  2  3
```

This experiment is equivalent to reaching in the urn, picking a pair, and looking to see what they are. This is the default setting of `urnsamples`, so we would have received the same output by simply typing `urnsamples(1:3, 2)`.

Unordered, With Replacement

The last possibility is perhaps the most interesting. We replace the balls after every draw, but we do not remember the order in which the draws came.

```
> urnsamples(1:3, size = 2, replace = TRUE, ordered = FALSE)

  X1 X2
1  1  1
2  1  2
3  1  3
4  2  2
5  2  3
6  3  3
```

We may interpret this experiment in a number of alternative ways. One way is to consider this as simply putting two 3-sided dice in a cup, shaking the cup, and looking inside – as in a game of *Liar's Dice*, for instance. Each row of the sample space is a potential pair we could observe. Another way is to view each outcome as a separate method to distribute two identical golf balls into three boxes labeled 1, 2, and 3. Regardless of the interpretation, `urnsamples` lists every possible way that the experiment can conclude.

Note that the urn does not need to contain numbers; we could have just as easily taken our urn to be `x = c("Red","Blue","Green")`. But, there is an **important** point to mention before proceeding. Astute readers will notice that in our example, the balls in the urn were *distinguishable* in the sense that each had a unique label to distinguish it from the others in the urn. A natural question would be, "What happens if your urn has indistinguishable elements, for example, what if `x = c("Red","Red","Blue")`?" The answer is that `urnsamples` behaves as if each ball in the urn is distinguishable, regardless of its actual contents. We may thus imagine that while there are two red balls in the urn, the balls are such that we can tell them apart (in principle) by looking closely enough at the imperfections on their surface.

In this way, when the `x` argument of `urnsamples` has repeated elements, the resulting sample space may appear to be `ordered = TRUE` even when, in fact, the call to the function was `urnsamples(..., ordered = FALSE)`. Similar remarks apply for the `replace` argument.

4.2 Events

An *event* A is merely a collection of outcomes, or in other words, a subset of the sample space[2]. After the performance of a random experiment E we say that the event A *occurred* if the experiment's outcome belongs to A. We say that a bunch of events $A_1, A_2, A_3, \ldots$ are *mutually exclusive* or *disjoint* if $A_i \cap A_j = \emptyset$ for any distinct pair $A_i \neq A_j$. For instance, in the coin-toss experiment the events $A = \{\text{Heads}\}$ and $B = \{\text{Tails}\}$ would be mutually exclusive. Now would be a good time to review the algebra of sets in Appendix E.1.

4.2.1 How to do it with R

Given a data frame sample/probability space S, we may extract rows using the `[]` operator:

```
> S <- tosscoin(2, makespace = TRUE)

  toss1 toss2 probs
1     H     H  0.25
2     T     H  0.25
3     H     T  0.25
4     T     T  0.25

> S[1:3, ]

  toss1 toss2 probs
1     H     H  0.25
2     T     H  0.25
3     H     T  0.25
```

[2]This naive definition works for finite or countably infinite sample spaces, but is inadequate for sample spaces in general. In this book, we will not address the subtleties that arise, but will refer the interested reader to any text on advanced probability or measure theory.

```
> S[c(2, 4), ]
  toss1 toss2 probs
2     T     H  0.25
4     T     T  0.25
```

and so forth. We may also extract rows that satisfy a logical expression using the `subset` function, for instance

```
> S <- cards()
```

```
> subset(S, suit == "Heart")
   rank  suit
27    2 Heart
28    3 Heart
29    4 Heart
30    5 Heart
31    6 Heart
32    7 Heart
33    8 Heart
34    9 Heart
35   10 Heart
36    J Heart
37    Q Heart
38    K Heart
39    A Heart
> subset(S, rank %in% 7:9)
   rank    suit
6     7    Club
7     8    Club
8     9    Club
19    7 Diamond
20    8 Diamond
21    9 Diamond
32    7   Heart
33    8   Heart
34    9   Heart
45    7   Spade
46    8   Spade
47    9   Spade
```

We could continue indefinitely. Also note that mathematical expressions are allowed:

```
> subset(rolldie(3), X1 + X2 + X3 > 16)
    X1 X2 X3
180  6  6  5
210  6  5  6
215  5  6  6
216  6  6  6
```

4.2.2 Functions for Finding Subsets

It does not take long before the subsets of interest become complicated to specify. Yet the main idea remains: we have a particular logical condition to apply to each row. If the row satisfies the condition, then it should be in the subset. It should not be in the subset otherwise. The ease with which the condition may be coded depends of course on the question being asked. Here are a few functions to get started.

The `%in%` function

The function `%in%` helps to learn whether each value of one vector lies somewhere inside another vector.

```
> x <- 1:10
> y <- 8:12
> y %in% x
```

```
[1]  TRUE  TRUE  TRUE FALSE FALSE
```

Notice that the returned value is a vector of length 5 which tests whether each element of `y` is in `x`, in turn.

The `isin` function

It is more common to want to know whether the *whole* vector `y` is in `x`. We can do this with the `isin` function.

```
> isin(x, y)
```

```
[1] FALSE
```

Of course, one may ask why we did not try something like `all(y %in% x)`, which would give a single result, `TRUE`. The reason is that the answers are different in the case that `y` has repeated values. Compare:

```
> x <- 1:10
> y <- c(3, 3, 7)
```

```
> all(y %in% x)
```

```
[1] TRUE
```

```
> isin(x, y)
```

```
[1] FALSE
```

The reason for the above is of course that `x` contains the value 3, but `x` does not have *two* 3's. The difference is important when rolling multiple dice, playing cards, *etc*. Note that there is an optional argument `ordered` which tests whether the elements of `y` appear in `x` in the order in which they are appear in `y`. The consequences are

```
> isin(x, c(3, 4, 5), ordered = TRUE)
```

```
[1] TRUE
> isin(x, c(3, 5, 4), ordered = TRUE)
[1] FALSE
```

The connection to probability is that have a data frame sample space and we would like to find a subset of that space. A `data.frame` method was written for `isin` that simply applies the function to each row of the data frame. We can see the method in action with the following:

```
> S <- rolldie(4)
> subset(S, isin(S, c(2, 2, 6), ordered = TRUE))
     X1 X2 X3 X4
188   2  2  6  1
404   2  2  6  2
620   2  2  6  3
836   2  2  6  4
1052  2  2  6  5
1088  2  2  1  6
1118  2  1  2  6
1123  1  2  2  6
1124  2  2  2  6
1125  3  2  2  6
1126  4  2  2  6
1127  5  2  2  6
1128  6  2  2  6
1130  2  3  2  6
1136  2  4  2  6
1142  2  5  2  6
1148  2  6  2  6
1160  2  2  3  6
1196  2  2  4  6
1232  2  2  5  6
1268  2  2  6  6
```

There are a few other functions written to find useful subsets, namely, `countrep` and `isrep`. Essentially these were written to test for (or count) a specific number of designated values in outcomes. See the documentation for details.

4.2.3 Set Union, Intersection, and Difference

Given subsets A and B, it is often useful to manipulate them in an algebraic fashion. To this end, we have three set operations at our disposal: union, intersection, and difference. Below is a table that summarizes the pertinent information about these operations.

Name	Denoted	Defined by elements	Code
Union	$A \cup B$	in A or B or both	`union(A,B)`
Intersection	$A \cap B$	in both A and B	`intersect(A,B)`
Difference	$A \backslash B$	in A but not in B	`setdiff(A,B)`

Some examples follow.

```
> S = cards()
> A = subset(S, suit == "Heart")
> B = subset(S, rank %in% 7:9)
```

We can now do some set algebra:

```
> union(A, B)
   rank    suit
6     7    Club
7     8    Club
8     9    Club
19    7 Diamond
20    8 Diamond
21    9 Diamond
27    2   Heart
28    3   Heart
29    4   Heart
30    5   Heart
31    6   Heart
32    7   Heart
33    8   Heart
34    9   Heart
35   10   Heart
36    J   Heart
37    Q   Heart
38    K   Heart
39    A   Heart
45    7   Spade
46    8   Spade
47    9   Spade
> intersect(A, B)
   rank  suit
32    7 Heart
33    8 Heart
34    9 Heart
> setdiff(A, B)
   rank  suit
27    2 Heart
28    3 Heart
29    4 Heart
30    5 Heart
31    6 Heart
35   10 Heart
36    J Heart
37    Q Heart
38    K Heart
39    A Heart
```

```
> setdiff(B, A)
   rank    suit
6     7    Club
7     8    Club
8     9    Club
19    7 Diamond
20    8 Diamond
21    9 Diamond
45    7   Spade
46    8   Spade
47    9   Spade
```

Notice that `setdiff` is not symmetric. Further, note that we can calculate the *complement* of a set A, denoted A^c and defined to be the elements of S that are not in A simply with `setdiff(S,A)`.

There have been methods written for `intersect`, `setdiff`, `subset`, and `union` in the case that the input objects are of class `ps`. See Section 4.6.3.

Note 4.3. When the `prob` package loads you will notice a message: "`The following object(s) are masked from package:base : intersect, setdiff, union`". The reason for this message is that there already exist methods for the functions `intersect`, `setdiff`, `subset`, and `union` in the `base` package which ships with R. However, these methods were designed for when the arguments are vectors of the same mode. Since we are manipulating sample spaces which are data frames and lists, it was necessary to write methods to handle those cases as well. When the `prob` package is loaded, R recognizes that there are multiple versions of the same function in the search path and acts to shield the new definitions from the existing ones. But there is no cause for alarm, thankfully, because the `prob` functions have been carefully defined to match the usual `base` package definition in the case that the arguments are vectors.

4.3 Model Assignment

Let us take a look at the coin-toss experiment more closely. What do we mean when we say "the probability of Heads" or write $\mathbb{P}$(Heads)? Given a coin and an itchy thumb, how do we go about finding what $\mathbb{P}$(Heads) should be?

4.3.1 The Measure Theory Approach

This approach states that the way to handle $\mathbb{P}$(Heads) is to define a mathematical function, called a *probability measure*, on the sample space. Probability measures satisfy certain axioms (to be introduced later) and have special mathematical properties, so not just any mathematical function will do. But in any given physical circumstance there are typically all sorts of probability measures from which to choose, and it is left to the experimenter to make a reasonable choice – usually based on considerations of objectivity. For the tossing coin example, a valid probability measure assigns probability p to the event {Heads}, where p is some number $0 \leq p \leq 1$. An experimenter that wishes to incorporate the symmetry of the coin would choose $p = 1/2$ to balance the likelihood of {Heads} and {Tails}.

Once the probability measure is chosen (or determined), there is not much left to do. All assignments of probability are made by the probability function, and the experimenter needs only to plug the event {Heads} into to the probability function to find $\mathbb{P}$(Heads). In this way, the probability of an event is simply a calculated value, nothing more, nothing less. Of course this is not the whole story; there are many theorems and consequences associated with this approach that will keep us occupied for the remainder of this book. The approach is called *measure theory* because the measure (probability) of a set (event) is associated with how big it is (how likely it is to occur).

The measure theory approach is well suited for situations where there is symmetry to the experiment, such as flipping a balanced coin or spinning an arrow around a circle with well-defined pie slices. It is also handy because of its mathematical simplicity, elegance, and flexibility. There are literally volumes of information that one can prove about probability measures, and the cold rules of mathematics allow us to analyze intricate probabilistic problems with vigor.

The large degree of flexibility is also a disadvantage, however. When symmetry fails it is not always obvious what an "objective" choice of probability measure should be; for instance, what probability should we assign to {Heads} if we spin the coin rather than flip it? (It is not 1/2.) Furthermore, the mathematical rules are restrictive when we wish to incorporate subjective knowledge into the model, knowledge which changes over time and depends on the experimenter, such as personal knowledge about the properties of the specific coin being flipped, or of the person doing the flipping.

The mathematician who revolutionized this way to do probability theory was Andrey Kolmogorov, who published a landmark monograph in 1933. See

`http://www-history.mcs.st-andrews.ac.uk/Mathematicians/Kolmogorov.html`

for more information.

4.3.2 Relative Frequency Approach

This approach states that the way to determine $\mathbb{P}$(Heads) is to flip the coin repeatedly, in exactly the same way each time. Keep a tally of the number of flips and the number of Heads observed. Then a good approximation to $\mathbb{P}$(Heads) will be

$$\mathbb{P}(\text{Heads}) \approx \frac{\text{number of observed Heads}}{\text{total number of flips}}. \tag{4.3.1}$$

The mathematical underpinning of this approach is the celebrated **Law of Large Numbers**, which may be loosely described as follows. Let E be a random experiment in which the event A either does or does not occur. Perform the experiment repeatedly, in an identical manner, in such a way that the successive experiments do not influence each other. After each experiment, keep a running tally of whether or not the event A occurred. Let S_n count the number of times that A occurred in the n experiments. Then the law of large numbers says that

$$\frac{S_n}{n} \to \mathbb{P}(A) \text{ as } n \to \infty. \tag{4.3.2}$$

As the reasoning goes, to learn about the probability of an event A we need only repeat the random experiment to get a reasonable estimate of the probability's value, and if we are not satisfied with our estimate then we may simply repeat the experiment more times all the while confident that with more and more experiments our estimate will stabilize to the true value.

The frequentist approach is good because it is relatively light on assumptions and does not worry about symmetry or claims of objectivity like the measure-theoretic approach does. It is perfect for the spinning coin experiment. One drawback to the method is that one can never know the exact value of a probability, only a long-run approximation. It also does not work well with experiments that can not be repeated indefinitely, say, the probability that it will rain today, the chances that you get will get an A in your Statistics class, or the probability that the world is destroyed by nuclear war.

This approach was espoused by Richard von Mises in the early twentieth century, and some of his main ideas were incorporated into the measure theory approach. See

`http://www-history.mcs.st-andrews.ac.uk/Biographies/Mises.html`

for more.

4.3.3 The Subjective Approach

The subjective approach interprets probability as the experimenter's *degree of belief* that the event will occur. The estimate of the probability of an event is based on the totality of the individual's knowledge at the time. As new information becomes available, the estimate is modified accordingly to best reflect his/her current knowledge. The method by which the probabilities are updated is commonly done with Bayes' Rule, discussed in Section 4.8.

So for the coin toss example, a person may have $\mathbb{P}(\text{Heads}) = 1/2$ in the absence of additional information. But perhaps the observer knows additional information about the coin or the thrower that would shift the probability in a certain direction. For instance, parlor magicians may be trained to be quite skilled at tossing coins, and some are so skilled that they may toss a fair coin and get nothing but Heads, indefinitely. I have *seen* this. It was similarly claimed in *Bringing Down the House* [65] that MIT students were accomplished enough with cards to be able to cut a deck to the same location, every single time. In such cases, one clearly should use the additional information to assign $\mathbb{P}(\text{Heads})$ away from the symmetry value of $1/2$.

This approach works well in situations that cannot be repeated indefinitely, for example, to assign your probability that you will get an A in this class, the chances of a devastating nuclear war, or the likelihood that a cure for the common cold will be discovered.

The roots of subjective probability reach back a long time. See

`http://en.wikipedia.org/wiki/Subjective_probability`

for a short discussion and links to references about the subjective approach.

4.3.4 Equally Likely Model (ELM)

We have seen several approaches to the assignment of a probability model to a given random experiment and they are very different in their underlying interpretation. But they all cross paths when it comes to the equally likely model which assigns equal probability to all elementary outcomes of the experiment.

The ELM appears in the measure theory approach when the experiment boasts symmetry of some kind. If symmetry guarantees that all outcomes have equal "size", and if outcomes with equal "size" should get the same probability, then the ELM is a logical objective choice for the experimenter. Consider the balanced 6-sided die, the fair coin, or the dart board with equal-sized wedges.

The ELM appears in the subjective approach when the experimenter resorts to indifference or ignorance with respect to his/her knowledge of the outcome of the experiment. If the experimenter has no prior knowledge to suggest that (s)he prefer Heads over Tails, then it is reasonable for the him/her to assign equal subjective probability to both possible outcomes.

The ELM appears in the relative frequency approach as a fascinating fact of Nature: when we flip balanced coins over and over again, we observe that the proportion of times that the coin comes up Heads tends to $1/2$. Of course if we assume that the measure theory applies then we can prove that the sample proportion must tend to 1/2 as expected, but that is putting the cart before the horse, in a manner of speaking.

The ELM is only available when there are finitely many elements in the sample space.

4.3.5 How to do it with R

In the `prob` package, a probability space is an object of outcomes S and a vector of probabilities (called "`probs`") with entries that correspond to each outcome in S. When S is a data frame, we may simply add a column called `probs` to S and we will be finished; the probability space will simply be a data frame which we may call S. In the case that S is a list, we may combine the `outcomes` and `probs` into a larger list, `space`; it will have two components: `outcomes` and `probs`. The only requirements we need are for the entries of `probs` to be nonnegative and `sum(probs)` to be one.

To accomplish this in R, we may use the `probspace` function. The general syntax is `probspace(x, probs)`, where `x` is a sample space of outcomes and `probs` is a vector (of the same length as the number of outcomes in `x`). The specific choice of `probs` depends on the context of the problem, and some examples follow to demonstrate some of the more common choices.

Example 4.4. The Equally Likely Model asserts that every outcome of the sample space has the same probability, thus, if a sample space has n outcomes, then `probs` would be a vector of length n with identical entries $1/n$. The quickest way to generate `probs` is with the `rep` function. We will start with the experiment of rolling a die, so that $n = 6$. We will construct the sample space, generate the `probs` vector, and put them together with `probspace`.

```
> outcomes <- rolldie(1)
  X1
1  1
2  2
3  3
4  4
5  5
6  6
> p <- rep(1/6, times = 6)
[1] 0.1666667 0.1666667 0.1666667 0.1666667 0.1666667 0.1666667
> probspace(outcomes, probs = p)
  X1     probs
1  1 0.1666667
2  2 0.1666667
3  3 0.1666667
4  4 0.1666667
5  5 0.1666667
6  6 0.1666667
```

The probspace function is designed to save us some time in many of the most common situations. For example, due to the especial simplicity of the sample space in this case, we could have achieved the same result with only (note the name change for the first column)

```
> probspace(1:6, probs = p)

  x     probs
1 1 0.1666667
2 2 0.1666667
3 3 0.1666667
4 4 0.1666667
5 5 0.1666667
6 6 0.1666667
```

Further, since the equally likely model plays such a fundamental role in the study of probability the probspace function will assume that the equally model is desired if no probs are specified. Thus, we get the same answer with only

```
> probspace(1:6)

  x     probs
1 1 0.1666667
2 2 0.1666667
3 3 0.1666667
4 4 0.1666667
5 5 0.1666667
6 6 0.1666667
```

And finally, since rolling dice is such a common experiment in probability classes, the rolldie function has an additional logical argument makespace that will add a column of equally likely probs to the generated sample space:

```
> rolldie(1, makespace = TRUE)

  X1     probs
1  1 0.1666667
2  2 0.1666667
3  3 0.1666667
4  4 0.1666667
5  5 0.1666667
6  6 0.1666667
```

or just rolldie(1, TRUE). Many of the other sample space functions (tosscoin, cards, roulette, *etc.*) have similar makespace arguments. Check the documentation for details.

One sample space function that does NOT have a makespace option is the urnsamples function. This was intentional. The reason is that under the varied sampling assumptions the outcomes in the respective sample spaces are NOT, in general, equally likely. It is important for the user to carefully consider the experiment to decide whether or not the outcomes are equally likely and then use probspace to assign the model.

Example 4.5. An unbalanced coin. While the `makespace` argument to `tosscoin` is useful to represent the tossing of a *fair* coin, it is not always appropriate. For example, suppose our coin is not perfectly balanced, for instance, maybe the "*H*" side is somewhat heavier such that the chances of a *H* appearing in a single toss is 0.70 instead of 0.5. We may set up the probability space with

```
> probspace(tosscoin(1), probs = c(0.7, 0.3))

  toss1 probs
1     H   0.7
2     T   0.3
```

The same procedure can be used to represent an unbalanced die, roulette wheel, *etc.*

4.3.6 Words of Warning

It should be mentioned that while the splendour of R is uncontested, it, like everything else, has limits both with respect to the sample/probability spaces it can manage and with respect to the finite accuracy of the representation of most numbers (see the R FAQ 7.31). When playing around with probability, one may be tempted to set up a probability space for tossing 100 coins or rolling 50 dice in an attempt to answer some scintillating question. (Bear in mind: rolling a die just 9 times has a sample space with over *10 million* outcomes.)

Alas, even if there were enough RAM to barely hold the sample space (and there were enough time to wait for it to be generated), the infinitesimal probabilities that are associated with *so many* outcomes make it difficult for the underlying machinery to handle reliably. In some cases, special algorithms need to be called just to give something that holds asymptotically. User beware.

4.4 Properties of Probability

4.4.1 Probability Functions

A *probability function* is a rule that associates with each event A of the sample space a unique number $\mathbb{P}(A) = p$, called the probability of A. Any probability function $\mathbb{P}$ satisfies the following three Kolmogorov Axioms:

Axiom 4.6. $\mathbb{P}(A) \geq 0$ *for any event* $A \subset S$.

Axiom 4.7. $\mathbb{P}(S) = 1$.

Axiom 4.8. *If the events* $A_1, A_2, A_3 \ldots$ *are disjoint then*

$$\mathbb{P}\left(\bigcup_{i=1}^{n} A_i\right) = \sum_{i=1}^{n} \mathbb{P}(A_i) \text{ for every } n, \tag{4.4.1}$$

and furthermore,

$$\mathbb{P}\left(\bigcup_{i=1}^{\infty} A_i\right) = \sum_{i=1}^{\infty} \mathbb{P}(A_i). \tag{4.4.2}$$

The intuition behind the axioms: first, the probability of an event should never be negative. And since the sample space contains all possible outcomes, its probability should be one, or 100%. The final axiom may look intimidating, but it simply means that for a sequence of disjoint events (in other words, sets that do not overlap), their total probability (measure) should equal the sum of its parts. For example, the chance of rolling a 1 or a 2 on a die is the chance of rolling a 1 plus the chance of rolling a 2. The connection to measure theory could not be more clear.

4.4.2 Properties

For any events A and B,

1. $\mathbb{P}(A^c) = 1 - \mathbb{P}(A)$.

   Proof. Since $A \cup A^c = S$ and $A \cap A^c = \emptyset$, we have

   $$1 = \mathbb{P}(S) = \mathbb{P}(A \cup A^c) = \mathbb{P}(A) + \mathbb{P}(A^c).$$

   □

2. $\mathbb{P}(\emptyset) = 0$.

   Proof. Note that $\emptyset = S^c$, and use Property 1. □

3. If $A \subset B$, then $\mathbb{P}(A) \leq \mathbb{P}(B)$.

   Proof. Write $B = A \cup (B \cap A^c)$, and notice that $A \cap (B \cap A^c) = \emptyset$; thus

   $$\mathbb{P}(B) = \mathbb{P}(A \cup (B \cap A^c)) = \mathbb{P}(A) + \mathbb{P}(B \cap A^c) \geq \mathbb{P}(A),$$

   since $\mathbb{P}(B \cap A^c) \geq 0$. □

4. $0 \leq \mathbb{P}(A) \leq 1$.

   Proof. The left inequality is immediate from Axiom 4.6, and the second inequality follows from Property 3 since $A \subset S$. □

5. ***The General Addition Rule.***

   $$\mathbb{P}(A \cup B) = \mathbb{P}(A) + \mathbb{P}(B) - \mathbb{P}(A \cap B). \tag{4.4.3}$$

   More generally, for events $A_1, A_2, A_3, \ldots, A_n$,

   $$\mathbb{P}\left(\bigcup_{i=1}^{n} A_i\right) = \sum_{i=1}^{n} \mathbb{P}(A_i) - \sum_{i=1}^{n-1} \sum_{j=i+1}^{n} \mathbb{P}(A_i \cap A_j) + \cdots + (-1)^{n-1}\, \mathbb{P}\left(\bigcap_{i=1}^{n} A_i\right) \tag{4.4.4}$$

6. ***The Theorem of Total Probability.*** Let $B_1, B_2, \ldots, B_n$ be mutually exclusive and exhaustive. Then

   $$\mathbb{P}(A) = \mathbb{P}(A \cap B_1) + \mathbb{P}(A \cap B_2) + \cdots + \mathbb{P}(A \cap B_n). \tag{4.4.5}$$

4.4.3 Assigning Probabilities

A model of particular interest is the *equally likely model.* The idea is to divide the sample space S into a finite collection of elementary events $\{a_1, a_2, \ldots, a_N\}$ that are equally likely in the sense that each a_i has equal chances of occurring. The probability function associated with this model must satisfy $\mathbb{P}(S) = 1$, by Axiom 2. On the other hand, it must also satisfy

$$\mathbb{P}(S) = \mathbb{P}(\{a_1, a_2, \ldots, a_N\}) = \mathbb{P}(a_1 \cup a_2 \cup \cdots \cup a_N) = \sum_{i=1}^{N} \mathbb{P}(a_i),$$

by Axiom 3. Since $\mathbb{P}(a_i)$ is the same for all i, each one necessarily equals $1/N$.

For an event $A \subset S$, we write it as a collection of elementary outcomes: if $A = \{a_{i_1}, a_{i_2}, \ldots, a_{i_k}\}$ then A has k elements and

$$\begin{aligned}\mathbb{P}(A) &= \mathbb{P}(a_{i_1}) + \mathbb{P}(a_{i_2}) + \cdots + \mathbb{P}(a_{i_k}),\\ &= \frac{1}{N} + \frac{1}{N} + \cdots + \frac{1}{N},\\ &= \frac{k}{N} = \frac{\#(A)}{\#(S)}.\end{aligned}$$

In other words, under the equally likely model, the probability of an event A is determined by the number of elementary events that A contains.

Example 4.9. Consider the random experiment E of tossing a coin. Then the sample space is $S = \{H, T\}$, and under the equally likely model, these two outcomes have $\mathbb{P}(H) = \mathbb{P}(T) = 1/2$. This model is taken when it is reasonable to assume that the coin is fair.

Example 4.10. Suppose the experiment E consists of tossing a fair coin twice. The sample space may be represented by $S = \{HH, HT, TH, TT\}$. Given that the coin is fair and that the coin is tossed in an independent and identical manner, it is reasonable to apply the equally likely model.

What is $\mathbb{P}$(at least 1 Head)? Looking at the sample space we see the elements HH, HT, and TH have at least one Head; thus, $\mathbb{P}$(at least 1 Head) $= 3/4$.

What is $\mathbb{P}$(no Heads)? Notice that the event {no Heads} = {at least one Head}^{c}, which by Property 1 means $\mathbb{P}$(no Heads) = 1 − $\mathbb{P}$(at least one Head) $= 1 - 3/4 = 1/4$. It is obvious in this simple example that the only outcome with no Heads is TT, however, this complementation trick is useful in more complicated circumstances.

Example 4.11. Imagine a three child family, each child being either Boy (B) or Girl (G). An example sequence of siblings would be BGB. The sample space may be written

$$S = \left\{ \begin{array}{cccc} BBB, & BGB, & GBB, & GGB, \\ BBG, & BGG, & GBG, & GGG \end{array} \right\}.$$

Note that for many reasons (for instance, it turns out that girls are slightly more likely to be born than boys), this sample space is *not* equally likely. For the sake of argument, however, we will assume that the elementary outcomes each have probability $1/8$.

What is $\mathbb{P}$(exactly 2 Boys)? Inspecting the sample space reveals three outcomes with exactly two boys: $\{BBG, BGB, GBB\}$. Therefore $\mathbb{P}$(exactly 2 Boys) $= 3/8$.

What is $\mathbb{P}$(at most 2 Boys)? One way to solve the problem would be to count the outcomes that have 2 or less Boys, but a quicker way would be to recognize that the only way that the event {at most 2 Boys} does *not* occur is the event {all Girls}. Thus

$$\mathbb{P}(\text{at most 2 Boys}) = 1 - \mathbb{P}(GGG) = 1 - 1/8 = 7/8.$$

Example 4.12. Consider the experiment of rolling a six-sided die, and let the outcome be the face showing up when the die comes to rest. Then $S = \{1, 2, 3, 4, 5, 6\}$. It is usually reasonable to suppose that the die is fair, so that the six outcomes are equally likely.

Example 4.13. Consider a standard deck of 52 cards. These are usually labeled with the four *suits*: Clubs, Diamonds, Hearts, and Spades, and the 13 *ranks*: 2, 3, 4, ..., 10, Jack (J), Queen (Q), King (K), and Ace (A). Depending on the game played, the Ace may be ranked below 2 or above King.

Let the random experiment E consist of drawing exactly one card from a well-shuffled deck, and let the outcome be the face of the card. Define the events $A = \{\text{draw an Ace}\}$ and $B = \{\text{draw a Club}\}$. Bear in mind: we are only drawing one card.

Immediately we have $\mathbb{P}(A) = 4/52$ since there are four Aces in the deck; similarly, there are 13 Clubs which implies $\mathbb{P}(B) = 13/52$.

What is $\mathbb{P}(A \cap B)$? We realize that there is only one card of the 52 which is an Ace and a Club at the same time, namely, the Ace of Clubs. Therefore $\mathbb{P}(A \cap B) = 1/52$.

To find $\mathbb{P}(A \cup B)$ we may use the above with the General Addition Rule to get

$$
\begin{aligned}
\mathbb{P}(A \cup B) &= \mathbb{P}(A) + \mathbb{P}(B) - \mathbb{P}(A \cap B), \\
&= 4/52 + 13/52 - 1/52, \\
&= 16/52.
\end{aligned}
$$

Example 4.14. Staying with the deck of cards, let another random experiment be the selection of a five card stud poker hand, where "five card stud" means that we draw exactly five cards from the deck without replacement, no more, and no less. It turns out that the sample space S is so large and complicated that we will be obliged to settle for the trivial description $S = \{\text{all possible 5 card hands}\}$ for the time being. We will have a more precise description later.

What is $\mathbb{P}(\text{Royal Flush})$, or in other words, $\mathbb{P}(\text{A, K, Q, J, 10 all in the same suit})$?

It should be clear that there are only four possible royal flushes. Thus, if we could only count the number of outcomes in S then we could simply divide four by that number and we would have our answer under the equally likely model. This is the subject of Section 4.5.

4.4.4 How to do it with R

Probabilities are calculated in the `prob` package with the `prob` function.

Consider the experiment of drawing a card from a standard deck of playing cards. Let's denote the probability space associated with the experiment as `S`, and let the subsets `A` and `B` be defined by the following:

```
> S <- cards(makespace = TRUE)
> A <- subset(S, suit == "Heart")
> B <- subset(S, rank %in% 7:9)
```

Now it is easy to calculate

```
> prob(A)
[1] 0.25
```

Note that we can get the same answer with

```
> prob(S, suit == "Heart")

[1] 0.25
```

We also find `prob(B)= 0.23` (listed here approximately, but 12/52 actually) and `prob(S)= 1`. Internally, the `prob` function operates by summing the `probs` column of its argument. It will find subsets on-the-fly if desired.

We have as yet glossed over the details. More specifically, `prob` has three arguments: `x`, which is a probability space (or a subset of one), `event`, which is a logical expression used to define a subset, and `given`, which is described in Section 4.6.

WARNING. The `event` argument is used to define a subset of `x`, that is, the only outcomes used in the probability calculation will be those that are elements of `x` and satisfy `event` simultaneously. In other words, `prob(x, event)` calculates

```
prob(intersect(x, subset(x, event)))
```

Consequently, `x` should be the entire probability space in the case that `event` is non-null.

4.5 Counting Methods

The equally-likely model is a convenient and popular way to analyze random experiments. And when the equally likely model applies, finding the probability of an event A amounts to nothing more than counting the number of outcomes that A contains (together with the number of events in S). Hence, to be a master of probability one must be skilled at counting outcomes in events of all kinds.

Proposition 4.15. *The Multiplication Principle. Suppose that an experiment is composed of two successive steps. Further suppose that the first step may be performed in n_1 distinct ways while the second step may be performed in n_2 distinct ways. Then the experiment may be performed in $n_1 n_2$ distinct ways.*

More generally, if the experiment is composed of k successive steps which may be performed in n_1, n_2, ..., n_k distinct ways, respectively, then the experiment may be performed in $n_1 n_2 \cdots n_k$ distinct ways.

Example 4.16. We would like to order a pizza. It will be sure to have cheese (and marinara sauce), but we may elect to add one or more of the following five (5) available toppings:

pepperoni, sausage, anchovies, olives, and green peppers.

How many distinct pizzas are possible?

There are many ways to approach the problem, but the quickest avenue employs the Multiplication Principle directly. We will separate the action of ordering the pizza into a series of stages. At the first stage, we will decide whether or not to include pepperoni on the pizza (two possibilities). At the next stage, we will decide whether or not to include sausage on the pizza (again, two possibilities). We will continue in this fashion until at last we will decide whether or not to include green peppers on the pizza.

At each stage we will have had two options, or ways, to select a pizza to be made. The Multiplication Principle says that we should multiply the 2's to find the total number of possible pizzas: $2 \cdot 2 \cdot 2 \cdot 2 \cdot 2 = 2^5 = 32$.

Example 4.17. We would like to buy a desktop computer to study statistics. We go to a website to build our computer our way. Given a line of products we have many options to customize our computer. In particular, there are 2 choices for a processor, 3 different operating systems, 4 levels of memory, 4 hard drives of differing sizes, and 10 choices for a monitor. How many possible types of computer must Gell be prepared to build? **Answer:** $2 \cdot 3 \cdot 4 \cdot 4 \cdot 10 = 960$.

4.5.1 Ordered Samples

Imagine a bag with n distinguishable balls inside. Now shake up the bag and select k balls at random. How many possible sequences might we observe?

Proposition 4.18. *The number of ways in which one may select an ordered sample of k subjects from a population that has n distinguishable members is*

- n^k *if sampling is done with replacement,*
- $n(n-1)(n-2)\cdots(n-k+1)$ *if sampling is done without replacement.*

Recall from calculus the notation for *factorials*:

$$\begin{aligned} 1! &= 1, \\ 2! &= 2 \cdot 1 = 2, \\ 3! &= 3 \cdot 2 \cdot 1 = 6, \\ &\vdots \\ n! &= n(n-1)(n-2)\cdots 3 \cdot 2 \cdot 1. \end{aligned}$$

Fact 4.19. *The number of permutations of n elements is* $n!$.

Example 4.20. Take a coin and flip it 7 times. How many sequences of Heads and Tails are possible? **Answer:** $2^7 = 128$.

Example 4.21. In a class of 20 students, we randomly select a class president, a class vice-president, and a treasurer. How many ways can this be done? **Answer:** $20 \cdot 19 \cdot 18 = 6840$.

Example 4.22. We rent five movies to watch over the span of two nights. We wish to watch 3 movies on the first night. How many distinct sequences of 3 movies could we possibly watch? **Answer:** $5 \cdot 4 \cdot 3 = 60$.

4.5.2 Unordered Samples

The number of ways in which one may select an unordered sample of k subjects from a population that has n distinguishable members is

- $(n-1+k)!/[(n-1)!k!]$ if sampling is done with replacement,
- $n!/[k!(n-k)!]$ if sampling is done without replacement.

The quantity $n!/[k!(n-k)!]$ is called a *binomial coefficient* and plays a special role in mathematics; it is denoted

$$\binom{n}{k} = \frac{n!}{k!(n-k)!} \tag{4.5.1}$$

and is read "n choose k".

	ordered = TRUE	ordered = FALSE
replace = TRUE	n^k	$\frac{(n-1+k)!}{(n-1)!k!}$
replace = FALSE	$\frac{n!}{(n-k)!}$	$\binom{n}{k}$

Table 4.1: Sampling k from n objects with `urnsamples`

Example 4.23. You rent five movies to watch over the span of two nights, but only wish to watch 3 movies the first night. Your friend, Fred, wishes to borrow some movies to watch at his house on the first night. You owe Fred a favor, and allow him to select 2 movies from the set of 5. How many choices does Fred have? **Answer:** $\binom{5}{2} = 10$.

Example 4.24. Place 3 six-sided dice into a cup. Next, shake the cup well and pour out the dice. How many distinct rolls are possible? **Answer:** $(6-1+3)!/[(6-1)!3!] = \binom{8}{5} = 56$.

4.5.3 How to do it with R

The factorial $n!$ is computed with the command `factorial(n)` and the binomial coefficient $\binom{n}{k}$ with the command `choose(n,k)`.

The sample spaces we have computed so far have been relatively small, and we can visually study them without much trouble. However, it is *very* easy to generate sample spaces that are prohibitively large. And while R is wonderful and powerful and does almost everything except wash windows, even R has limits of which we should be mindful.

But we often do not need to actually generate the sample space; it suffices to count the number of outcomes. The `nsamp` function will calculate the number of rows in a sample space made by `urnsamples` without actually devoting the memory resources necessary to generate the space. The arguments are `n`, the number of (distinguishable) objects in the urn, `k`, the sample size, and `replace`, `ordered`, as above.

Example 4.25. We will compute the number of outcomes for each of the four `urnsamples` examples that we saw in Example 4.2. Recall that we took a sample of size two from an urn with three distinguishable elements.

```
> nsamp(n = 3, k = 2, replace = TRUE, ordered = TRUE)
[1] 9
> nsamp(n = 3, k = 2, replace = FALSE, ordered = TRUE)
[1] 6
> nsamp(n = 3, k = 2, replace = FALSE, ordered = FALSE)
[1] 3
> nsamp(n = 3, k = 2, replace = TRUE, ordered = FALSE)
[1] 6
```

Compare these answers with the length of the data frames generated above.

The Multiplication Principle

A benefit of `nsamp` is that it is *vectorized* so that entering vectors instead of numbers for `n`, `k`, `replace`, and `ordered` results in a vector of corresponding answers. This becomes particularly convenient for combinatorics problems.

Example 4.26. There are 11 artists who each submit a portfolio containing 7 paintings for competition in an art exhibition. Unfortunately, the gallery director only has space in the winners' section to accommodate 12 paintings in a row equally spread over three consecutive walls. The director decides to give the first, second, and third place winners each a wall to display the work of their choice. The walls boast 31 separate lighting options apiece. How many displays are possible?

Answer: The judges will pick 3 (ranked) winners out of 11 (with `rep = FALSE`, `ord = TRUE`). Each artist will select 4 of his/her paintings from 7 for display in a row (`rep = FALSE`, `ord = TRUE`), and lastly, each of the 3 walls has 31 lighting possibilities (`rep = TRUE`, `ord = TRUE`). These three numbers can be calculated quickly with

```
> n <- c(11, 7, 31)
> k <- c(3, 4, 3)
> r <- c(FALSE, FALSE, TRUE)
```

```
> x <- nsamp(n, k, rep = r, ord = TRUE)
[1]   990   840 29791
```

(Notice that `ordered` is always `TRUE`; `nsamp` will recycle `ordered` and `replace` to the appropriate length.) By the Multiplication Principle, the number of ways to complete the experiment is the product of the entries of `x`:

```
> prod(x)
[1] 24774195600
```

Compare this with the some other ways to compute the same thing:

```
> (11 * 10 * 9) * (7 * 6 * 5 * 4) * 313
[1] 260290800
```

or alternatively

```
> prod(9:11) * prod(4:7) * 313
[1] 260290800
```

or even

```
> prod(factorial(c(11, 7))/factorial(c(8, 3))) * 313
[1] 260290800
```

As one can guess, in many of the standard counting problems there aren't substantial savings in the amount of typing; it is about the same using `nsamp` versus `factorial` and `choose`. But the virtue of `nsamp` lies in its collecting the relevant counting formulas in a one-stop shop. Ultimately, it is up to the user to choose the method that works best for him/herself.

Example 4.27. The Birthday Problem. Suppose that there are n people together in a room. Each person announces the date of his/her birthday in turn. The question is: what is the probability of at least one match? If we let the event A represent {there is at least one match}, then would like to know $\mathbb{P}(A)$, but as we will see, it is more convenient to calculate $\mathbb{P}(A^c)$.

For starters we will ignore leap years and assume that there are only 365 days in a year. Second, we will assume that births are equally distributed over the course of a year (which is not true due to all sorts of complications such as hospital delivery schedules). See `http://en.wikipedia.org` for more.

Let us next think about the sample space. There are 365 possibilities for the first person's birthday, 365 possibilities for the second, and so forth. The total number of possible birthday sequences is therefore $\#(S) = 365^n$.

Now we will use the complementation trick we saw in Example 4.11. We realize that the only situation in which A does *not* occur is if there are *no* matches among all people in the room, that is, only when everybody's birthday is different, so

$$\mathbb{P}(A) = 1 - \mathbb{P}(A^c) = 1 - \frac{\#(A^c)}{\#(S)},$$

since the outcomes are equally likely. Let us then suppose that there are no matches. The first person has one of 365 possible birthdays. The second person must not match the first, thus, the second person has only 364 available birthdays from which to choose. Similarly, the third person has only 363 possible birthdays, and so forth, until we reach the nth person, who has only $365 - n + 1$ remaining possible days for a birthday. By the Multiplication Principle, we have $\#(A^c) = 365 \cdot 364 \cdots (365 - n + 1)$, and

$$\mathbb{P}(A) = 1 - \frac{365 \cdot 364 \cdots (365 - n + 1)}{365^n} = 1 - \frac{364}{365} \cdot \frac{363}{365} \cdots \frac{(365 - n + 1)}{365}. \tag{4.5.2}$$

As a surprising consequence, consider this: how many people does it take to be in the room so that the probability of at least one match is at least 0.50? Clearly, if there is only $n = 1$ person in the room then the probability of a match is zero, and when there are $n = 366$ people in the room there is a 100% chance of a match (recall that we are ignoring leap years). So how many people does it take so that there is an equal chance of a match and no match?

When I have asked this question to students, the usual response is "somewhere around $n = 180$ people" in the room. The reasoning seems to be that in order to get a 50% chance of a match, there should be 50% of the available days to be occupied. The number of students in a typical classroom is 25, so as a companion question I ask students to estimate the probability of a match when there are $n = 25$ students in the room. Common estimates are a 1%, or 0.5%, or even 0.1% chance of a match. After they have given their estimates, we go around the room and each student announces their birthday. More often than not, we observe a match in the class, to the students' disbelief.

Students are usually surprised to hear that, using the formula above, one needs only $n = 23$ students to have a greater than 50% chance of at least one match. Figure 4.5.1 shows a graph of the birthday probabilities:

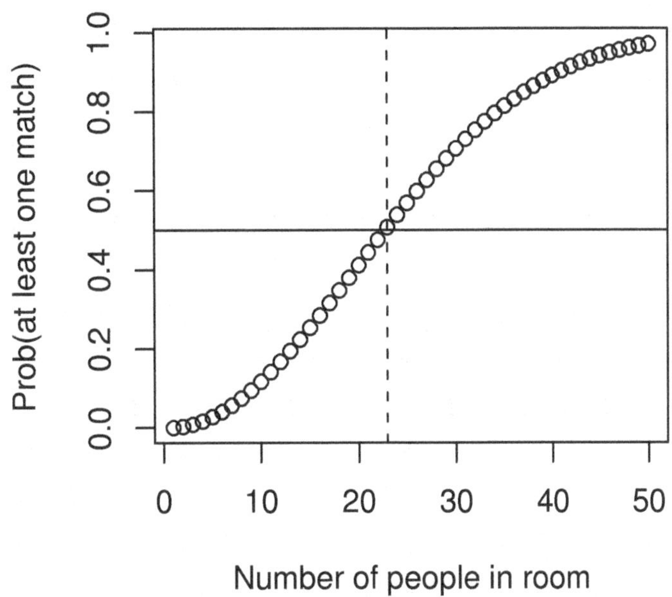

Figure 4.5.1: The birthday problem
The horizontal line is at $p = 0.50$ and the vertical line is at $n = 23$.

4.5.4 How to do it with R

We can make the plot in Figure 4.5.1 with the following sequence of commands.

```
g <- Vectorize(pbirthday.ipsur)
plot(1:50, g(1:50),
     xlab = "Number of people in room",
     ylab = "Prob(at least one match)",
     main = "The Birthday Problem")
abline(h = 0.5)
abline(v = 23, lty = 2) # dashed line
```

There is a Birthday problem item in the Probability menu of `RcmdrPlugin.IPSUR`.

In the base R version, one can compute approximate probabilities for the more general case of probabilities other than 1/2, for differing total number of days in the year, and even for more than two matches.

4.6 Conditional Probability

Consider a full deck of 52 standard playing cards. Now select two cards from the deck, in succession. Let $A = \{\text{first card drawn is an Ace}\}$ and $B = \{\text{second card drawn is an Ace}\}$. Since there are four Aces in the deck, it is natural to assign $\mathbb{P}(A) = 4/52$. Suppose we look at the first card. What now is the probability of B? Of course, the answer depends on the value of the first card. If the first card is an Ace, then the probability that the second also is an Ace should be $3/51$, but if the first card is not an Ace, then the probability that the second is an Ace should

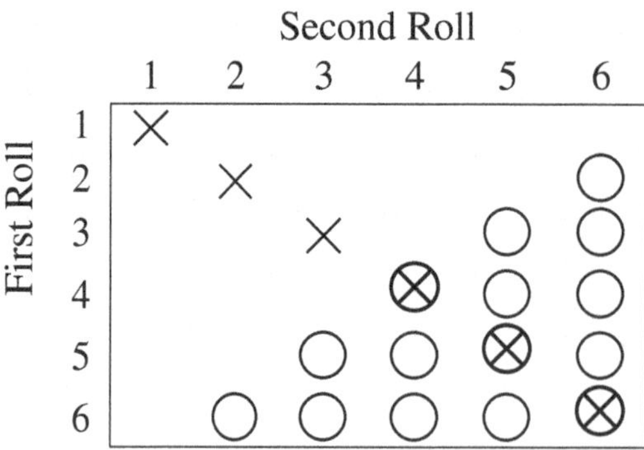

Table 4.2: Rolling two dice

be 4/51. As notation for these two situations we write

$$\mathbb{P}(B|A) = 3/51, \quad \mathbb{P}(B|A^c) = 4/51.$$

Definition 4.28. The conditional probability of B given A, denoted $\mathbb{P}(B|A)$, is defined by

$$\mathbb{P}(B|A) = \frac{\mathbb{P}(A \cap B)}{\mathbb{P}(A)}, \quad \text{if } \mathbb{P}(A) > 0. \tag{4.6.1}$$

We will not be discussing a conditional probability of B given A when $\mathbb{P}(A) = 0$, even though this theory exists, is well developed, and forms the foundation for the study of stochastic processes[3].

Example 4.29. Toss a coin twice. The sample space is given by $S = \{HH, HT, TH, TT\}$. Let $A = \{\text{a head occurs}\}$ and $B = \{\text{a head and tail occur}\}$. It should be clear that $\mathbb{P}(A) = 3/4$, $\mathbb{P}(B) = 2/4$, and $\mathbb{P}(A \cap B) = 2/4$. What now are the probabilities $\mathbb{P}(A|B)$ and $\mathbb{P}(B|A)$?

$$\mathbb{P}(A|B) = \frac{\mathbb{P}(A \cap B)}{\mathbb{P}(B)} = \frac{2/4}{2/4} = 1,$$

in other words, once we know that a Head and Tail occur, we may be certain that a Head occurs. Next

$$\mathbb{P}(B|A) = \frac{\mathbb{P}(A \cap B)}{\mathbb{P}(A)} = \frac{2/4}{3/4} = \frac{2}{3},$$

which means that given the information that a Head has occurred, we no longer need to account for the outcome TT, and the remaining three outcomes are equally likely with exactly two outcomes lying in the set B.

Example 4.30. Toss a six-sided die twice. The sample space consists of all ordered pairs (i, j) of the numbers $1, 2, \ldots, 6$, that is, $S = \{(1,1), (1,2), \ldots, (6,6)\}$. We know from Section 4.5 that $\#(S) = 6^2 = 36$. Let $A = \{\text{outcomes match}\}$ and $B = \{\text{sum of outcomes at least 8}\}$. The sample space may be represented by a matrix:

The outcomes lying in the event A are marked with the symbol "×", the outcomes falling in B are marked with "○", and those in both A and B are marked "⊗". Now it is clear that $\mathbb{P}(A) = 6/36$, $\mathbb{P}(B) = 15/36$, and $\mathbb{P}(A \cap B) = 3/36$. Finally,

$$\mathbb{P}(A|B) = \frac{3/36}{15/36} = \frac{1}{5}, \quad \mathbb{P}(B|A) = \frac{3/36}{6/36} = \frac{1}{2}.$$

[3]Conditional probability in this case is defined by means of *conditional expectation*, a topic that is well beyond the scope of this text. The interested reader should consult an advanced text on probability theory, such as Billingsley, Resnick, or Ash Dooleans-Dade.

Again, we see that given the knowledge that B occurred (the 15 outcomes in the lower right triangle), there are 3 of the 15 that fall into the set A, thus the probability is $3/15$. Similarly, given that A occurred (we are on the diagonal), there are 3 out of 6 outcomes that also fall in B, thus, the probability of B given A is 1/2.

4.6.1 How to do it with R

Continuing with Example 4.30, the first thing to do is set up the probability space with the `rolldie` function.

```
> library(prob)
> S <- rolldie(2, makespace = TRUE)  # assumes ELM
> head(S)                            #  first few rows
```

```
  X1 X2      probs
1  1  1 0.02777778
2  2  1 0.02777778
3  3  1 0.02777778
4  4  1 0.02777778
5  5  1 0.02777778
6  6  1 0.02777778
```

Next we define the events

```
> A <- subset(S, X1 == X2)
> B <- subset(S, X1 + X2 >= 8)
```

And now we are ready to calculate probabilities. To do conditional probability, we use the `given` argument of the `prob` function:

```
> prob(A, given = B)
```

```
[1] 0.2
```

```
> prob(B, given = A)
```

```
[1] 0.5
```

Note that we do not actually need to define the events A and B separately as long as we reference the original probability space S as the first argument of the `prob` calculation:

```
> prob(S, X1==X2, given = (X1 + X2 >= 8) )
```

```
[1] 0.2
```

```
> prob(S, X1+X2 >= 8, given = (X1==X2) )
```

```
[1] 0.5
```

4.6.2 Properties and Rules

The following theorem establishes that conditional probabilities behave just like regular probabilities when the conditioned event is fixed.

Theorem 4.31. *For any fixed event A with $\mathbb{P}(A) > 0$,*

1. $\mathbb{P}(B|A) \geq 0$, *for all events $B \subset S$,*
2. $\mathbb{P}(S|A) = 1$, *and*
3. *If B_1, B_2, B_3,... are disjoint events, then*

$$\mathbb{P}\left(\bigcup_{k=1}^{\infty} B_k \middle| A\right) = \sum_{k=1}^{\infty} \mathbb{P}(B_k|A). \tag{4.6.2}$$

In other words, $\mathbb{P}(\cdot|A)$ is a legitimate probability function. With this fact in mind, the following properties are immediate:

Proposition 4.32. *For any events A, B, and C with $\mathbb{P}(A) > 0$,*

1. $\mathbb{P}(B^c|A) = 1 - \mathbb{P}(B|A)$.
2. *If $B \subset C$ then $\mathbb{P}(B|A) \leq \mathbb{P}(C|A)$.*
3. $\mathbb{P}[(B \cup C)|A] = \mathbb{P}(B|A) + \mathbb{P}(C|A) - \mathbb{P}[(B \cap C|A)]$.
4. ***The Multiplication Rule.*** *For any two events A and B,*

$$\mathbb{P}(A \cap B) = \mathbb{P}(A)\,\mathbb{P}(B|A). \tag{4.6.3}$$

And more generally, for events A_1, A_2, A_3,..., A_n,

$$\mathbb{P}(A_1 \cap A_2 \cap \cdots \cap A_n) = \mathbb{P}(A_1)\,\mathbb{P}(A_2|A_1) \cdots \mathbb{P}(A_n|A_1 \cap A_2 \cap \cdots \cap A_{n-1}). \tag{4.6.4}$$

The Multiplication Rule is very important because it allows us to find probabilities in random experiments that have a sequential structure, as the next example shows.

Example 4.33. At the beginning of the section we drew two cards from a standard playing deck. Now we may answer our original question, what is $\mathbb{P}(\text{both Aces})$?

$$\mathbb{P}(\text{both Aces}) = \mathbb{P}(A \cap B) = \mathbb{P}(A)\,\mathbb{P}(B|A) = \frac{4}{52} \cdot \frac{3}{51} \approx 0.00452.$$

4.6.3 How to do it with R

Continuing Example 4.33, we set up the probability space by way of a three step process. First we employ the `cards` function to get a data frame `L` with two columns: `rank` and `suit`. Both columns are stored internally as factors with 13 and 4 levels, respectively.

Next we sample two cards randomly from the `L` data frame by way of the `urnsamples` function. It returns a list `M` which contains all possible pairs of rows from `L` (there are `choose(52,2)` of them). The sample space for this experiment is exactly the list `M`.

At long last we associate a probability model with the sample space. This is right down the `probspace` function's alley. It assumes the equally likely model by default. We call this result `N` which is an object of class `ps` – short for "probability space".

But do not be intimidated. The object `N` is nothing more than a list with two elements: `outcomes` and `probs`. The `outcomes` element is itself just another list, with `choose(52,2)` entries, each one a data frame with two rows which correspond to the pair of cards chosen. The `probs` element is just a vector with `choose(52,2)` entries all the same: `1/choose(52,2)`.

Putting all of this together we do

```
> library(prob)
> L <- cards()
> M <- urnsamples(L, size = 2)
> N <- probspace(M)
```

Now that we have the probability space `N` we are ready to do some probability. We use the `prob` function, just like before. The only trick is to specify the event of interest correctly, and recall that we were interested in $\mathbb{P}$(both Aces). But if the cards are both Aces then the `rank` of both cards should be `"A"`, which sounds like a job for the `all` function:

```
> prob(N, all(rank == "A"))

[1] 0.004524887
```

Note that this value matches what we found in Example 4.33, above. We could calculate all sorts of probabilities at this point; we are limited only by the complexity of the event's computer representation.

Example 4.34. Consider an urn with 10 balls inside, 7 of which are red and 3 of which are green. Select 3 balls successively from the urn. Let $A = \{1^{\text{st}} \text{ ball is red}\}$, $B = \left\{2^{\text{nd}} \text{ ball is red}\right\}$, and $C = \left\{3^{\text{rd}} \text{ ball is red}\right\}$. Then

$$\mathbb{P}(\text{all 3 balls are red}) = \mathbb{P}(A \cap B \cap C) = \frac{7}{10} \cdot \frac{6}{9} \cdot \frac{5}{8} \approx 0.2917.$$

4.6.4 How to do it with R

Example 4.34 is similar to Example 4.33, but it is even easier. We need to set up an urn (vector `L`) to hold the balls, we sample from `L` to get the sample space (data frame `M`), and we associate a probability vector (column `probs`) with the outcomes (rows of `M`) of the sample space. The final result is a probability space (an ordinary data frame `N`).

It is easier for us this time because our urn is a vector instead of a `cards()` data frame. Before there were two dimensions of information associated with the outcomes (rank and suit) but presently we have only one dimension (color).

```
> library(prob)
> L <- rep(c("red", "green"), times = c(7, 3))
> M <- urnsamples(L, size = 3, replace = FALSE, ordered = TRUE)
> N <- probspace(M)
```

Now let us think about how to set up the event {all 3 balls are red}. Rows of `N` that satisfy this condition have `X1=="red"&X2=="red"&X3=="red"`, but there must be an easier way. Indeed, there is. The `isrep` function (short for "is repeated") in the `prob` package was written for this purpose. The command `isrep(N,"red",3)` will test each row of `N` to see whether the value `"red"` appears `3` times. The result is exactly what we need to define an event with the `prob` function. Observe

```
> prob(N, isrep(N, "red", 3))
[1] 0.2916667
```

Note that this answer matches what we found in Example 4.34. Now let us try some other probability questions. What is the probability of getting two `"red"`s?

```
> prob(N, isrep(N, "red", 2))
[1] 0.525
```

Note that the exact value is $21/40$; we will learn a quick way to compute this in Section 5.6. What is the probability of observing `"red"`, then `"green"`, then `"red"`?

```
> prob(N, isin(N, c("red", "green", "red"), ordered = TRUE))
[1] 0.175
```

Note that the exact value is $7/20$ (do it with the Multiplication Rule). What is the probability of observing `"red"`, `"green"`, and `"red"`, in no particular order?

```
> prob(N, isin(N, c("red", "green", "red")))
[1] 0.525
```

We already knew this. It is the probability of observing two `"red"`s, above.

Example 4.35. Consider two urns, the first with 5 red balls and 3 green balls, and the second with 2 red balls and 6 green balls. Your friend randomly selects one ball from the first urn and transfers it to the second urn, without disclosing the color of the ball. You select one ball from the second urn. What is the probability that the selected ball is red? Let $A = \{\text{transferred ball is red}\}$ and $B = \{\text{selected ball is red}\}$. Write

$$\begin{aligned} B &= S \cap B \\ &= (A \cup A^c) \cap B \\ &= (A \cap B) \cup (A^c \cap B) \end{aligned}$$

and notice that $A \cap B$ and $A^c \cap B$ are disjoint. Therefore

$$\begin{aligned} \mathbb{P}(B) &= \mathbb{P}(A \cap B) + \mathbb{P}(A^c \cap B) \\ &= \mathbb{P}(A)\,\mathbb{P}(B|A) + \mathbb{P}(A^c)\,\mathbb{P}(B|A^c) \\ &= \frac{5}{8} \cdot \frac{3}{9} + \frac{3}{8} \cdot \frac{2}{9} \\ &= \frac{21}{72} \end{aligned}$$

(which is 7/24 in lowest terms).

Example 4.36. We saw the `RcmdrTestDrive` data set in Chapter 2 in which a two-way table of the smoking status versus the gender was

```
      gender
smoke Female Male Sum
  No      80   54 134
  Yes     15   19  34
  Sum     95   73 168
```

If one person were selected at random from the data set, then we see from the two-way table that $\mathbb{P}(\text{Female}) = 70/168$ and $\mathbb{P}(\text{Smoker}) = 32/168$. Now suppose that one of the subjects quits smoking, but we do not know the person's gender. If we select one subject at random, what now is $\mathbb{P}(\text{Female})$? Let $A = \{\text{the quitter is a female}\}$ and $B = \{\text{selected person is a female}\}$. Write

$$\begin{aligned} B &= S \cap B \\ &= (A \cup A^c) \cap B \\ &= (A \cap B) \cup (A^c \cap B) \end{aligned}$$

and notice that $A \cap B$ and $A^c \cap B$ are disjoint. Therefore

$$\begin{aligned} \mathbb{P}(B) &= \mathbb{P}(A \cap B) + \mathbb{P}(A^c \cap B), \\ &= \mathbb{P}(A)\,\mathbb{P}(B|A) + \mathbb{P}(A^c)\,\mathbb{P}(B|A^c), \\ &= \frac{5}{8} \cdot \frac{3}{9} + \frac{3}{8} \cdot \frac{2}{9}, \\ &= \frac{21}{72}, \end{aligned}$$

(which is 7/24 in lowest terms).

Using the same reasoning, we can return to the example from the beginning of the section and show that

$$\mathbb{P}(\{\text{second card is an Ace}\}) = 4/52.$$

.

4.7 Independent Events

Toss a coin twice. The sample space is $S = \{HH,\ HT,\ TH,\ TT\}$. We know that $\mathbb{P}(1^{\text{st}} \text{ toss is } H) = 2/4$, $\mathbb{P}(2^{\text{nd}} \text{ toss is } H) = 2/4$, and $\mathbb{P}(\text{both } H) = 1/4$. Then

$$\begin{aligned} \mathbb{P}(2^{\text{nd}} \text{ toss is } H \mid 1^{\text{st}} \text{ toss is } H) &= \frac{\mathbb{P}(\text{both } H)}{\mathbb{P}(1^{\text{st}} \text{ toss is } H)}, \\ &= \frac{1/4}{2/4}, \\ &= \mathbb{P}(2^{\text{nd}} \text{ toss is } H). \end{aligned}$$

Intuitively, this means that the information that the first toss is H has no bearing on the probability that the second toss is H. The coin does not remember the result of the first toss.

Definition 4.37. Events A and B are said to be *independent* if

$$\mathbb{P}(A \cap B) = \mathbb{P}(A)\,\mathbb{P}(B). \tag{4.7.1}$$

Otherwise, the events are said to be *dependent*.

The connection with the above example stems from the following. We know from Section 4.6 that when $\mathbb{P}(B) > 0$ we may write

$$\mathbb{P}(A|B) = \frac{\mathbb{P}(A \cap B)}{\mathbb{P}(B)}. \tag{4.7.2}$$

In the case that A and B are independent, the numerator of the fraction factors so that $\mathbb{P}(B)$ cancels with the result:

$$\mathbb{P}(A|B) = \mathbb{P}(A) \quad \text{when } A, B \text{ are independent.} \tag{4.7.3}$$

The interpretation in the case of independence is that the information that the event B occurred does not influence the probability of the event A occurring. Similarly, $\mathbb{P}(B|A) = \mathbb{P}(B)$, and so the occurrence of the event A likewise does not affect the probability of event B. It may seem more natural to define A and B to be independent when $\mathbb{P}(A|B) = \mathbb{P}(A)$; however, the conditional probability $\mathbb{P}(A|B)$ is only defined when $\mathbb{P}(B) > 0$. Our definition is not limited by this restriction. It can be shown that when $\mathbb{P}(A),\ \mathbb{P}(B) > 0$ the two notions of independence are equivalent.

Proposition 4.38. *If the events A and B are independent then*

- *A and B^c are independent,*
- *A^c and B are independent,*
- *A^c and B^c are independent.*

Proof. Suppose that A and B are independent. We will show the second one; the others are similar. We need to show that

$$\mathbb{P}(A^c \cap B) = \mathbb{P}(A^c)\,\mathbb{P}(B).$$

To this end, note that the Multiplication Rule, Equation 4.6.3 implies

$$\begin{aligned} \mathbb{P}(A^c \cap B) &= \mathbb{P}(B)\,\mathbb{P}(A^c|B), \\ &= \mathbb{P}(B)[1 - \mathbb{P}(A|B)], \\ &= \mathbb{P}(B)\,\mathbb{P}(A^c). \end{aligned}$$

□

Definition 4.39. The events A, B, and C are *mutually independent* if the following four conditions are met:

$$\begin{aligned} \mathbb{P}(A \cap B) &= \mathbb{P}(A)\,\mathbb{P}(B), \\ \mathbb{P}(A \cap C) &= \mathbb{P}(A)\,\mathbb{P}(C), \\ \mathbb{P}(B \cap C) &= \mathbb{P}(B)\,\mathbb{P}(C), \end{aligned}$$

and

$$\mathbb{P}(A \cap B \cap C) = \mathbb{P}(A)\,\mathbb{P}(B)\,\mathbb{P}(C).$$

If only the first three conditions hold then A, B, and C are said to be independent *pairwise*. Note that pairwise independence is not the same as mutual independence when the number of events is larger than two.

We can now deduce the pattern for n events, $n > 3$. The events will be mutually independent only if they satisfy the product equality pairwise, then in groups of three, in groups of four, and so forth, up to all n events at once. For n events, there will be $2^n - n - 1$ equations that must be satisfied (see Exercise 4.1). Although these requirements for a set of events to be mutually independent may seem stringent, the good news is that for most of the situations considered in this book the conditions will all be met (or at least we will suppose that they are).

Example 4.40. Toss ten coins. What is the probability of observing at least one Head? Answer: Let $A_i = \left\{\text{the } i^{\text{th}} \text{ coin shows } H\right\},\ i = 1, 2, \ldots, 10$. Supposing that we toss the coins in such a way that they do not interfere with each other, this is one of the situations where all of the A_i may be considered mutually independent due to the nature of the tossing. Of course, the only way that there will not be at least one Head showing is if all tosses are Tails. Therefore,

$$\begin{aligned}\mathbb{P}(\text{at least one } H) &= 1 - \mathbb{P}(\text{all } T),\\ &= 1 - \mathbb{P}(A_1^c \cap A_2^c \cap \cdots \cap A_{10}^c),\\ &= 1 - \mathbb{P}(A_1^c)\,\mathbb{P}(A_2^c)\cdots\mathbb{P}(A_{10}^c),\\ &= 1 - \left(\frac{1}{2}\right)^{10},\end{aligned}$$

which is approximately 0.9990234.

4.7.1 How to do it with R

Example 4.41. Toss ten coins. What is the probability of observing at least one Head?

```
> S <- tosscoin(10, makespace = TRUE)
> A <- subset(S, isrep(S, vals = "T", nrep = 10))
> 1 - prob(A)
[1] 0.9990234
```

Compare this answer to what we got in Example 4.40.

Independent, Repeated Experiments

Generalizing from above it is common to repeat a certain experiment multiple times under identical conditions and in an independent manner. We have seen many examples of this already: tossing a coin repeatedly, rolling a die or dice, *etc.*

The `iidspace` function was designed specifically for this situation. It has three arguments: `x`, which is a vector of outcomes, `ntrials`, which is an integer telling how many times to repeat the experiment, and `probs` to specify the probabilities of the outcomes of `x` in a single trial.

Example 4.42. An unbalanced coin (continued, see Example 4.5). It was easy enough to set up the probability space for one unbalanced toss, however, the situation becomes more complicated when there are many tosses involved. Clearly, the outcome HHH should not have the same probability as TTT, which should again not have the same probability as HTH. At the same time, there is symmetry in the experiment in that the coin does not remember the face it shows from toss to toss, and it is easy enough to toss the coin in a similar way repeatedly.

We may represent tossing our unbalanced coin three times with the following:

```
> iidspace(c("H","T"), ntrials = 3, probs = c(0.7, 0.3))
  X1 X2 X3 probs
1  H  H  H 0.343
2  T  H  H 0.147
3  H  T  H 0.147
4  T  T  H 0.063
5  H  H  T 0.147
6  T  H  T 0.063
7  H  T  T 0.063
8  T  T  T 0.027
```

As expected, the outcome HHH has the largest probability, while TTT has the smallest. (Since the trials are independent, $\mathbb{P}(HHH) = 0.7^3$ and $\mathbb{P}(TTT) = 0.3^3$, *etc.*) Note that the result of the function call is a probability space, not a sample space (which we could construct already with the `tosscoin` or `urnsamples` functions). The same procedure could be used to model an unbalanced die or any other experiment that may be represented with a vector of possible outcomes.

Note that `iidspace` will assume `x` has equally likely outcomes if no `probs` argument is specified. Also note that the argument `x` is a *vector*, not a data frame. Something like `iidspace(tosscoin(1),...)` would give an error.

4.8 Bayes' Rule

We mentioned the subjective view of probability in Section 4.3. In this section we introduce a rule that allows us to update our probabilities when new information becomes available.

Theorem 4.43. (Bayes' Rule). *Let B_1, B_2, ..., B_n be mutually exclusive and exhaustive and let A be an event with $\mathbb{P}(A) > 0$. Then*

$$\mathbb{P}(B_k|A) = \frac{\mathbb{P}(B_k)\,\mathbb{P}(A|B_k)}{\sum_{i=1}^{n} \mathbb{P}(B_i)\,\mathbb{P}(A|B_i)}, \quad k = 1, 2, \ldots, n. \tag{4.8.1}$$

Proof. The proof follows from looking at $\mathbb{P}(B_k \cap A)$ in two different ways. For simplicity, suppose that $P(B_k) > 0$ for all k. Then

$$\mathbb{P}(A)\,\mathbb{P}(B_k|A) = \mathbb{P}(B_k \cap A) = \mathbb{P}(B_k)\,\mathbb{P}(A|B_k).$$

Since $\mathbb{P}(A) > 0$ we may divide through to obtain

$$\mathbb{P}(B_k|A) = \frac{\mathbb{P}(B_k)\,\mathbb{P}(A|B_k)}{\mathbb{P}(A)}.$$

Now remembering that $\{B_k\}$ is a partition, the Theorem of Total Probability (Equation 4.4.5) gives the denominator of the last expression to be

$$\mathbb{P}(A) = \sum_{k=1}^{n} \mathbb{P}(B_k \cap A) = \sum_{k=1}^{n} \mathbb{P}(B_k)\,\mathbb{P}(A|B_k).$$

□

What does it mean? Usually in applications we are given (or know) *a priori* probabilities $\mathbb{P}(B_k)$. We go out and collect some data, which we represent by the event A. We want to know: how do we **update** $\mathbb{P}(B_k)$ to $\mathbb{P}(B_k|A)$? The answer: Bayes' Rule.

Example 4.44. Misfiling Assistants. In this problem, there are three assistants working at a company: Moe, Larry, and Curly. Their primary job duty is to file paperwork in the filing cabinet when papers become available. The three assistants have different work schedules:

	Moe	Larry	Curly
Workload	60%	30%	10%

That is, Moe works 60% of the time, Larry works 30% of the time, and Curly does the remaining 10%, and they file documents at approximately the same speed. Suppose a person were to select one of the documents from the cabinet at random. Let M be the event

$$M = \{\text{Moe filed the document}\}$$

and let L and C be the events that Larry and Curly, respectively, filed the document. What are these events' respective probabilities? In the absence of additional information, reasonable prior probabilities would just be

	Moe	Larry	Curly
Prior Probability	$\mathbb{P}(M) = 0.60$	$\mathbb{P}(L) = 0.30$	$\mathbb{P}(C) = 0.10$

Now, the boss comes in one day, opens up the file cabinet, and selects a file at random. The boss discovers that the file has been misplaced. The boss is so angry at the mistake that (s)he threatens to fire the one who erred. The question is: who misplaced the file?

The boss decides to use probability to decide, and walks straight to the workload schedule. (S)he reasons that, since the three employees work at the same speed, the probability that a randomly selected file would have been filed by each one would be proportional to his workload. The boss notifies **Moe** that he has until the end of the day to empty his desk.

But Moe argues in his defense that the boss has ignored additional information. Moe's likelihood of having misfiled a document is smaller than Larry's and Curly's, since he is a diligent worker who pays close attention to his work. Moe admits that he works longer than the others, but he doesn't make as many mistakes as they do. Thus, Moe recommends that – before making a decision – the boss should update the probability (initially based on workload alone) to incorporate the likelihood of having observed a misfiled document.

And, as it turns out, the boss has information about Moe, Larry, and Curly's filing accuracy in the past (due to historical performance evaluations). The performance information may be represented by the following table:

	Moe	Larry	Curly
Misfile Rate	0.003	0.007	0.010

In other words, on the average, Moe misfiles 0.3% of the documents he is supposed to file. Notice that Moe was correct: he is the most accurate filer, followed by Larry, and lastly Curly. If the boss were to make a decision based only on the worker's overall accuracy, then **Curly** should get the axe. But Curly hears this and interjects that he only works a short period during the day, and consequently makes mistakes only very rarely; there is only the tiniest chance that he misfiled this particular document.

The boss would like to use this updated information to update the probabilities for the three assistants, that is, (s)he wants to use the additional likelihood that the document was misfiled to update his/her beliefs about the likely culprit. Let A be the event that a document is misfiled. What the boss would like to know are the three probabilities

$$\mathbb{P}(M|A),\quad \mathbb{P}(L|A),\ \text{and}\ \mathbb{P}(C|A).$$

We will show the calculation for $\mathbb{P}(M|A)$, the other two cases being similar. We use Bayes' Rule in the form

$$\mathbb{P}(M|A) = \frac{\mathbb{P}(M \cap A)}{\mathbb{P}(A)}.$$

Let's try to find $\mathbb{P}(M \cap A)$, which is just $\mathbb{P}(M) \cdot \mathbb{P}(A|M)$ by the Multiplication Rule. We already know $\mathbb{P}(M) = 0.6$ and $\mathbb{P}(A|M)$ is nothing more than Moe's misfile rate, given above to be $\mathbb{P}(A|M) = 0.003$. Thus, we compute

$$\mathbb{P}(M \cap A) = (0.6)(0.003) = 0.0018.$$

Using the same procedure we may calculate

$$\mathbb{P}(L|A) = 0.0021 \text{ and } \mathbb{P}(C|A) = 0.0010.$$

Now let's find the denominator, $\mathbb{P}(A)$. The key here is the notion that if a file is misplaced, then either Moe or Larry or Curly must have filed it; there is no one else around to do the misfiling. Further, these possibilities are mutually exclusive. We may use the Theorem of Total Probability 4.4.5 to write

$$\mathbb{P}(A) = \mathbb{P}(A \cap M) + \mathbb{P}(A \cap L) + \mathbb{P}(A \cap C).$$

Luckily, we have computed these above. Thus

$$\mathbb{P}(A) = 0.0018 + 0.0021 + 0.0010 = 0.0049.$$

Therefore, Bayes' Rule yields

$$\mathbb{P}(M|A) = \frac{0.0018}{0.0049} \approx 0.37.$$

This last quantity is called the posterior probability that Moe misfiled the document, since it incorporates the observed data that a randomly selected file was misplaced (which is governed by the misfile rate). We can use the same argument to calculate

	Moe	Larry	Curly
Posterior Probability	$\mathbb{P}(M\|A) \approx 0.37$	$\mathbb{P}(L\|A) \approx 0.43$	$\mathbb{P}(C\|A) \approx 0.20$

The conclusion: **Larry** gets the axe. What is happening is an intricate interplay between the time on the job and the misfile rate. It is not obvious who the winner (or in this case, loser) will be, and the statistician needs to consult Bayes' Rule to determine the best course of action.

Example 4.45. Suppose the boss gets a change of heart and does not fire anybody. But the next day (s)he randomly selects another file and again finds it to be misplaced. To decide whom to fire now, the boss would use the same procedure, with one small change. (S)he would not use the prior probabilities 60%, 30%, and 10%; those are old news. Instead, she would replace the prior probabilities with the posterior probabilities just calculated. After the math she will have new posterior probabilities, updated even more from the day before.

In this way, probabilities found by Bayes' rule are always on the cutting edge, always updated with respect to the best information available at the time.

4.8.1 How to do it with R

There are not any special functions for Bayes' Rule in the prob package, but problems like the ones above are easy enough to do by hand.

Example 4.46. Misfiling assistants (continued from Example 4.44). We store the prior probabilities and the likelihoods in vectors and go to town.

```
> prior <- c(0.6, 0.3, 0.1)
> like <- c(0.003, 0.007, 0.01)
> post <- prior * like
> post/sum(post)
[1] 0.3673469 0.4285714 0.2040816
```

Compare these answers with what we got in Example 4.44. We would replace prior with post in a future calculation. We could raise like to a power to see how the posterior is affected by future document mistakes. (Do you see why? Think back to Section 4.7.)

Example 4.47. Let us incorporate the posterior probability (post) information from the last example and suppose that the assistants misfile seven more documents. Using Bayes' Rule, what would the new posterior probabilities be?

```
> newprior <- post
> post <- newprior * like^7
> post/sum(post)
[1] 0.0003355044 0.1473949328 0.8522695627
```

We see that the individual with the highest probability of having misfiled all eight documents given the observed data is no longer Larry, but Curly.

There are two important points. First, we did not divide post by the sum of its entries until the very last step; we do not need to calculate it, and it will save us computing time to postpone normalization until absolutely necessary, namely, until we finally want to interpret them as probabilities.

Second, the reader might be wondering what the boss would get if (s)he skipped the intermediate step of calculating the posterior after only one misfiled document. What if she started from the *original* prior, then observed eight misfiled documents, and calculated the posterior? What would she get? It must be the same answer, of course.

```
> fastpost <- prior * like^8
> fastpost/sum(fastpost)
[1] 0.0003355044 0.1473949328 0.8522695627
```

Compare this to what we got in Example 4.45.

4.9 Random Variables

We already know about experiments, sample spaces, and events. In this section, we are interested in a *number* that is associated with the experiment. We conduct a random experiment E and after learning the outcome ω in S we calculate a number X. That is, to each outcome ω in the sample space we associate a number $X(\omega) = x$.

Definition 4.48. A *random variable* X is a function $X : S \to \mathbb{R}$ that associates to each outcome $\omega \in S$ exactly one number $X(\omega) = x$.

We usually denote random variables by uppercase letters such as X, Y, and Z, and we denote their observed values by lowercase letters x, y, and z. Just as S is the set of all possible outcomes of E, we call the set of all possible values of X the *support* of X and denote it by S_X.

Example 4.49. Let E be the experiment of flipping a coin twice. We have seen that the sample space is $S = \{HH, HT, TH, TT\}$. Now define the random variable X = the number of heads. That is, for example, $X(HH) = 2$, while $X(HT) = 1$. We may make a table of the possibilities:

$\omega \in S$	HH	HT	TH	TT
$X(\omega) = x$	2	1	1	0

Taking a look at the second row of the table, we see that the support of X – the set of all numbers that X assumes – would be $S_X = \{0, 1, 2\}$.

Example 4.50. Let E be the experiment of flipping a coin repeatedly until observing a Head. The sample space would be $S = \{H, TH, TTH, TTTH, \ldots\}$. Now define the random variable Y = the number of Tails before the first head. Then the support of Y would be $S_Y = \{0, 1, 2, \ldots\}$.

Example 4.51. Let E be the experiment of tossing a coin in the air, and define the random variable Z = the time (in seconds) until the coin hits the ground. In this case, the sample space is inconvenient to describe. Yet the support of Z would be $(0, \infty)$. Of course, it is reasonable to suppose that the coin will return to Earth in a short amount of time; in practice, the set $(0, \infty)$ is admittedly too large. However, we will find that in many circumstances it is mathematically convenient to study the extended set rather than a restricted one.

There are important differences between the supports of X, Y, and Z. The support of X is a finite collection of elements that can be inspected all at once. And while the support of Y cannot be exhaustively written down, its elements can nevertheless be listed in a naturally ordered sequence. Random variables with supports similar to those of X and Y are called *discrete random variables*. We study these in Chapter 5.

In contrast, the support of Z is a continuous interval, containing all rational and irrational positive real numbers. For this reason[4], random variables with supports like Z are called *continuous random variables*, to be studied in Chapter 6.

4.9.1 How to do it with R

The primary vessel for this task is the `addrv` function. There are two ways to use it, and we will describe both.

[4]This isn't really the reason, but it serves as an effective litmus test at the introductory level. See Billingsley or Resnick.

Supply a Defining Formula

The first method is based on the `transform` function. See `?transform`. The idea is to write a formula defining the random variable inside the function, and it will be added as a column to the data frame. As an example, let us roll a 4-sided die three times, and let us define the random variable $U = X1 - X2 + X3$.

```
> S <- rolldie(3, nsides = 4, makespace = TRUE)
> S <- addrv(S, U = X1 - X2 + X3)
```

Now let's take a look at the values of U. In the interest of space, we will only reproduce the first few rows of S (there are $4^3 = 64$ rows in total).

```
> head(S)
  X1 X2 X3 U    probs
1  1  1  1 1 0.015625
2  2  1  1 2 0.015625
3  3  1  1 3 0.015625
4  4  1  1 4 0.015625
5  1  2  1 0 0.015625
6  2  2  1 1 0.015625
```

We see from the U column it is operating just like it should. We can now answer questions like

```
> prob(S, U > 6)
[1] 0.015625
```

Supply a Function

Sometimes we have a function laying around that we would like to apply to some of the outcome variables, but it is unfortunately tedious to write out the formula defining what the new variable would be. The `addrv` function has an argument `FUN` specifically for this case. Its value should be a legitimate function from R, such as `sum`, `mean`, `median`, *etc.* Or, you can define your own function. Continuing the previous example, let's define $V = \max(X1, X2, X3)$ and $W = X1 + X2 + X3$.

```
> S <- addrv(S, FUN = max, invars = c("X1", "X2", "X3"), name = "V")
> S <- addrv(S, FUN = sum, invars = c("X1", "X2", "X3"), name = "W")
> head(S)
  X1 X2 X3 U V W    probs
1  1  1  1 1 1 3 0.015625
2  2  1  1 2 2 4 0.015625
3  3  1  1 3 3 5 0.015625
4  4  1  1 4 4 6 0.015625
5  1  2  1 0 2 4 0.015625
6  2  2  1 1 2 5 0.015625
```

Notice that `addrv` has an `invars` argument to specify exactly to which columns one would like to apply the function `FUN`. If no input variables are specified, then `addrv` will apply `FUN` to all non-`probs` columns. Further, `addrv` has an optional argument `name` to give the new variable; this can be useful when adding several random variables to a probability space (as above). If not specified, the default name is "`X`".

Marginal Distributions

As we can see above, often after adding a random variable V to a probability space one will find that V has values that are repeated, so that it becomes difficult to understand what the ultimate behavior of V actually is. We can use the `marginal` function to aggregate the rows of the sample space by values of V, all the while accumulating the probability associated with V's distinct values. Continuing our example from above, suppose we would like to focus entirely on the values and probabilities of $V = \max(X1, X2, X3)$.

```
> marginal(S, vars = "V")
```

```
  V    probs
1 1 0.015625
2 2 0.109375
3 3 0.296875
4 4 0.578125
```

We could save the probability space of V in a data frame and study it further, if we wish. As a final remark, we can calculate the marginal distributions of multiple variables desired using the `vars` argument. For example, suppose we would like to examine the joint distribution of V and W.

```
> marginal(S, vars = c("V", "W"))
```

```
   V  W    probs
1  1  3 0.015625
2  2  4 0.046875
3  2  5 0.046875
4  3  5 0.046875
5  2  6 0.015625
6  3  6 0.093750
7  4  6 0.046875
8  3  7 0.093750
9  4  7 0.093750
10 3  8 0.046875
11 4  8 0.140625
12 3  9 0.015625
13 4  9 0.140625
14 4 10 0.093750
15 4 11 0.046875
16 4 12 0.015625
```

Note that the default value of `vars` is the names of all columns except `probs`. This can be useful if there are duplicated rows in the probability space.

Chapter Exercises

Exercise 4.1. Prove the assertion given in the text: the number of conditions that the events A_1, $A_2, \ldots, A_n$ must satisfy in order to be mutually independent is $2^n - n - 1$. (*Hint*: think about Pascal's triangle.)

Answer: The events must satisfy the product equalities two at a time, of which there are $\binom{n}{2}$, then they must satisfy an additional $\binom{n}{3}$ conditions three at a time, and so on, until they satisfy the $\binom{n}{n} = 1$ condition including all n events. In total, there are

$$\binom{n}{2} + \binom{n}{3} + \cdots + \binom{n}{n} = \sum_{k=0}^{n} \binom{n}{k} - \left[\binom{n}{0} + \binom{n}{1}\right]$$

conditions to be satisfied, but the binomial series in the expression on the right is the sum of the entries of the nth row of Pascal's triangle, which is 2^n.

Chapter 5

Discrete Distributions

In this chapter we introduce discrete random variables, those who take values in a finite or countably infinite support set. We discuss probability mass functions and some special expectations, namely, the mean, variance and standard deviation. Some of the more important discrete distributions are explored in detail, and the more general concept of expectation is defined, which paves the way for moment generating functions.

We give special attention to the empirical distribution since it plays such a fundamental role with respect to re sampling and Chapter 13; it will also be needed in Section 10.5.1 where we discuss the Kolmogorov-Smirnov test. Following this is a section in which we introduce a catalogue of discrete random variables that can be used to model experiments.

There are some comments on simulation, and we mention transformations of random variables in the discrete case. The interested reader who would like to learn more about any of the assorted discrete distributions mentioned here should take a look at *Univariate Discrete Distributions* by Johnson *et al* [50].

What do I want them to know?

- how to choose a reasonable discrete model under a variety of physical circumstances
- the notion of mathematical expectation, how to calculate it, and basic properties
- moment generating functions (yes, I want them to hear about those)
- the general tools of the trade for manipulation of continuous random variables, integration, *etc.*
- some details on a couple of discrete models, and exposure to a bunch of other ones
- how to make new discrete random variables from old ones

5.1 Discrete Random Variables

5.1.1 Probability Mass Functions

Discrete random variables are characterized by their supports which take the form

$$S_X = \{u_1, u_2, \ldots, u_k\} \text{ or } S_X = \{u_1, u_2, u_3 \ldots\}. \tag{5.1.1}$$

Every discrete random variable X has associated with it a probability mass function (PMF) $f_X : S_X \to [0,1]$ defined by

$$f_X(x) = \mathbb{P}(X = x), \quad x \in S_X. \tag{5.1.2}$$

Since values of the PMF represent probabilities, we know from Chapter 4 that PMFs enjoy certain properties. In particular, all PMFs satisfy

1. $f_X(x) > 0$ for $x \in S$,
2. $\sum_{x \in S} f_X(x) = 1$, and
3. $\mathbb{P}(X \in A) = \sum_{x \in A} f_X(x)$, for any event $A \subset S$.

Example 5.1. Toss a coin 3 times. The sample space would be

$$S = \{HHH, HTH, THH, TTH, HHT, HTT, THT, TTT\}.$$

Now let X be the number of Heads observed. Then X has support $S_X = \{0, 1, 2, 3\}$. Assuming that the coin is fair and was tossed in exactly the same way each time, it is not unreasonable to suppose that the outcomes in the sample space are all equally likely. What is the PMF of X? Notice that X is zero exactly when the outcome TTT occurs, and this event has probability $1/8$. Therefore, $f_X(0) = 1/8$, and the same reasoning shows that $f_X(3) = 1/8$. Exactly three outcomes result in $X = 1$, thus, $f_X(1) = 3/8$ and $f_X(3)$ holds the remaining $3/8$ probability (the total is 1). We can represent the PMF with a table:

$x \in S_X$	0	1	2	3	Total
$f_X(x) = \mathbb{P}(X = x)$	1/8	3/8	3/8	1/8	1

5.1.2 Mean, Variance, and Standard Deviation

There are numbers associated with PMFs. One important example is the mean μ, also known as $\mathbb{E}\,X$:

$$\mu = \mathbb{E}\,X = \sum_{x \in S} x f_X(x), \tag{5.1.3}$$

provided the (potentially infinite) series $\sum |x| f_X(x)$ is convergent. Another important number is the variance:

$$\sigma^2 = \mathbb{E}(X - \mu)^2 = \sum_{x \in S} (x - \mu)^2 f_X(x), \tag{5.1.4}$$

which can be computed (see Exercise 5.4) with the alternate formula $\sigma^2 = \mathbb{E}\,X^2 - (\mathbb{E}\,X)^2$. Directly defined from the variance is the standard deviation $\sigma = \sqrt{\sigma^2}$.

Example 5.2. We will calculate the mean of X in Example 5.1.

$$\mu = \sum_{x=0}^{3} x f_X(x) = 0 \cdot \frac{1}{8} + 1 \cdot \frac{3}{8} + 2 \cdot \frac{3}{8} + 3 \cdot \frac{1}{8} = 3.5.$$

We interpret $\mu = 3.5$ by reasoning that if we were to repeat the random experiment many times, independently each time, observe many corresponding outcomes of the random variable X, and take the sample mean of the observations, then the calculated value would fall close to 3.5. The approximation would get better as we observe more and more values of X (another form of the Law of Large Numbers; see Section 4.3). Another way it is commonly stated is that X is 3.5 "on the average" or "in the long run".

Remark 5.3. Note that although we say X is 3.5 on the average, we must keep in mind that our X never actually equals 3.5 (in fact, it is impossible for X to equal 3.5).

Related to the probability mass function $f_X(x) = \mathbb{P}(X = x)$ is another important function called the cumulative distribution function (CDF), F_X. It is defined by the formula

$$F_X(t) = \mathbb{P}(X \leq t), \quad -\infty < t < \infty. \tag{5.1.5}$$

We know that all PMFs satisfy certain properties, and a similar statement may be made for CDFs. In particular, any CDF F_X satisfies

- F_X is nondecreasing ($t_1 \leq t_2$ implies $F_X(t_1) \leq F_X(t_2)$).
- F_X is right-continuous ($\lim_{t \to a^+} F_X(t) = F_X(a)$ for all $a \in \mathbb{R}$).
- $\lim_{t \to -\infty} F_X(t) = 0$ and $\lim_{t \to \infty} F_X(t) = 1$.

We say that X has the distribution F_X and we write $X \sim F_X$. In an abuse of notation we will also write $X \sim f_X$ and for the named distributions the PMF or CDF will be identified by the family name instead of the defining formula.

5.1.3 How to do it with R

The mean and variance of a discrete random variable is easy to compute at the console. Let's return to Example 5.2. We will start by defining a vector `x` containing the support of X, and a vector `f` to contain the values of f_X at the respective outcomes in `x`:

```
> x <- c(0,1,2,3)
> f <- c(1/8, 3/8, 3/8, 1/8)
```

To calculate the mean μ, we need to multiply the corresponding values of `x` and `f` and add them. This is easily accomplished in R since operations on vectors are performed *element-wise* (see Section 2.3.4):

```
> mu <- sum(x * f)
> mu
[1] 1.5
```

To compute the variance σ^2, we subtract the value of `mu` from each entry in `x`, square the answers, multiply by `f`, and `sum`. The standard deviation σ is simply the square root of σ^2.

```
> sigma2 <- sum((x-mu)^2 * f)
> sigma2
[1] 0.75
> sigma <- sqrt(sigma2)
> sigma
[1] 0.8660254
```

Finally, we may find the values of the CDF F_X on the support by accumulating the probabilities in f_X with the `cumsum` function.

```
> F = cumsum(f)
> F
[1] 0.125 0.500 0.875 1.000
```

As easy as this is, it is even easier to do with the `distrEx` package [74]. We define a random variable `X` as an object, then compute things from the object such as mean, variance, and standard deviation with the functions `E`, `var`, and `sd`:

```
> library(distrEx)
> X <- DiscreteDistribution(supp = 0:3, prob = c(1,3,3,1)/8)
> E(X); var(X); sd(X)
[1] 1.5
[1] 0.75
[1] 0.8660254
```

5.2 The Discrete Uniform Distribution

We have seen the basic building blocks of discrete distributions and we now study particular models that statisticians often encounter in the field. Perhaps the most fundamental of all is the *discrete uniform* distribution.

A random variable X with the discrete uniform distribution on the integers $1, 2, \ldots, m$ has PMF

$$f_X(x) = \frac{1}{m}, \quad x = 1, 2, \ldots, m. \tag{5.2.1}$$

We write $X \sim \mathsf{disunif}(m)$. A random experiment where this distribution occurs is the choice of an integer at random between 1 and 100, inclusive. Let X be the number chosen. Then $X \sim \mathsf{disunif}(m = 100)$ and

$$\mathbb{P}(X = x) = \frac{1}{100}, \quad x = 1, \ldots, 100.$$

We find a direct formula for the mean of $X \sim \mathsf{disunif}(m)$:

$$\mu = \sum_{x=1}^{m} x f_X(x) = \sum_{x=1}^{m} x \cdot \frac{1}{m} = \frac{1}{m}(1 + 2 + \cdots + m) = \frac{m+1}{2}, \tag{5.2.2}$$

where we have used the famous identity $1 + 2 + \cdots + m = m(m+1)/2$. That is, if we repeatedly choose integers at random from 1 to m then, on the average, we expect to get $(m+1)/2$. To get the variance we first calculate

$$\mathbb{E}\,X^2 = \frac{1}{m}\sum_{x=1}^{m} x^2 = \frac{1}{m}\frac{m(m+1)(2m+3)}{6} = \frac{(m+1)(2m+1)}{6},$$

and finally,

$$\sigma^2 = \mathbb{E}\,X^2 - (\mathbb{E}\,X)^2 = \frac{(m+1)(2m+1)}{6} - \left(\frac{m+1}{2}\right)^2 = \cdots = \frac{m^2-1}{12}. \tag{5.2.3}$$

Example 5.4. Roll a die and let X be the upward face showing. Then $m = 6$, $\mu = 7/2 = 3.5$, and $\sigma^2 = (6^2 - 1)/12 = 35/12$.

5.2.1 How to do it with R

From the console: One can choose an integer at random with the `sample` function. The general syntax to simulate a discrete uniform random variable is `sample(x, size, replace = TRUE)`.

The argument `x` identifies the numbers from which to randomly sample. If `x` is a number, then sampling is done from 1 to `x`. The argument `size` tells how big the sample size should be, and `replace` tells whether or not numbers should be replaced in the urn after having been sampled. The default option is `replace = FALSE` but for discrete uniforms the sampled values should be replaced. Some examples follow.

5.2.2 Examples

- To roll a fair die 3000 times, do `sample(6, size = 3000, replace = TRUE)`.
- To choose 27 random numbers from 30 to 70, do `sample(30:70, size = 27, replace = TRUE)`.
- To flip a fair coin 1000 times, do `sample(c("H","T"), size = 1000, replace = TRUE)`.

With the R Commander: Follow the sequence Probability ▹ Discrete Distributions ▹ Discrete Uniform distribution ▹ Simulate Discrete uniform variates. . . .

Suppose we would like to roll a fair die 3000 times. In the `Number of samples` field we enter `1`. Next, we describe what interval of integers to be sampled. Since there are six faces numbered 1 through 6, we set `from = 1`, we set `to = 6`, and set `by = 1` (to indicate that we travel from 1 to 6 in increments of 1 unit). We will generate a list of 3000 numbers selected from among 1, 2, . . . , 6, and we store the results of the simulation. For the time being, we select `New Data set`. Click OK.

Since we are defining a new data set, the R Commander requests a name for the data set. The default name is `Simset1`, although in principle you could name it whatever you like (according to R's rules for object names). We wish to have a list that is 3000 long, so we set `Sample Size = 3000` and click OK.

In the R Console window, the R Commander should tell you that `Simset1` has been initialized, and it should also alert you that `There was 1 discrete uniform variate sample stored in Simset 1.`. To take a look at the rolls of the die, we click View data set and a window opens.

The default name for the variable is `disunif.sim1`.

5.3 The Binomial Distribution

The binomial distribution is based on a *Bernoulli trial*, which is a random experiment in which there are only two possible outcomes: success (S) and failure (F). We conduct the Bernoulli trial and let

$$X = \begin{cases} 1 & \text{if the outcome is } S, \\ 0 & \text{if the outcome is } F. \end{cases} \tag{5.3.1}$$

If the probability of success is p then the probability of failure must be $1 - p = q$ and the PMF of X is

$$f_X(x) = p^x(1-p)^{1-x}, \quad x = 0, 1. \tag{5.3.2}$$

It is easy to calculate $\mu = \mathbb{E}\,X = p$ and $\mathbb{E}\,X^2 = p$ so that $\sigma^2 = p - p^2 = p(1-p)$.

5.3.1 The Binomial Model

The Binomial model has three defining properties:

- Bernoulli trials are conducted n times,
- the trials are independent,
- the probability of success p does not change between trials.

If X counts the number of successes in the n independent trials, then the PMF of X is

$$f_X(x) = \binom{n}{x} p^x(1-p)^{n-x}, \quad x = 0, 1, 2, \ldots, n. \tag{5.3.3}$$

We say that X has a *binomial distribution* and we write $X \sim$ `binom(size` $= n$, `prob` $= p$). It is clear that $f_X(x) \geq 0$ for all x in the support because the value is the product of nonnegative numbers. We next check that $\sum f(x) = 1$:

$$\sum_{x=0}^{n} \binom{n}{x} p^x(1-p)^{n-x} = [p + (1-p)]^n = 1^n = 1.$$

We next find the mean:

$$\begin{aligned}
\mu =& \sum_{x=0}^{n} x \binom{n}{x} p^x(1-p)^{n-x},\\
=& \sum_{x=1}^{n} x \frac{n!}{x!(n-x)!} p^x q^{n-x},\\
=& n \cdot p \sum_{x=1}^{n} \frac{(n-1)!}{(x-1)!(n-x)!} p^{x-1} q^{n-x},\\
=& np \sum_{x-1=0}^{n-1} \binom{n-1}{x-1} p^{(x-1)}(1-p)^{(n-1)-(x-1)},\\
=& np.
\end{aligned}$$

A similar argument shows that $\mathbb{E}\,X(X-1) = n(n-1)p^2$ (see Exercise 5.5). Therefore

$$\begin{aligned}
\sigma^2 =& \mathbb{E}\,X(X-1) + \mathbb{E}\,X - [\mathbb{E}\,X]^2,\\
=& n(n-1)p^2 + np - (np)^2,\\
=& n^2p^2 - np^2 + np - n^2p^2,\\
=& np - np^2 = np(1-p).
\end{aligned}$$

Example 5.5. A four-child family. Each child may be either a boy (B) or a girl (G). For simplicity we suppose that $\mathbb{P}(B) = \mathbb{P}(G) = 1/2$ and that the genders of the children are determined independently. If we let X count the number of B's, then $X \sim$ binom(`size` = 4, `prob` = 1/2). Further, $\mathbb{P}(X = 2)$ is

$$f_X(2) = \binom{4}{2}(1/2)^2(1/2)^2 = \frac{6}{2^4}.$$

The mean number of boys is $4(1/2) = 2$ and the variance of X is $4(1/2)(1/2) = 1$.

5.3.2 How to do it with R

The corresponding R function for the PMF and CDF are `dbinom` and `pbinom`, respectively. We demonstrate their use in the following examples.

Example 5.6. We can calculate it in R Commander under the Binomial Distribution menu with the Binomial probabilities menu item.

```
      Pr
0 0.0625
1 0.2500
2 0.3750
3 0.2500
4 0.0625
```

We know that the binom(`size` = 4, `prob` = 1/2) distribution is supported on the integers 0, 1, 2, 3, and 4; thus the table is complete. We can read off the answer to be $\mathbb{P}(X = 2) = 0.3750$.

Example 5.7. Roll 12 dice simultaneously, and let X denote the number of 6's that appear. We wish to find the probability of getting seven, eight, or nine 6's. If we let $S = \{\text{get a 6 on one roll}\}$, then $\mathbb{P}(S) = 1/6$ and the rolls constitute Bernoulli trials; thus $X \sim$ binom(`size` =12, `prob` =1/6) and our task is to find $\mathbb{P}(7 \leq X \leq 9)$. This is just

$$\mathbb{P}(7 \leq X \leq 9) = \sum_{x=7}^{9} \binom{12}{x}(1/6)^x(5/6)^{12-x}.$$

Again, one method to solve this problem would be to generate a probability mass table and add up the relevant rows. However, an alternative method is to notice that $\mathbb{P}(7 \leq X \leq 9) = \mathbb{P}(X \leq 9) - \mathbb{P}(X \leq 6) = F_X(9) - F_X(6)$, so we could get the same answer by using the Binomial tail probabilities... menu in the R Commander or the following from the command line:

```
> pbinom(9, size=12, prob=1/6) - pbinom(6, size=12, prob=1/6)
[1] 0.001291758
> diff(pbinom(c(6,9), size = 12, prob = 1/6))  # same thing
[1] 0.001291758
```

Example 5.8. Toss a coin three times and let X be the number of Heads observed. We know from before that $X \sim$ `binom(size = 3, prob = 1/2)` which implies the following PMF:

x = #of Heads	0	1	2	3
$f(x) = \mathbb{P}(X = x)$	1/8	3/8	3/8	1/8

Our next goal is to write down the CDF of X explicitly. The first case is easy: it is impossible for X to be negative, so if $x < 0$ then we should have $\mathbb{P}(X \leq x) = 0$. Now choose a value x satisfying $0 \leq x < 1$, say, $x = 0.3$. The only way that $X \leq x$ could happen would be if $X = 0$, therefore, $\mathbb{P}(X \leq x)$ should equal $\mathbb{P}(X = 0)$, and the same is true for any $0 \leq x < 1$. Similarly, for any $1 \leq x < 2$, say, $x = 1.73$, the event $\{X \leq x\}$ is exactly the event $\{X = 0 \text{ or } X = 1\}$. Consequently, $\mathbb{P}(X \leq x)$ should equal $\mathbb{P}(X = 0 \text{ or } X = 1) = \mathbb{P}(X = 0) + \mathbb{P}(X = 1)$. Continuing in this fashion, we may figure out the values of $F_X(x)$ for all possible inputs $-\infty < x < \infty$, and we may summarize our observations with the following piecewise defined function:

$$F_X(x) = \mathbb{P}(X \leq x) = \begin{cases} 0, & x < 0, \\ \frac{1}{8}, & 0 \leq x < 1, \\ \frac{1}{8} + \frac{3}{8} = \frac{4}{8}, & 1 \leq x < 2, \\ \frac{4}{8} + \frac{3}{8} = \frac{7}{8}, & 2 \leq x < 3, \\ 1, & x \geq 3. \end{cases}$$

In particular, the CDF of X is defined for the entire real line, $\mathbb{R}$. The CDF is right continuous and nondecreasing. A graph of the `binom(size = 3, prob = 1/2)` CDF is shown in Figure 5.3.1.

Example 5.9. Another way to do Example 5.8 is with the `distr` family of packages [74]. They use an object oriented approach to random variables, that is, a random variable is stored in an object `X`, and then questions about the random variable translate to functions on and involving `X`. Random variables with distributions from the `base` package are specified by capitalizing the name of the distribution.

```
> library(distr)
> X <- Binom(size = 3, prob = 1/2)
> X

Distribution Object of Class: Binom
 size: 3
 prob: 0.5
```

The analogue of the `dbinom` function for `X` is the `d(X)` function, and the analogue of the `pbinom` function is the `p(X)` function. Compare the following:

```
> d(X)(1)   # pmf of X evaluated at x = 1

[1] 0.375

> p(X)(2)   # cdf of X evaluated at x = 2

[1] 0.875
```

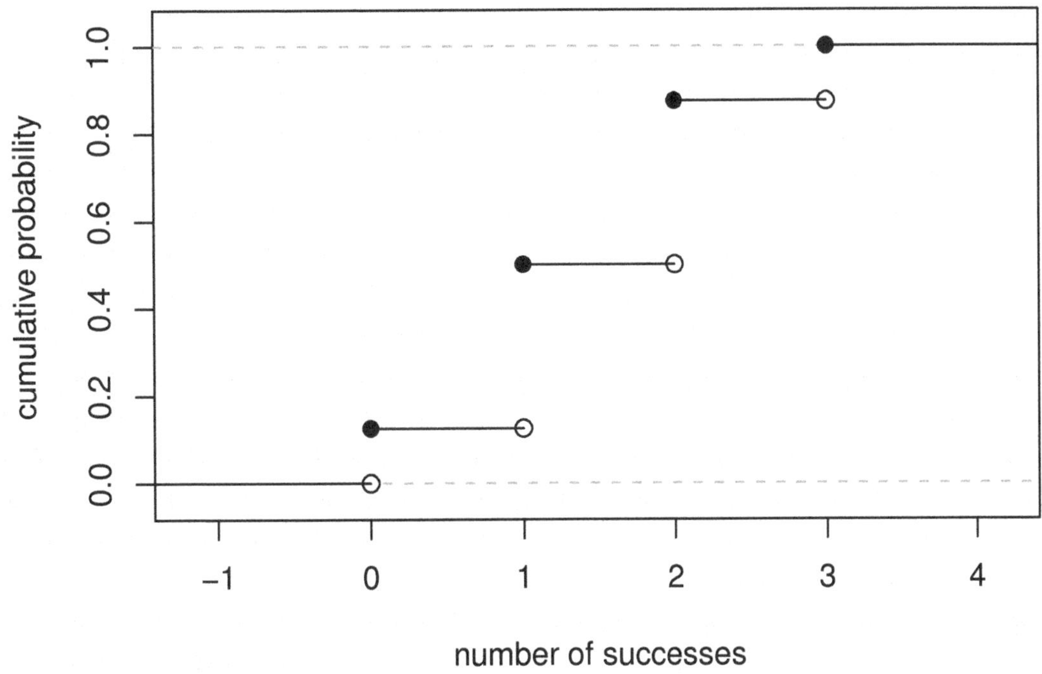

Figure 5.3.1: Graph of the binom(`size` = 3, `prob` = 1/2) CDF

Random variables defined via the `distr` package may be *plotted*, which will return graphs of the PMF, CDF, and quantile function (introduced in Section 6.3.1). See Figure 5.3.2 for an example.

Given $X \sim$ dbinom(`size` $= n$, `prob` $= p$).

How to do:	with `stats` (default)	with `distr`
PMF: $\mathbb{P}(X = x)$	`dbinom(x, size = n, prob = p)`	`d(X)(x)`
CDF: $\mathbb{P}(X \leq x)$	`pbinom(x, size = n, prob = p)`	`p(X)(x)`
Simulate k variates	`rbinom(k, size = n, prob = p)`	`r(X)(k)`

For `distr` need `X <- Binom(size =`n`, prob =`p`)`

Table 5.1: Correspondence between `stats` and `distr`

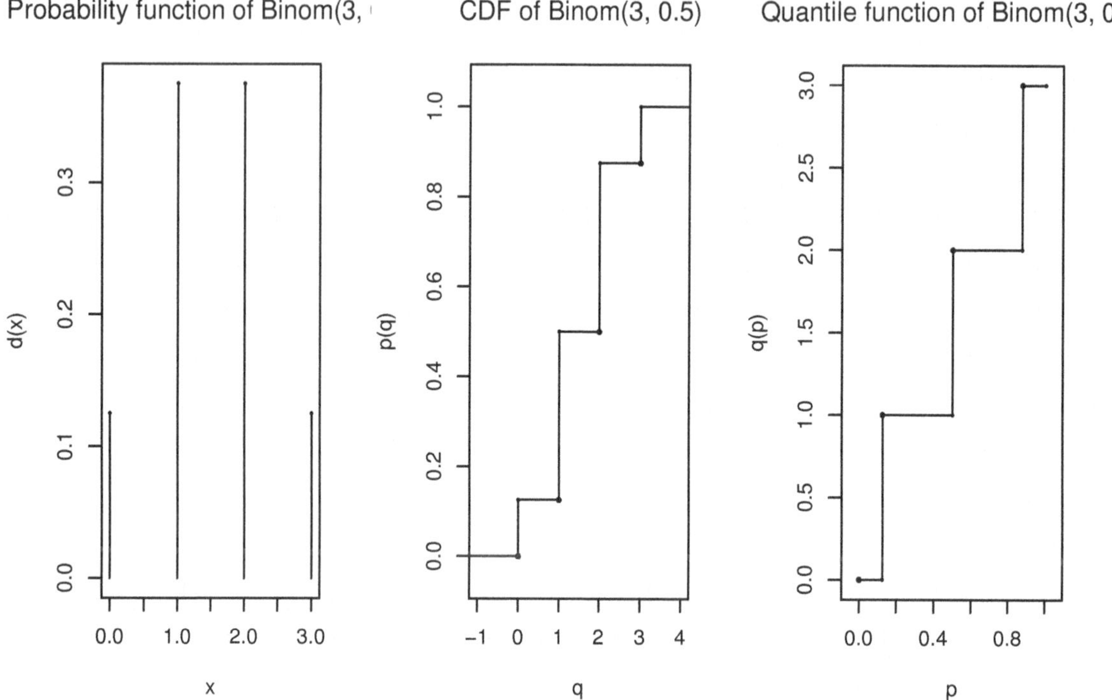

Figure 5.3.2: The binom(`size` = 3, `prob` = 0.5) distribution from the `distr` package

5.4 Expectation and Moment Generating Functions

5.4.1 The Expectation Operator

We next generalize some of the concepts from Section 5.1.2. There we saw that every[1] PMF has two important numbers associated with it:

$$\mu = \sum_{x \in S} x f_X(x), \quad \sigma^2 = \sum_{x \in S} (x - \mu)^2 f_X(x). \tag{5.4.1}$$

Intuitively, for repeated observations of X we would expect the sample mean to closely approximate μ as the sample size increases without bound. For this reason we call μ the *expected value* of X and we write $\mu = \mathbb{E}\, X$, where $\mathbb{E}$ is an *expectation operator*.

[1]Not every, only those PMFs for which the (potentially infinite) series converges.

Definition 5.10. More generally, given a function g we define the *expected value of* $g(X)$ by

$$\mathbb{E}\, g(X) = \sum_{x \in S} g(x) f_X(x), \tag{5.4.2}$$

provided the (potentially infinite) series $\sum_x |g(x)| f(x)$ is convergent. We say that $\mathbb{E}\, g(X)$ *exists.*

In this notation the variance is $\sigma^2 = \mathbb{E}(X - \mu)^2$ and we prove the identity

$$\mathbb{E}(X - \mu)^2 = \mathbb{E}\, X^2 - (\mathbb{E}\, X)^2 \tag{5.4.3}$$

in Exercise 5.4. Intuitively, for repeated observations of X we would expect the sample mean of the $g(X)$ values to closely approximate $\mathbb{E}\, g(X)$ as the sample size increases without bound.

Let us take the analogy further. If we expect $g(X)$ to be close to $\mathbb{E}\, g(X)$ on the average, where would we expect $3g(X)$ to be on the average? It could only be $3\, \mathbb{E}\, g(X)$. The following theorem makes this idea precise.

Proposition 5.11. *For any functions g and h, any random variable X, and any constant c:*

1. $\mathbb{E}\, c = c$,
2. $\mathbb{E}[c \cdot g(X)] = c\, \mathbb{E}\, g(X)$
3. $\mathbb{E}[g(X) + h(X)] = \mathbb{E}\, g(X) + \mathbb{E}\, h(X)$,

provided $\mathbb{E}\, g(X)$ and $\mathbb{E}\, h(X)$ exist.

Proof. Go directly from the definition. For example,

$$\mathbb{E}[c \cdot g(X)] = \sum_{x \in S} c \cdot g(x) f_X(x) = c \cdot \sum_{x \in S} g(x) f_X(x) = c\, \mathbb{E}\, g(X).$$

□

5.4.2 Moment Generating Functions

Definition 5.12. Given a random variable X, its *moment generating function* (abbreviated MGF) is defined by the formula

$$M_X(t) = \mathbb{E}\, \mathrm{e}^{tX} = \sum_{x \in S} \mathrm{e}^{tx} f_X(x), \tag{5.4.4}$$

provided the (potentially infinite) series is convergent for all t in a neighborhood of zero (that is, for all $-\epsilon < t < \epsilon$, for some $\epsilon > 0$).

Note that for any MGF M_X,

$$M_X(0) = \mathbb{E}\, \mathrm{e}^{0 \cdot X} = \mathbb{E}\, 1 = 1. \tag{5.4.5}$$

We will calculate the MGF for the two distributions introduced above.

Example 5.13. Find the MGF for $X \sim \mathsf{disunif}(m)$.

Since $f(x) = 1/m$, the MGF takes the form

$$M(t) = \sum_{x=1}^{m} \mathrm{e}^{tx} \frac{1}{m} = \frac{1}{m}(\mathrm{e}^{t} + \mathrm{e}^{2t} + \cdots + \mathrm{e}^{mt}), \quad \text{for any } t.$$

Example 5.14. Find the MGF for $X \sim$ binom(`size` $= n$, `prob` $= p$).

$$\begin{aligned} M_X(t) &= \sum_{x=0}^{n} \mathrm{e}^{tx} \binom{n}{x} p^x (1-p)^{n-x}, \\ &= \sum_{x=0}^{n-x} \binom{n}{x} (p\mathrm{e}^t)^x q^{n-x}, \\ &= (p\mathrm{e}^t + q)^n, \quad \text{for any } t. \end{aligned}$$

Applications

We will discuss three applications of moment generating functions in this book. The first is the fact that an MGF may be used to accurately identify the probability distribution that generated it, which rests on the following:

Theorem 5.15. *The moment generating function, if it exists in a neighborhood of zero, determines a probability distribution* uniquely.

Proof. Unfortunately, the proof of such a theorem is beyond the scope of a text like this one. Interested readers could consult Billingsley [8]. □

We will see an example of Theorem 5.15 in action.

Example 5.16. Suppose we encounter a random variable which has MGF

$$M_X(t) = (0.3 + 0.7\mathrm{e}^t)^{13}.$$

Then $X \sim$ binom(`size` $= 13$, `prob` $= 0.7$).

An MGF is also known as a "Laplace Transform" and is manipulated in that context in many branches of science and engineering.

Why is it called a Moment Generating Function?

This brings us to the second powerful application of MGFs. Many of the models we study have a simple MGF, indeed, which permits us to determine the mean, variance, and even higher moments very quickly. Let us see why. We already know that

$$M(t) = \sum_{x \in S} \mathrm{e}^{tx} f(x).$$

Take the derivative with respect to t to get

$$M'(t) = \frac{\mathrm{d}}{\mathrm{d}t}\left(\sum_{x \in S} \mathrm{e}^{tx} f(x)\right) = \sum_{x \in S} \frac{\mathrm{d}}{\mathrm{d}t}\left(\mathrm{e}^{tx} f(x)\right) = \sum_{x \in S} x\mathrm{e}^{tx} f(x), \tag{5.4.6}$$

and so if we plug in zero for t we see

$$M'(0) = \sum_{x \in S} x\mathrm{e}^0 f(x) = \sum_{x \in S} x f(x) = \mu = \mathbb{E}\, X. \tag{5.4.7}$$

Similarly, $M''(t) = \sum x^2 e^{tx} f(x)$ so that $M''(0) = \mathbb{E}\, X^2$. And in general, we can see[2] that

$$M_X^{(r)}(0) = \mathbb{E}\, X^r = r^{th}\text{moment of } X \text{about the origin.} \tag{5.4.8}$$

These are also known as *raw moments* and are sometimes denoted μ_r'. In addition to these are the so called *central moments* μ_r defined by

$$\mu_r = \mathbb{E}(X - \mu)^r, \quad r = 1, 2, \ldots \tag{5.4.9}$$

Example 5.17. Let $X \sim$ `binom(size` $= n$, `prob` $= p)$ with $M(t) = (q + pe^t)^n$. We calculated the mean and variance of a binomial random variable in Section 5.3 by means of the binomial series. But look how quickly we find the mean and variance with the moment generating function.

$$\begin{aligned} M'(t) =& n(q + pe^t)^{n-1} pe^t \,|_{t=0}\,, \\ =& n \cdot 1^{n-1} p, \\ =& np. \end{aligned}$$

And

$$\begin{aligned} M''(0) =& n(n-1)[q + pe^t]^{n-2}(pe^t)^2 + n[q + pe^t]^{n-1} pe^t \,|_{t=0}\,, \\ \mathbb{E}\, X^2 =& n(n-1)p^2 + np. \end{aligned}$$

Therefore

$$\begin{aligned} \sigma^2 =& \mathbb{E}\, X^2 - (\mathbb{E}\, X)^2, \\ =& n(n-1)p^2 + np - n^2p^2, \\ =& np - np^2 = npq. \end{aligned}$$

See how much easier that was?

Remark 5.18. We learned in this section that $M^{(r)}(0) = \mathbb{E}\, X^r$. We remember from Calculus II that certain functions f can be represented by a Taylor series expansion about a point a, which takes the form

$$f(x) = \sum_{r=0}^{\infty} \frac{f^{(r)}(a)}{r!}(x - a)^r, \quad \text{for all } |x - a| < R, \tag{5.4.10}$$

where R is called the *radius of convergence* of the series (see Appendix E.3). We combine the two to say that if an MGF exists for all t in the interval $(-\epsilon, \epsilon)$, then we can write

$$M_X(t) = \sum_{r=0}^{\infty} \frac{\mathbb{E}\, X^r}{r!} t^r, \quad \text{for all } |t| < \epsilon. \tag{5.4.11}$$

[2]We are glossing over some significant mathematical details in our derivation. Suffice it to say that when the MGF exists in a neighborhood of $t = 0$, the exchange of differentiation and summation is valid in that neighborhood, and our remarks hold true.

5.4.3 How to do it with R

The `distrEx` package provides an expectation operator `E` which can be used on random variables that have been defined in the ordinary `distr` sense:

```
> X <- Binom(size = 3, prob = 0.45)
> library(distrEx)
> E(X)
[1] 1.35
> E(3 * X + 4)
[1] 8.05
```

For discrete random variables with finite support, the expectation is simply computed with direct summation. In the case that the random variable has infinite support and the function is crazy, then the expectation is not computed directly, rather, it is estimated by first generating a random sample from the underlying model and next computing a sample mean of the function of interest.

There are methods for other population parameters:

```
> var(X)
[1] 0.7425
> sd(X)
[1] 0.8616844
```

There are even methods for `IQR`, `mad`, `skewness`, and `kurtosis`.

5.5 The Empirical Distribution

Do an experiment n times and observe n values $x_1, x_2, \ldots, x_n$ of a random variable X. For simplicity in most of the discussion that follows it will be convenient to imagine that the observed values are distinct, but the remarks are valid even when the observed values are repeated.

Definition 5.19. The *empirical cumulative distribution function* F_n (written ECDF) is the probability distribution that places probability mass $1/n$ on each of the values $x_1, x_2, \ldots, x_n$. The empirical PMF takes the form

$$f_X(x) = \frac{1}{n}, \quad x \in \{x_1, x_2, ..., x_n\}. \tag{5.5.1}$$

If the value x_i is repeated k times, the mass at x_i is accumulated to k/n.

The mean of the empirical distribution is

$$\mu = \sum_{x \in S} x f_X(x) = \sum_{i=1}^{n} x_i \cdot \frac{1}{n} \tag{5.5.2}$$

and we recognize this last quantity to be the sample mean, $\overline{x}$. The variance of the empirical distribution is

$$\sigma^2 = \sum_{x \in S} (x - \mu)^2 f_X(x) = \sum_{i=1}^{n} (x_i - \overline{x})^2 \cdot \frac{1}{n} \tag{5.5.3}$$

and this last quantity looks very close to what we already know to be the sample variance.

$$s^2 = \frac{1}{n-1}\sum_{i=1}^{n}(x_i - \overline{x})^2. \tag{5.5.4}$$

The *empirical quantile function* is the inverse of the ECDF. See Section 6.3.1.

5.5.1 How to do it with R

The empirical distribution is not directly available as a distribution in the same way that the other base probability distributions are, but there are plenty of resources available for the determined investigator.

Given a data vector of observed values `x`, we can see the empirical CDF with the `ecdf` function:

```
> x <- c(4, 7, 9, 11, 12)
> ecdf(x)
```

```
Empirical CDF
Call: ecdf(x)
 x[1:5] =      4,      7,      9,     11,     12
```

The above shows that the returned value of `ecdf(x)` is not a *number* but rather a *function*. The ECDF is not usually used by itself in this form, by itself. More commonly it is used as an intermediate step in a more complicated calculation, for instance, in hypothesis testing (see Chapter 10) or resampling (see Chapter 13). It is nevertheless instructive to see what the `ecdf` looks like, and there is a special plot method for `ecdf` objects.

```
> plot(ecdf(x))
```

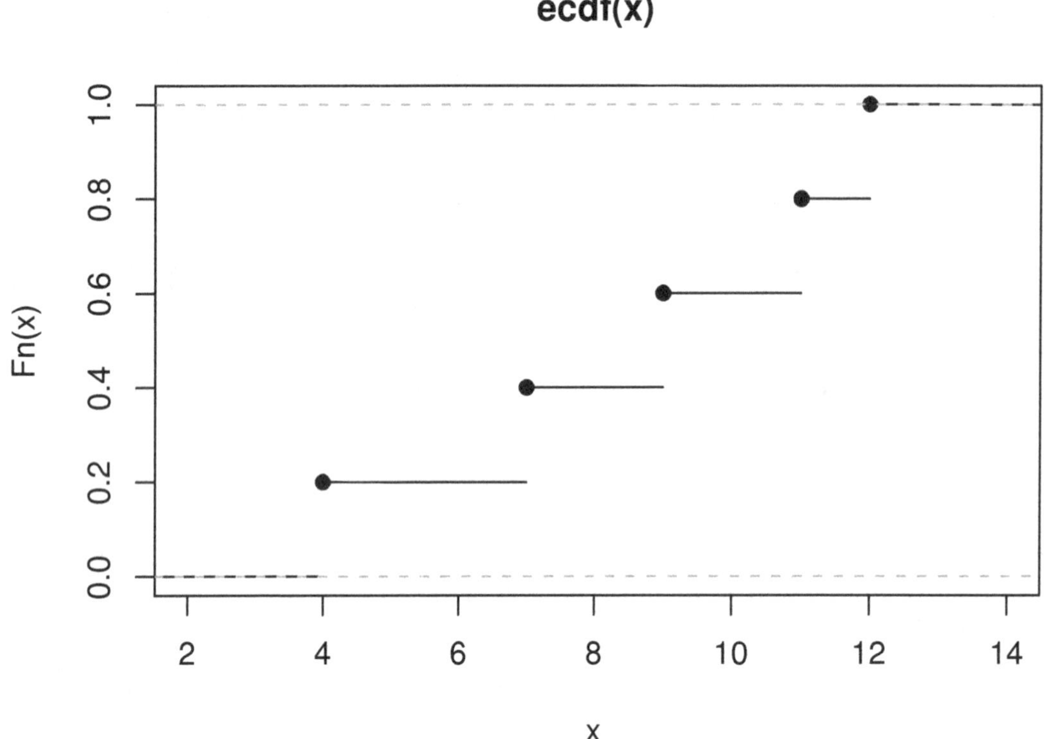

Figure 5.5.1: The empirical CDF

See Figure 5.5.1. The graph is of a right-continuous function with jumps exactly at the locations stored in `x`. There are no repeated values in `x` so all of the jumps are equal to $1/5 = 0.2$.

The empirical PDF is not usually of particular interest in itself, but if we really wanted we could define a function to serve as the empirical PDF:

```
> epdf <- function(x) function(t){sum(x %in% t)/length(x)}
> x <- c(0,0,1)
> epdf(x)(0)        # should be 2/3
[1] 0.6666667
```

To simulate from the empirical distribution supported on the vector `x`, we use the `sample` function.

```
> x <- c(0, 0, 1)
> sample(x, size = 7, replace = TRUE)
[1] 0 1 0 1 1 0 0
```

We can get the empirical quantile function in R with `quantile(x, probs = p, type = 1)`; see Section 6.3.1.

As we hinted above, the empirical distribution is significant more because of how and where it appears in more sophisticated applications. We will explore some of these in later chapters – see, for instance, Chapter 13.

5.6 Other Discrete Distributions

The binomial and discrete uniform distributions are popular, and rightly so; they are simple and form the foundation for many other more complicated distributions. But the particular uniform and binomial models only apply to a limited range of problems. In this section we introduce situations for which we need more than what the uniform and binomial offer.

5.6.1 Dependent Bernoulli Trials

The Hypergeometric Distribution

Consider an urn with 7 white balls and 5 black balls. Let our random experiment be to randomly select 4 balls, without replacement, from the urn. Then the probability of observing 3 white balls (and thus 1 black ball) would be

$$\mathbb{P}(3W, 1B) = \frac{\binom{7}{3}\binom{5}{1}}{\binom{12}{4}}. \tag{5.6.1}$$

More generally, we sample without replacement K times from an urn with M white balls and N black balls. Let X be the number of white balls in the sample. The PMF of X is

$$f_X(x) = \frac{\binom{M}{x}\binom{N}{K-x}}{\binom{M+N}{K}}. \tag{5.6.2}$$

We say that X has a *hypergeometric distribution* and write $X \sim \mathsf{hyper}(\mathtt{m} = M,\ \mathtt{n} = N,\ \mathtt{k} = K)$.

The support set for the hypergeometric distribution is a little bit tricky. It is tempting to say that x should go from 0 (no white balls in the sample) to K (no black balls in the sample), but that does not work if $K > M$, because it is impossible to have more white balls in the sample than there were white balls originally in the urn. We have the same trouble if $K > N$. The good news is that the majority of examples we study have $K \leq M$ and $K \leq N$ and we will happily take the support to be $x = 0,\ 1,\ \ldots,\ K$.

It is shown in Exercise 5.6 that

$$\mu = K\frac{M}{M+N}, \quad \sigma^2 = K\frac{MN}{(M+N)^2}\,\frac{M+N-K}{M+N-1}. \tag{5.6.3}$$

The associated R functions for the PMF and CDF are `dhyper(x, m, n, k)` and `phyper`, respectively. There are two more functions: `qhyper`, which we will discuss in Section 6.3.1, and `rhyper`, discussed below.

Example 5.20. Suppose in a certain shipment of 250 Pentium processors there are 17 defective processors. A quality control consultant randomly collects 5 processors for inspection to determine whether or not they are defective. Let X denote the number of defectives in the sample.

1. Find the probability of exactly 3 defectives in the sample, that is, find $\mathbb{P}(X = 3)$.

   Solution: We know that $X \sim \mathsf{hyper}(\mathtt{m} = 17,\ \mathtt{n} = 233,\ \mathtt{k} = 5)$. So the required probability is just

   $$f_X(3) = \frac{\binom{17}{3}\binom{233}{2}}{\binom{250}{5}}.$$

   To calculate it in R we just type

```
> dhyper(3, m = 17, n = 233, k = 5)

[1] 0.002351153
```

To find it with the R Commander we go Probability ▹ Discrete Distributions ▹ Hypergeometric distribution ▹ Hypergeometric probabilities.... We fill in the parameters $m = 17$, $n = 233$, and $k = 5$. Click OK, and the following table is shown in the window.

```
> A <- data.frame(Pr = dhyper(0:4, m = 17, n = 233, k = 5))
> rownames(A) <- 0:4
> A

            Pr
0 7.011261e-01
1 2.602433e-01
2 3.620776e-02
3 2.351153e-03
4 7.093997e-05
```

We wanted $\mathbb{P}(X = 3)$, and this is found from the table to be approximately 0.0024. The value is rounded to the fourth decimal place.

We know from our above discussion that the sample space should be $x = 0, 1, 2, 3, 4, 5$, yet, in the table the probabilities are only displayed for $x = 1, 2, 3$, and 4. What is happening? As it turns out, the R Commander will only display probabilities that are 0.00005 or greater. Since $x = 5$ is not shown, it suggests that the outcome has a tiny probability. To find its exact value we use the `dhyper` function:

```
> dhyper(5, m = 17, n = 233, k = 5)

[1] 7.916049e-07
```

In other words, $\mathbb{P}(X = 5) \approx 0.0000007916049$, a small number indeed.

2. Find the probability that there are at most 2 defectives in the sample, that is, compute $\mathbb{P}(X \leq 2)$.

   Solution: Since $\mathbb{P}(X \leq 2) = \mathbb{P}(X = 0, 1, 2)$, one way to do this would be to add the 0, 1, and 2 entries in the above table. this gives $0.7011 + 0.2602 + 0.0362 = 0.9975$. Our answer should be correct up to the accuracy of 4 decimal places. However, a more precise method is provided by the R Commander. Under the Hypergeometric distribution menu we select Hypergeometric tail probabilities.... We fill in the parameters m, n, and k as before, but in the Variable value(s) dialog box we enter the value 2. We notice that the `Lower tail` option is checked, and we leave that alone. Click OK.

```
> phyper(2, m = 17, n = 233, k = 5)

[1] 0.9975771
```

   And thus $\mathbb{P}(X \leq 2) \approx 0.9975771$. We have confirmed that the above answer was correct up to four decimal places.

3. Find $\mathbb{P}(X > 1)$.

   The table did not give us the explicit probability $\mathbb{P}(X = 5)$, so we can not use the table to give us this probability. We need to use another method. Since $\mathbb{P}(X > 1) = 1 - \mathbb{P}(X \leq 1) = 1 - F_X(1)$, we can find the probability with Hypergeometric tail probabilities.... We enter 1 for Variable Value(s), we enter the parameters as before, and in this case we choose the `Upper tail` option. This results in the following output.

```
> phyper(1, m = 17, n = 233, k = 5, lower.tail = FALSE)

[1] 0.03863065
```

   In general, the `Upper tail` option of a tail probabilities dialog computes $\mathbb{P}(X > x)$ for all given Variable Value(s) x.

4. Generate 100, 000 observations of the random variable X.

   We can randomly simulate as many observations of X as we want in R Commander. Simply choose Simulate hypergeometric variates... in the Hypergeometric distribution dialog.

   In the Number of samples dialog, type 1. Enter the parameters as above. Under the Store Values section, make sure New Data set is selected. Click OK.

   A new dialog should open, with the default name `Simset1`. We could change this if we like, according to the rules for R object names. In the sample size box, enter 100000. Click OK.

   In the Console Window, R Commander should issue an alert that `Simset1` has been initialized, and in a few seconds, it should also state that 100,000 hypergeometric variates were stored in `hyper.sim1`. We can view the sample by clicking the View Data Set button on the R Commander interface.

   We know from our formulas that $\mu = K \cdot M/(M + N) = 5 * 17/250 = 0.34$. We can check our formulas using the fact that with repeated observations of X we would expect about 0.34 defectives on the average. To see how our sample reflects the true mean, we can compute the sample mean

```
Rcmdr> mean(Simset2$hyper.sim1, na.rm=TRUE)
[1] 0.340344

Rcmdr> sd(Simset2$hyper.sim1, na.rm=TRUE)
[1] 0.5584982

⋮
```

   We see that when given many independent observations of X, the sample mean is very close to the true mean μ. We can repeat the same idea and use the sample standard deviation to estimate the true standard deviation of X. From the output above our estimate is 0.5584982, and from our formulas we get

$$\sigma^2 = K \frac{MN}{(M + N)^2} \frac{M + N - K}{M + N - 1} \approx 0.3117896,$$

   with $\sigma = \sqrt{\sigma^2} \approx 0.5583811944$. Our estimate was pretty close.

   From the console we can generate random hypergeometric variates with the `rhyper` function, as demonstrated below.

```
> rhyper(10, m = 17, n = 233, k = 5)
 [1] 0 0 0 0 0 2 0 0 0 1
```

Sampling With and Without Replacement

Suppose that we have a large urn with, say, M white balls and N black balls. We take a sample of size n from the urn, and let X count the number of white balls in the sample. If we sample

without replacement, then $X \sim$ hyper(`m` $=M$, `n` $= N$, `k` $= n$) and has mean and variance

$$\begin{aligned}\mu =& n\frac{M}{M+N},\\ \sigma^2 =& n\frac{MN}{(M+N)^2}\frac{M+N-n}{M+N-1},\\ =& n\frac{M}{M+N}\left(1-\frac{M}{M+N}\right)\frac{M+N-n}{M+N-1}.\end{aligned}$$

On the other hand, if we sample

with replacement, then $X \sim$ binom(`size` $= n$, `prob` $= M/(M+N)$) with mean and variance

$$\begin{aligned}\mu =& n\frac{M}{M+N},\\ \sigma^2 =& n\frac{M}{M+N}\left(1-\frac{M}{M+N}\right).\end{aligned}$$

We see that both sampling procedures have the same mean, and the method with the larger variance is the "with replacement" scheme. The factor by which the variances differ,

$$\frac{M+N-n}{M+N-1}, \tag{5.6.4}$$

is called a *finite population correction*. For a fixed sample size n, as $M, N \to \infty$ it is clear that the correction goes to 1, that is, for infinite populations the sampling schemes are essentially the same with respect to mean and variance.

5.6.2 Waiting Time Distributions

Another important class of problems is associated with the amount of time it takes for a specified event of interest to occur. For example, we could flip a coin repeatedly until we observe Heads. We could toss a piece of paper repeatedly until we make it in the trash can.

The Geometric Distribution

Suppose that we conduct Bernoulli trials repeatedly, noting the successes and failures. Let X be the number of failures before a success. If $\mathbb{P}(S) = p$ then X has PMF

$$f_X(x) = p(1-p)^x, \quad x = 0, 1, 2, \ldots \tag{5.6.5}$$

(Why?) We say that X has a *Geometric distribution* and we write $X \sim$ geom(`prob` $= p$). The associated R functions are `dgeom(x, prob)`, `pgeom`, `qgeom`, and `rhyper`, which give the PMF, CDF, quantile function, and simulate random variates, respectively.

Again it is clear that $f(x) \geq 0$ and we check that $\sum f(x) = 1$ (see Equation E.3.9 in Appendix E.3):

$$\sum_{x=0}^{\infty} p(1-p)^x = p \sum_{x=0}^{\infty} q^x = p \frac{1}{1-q} = 1.$$

We will find in the next section that the mean and variance are

$$\mu = \frac{1-p}{p} = \frac{q}{p} \text{ and } \sigma^2 = \frac{q}{p^2}. \tag{5.6.6}$$

Example 5.21. The Pittsburgh Steelers place kicker, Jeff Reed, made 81.2% of his attempted field goals in his career up to 2006. Assuming that his successive field goal attempts are approximately Bernoulli trials, find the probability that Jeff misses at least 5 field goals before his first successful goal.

Solution: If X = the number of missed goals until Jeff's first success, then $X \sim$ geom(prob = 0.812) and we want $\mathbb{P}(X \geq 5) = \mathbb{P}(X > 4)$. We can find this in R with

```
> pgeom(4, prob = 0.812, lower.tail = FALSE)
[1] 0.0002348493
```

Note 5.22. Some books use a slightly different definition of the geometric distribution. They consider Bernoulli trials and let Y count instead the number of trials until a success, so that Y has PMF

$$f_Y(y) = p(1-p)^{y-1}, \quad y = 1, 2, 3, \ldots \tag{5.6.7}$$

When they say "geometric distribution", this is what they mean. It is not hard to see that the two definitions are related. In fact, if X denotes our geometric and Y theirs, then $Y = X + 1$. Consequently, they have $\mu_Y = \mu_X + 1$ and $\sigma_Y^2 = \sigma_X^2$.

The Negative Binomial Distribution

We may generalize the problem and consider the case where we wait for *more* than one success. Suppose that we conduct Bernoulli trials repeatedly, noting the respective successes and failures. Let X count the number of failures before r successes. If $\mathbb{P}(S) = p$ then X has PMF

$$f_X(x) = \binom{r+x-1}{r-1} p^r (1-p)^x, \quad x = 0, 1, 2, \ldots \tag{5.6.8}$$

We say that X has a *Negative Binomial distribution* and write $X \sim$ nbinom(size = r, prob = p). The associated R functions are `dnbinom(x, size, prob)`, `pnbinom`, `qnbinom`, and `rnbinom`, which give the PMF, CDF, quantile function, and simulate random variates, respectively.

As usual it should be clear that $f_X(x) \geq 0$ and the fact that $\sum f_X(x) = 1$ follows from a generalization of the geometric series by means of a Maclaurin's series expansion:

$$\frac{1}{1-t} = \sum_{k=0}^{\infty} t^k, \quad \text{for } -1 < t < 1, \text{ and} \tag{5.6.9}$$

$$\frac{1}{(1-t)^r} = \sum_{k=0}^{\infty} \binom{r+k-1}{r-1} t^k, \quad \text{for } -1 < t < 1. \tag{5.6.10}$$

Therefore

$$\sum_{x=0}^{\infty} f_X(x) = p^r \sum_{x=0}^{\infty} \binom{r+x-1}{r-1} q^x = p^r (1-q)^{-r} = 1, \tag{5.6.11}$$

since $|q| = |1 - p| < 1$.

Example 5.23. We flip a coin repeatedly and let X count the number of Tails until we get seven Heads. What is $\mathbb{P}(X = 5)$?

Solution: We know that $X \sim$ nbinom(`size` = 7, `prob` = 1/2).

$$\mathbb{P}(X = 5) = f_X(5) = \binom{7+5-1}{7-1}(1/2)^7(1/2)^5 = \binom{11}{6}2^{-12}$$

and we can get this in R with

```
> dnbinom(5, size = 7, prob = 0.5)
[1] 0.1127930
```

Let us next compute the MGF of $X \sim$ nbinom(`size` = r, `prob` = p).

$$\begin{aligned}
M_X(t) &= \sum_{x=0}^{\infty} e^{tx} \binom{r+x-1}{r-1} p^r q^x \\
&= p^r \sum_{x=0}^{\infty} \binom{r+x-1}{r-1} [qe^t]^x \\
&= p^r (1 - qe^t)^{-r}, \quad \text{provided } |qe^t| < 1,
\end{aligned}$$

and so

$$M_X(t) = \left(\frac{p}{1 - qe^t}\right)^r, \quad \text{for } qe^t < 1. \tag{5.6.12}$$

We see that $qe^t < 1$ when $t < -\ln(1 - p)$.

Let $X \sim$ nbinom(`size` = r, `prob` = p) with $M(t) = p^r(1 - qe^t)^{-r}$. We proclaimed above the values of the mean and variance. Now we are equipped with the tools to find these directly.

$$\begin{aligned}
M'(t) &= p^r(-r)(1 - qe^t)^{-r-1}(-qe^t), \\
&= rqe^t p^r (1 - qe^t)^{-r-1}, \\
&= \frac{rqe^t}{1 - qe^t} M(t), \text{ and so} \\
M'(0) &= \frac{rq}{1-q} \cdot 1 = \frac{rq}{p}.
\end{aligned}$$

Thus $\mu = rq/p$. We next find $\mathbb{E}\,X^2$.

$$\begin{aligned}
M''(0) &= \frac{rqe^t(1 - qe^t) - rqe^t(-qe^t)}{(1 - qe^t)^2} M(t) + \left.\frac{rqe^t}{1 - qe^t} M'(t)\right|_{t=0}, \\
&= \frac{rqp + rq^2}{p^2} \cdot 1 + \frac{rq}{p}\left(\frac{rq}{p}\right), \\
&= \frac{rq}{p^2} + \left(\frac{rq}{p}\right)^2.
\end{aligned}$$

Finally we may say $\sigma^2 = M''(0) - [M'(0)]^2 = rq/p^2$.

Example 5.24. A random variable has MGF

$$M_X(t) = \left(\frac{0.19}{1 - 0.81e^t}\right)^{31}.$$

Then $X \sim$ nbinom(`size` = 31, `prob` = 0.19).

Note 5.25. As with the Geometric distribution, some books use a slightly different definition of the Negative Binomial distribution. They consider Bernoulli trials and let Y be the number of trials until r successes, so that Y has PMF

$$f_Y(y) = \binom{y-1}{r-1} p^r (1-p)^{y-r}, \quad y = r, r+1, r+2, \ldots \tag{5.6.13}$$

It is again not hard to see that if X denotes our Negative Binomial and Y theirs, then $Y = X + r$. Consequently, they have $\mu_Y = \mu_X + r$ and $\sigma_Y^2 = \sigma_X^2$.

5.6.3 Arrival Processes

The Poisson Distribution

This is a distribution associated with "rare events", for reasons which will become clear in a moment. The events might be:

- traffic accidents,
- typing errors, or
- customers arriving in a bank.

Let λ be the average number of events in the time interval $[0, 1]$. Let the random variable X count the number of events occurring in the interval. Then under certain reasonable conditions it can be shown that

$$f_X(x) = \mathbb{P}(X = x) = e^{-\lambda}\frac{\lambda^x}{x!}, \quad x = 0, 1, 2, \ldots \tag{5.6.14}$$

We use the notation $X \sim$ pois(`lambda` = λ). The associated R functions are `dpois(x, lambda)`, `ppois`, `qpois`, and `rpois`, which give the PMF, CDF, quantile function, and simulate random variates, respectively.

What are the reasonable conditions? Divide $[0, 1]$ into subintervals of length $1/n$. A *Poisson process* satisfies the following conditions:

- the probability of an event occurring in a particular subinterval is $\approx \lambda/n$.
- the probability of two or more events occurring in any subinterval is ≈ 0.
- occurrences in disjoint subintervals are independent.

Remark 5.26. If X counts the number of events in the interval $[0, t]$ and λ is the average number that occur in unit time, then $X \sim$ pois(`lambda` = λt), that is,

$$\mathbb{P}(X = x) = e^{-\lambda t}\frac{(\lambda t)^x}{x!}, \quad x = 0, 1, 2, 3 \ldots \tag{5.6.15}$$

Example 5.27. On the average, five cars arrive at a particular car wash every hour. Let X count the number of cars that arrive from 10AM to 11AM. Then $X \sim$ `pois(lambda = 5)`. Also, $\mu = \sigma^2 = 5$. What is the probability that no car arrives during this period?

Solution: The probability that no car arrives is

$$\mathbb{P}(X = 0) = \mathrm{e}^{-5}\frac{5^0}{0!} = \mathrm{e}^{-5} \approx 0.0067.$$

Example 5.28. Suppose the car wash above is in operation from 8AM to 6PM, and we let Y be the number of customers that appear in this period. Since this period covers a total of 10 hours, from Remark 5.26 we get that $Y \sim$ `pois(lambda = 5 * 10 = 50)`. What is the probability that there are between 48 and 50 customers, inclusive?

Solution: We want $\mathbb{P}(48 \leq Y \leq 50) = \mathbb{P}(X \leq 50) - \mathbb{P}(X \leq 47)$.

```
> diff(ppois(c(47, 50), lambda = 50))
[1] 0.1678485
```

5.7 Functions of Discrete Random Variables

We have built a large catalogue of discrete distributions, but the tools of this section will give us the ability to consider infinitely many more. Given a random variable X and a given function h, we may consider $Y = h(X)$. Since the values of X are determined by chance, so are the values of Y. The question is, what is the PMF of the random variable Y? The answer, of course, depends on h. In the case that h is one-to-one (see Appendix E.2), the solution can be found by simple substitution.

Example 5.29. Let $X \sim$ `nbinom(size = r, prob = p)`. We saw in 5.6 that X represents the number of failures until r successes in a sequence of Bernoulli trials. Suppose now that instead we were interested in counting the number of trials (successes and failures) until the rth success occurs, which we will denote by Y. In a given performance of the experiment, the number of failures (X) and the number of successes (r) together will comprise the total number of trials (Y), or in other words, $X + r = Y$. We may let h be defined by $h(x) = x + r$ so that $Y = h(X)$, and we notice that h is linear and hence one-to-one. Finally, X takes values $0,\ 1,\ 2, \ldots$ implying that the support of Y would be $\{r,\ r+1,\ r+2, \ldots\}$. Solving for X we get $X = Y - r$. Examining the PMF of X

$$f_X(x) = \binom{r+x-1}{r-1} p^r (1-p)^x, \tag{5.7.1}$$

we can substitute $x = y - r$ to get

$$\begin{aligned} f_Y(y) &= f_X(y-r), \\ &= \binom{r+(y-r)-1}{r-1} p^r (1-p)^{y-r}, \\ &= \binom{y-1}{r-1} p^r (1-p)^{y-r}, \quad y = r,\ r+1, \ldots \end{aligned}$$

Even when the function h is not one-to-one, we may still find the PMF of Y simply by accumulating, for each y, the probability of all the x's that are mapped to that y.

Proposition 5.30. *Let X be a discrete random variable with PMF f_X supported on the set S_X. Let $Y = h(X)$ for some function h. Then Y has PMF f_Y defined by*

$$f_Y(y) = \sum_{\{x \in S_X \mid h(x) = y\}} f_X(x) \tag{5.7.2}$$

Example 5.31. Let $X \sim$ `binom(size` $= 4$, `prob` $= 1/2)$, and let $Y = (X - 1)^2$. Consider the following table:

x	0	1	2	3	4
$f_X(x)$	1/16	1/4	6/16	1/4	1/16
$y = (x - 2)^2$	1	0	1	4	9

From this we see that Y has support $S_Y = \{0, 1, 4, 9\}$. We also see that $h(x) = (x - 1)^2$ is not one-to-one on the support of X, because both $x = 0$ and $x = 2$ are mapped by h to $y = 1$. Nevertheless, we see that $Y = 0$ only when $X = 1$, which has probability $1/4$; therefore, $f_Y(0)$ should equal $1/4$. A similar approach works for $y = 4$ and $y = 9$. And $Y = 1$ exactly when $X = 0$ or $X = 2$, which has total probability $7/16$. In summary, the PMF of Y may be written:

y	0	1	4	9
$f_X(x)$	1/4	7/16	1/4	1/16

Note that there is not a special name for the distribution of Y, it is just an example of what to do when the transformation of a random variable is not one-to-one. The method is the same for more complicated problems.

Proposition 5.32. *If X is a random variable with $\mathbb{E} X = \mu$ and $Var(X) = \sigma^2$, then the mean and variance of $Y = mX + b$ is*

$$\mu_Y = m\mu + b, \quad \sigma_Y^2 = m^2\sigma^2, \quad \sigma_Y = |m|\sigma. \tag{5.7.3}$$

Chapter Exercises

Exercise 5.1. A recent national study showed that approximately 44.7% of college students have used Wikipedia as a source in at least one of their term papers. Let X equal the number of students in a random sample of size $n = 31$ who have used Wikipedia as a source.

1. How is X distributed?

$$X \sim \mathsf{binom}(\mathtt{size} = 31, \mathtt{prob} = 0.447)$$

2. Sketch the probability mass function (roughly).

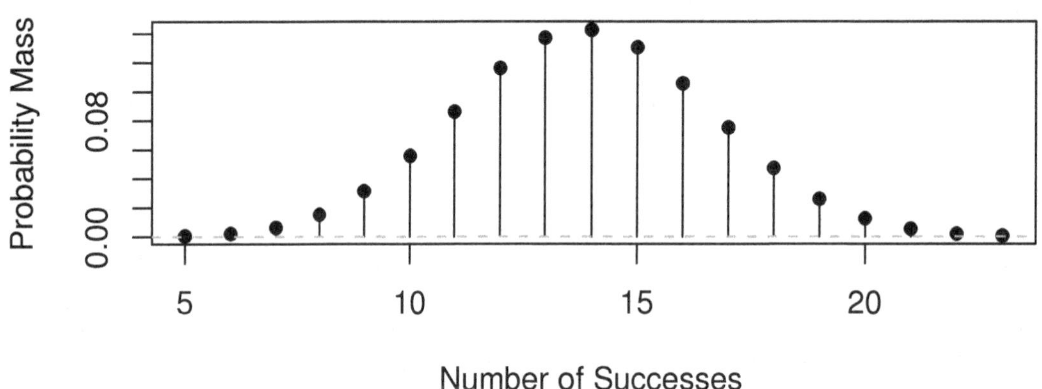

3. Sketch the cumulative distribution function (roughly).

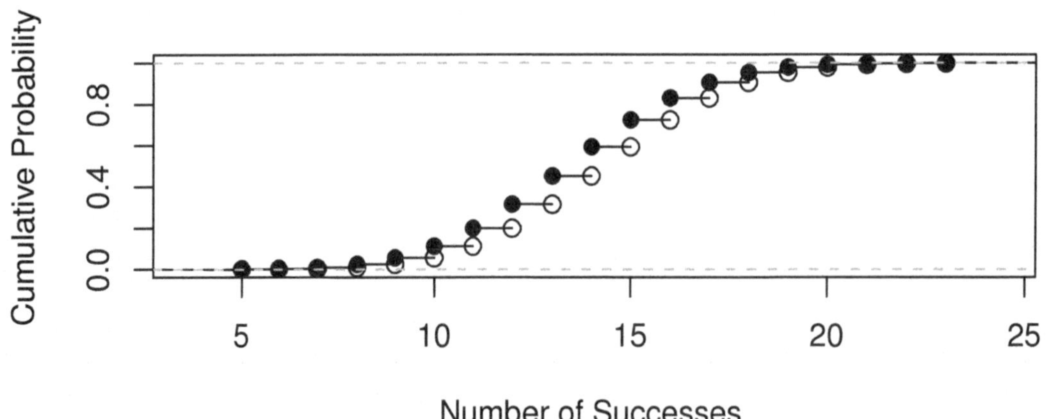

4. Find the probability that X is equal to 17.

```
> dbinom(17, size = 31, prob = 0.447)
```

```
[1] 0.07532248
```

5. Find the probability that X is at most 13.

```
> pbinom(13, size = 31, prob = 0.447)
```

```
[1] 0.451357
```

6. Find the probability that X is bigger than 11.

```
> pbinom(11, size = 31, prob = 0.447, lower.tail = FALSE)
```

```
[1] 0.8020339
```

7. Find the probability that X is at least 15.

```
> pbinom(14, size = 31, prob = 0.447, lower.tail = FALSE)
```

```
[1] 0.406024
```

8. Find the probability that X is between 16 and 19, inclusive.

```
> sum(dbinom(16:19, size = 31, prob = 0.447))
```

```
[1] 0.2544758
```

```
> diff(pbinom(c(19, 15), size = 31, prob = 0.447, lower.tail = FALSE))
```

```
[1] 0.2544758
```

9. Give the mean of X, denoted $\mathbb{E}X$.

```
> library(distrEx)
> X = Binom(size = 31, prob = 0.447)
> E(X)
```

```
[1] 13.857
```

10. Give the variance of X.

```
> var(X)
```

```
[1] 7.662921
```

11. Give the standard deviation of X.

```
> sd(X)
[1] 2.768198
```

12. Find $\mathbb{E}(4X + 51.324)$

```
> E(4 * X + 51.324)
[1] 106.752
```

Exercise 5.2. For the following situations, decide what the distribution of X should be. In nearly every case, there are additional assumptions that should be made for the distribution to apply; identify those assumptions (which may or may not hold in practice.)

1. We shoot basketballs at a basketball hoop, and count the number of shots until we make a goal. Let X denote the number of missed shots. On a normal day we would typically make about 37% of the shots.

2. In a local lottery in which a three digit number is selected randomly, let X be the number selected.

3. We drop a Styrofoam cup to the floor twenty times, each time recording whether the cup comes to rest perfectly right side up, or not. Let X be the number of times the cup lands perfectly right side up.

4. We toss a piece of trash at the garbage can from across the room. If we miss the trash can, we retrieve the trash and try again, continuing to toss until we make the shot. Let X denote the number of missed shots.

5. Working for the border patrol, we inspect shipping cargo as when it enters the harbor looking for contraband. A certain ship comes to port with 557 cargo containers. Standard practice is to select 10 containers randomly and inspect each one very carefully, classifying it as either having contraband or not. Let X count the number of containers that illegally contain contraband.

6. At the same time every year, some migratory birds land in a bush outside for a short rest. On a certain day, we look outside and let X denote the number of birds in the bush.

7. We count the number of rain drops that fall in a circular area on a sidewalk during a ten minute period of a thunder storm.

8. We count the number of moth eggs on our window screen.

9. We count the number of blades of grass in a one square foot patch of land.

10. We count the number of pats on a baby's back until (s)he burps.

Exercise 5.3. Find the constant c so that the given function is a valid PDF of a random variable X.

1. $f(x) = Cx^n, \quad 0 < x < 1.$
2. $f(x) = Cx\mathrm{e}^{-x}, \quad 0 < x < \infty.$
3. $f(x) = \mathrm{e}^{-(x-C)}, \quad 7 < x < \infty.$
4. $f(x) = Cx^3(1-x)^2, \quad 0 < x < 1.$
5. $f(x) = C(1 + x^2/4)^{-1}, \quad -\infty < x < \infty.$

Exercise 5.4. Show that $\mathbb{E}(X - \mu)^2 = \mathbb{E}X^2 - \mu^2$. *Hint*: expand the quantity $(X - \mu)^2$ and distribute the expectation over the resulting terms.

Exercise 5.5. If $X \sim$ `binom(size` $= n$, `prob` $= p$) show that $\mathbb{E}X(X-1) = n(n-1)p^2$.

Exercise 5.6. Calculate the mean and variance of the hypergeometric distribution. Show that

$$\mu = K\frac{M}{M+N}, \quad \sigma^2 = K\frac{MN}{(M+N)^2}\frac{M+N-K}{M+N-1}. \tag{5.7.4}$$

Chapter 6

Continuous Distributions

The focus of the last chapter was on random variables whose support can be written down in a list of values (finite or countably infinite), such as the number of successes in a sequence of Bernoulli trials. Now we move to random variables whose support is a whole range of values, say, an interval (a, b). It is shown in later classes that it is impossible to write all of the numbers down in a list; there are simply too many of them.

This chapter begins with continuous random variables and the associated PDFs and CDFs The continuous uniform distribution is highlighted, along with the Gaussian, or normal, distribution. Some mathematical details pave the way for a catalogue of models.

The interested reader who would like to learn more about any of the assorted discrete distributions mentioned below should take a look at *Continuous Univariate Distributions, Volumes 1* and *2* by Johnson *et al* [47, 48].

What do I want them to know?

- how to choose a reasonable continuous model under a variety of physical circumstances
- basic correspondence between continuous versus discrete random variables
- the general tools of the trade for manipulation of continuous random variables, integration, *etc.*
- some details on a couple of continuous models, and exposure to a bunch of other ones
- how to make new continuous random variables from old ones

6.1 Continuous Random Variables

6.1.1 Probability Density Functions

Continuous random variables have supports that look like

$$S_X = [a, b] \text{ or } (a, b), \tag{6.1.1}$$

or unions of intervals of the above form. Examples of random variables that are often taken to be continuous are:

- the height or weight of an individual,

- other physical measurements such as the length or size of an object, and
- durations of time (usually).

Every continuous random variable X has a *probability density function* (PDF) denoted f_X associated with it[1] that satisfies three basic properties:

1. $f_X(x) > 0$ for $x \in S_X$,
2. $\int_{x \in S_X} f_X(x)\,\mathrm{d}x = 1$, and
3. $\mathbb{P}(X \in A) = \int_{x \in A} f_X(x)\,\mathrm{d}x$, for an event $A \subset S_X$.

Remark 6.1. We can say the following about continuous random variables:

- Usually, the set A in 3 takes the form of an interval, for example, $A = [c, d]$, in which case
$$\mathbb{P}(X \in A) = \int_c^d f_X(x)\,\mathrm{d}x. \tag{6.1.2}$$
- It follows that the probability that X falls in a given interval is simply the *area under the curve* of f_X over the interval.
- Since the area of a line $x = c$ in the plane is zero, $\mathbb{P}(X = c) = 0$ for any value c. In other words, the chance that X equals a particular value c is zero, and this is true for any number c. Moreover, when $a < b$ all of the following probabilities are the same:
$$\mathbb{P}(a \leq X \leq b) = \mathbb{P}(a < X \leq b) = \mathbb{P}(a \leq X < b) = \mathbb{P}(a < X < b). \tag{6.1.3}$$
- The PDF f_X can sometimes be greater than 1. This is in contrast to the discrete case; every nonzero value of a PMF is a probability which is restricted to lie in the interval $[0, 1]$.

We met the cumulative distribution function, F_X, in Chapter 5. Recall that it is defined by $F_X(t) = \mathbb{P}(X \leq t)$, for $-\infty < t < \infty$. While in the discrete case the CDF is unwieldy, in the continuous case the CDF has a relatively convenient form:
$$F_X(t) = \mathbb{P}(X \leq t) = \int_{-\infty}^{t} f_X(x)\,\mathrm{d}x, \quad -\infty < t < \infty. \tag{6.1.4}$$

Remark 6.2. For any continuous CDF F_X the following are true.

- F_X is nondecreasing , that is, $t_1 \leq t_2$ implies $F_X(t_1) \leq F_X(t_2)$.
- F_X is continuous (see Appendix E.2). Note the distinction from the discrete case: CDFs of discrete random variables are not continuous, they are only right continuous.
- $\lim_{t \to -\infty} F_X(t) = 0$ and $\lim_{t \to \infty} F_X(t) = 1$.

There is a handy relationship between the CDF and PDF in the continuous case. Consider the derivative of F_X:
$$F'_X(t) = \frac{\mathrm{d}}{\mathrm{d}t} F_X(t) = \frac{\mathrm{d}}{\mathrm{d}t} \int_{-\infty}^{t} f_X(x)\,\mathrm{d}x = f_X(t), \tag{6.1.5}$$
the last equality being true by the Fundamental Theorem of Calculus, part (2) (see Appendix E.2). In short, $(F_X)' = f_X$ in the continuous case[2].

[1] Not true. There are pathological random variables with no density function. (This is one of the crazy things that can happen in the world of measure theory). But in this book we will not get even close to these anomalous beasts, and regardless it can be proved that the CDF always exists.

[2] In the discrete case, $f_X(x) = F_X(x) - \lim_{t \to x^-} F_X(t)$.

6.1.2 Expectation of Continuous Random Variables

For a continuous random variable X the expected value of $g(X)$ is

$$\mathbb{E}\, g(X) = \int_{x \in S} g(x) f_X(x)\, \mathrm{d}x, \tag{6.1.6}$$

provided the (potentially improper) integral $\int_S |g(x)|\, f(x)\mathrm{d}x$ is convergent. One important example is the mean μ, also known as $\mathbb{E}\, X$:

$$\mu = \mathbb{E}\, X = \int_{x \in S} x f_X(x)\, \mathrm{d}x, \tag{6.1.7}$$

provided $\int_S |x| f(x)\mathrm{d}x$ is finite. Also there is the variance

$$\sigma^2 = \mathbb{E}(X - \mu)^2 = \int_{x \in S} (x - \mu)^2 f_X(x)\, \mathrm{d}x, \tag{6.1.8}$$

which can be computed with the alternate formula $\sigma^2 = \mathbb{E}\, X^2 - (\mathbb{E}\, X)^2$. In addition, there is the standard deviation $\sigma = \sqrt{\sigma^2}$. The moment generating function is given by

$$M_X(t) = \mathbb{E}\ \mathrm{e}^{tX} = \int_{-\infty}^{\infty} \mathrm{e}^{tx} f_X(x)\, \mathrm{d}x, \tag{6.1.9}$$

provided the integral exists (is finite) for all t in a neighborhood of $t = 0$.

Example 6.3. Let the continuous random variable X have PDF

$$f_X(x) = 3x^2, \quad 0 \leq x \leq 1.$$

We will see later that f_X belongs to the *Beta* family of distributions. It is easy to see that $\int_{-\infty}^{\infty} f(x)\mathrm{d}x = 1$.

$$\begin{aligned}
\int_{-\infty}^{\infty} f_X(x)\mathrm{d}x &= \int_0^1 3x^2\, \mathrm{d}x \\
&= x^3 \Big|_{x=0}^{1} \\
&= 1^3 - 0^3 \\
&= 1.
\end{aligned}$$

This being said, we may find $\mathbb{P}(0.14 \leq X < 0.71)$.

$$\begin{aligned}
\mathbb{P}(0.14 \leq X < 0.71) &= \int_{0.14}^{0.71} 3x^2 \mathrm{d}x, \\
&= x^3 \Big|_{x=0.14}^{0.71} \\
&= 0.71^3 - 0.14^3 \\
&\approx 0.355167.
\end{aligned}$$

We can find the mean and variance in an identical manner.

$$\begin{aligned}
\mu = \int_{-\infty}^{\infty} x f_X(x)\mathrm{d}x &= \int_0^1 x \cdot 3x^2\, \mathrm{d}x, \\
&= \frac{3}{4} x^4 \Big|_{x=0}^{1}, \\
&= \frac{3}{4}.
\end{aligned}$$

It would perhaps be best to calculate the variance with the shortcut formula $\sigma^2 = \mathbb{E}\, X^2 - \mu^2$:

$$\begin{aligned}
\mathbb{E}\,X^2 = \int_{-\infty}^{\infty} x^2 f_X(x)\mathrm{d}x &= \int_0^1 x^2 \cdot 3x^2\,\mathrm{d}x \\
&= \left.\frac{3}{5}x^5\right|_{x=0}^{1} \\
&= 3/5.
\end{aligned}$$

which gives $\sigma^2 = 3/5 - (3/4)^2 = 3/80$.

Example 6.4. We will try one with unbounded support to brush up on improper integration. Let the random variable X have PDF

$$f_X(x) = \frac{3}{x^4}, \qquad x > 1.$$

We can show that $\int_{-\infty}^{\infty} f(x)\mathrm{d}x = 1$:

$$\begin{aligned}
\int_{-\infty}^{\infty} f_X(x)\mathrm{d}x &= \int_1^{\infty} \frac{3}{x^4}\,\mathrm{d}x \\
&= \lim_{t\to\infty} \int_1^{t} \frac{3}{x^4}\,\mathrm{d}x \\
&= \lim_{t\to\infty} \left. 3\,\frac{1}{-3}x^{-3}\right|_{x=1}^{t} \\
&= -\left(\lim_{t\to\infty} \frac{1}{t^3} - 1\right) \\
&= 1.
\end{aligned}$$

We calculate $\mathbb{P}(3.4 \leq X < 7.1)$:

$$\begin{aligned}
\mathbb{P}(3.4 \leq X < 7.1) &= \int_{3.4}^{7.1} 3x^{-4}\mathrm{d}x \\
&= \left. 3\,\frac{1}{-3}x^{-3}\right|_{x=3.4}^{7.1} \\
&= -1(7.1^{-3} - 3.4^{-3}) \\
&\approx 0.0226487123.
\end{aligned}$$

We locate the mean and variance just like before.

$$\begin{aligned}
\mu = \int_{-\infty}^{\infty} x f_X(x)\mathrm{d}x &= \int_1^{\infty} x \cdot \frac{3}{x^4}\,\mathrm{d}x \\
&= \left. 3\,\frac{1}{-2}x^{-2}\right|_{x=1}^{\infty} \\
&= -\frac{3}{2}\left(\lim_{t\to\infty} \frac{1}{t^2} - 1\right) \\
&= \frac{3}{2}.
\end{aligned}$$

Again we use the shortcut $\sigma^2 = \mathbb{E}X^2 - \mu^2$:

$$
\begin{aligned}
\mathbb{E}X^2 = \int_{-\infty}^{\infty} x^2 f_X(x)\mathrm{d}x &= \int_1^{\infty} x^2 \cdot \frac{3}{x^4}\,\mathrm{d}x \\
&= 3\,\frac{1}{-1}x^{-1}\Big|_{x=1}^{\infty} \\
&= -3\left(\lim_{t\to\infty}\frac{1}{t^2} - 1\right) \\
&= 3,
\end{aligned}
$$

which closes the example with $\sigma^2 = 3 - (3/2)^2 = 3/4$.

6.1.3 How to do it with R

There exist utilities to calculate probabilities and expectations for general continuous random variables, but it is better to find a built-in model, if possible. Sometimes it is not possible. We show how to do it the long way, and the `distr` package way.

Example 6.5. Let X have PDF $f(x) = 3x^2$, $0 < x < 1$ and find $\mathbb{P}(0.14 \leq X \leq 0.71)$. (We will ignore that X is a beta random variable for the sake of argument.)

```
> f <- function(x) 3 * x^2
> integrate(f, lower = 0.14, upper = 0.71)

0.355167 with absolute error < 3.9e-15
```

Compare this to the answer we found in Example 6.3. We could integrate the function $xf(x) =$ `3*x^3` from zero to one to get the mean, and use the shortcut $\sigma^2 = \mathbb{E}X^2 - (\mathbb{E}X)^2$ for the variance.

Example 6.6. Let X have PDF $f(x) = 3/x^4$, $x > 1$. We may integrate the function $xf(x) =$ `3/x^3` from zero to infinity to get the mean of X.

```
> g <- function(x) 3/x^3
> integrate(g, lower = 1, upper = Inf)

1.5 with absolute error < 1.7e-14
```

Compare this to the answer we got in Example 6.4. Use `-Inf` for $-\infty$.

Example 6.7. Let us redo Example 6.3 with the `distr` package. The method is similar to that encountered in Section 5.1.3 in Chapter 5. We define an absolutely continuous random variable:

```
> library(distr)
> f <- function(x) 3 * x^2
> X <- AbscontDistribution(d = f, low1 = 0, up1 = 1)
> p(X)(0.71) - p(X)(0.14)

[1] 0.355167
```

Compare this answers we found earlier. Now let us try expectation with the `distrEx` package [74]:

```
> library(distrEx)
> E(X)
[1] 0.7496337
> var(X)
[1] 0.03768305
> 3/80
[1] 0.0375
```

Compare these answers to the ones we found in Example 6.3. Why are they different? Because the `distrEx` package resorts to numerical methods when it encounters a model it does not recognize. This means that the answers we get for calculations may not exactly match the theoretical values. Be careful.

6.2 The Continuous Uniform Distribution

A random variable X with the continuous uniform distribution on the interval (a, b) has PDF

$$f_X(x) = \frac{1}{b-a}, \quad a < x < b. \tag{6.2.1}$$

The associated R function is dunif(`min` $= a$, `max` $= b$). We write $X \sim$ unif(`min` $= a$, `max` $= b$). Due to the particularly simple form of this PDF we can also write down explicitly a formula for the CDF F_X:

$$F_X(t) = \begin{cases} 0, & t < 0, \\ \frac{t-a}{b-a}, & a \leq t < b, \\ 1, & t \geq b. \end{cases} \tag{6.2.2}$$

The continuous uniform distribution is the continuous analogue of the discrete uniform distribution; it is used to model experiments whose outcome is an interval of numbers that are "equally likely" in the sense that any two intervals of equal length in the support have the same probability associated with them.

Example 6.8. Choose a number in [0,1] at random, and let X be the number chosen. Then $X \sim$ unif(`min` $= 0$, `max` $= 1$).

The mean of $X \sim$ unif(`min` $= a$, `max` $= b$) is relatively simple to calculate:

$$\begin{aligned} \mu = \mathbb{E}X &= \int_{-\infty}^{\infty} x\, f_X(x)\, \mathrm{d}x, \\ &= \int_a^b x\, \frac{1}{b-a}\, \mathrm{d}x, \\ &= \frac{1}{b-a}\, \frac{x^2}{2}\bigg|_{x=a}^{b}, \\ &= \frac{1}{b-a}\, \frac{b^2-a^2}{2}, \\ &= \frac{b+a}{2}, \end{aligned}$$

using the popular formula for the difference of squares. The variance is left to Exercise 6.4.

6.3 The Normal Distribution

We say that X has a *normal distribution* if it has PDF

$$f_X(x) = \frac{1}{\sigma\sqrt{2\pi}} \exp\left\{\frac{-(x-\mu)^2}{2\sigma^2}\right\}, \quad -\infty < x < \infty. \tag{6.3.1}$$

We write $X \sim \mathsf{norm(mean} = \mu,\ \mathsf{sd} = \sigma)$, and the associated R function is `dnorm(x, mean = 0, sd = 1)`.

The familiar bell-shaped curve, the normal distribution is also known as the *Gaussian distribution* because the German mathematician C. F. Gauss largely contributed to its mathematical development. This distribution is by far the most important distribution, continuous or discrete. The normal model appears in the theory of all sorts of natural phenomena, from to the way particles of smoke dissipate in a closed room, to the journey of a bottle in the ocean to the white noise of cosmic background radiation.

When $\mu = 0$ and $\sigma = 1$ we say that the random variable has a *standard normal* distribution and we typically write $Z \sim \mathsf{norm(mean} = 0,\ \mathsf{sd} = 1)$. The lowercase Greek letter phi (ϕ) is used to denote the standard normal PDF and the capital Greek letter phi Φ is used to denote the standard normal CDF: for $-\infty < z < \infty$,

$$\phi(z) = \frac{1}{\sqrt{2\pi}} \mathrm{e}^{-z^2/2} \text{ and } \Phi(t) = \int_{-\infty}^{t} \phi(z)\,\mathrm{d}z. \tag{6.3.2}$$

Proposition 6.9. *If* $X \sim \mathsf{norm(mean} = \mu,\ \mathsf{sd} = \sigma)$ *then*

$$Z = \frac{X-\mu}{\sigma} \sim \mathsf{norm(mean} = 0,\ \mathsf{sd} = 1). \tag{6.3.3}$$

The MGF of $Z \sim \mathsf{norm(mean} = 0,\ \mathsf{sd} = 1)$ is relatively easy to derive:

$$\begin{aligned} M_Z(t) &= \int_{-\infty}^{\infty} \mathrm{e}^{tz} \frac{1}{\sqrt{2\pi}} \mathrm{e}^{-z^2/2} \mathrm{d}z, \\ &= \int_{-\infty}^{\infty} \frac{1}{\sqrt{2\pi}} \exp\left\{-\frac{1}{2}\left(z^2 + 2tz + t^2\right) + \frac{t^2}{2}\right\} \mathrm{d}z, \\ &= \mathrm{e}^{t^2/2}\left(\int_{-\infty}^{\infty} \frac{1}{\sqrt{2\pi}} \mathrm{e}^{-[z-(-t)]^2/2} \mathrm{d}z\right), \end{aligned}$$

and the quantity in the parentheses is the total area under a $\mathsf{norm(mean} = -t,\ \mathsf{sd} = 1)$ density, which is one. Therefore,

$$M_Z(t) = \mathrm{e}^{-t^2/2}, \quad -\infty < t < \infty. \tag{6.3.4}$$

Example 6.10. The MGF of $X \sim \mathsf{norm(mean} = \mu,\ \mathsf{sd} = \sigma)$ is then not difficult either because

$$Z = \frac{X-\mu}{\sigma}, \text{ or rewriting, } X = \sigma Z + \mu.$$

Therefore:

$$M_X(t) = \mathbb{E}\,\mathrm{e}^{tX} = \mathbb{E}\,\mathrm{e}^{t(\sigma Z+\mu)} = \mathbb{E}\,\mathrm{e}^{\sigma t X}\mathrm{e}^{\mu} = \mathrm{e}^{t\mu} M_Z(\sigma t),$$

and we know that $M_Z(t) = \mathrm{e}^{t^2/2}$, thus substituting we get

$$M_X(t) = \mathrm{e}^{t\mu}\mathrm{e}^{(\sigma t)^2/2} = \exp\left\{\mu t + \sigma^2 t^2/2\right\},$$

for $-\infty < t < \infty$.

Fact 6.11. *The same argument above shows that if X has MGF $M_X(t)$ then the MGF of $Y = a + bX$ is*

$$M_Y(t) = \mathrm{e}^{ta} M_X(bt). \tag{6.3.5}$$

Example 6.12. The 68-95-99.7 Rule. We saw in Section 3.3.6 that when an empirical distribution is approximately bell shaped there are specific proportions of the observations which fall at varying distances from the (sample) mean. We can see where these come from – and obtain more precise proportions – with the following:

```
> pnorm(1:3) - pnorm(-(1:3))
[1] 0.6826895 0.9544997 0.9973002
```

Example 6.13. Let the random experiment consist of a person taking an IQ test, and let X be the score on the test. The scores on such a test are typically standardized to have a mean of 100 and a standard deviation of 15. What is $\mathbb{P}(85 \leq X \leq 115)$?

Solution: this one is easy because the limits 85 and 115 fall exactly one standard deviation (below and above, respectively) from the mean of 100. The answer is therefore approximately 68%.

6.3.1 Normal Quantiles and the Quantile Function

Until now we have been given two values and our task has been to find the area under the PDF between those values. In this section, we go in reverse: we are given an area, and we would like to find the value(s) that correspond to that area.

Example 6.14. Assuming the IQ model of Example 6.13, what is the lowest possible IQ score that a person can have and still be in the top 1% of all IQ scores?

Solution: If a person is in the top 1%, then that means that 99% of the people have lower IQ scores. So, in other words, we are looking for a value x such that $F(x) = \mathbb{P}(X \leq x)$ satisfies $F(x) = 0.99$, or yet another way to say it is that we would like to solve the equation $F(x) - 0.99 = 0$. For the sake of argument, let us see how to do this the long way. We define the function $g(x) = F(x) - 0.99$, and then look for the root of g with the `uniroot` function. It uses numerical procedures to find the root so we need to give it an interval of x values in which to search for the root. We can get an educated guess from the Empirical Rule 3.13; the root should be somewhere between two and three standard deviations (15 each) above the mean (which is 100).

```
> g <- function(x) pnorm(x, mean = 100, sd = 15) - 0.99
> uniroot(g, interval = c(130, 145))
$root
[1] 134.8952


$f.root
[1] -4.873083e-09


$iter
[1] 6


$estim.prec
[1] 6.103516e-05
```

The answer is shown in `$root` which is approximately 134.8952, that is, a person with this IQ score or higher falls in the top 1% of all IQ scores.

The discussion in example 6.14 was centered on the search for a value x that solved an equation $F(x) = p$, for some given probability p, or in mathematical parlance, the search for F^{-1}, the inverse of the CDF of X, evaluated at p. This is so important that it merits a definition all its own.

Definition 6.15. The *quantile function*[3] of a random variable X is the inverse of its cumulative distribution function:

$$Q_X(p) = \min\{x : F_X(x) \geq p\}, \quad 0 < p < 1. \tag{6.3.6}$$

Remark 6.16. Here are some properties of quantile functions:

1. The quantile function is defined and finite for all $0 < p < 1$.

2. Q_X is left-continuous (see Appendix E.2). For discrete random variables it is a step function, and for continuous random variables it is a continuous function.

3. In the continuous case the graph of Q_X may be obtained by reflecting the graph of F_X about the line $y = x$. In the discrete case, before reflecting one should: 1) connect the dots to get rid of the jumps – this will make the graph look like a set of stairs, 2) erase the horizontal lines so that only vertical lines remain, and finally 3) swap the open circles with the solid dots. Please see Figure 5.3.2 for a comparison.

4. The two limits
$$\lim_{p\to 0^+} Q_X(p) \quad \text{and} \quad \lim_{p\to 1^-} Q_X(p)$$
always exist, but may be infinite (that is, sometimes $\lim_{p\to 0} Q(p) = -\infty$ and/or $\lim_{p\to 1} Q(p) = \infty$).

As the reader might expect, the standard normal distribution is a very special case and has its own special notation.

Definition 6.17. For $0 < \alpha < 1$, the symbol z_α denotes the unique solution of the equation $\mathbb{P}(Z > z_\alpha) = \alpha$, where $Z \sim$ norm(mean $= 0$, sd $= 1$). It can be calculated in one of two equivalent ways: qnorm($1 - \alpha$) and qnorm(α, lower.tail = FALSE).

There are a few other very important special cases which we will encounter in later chapters.

6.3.2 How to do it with R

Quantile functions are defined for all of the base distributions with the q prefix to the distribution name, except for the ECDF whose quantile function is exactly the $Q_x(p)$ =quantile(x, probs = p , type = 1) function.

Example 6.18. Back to Example 6.14, we are looking for $Q_X(0.99)$, where $X \sim$ norm(mean = 100, sd = 15). It could not be easier to do with R.

```
> qnorm(0.99, mean = 100, sd = 15)
```

[3]The precise definition of the quantile function is $Q_X(p) = \inf\{x : F_X(x) \geq p\}$, so at least it is well defined (though perhaps infinite) for the values $p = 0$ and $p = 1$.

```
[1] 134.8952
```

Compare this answer to the one obtained earlier with `uniroot`.

Example 6.19. Find the values $z_{0.025}$, $z_{0.01}$, and $z_{0.005}$ (these will play an important role from Chapter 9 onward).

```
> qnorm(c(0.025, 0.01, 0.005), lower.tail = FALSE)
[1] 1.959964 2.326348 2.575829
```

Note the `lower.tail` argument. We would get the same answer with

```
qnorm(c(0.975, 0.99, 0.995))
```

6.4 Functions of Continuous Random Variables

The goal of this section is to determine the distribution of $U = g(X)$ based on the distribution of X. In the discrete case all we needed to do was back substitute for $x = g^{-1}(u)$ in the PMF of X (sometimes accumulating probability mass along the way). In the continuous case, however, we need more sophisticated tools. Now would be a good time to review Appendix E.2.

6.4.1 The PDF Method

Proposition 6.20. *Let X have PDF f_X and let g be a function which is one-to-one with a differentiable inverse g^{-1}. Then the PDF of $U = g(X)$ is given by*

$$f_U(u) = f_X\left[g^{-1}(u)\right]\left|\frac{\mathrm{d}}{\mathrm{d}u}g^{-1}(u)\right|. \tag{6.4.1}$$

Remark 6.21. The formula in Equation 6.4.1 is nice, but does not really make any sense. It is better to write in the intuitive form

$$f_U(u) = f_X(x)\left|\frac{\mathrm{d}x}{\mathrm{d}u}\right|. \tag{6.4.2}$$

Example 6.22. Let $X \sim \mathsf{norm}(\mathtt{mean} = \mu,\ \mathsf{sd} = \sigma)$, and let $Y = \mathrm{e}^X$. What is the PDF of Y?

Solution: Notice first that $\mathrm{e}^x > 0$ for any x, so the support of Y is $(0, \infty)$. Since the transformation is monotone, we can solve $y = \mathrm{e}^x$ for x to get $x = \ln y$, giving $\mathrm{d}x/\mathrm{d}y = 1/y$. Therefore, for any $y > 0$,

$$f_Y(y) = f_X(\ln y) \cdot \left|\frac{1}{y}\right| = \frac{1}{\sigma\sqrt{2\pi}}\exp\left\{\frac{(\ln y - \mu)^2}{2\sigma^2}\right\} \cdot \frac{1}{y},$$

where we have dropped the absolute value bars since $y > 0$. The random variable Y is said to have a *lognormal distribution*; see Section 6.5.

Example 6.23. Suppose $X \sim \mathsf{norm}(\mathtt{mean} = 0,\ \mathsf{sd} = 1)$ and let $Y = 4 - 3X$. What is the PDF of Y?

The support of X is $(-\infty, \infty)$, and as x goes from $-\infty$ to ∞, the quantity $y = 4 - 3x$ also traverses $(-\infty, \infty)$. Solving for x in the equation $y = 4 - 3x$ yields $x = -(y - 4)/3$ giving $\mathrm{d}x/\mathrm{d}y = -1/3$. And since

$$f_X(x) = \frac{1}{\sqrt{2\pi}} \mathrm{e}^{-x^2/2}, \quad -\infty < x < \infty,$$

we have

$$\begin{aligned} f_Y(y) &= f_X\left(\frac{y-4}{3}\right) \cdot \left|-\frac{1}{3}\right|, \quad -\infty < y < \infty, \\ &= \frac{1}{3\sqrt{2\pi}} \mathrm{e}^{-(y-4)^2/2\cdot 3^2}, \quad -\infty < y < \infty. \end{aligned}$$

We recognize the PDF of Y to be that of a `norm(mean = 4, sd = 3)` distribution. Indeed, we may use an identical argument as the above to prove the following fact:

Fact 6.24. *If $X \sim$ `norm(mean` $= \mu$, `sd` $= \sigma)$ and if $Y = a + bX$ for constants a and b, with $b \neq 0$, then $Y \sim$ `norm(mean` $= a + b\mu$, `sd` $= |b|\sigma)$.*

Note that it is sometimes easier to *postpone* solving for the inverse transformation $x = x(u)$. Instead, leave the transformation in the form $u = u(x)$ and calculate the derivative of the *original* transformation

$$\mathrm{d}u/\mathrm{d}x = g'(x). \tag{6.4.3}$$

Once this is known, we can get the PDF of U with

$$f_U(u) = f_X(x) \left| \frac{1}{\mathrm{d}u/\mathrm{d}x} \right|. \tag{6.4.4}$$

In many cases there are cancellations and the work is shorter. Of course, it is not always true that

$$\frac{\mathrm{d}x}{\mathrm{d}u} = \frac{1}{\mathrm{d}u/\mathrm{d}x}, \tag{6.4.5}$$

but for the well-behaved examples in this book the trick works just fine.

Remark 6.25. In the case that g is not monotone we cannot apply Proposition 6.20 directly. However, hope is not lost. Rather, we break the support of X into pieces such that g is monotone on each one. We apply Proposition 6.20 on each piece, and finish up by adding the results together.

6.4.2 The CDF method

We know from Section 6.1 that $f_X = F_X'$ in the continuous case. Starting from the equation $F_Y(y) = \mathbb{P}(Y \leq y)$, we may substitute $g(X)$ for Y, then solve for X to obtain $\mathbb{P}[X \leq g^{-1}(y)]$, which is just another way to write $F_X[g^{-1}(y)]$. Differentiating this last quantity with respect to y will yield the PDF of Y.

Example 6.26. Suppose $X \sim$ `unif(min = 0, max = 1)` and suppose that we let $Y = -\ln X$. What is the PDF of Y?

The support set of X is $(0, 1)$, and y traverses $(0, \infty)$ as x ranges from 0 to 1, so the support set of Y is $S_Y = (0, \infty)$. For any $y > 0$, we consider

$$F_Y(y) = \mathbb{P}(Y \leq y) = \mathbb{P}(-\ln X \leq y) = \mathbb{P}(X \geq \mathrm{e}^{-y}) = 1 - \mathbb{P}(X < \mathrm{e}^{-y}),$$

where the next to last equality follows because the exponential function is *monotone* (this point will be revisited later). Now since X is continuous the two probabilities $\mathbb{P}(X < \mathrm{e}^{-y})$ and $\mathbb{P}(X \leq \mathrm{e}^{-y})$ are equal; thus

$$1 - \mathbb{P}(X < \mathrm{e}^{-y}) = 1 - \mathbb{P}(X \leq \mathrm{e}^{-y}) = 1 - F_X(\mathrm{e}^{-y}).$$

Now recalling that the CDF of a unif(`min` = 0, `max` = 1) random variable satisfies $F(u) = u$ (see Equation 6.2.2), we can say

$$F_Y(y) = 1 - F_X(\mathrm{e}^{-y}) = 1 - \mathrm{e}^{-y}, \quad \text{for } y > 0.$$

We have consequently found the formula for the CDF of Y; to obtain the PDF f_Y we need only differentiate F_Y:

$$f_Y(y) = \frac{\mathrm{d}}{\mathrm{d}y}\left(1 - \mathrm{e}^{-y}\right) = 0 - \mathrm{e}^{-y}(-1),$$

or $f_Y(y) = \mathrm{e}^{-y}$ for $y > 0$. This turns out to be a member of the exponential family of distributions, see Section 6.5.

Example 6.27. ***The Probability Integral Transform.*** Given a continuous random variable X with strictly increasing CDF F_X, let the random variable Y be defined by $Y = F_X(X)$. Then the distribution of Y is unif(`min` = 0, `max` = 1).

Proof. We employ the CDF method. First note that the support of Y is $(0, 1)$. Then for any $0 < y < 1$,

$$F_Y(y) = \mathbb{P}(Y \leq y) = \mathbb{P}(F_X(X) \leq y).$$

Now since F_X is strictly increasing, it has a well defined inverse function F_X^{-1}. Therefore,

$$\mathbb{P}(F_X(X) \leq y) = \mathbb{P}(X \leq F_X^{-1}(y)) = F_X[F_X^{-1}(y)] = y.$$

Summarizing, we have seen that $F_Y(y) = y$, $0 < y < 1$. But this is exactly the CDF of a unif(`min` = 0, `max` = 1) random variable. □

Fact 6.28. *The Probability Integral Transform is true for all continuous random variables with continuous CDFs, not just for those with strictly increasing CDFs (but the proof is more complicated). The transform is **not** true for discrete random variables, or for continuous random variables having a discrete component (that is, with jumps in their CDF).*

Example 6.29. Let $Z \sim$ norm(`mean` = 0, `sd` = 1) and let $U = Z^2$. What is the PDF of U?

Notice first that $Z^2 \geq 0$, and thus the support of U is $[0, \infty)$. And for any $u \geq 0$,

$$F_U(u) = \mathbb{P}(U \leq u) = \mathbb{P}(Z^2 \leq u).$$

But $Z^2 \leq u$ occurs if and only if $-\sqrt{u} \leq Z \leq \sqrt{u}$. The last probability above is simply the area under the standard normal PDF from $-\sqrt{u}$ to $\sqrt{u}$, and since ϕ is symmetric about 0, we have

$$\mathbb{P}(Z^2 \leq u) = 2\,\mathbb{P}(0 \leq Z \leq \sqrt{u}) = 2\left[F_Z(\sqrt{u}) - F_Z(0)\right] = 2\Phi(\sqrt{u}) - 1,$$

because $\Phi(0) = 1/2$. To find the PDF of U we differentiate the CDF recalling that $\Phi' = \phi$.

$$f_U(u) = \left(2\Phi(\sqrt{u}) - 1\right)' = 2\phi(\sqrt{u}) \cdot \frac{1}{2\sqrt{u}} = u^{-1/2}\phi(\sqrt{u}).$$

Substituting,

$$f_U(u) = u^{-1/2}\frac{1}{\sqrt{2\pi}}\mathrm{e}^{-(\sqrt{u})^2/2} = (2\pi u)^{-1/2}\mathrm{e}^{-u}, \quad u > 0.$$

This is what we will later call a *chi-square distribution with 1 degree of freedom*. See Section 6.5.

6.4.3 How to do it with R

The distr package has functionality to investigate transformations of univariate distributions. There are exact results for ordinary transformations of the standard distributions, and distr takes advantage of these in many cases. For instance, the distr package can handle the transformation in Example 6.23 quite nicely:

```
> library(distr)
> X <- Norm(mean = 0, sd = 1)
> Y <- 4 - 3 * X
> Y
```

```
Distribution Object of Class: Norm
 mean: 4
 sd: 3
```

So distr "knows" that a linear transformation of a normal random variable is again normal, and it even knows what the correct mean and sd should be. But it is impossible for distr to know everything, and it is not long before we venture outside of the transformations that distr recognizes. Let us try Example 6.22:

```
> Y <- exp(X)
> Y
```

```
Distribution Object of Class: AbscontDistribution
```

The result is an object of class AbscontDistribution, which is one of the classes that distr uses to denote general distributions that it does not recognize (it turns out that Z has a *lognormal* distribution; see Section 6.5). A simplified description of the process that distr undergoes when it encounters a transformation $Y = g(X)$ that it does not recognize is

1. Randomly generate many, many copies $X_1, X_2, \ldots, X_n$ from the distribution of X,
2. Compute $Y_1 = g(X_1)$, $Y_2 = g(X_2)$, $\ldots$, $Y_n = g(X_n)$ and store them for use.
3. Calculate the PDF, CDF, quantiles, and random variates using the simulated values of Y.

As long as the transformation is sufficiently nice, such as a linear transformation, the exponential, absolute value, *etc.*, the d-p-q functions are calculated analytically based on the d-p-q functions associated with X. But if we try a crazy transformation then we are greeted by a warning:

```
> W <- sin(exp(X) + 27)
> W
```

```
Distribution Object of Class: AbscontDistribution
```

The warning confirms that the d-p-q functions are not calculated analytically, but are instead based on the randomly simulated values of Y. *We must be careful to remember this.* The nature of random simulation means that we can get different answers to the same question: watch what happens when we compute $\mathbb{P}(W \leq 0.5)$ using the W above, then define W again, and compute the (supposedly) same $\mathbb{P}(W \leq 0.5)$ a few moments later.

```
> p(W)(0.5)
[1] 0.57988
> W <- sin(exp(X) + 27)
> p(W)(0.5)
[1] 0.5804
```

The answers are not the same! Furthermore, if we were to repeat the process we would get yet another answer for $\mathbb{P}(W \leq 0.5)$.

The answers were close, though. And the underlying randomly generated X's were not the same so it should hardly be a surprise that the calculated W's were not the same, either. This serves as a warning (in concert with the one that `distr` provides) that we should be careful to remember that complicated transformations computed by R are only approximate and may fluctuate slightly due to the nature of the way the estimates are calculated.

6.5 Other Continuous Distributions

6.5.1 Waiting Time Distributions

In some experiments, the random variable being measured is the time until a certain event occurs. For example, a quality control specialist may be testing a manufactured product to see how long it takes until it fails. An efficiency expert may be recording the customer traffic at a retail store to streamline scheduling of staff.

The Exponential Distribution

We say that X has an *exponential distribution* and write $X \sim \mathsf{exp}(\mathtt{rate} = \lambda)$.

$$f_X(x) = \lambda \mathrm{e}^{-\lambda x}, \quad x > 0 \tag{6.5.1}$$

The associated R functions are `dexp(x, rate = 1)`, `pexp`, `qexp`, and `rexp`, which give the PDF, CDF, quantile function, and simulate random variates, respectively.

The parameter λ measures the rate of arrivals (to be described later) and must be positive. The CDF is given by the formula

$$F_X(t) = 1 - \mathrm{e}^{-\lambda t}, \quad t > 0. \tag{6.5.2}$$

The mean is $\mu = 1/\lambda$ and the variance is $\sigma^2 = 1/\lambda^2$.

The exponential distribution is closely related to the Poisson distribution. If customers arrive at a store according to a Poisson process with rate λ and if Y counts the number of customers that arrive in the time interval $[0, t)$, then we saw in Section 5.6 that $Y \sim \mathsf{pois}(\mathtt{lambda} = \lambda t)$. Now consider a different question: let us start our clock at time 0 and stop the clock when the first customer arrives. Let X be the length of this random time interval. Then $X \sim \mathsf{exp}(\mathtt{rate} = \lambda)$. Observe the following string of equalities:

$$\begin{aligned}
\mathbb{P}(X > t) &= \mathbb{P}(\text{first arrival after time } t), \\
&= \mathbb{P}(\text{no events in } [0,t)), \\
&= \mathbb{P}(Y = 0), \\
&= \mathrm{e}^{-\lambda t},
\end{aligned}$$

where the last line is the PMF of Y evaluated at $y = 0$. In other words, $\mathbb{P}(X \leq t) = 1 - e^{-\lambda t}$, which is exactly the CDF of an exp(`rate` = λ) distribution.

The exponential distribution is said to be *memoryless* because exponential random variables "forget" how old they are at every instant. That is, the probability that we must wait an additional five hours for a customer to arrive, given that we have already waited seven hours, is exactly the probability that we needed to wait five hours for a customer in the first place. In mathematical symbols, for any $s, t > 0$,

$$\mathbb{P}(X > s + t \mid X > t) = \mathbb{P}(X > s). \tag{6.5.3}$$

See Exercise 6.5.

The Gamma Distribution

This is a generalization of the exponential distribution. We say that X has a gamma distribution and write $X \sim$ gamma(`shape` = α, `rate` = λ). It has PDF

$$f_X(x) = \frac{\lambda^\alpha}{\Gamma(\alpha)} x^{\alpha-1} e^{-\lambda x}, \quad x > 0. \tag{6.5.4}$$

The associated R functions are `dgamma(x, shape, rate = 1)`, `pgamma`, `qgamma`, and `rgamma`, which give the PDF, CDF, quantile function, and simulate random variates, respectively. If $\alpha = 1$ then $X \sim$ exp(`rate` = λ). The mean is $\mu = \alpha/\lambda$ and the variance is $\sigma^2 = \alpha/\lambda^2$.

To motivate the gamma distribution recall that if X measures the length of time until the first event occurs in a Poisson process with rate λ then $X \sim$ exp(`rate` = λ). If we let Y measure the length of time until the αth event occurs then $Y \sim$ gamma(`shape` = α, `rate` = λ). When α is an integer this distribution is also known as the *Erlang* distribution.

Example 6.30. At a car wash, two customers arrive per hour on the average. We decide to measure how long it takes until the third customer arrives. If Y denotes this random time then $Y \sim$ gamma(`shape` = 3, `rate` = 1/2).

6.5.2 The Chi square, Student's t, and Snedecor's F Distributions

The Chi square Distribution

A random variable X with PDF

$$f_X(x) = \frac{1}{\Gamma(p/2)2^{p/2}} x^{p/2-1} e^{-x/2}, \quad x > 0, \tag{6.5.5}$$

is said to have a *chi-square distribution* with *p degrees of freedom*. We write $X \sim$ chisq(`df` = p). The associated R functions are `dchisq(x, df)`, `pchisq`, `qchisq`, and `rchisq`, which give the PDF, CDF, quantile function, and simulate random variates, respectively. See Figure 6.5.1. In an obvious notation we may define $\chi^2_\alpha(p)$ as the number on the x-axis such that there is exactly α area under the chisq(`df` = p) curve to its right.

The code to produce Figure 6.5.1 is

```
> curve(dchisq(x, df = 3), from = 0, to = 20, ylab = "y")
> ind <- c(4, 5, 10, 15)
> for (i in ind) curve(dchisq(x, df = i), 0, 20, add = TRUE)
```

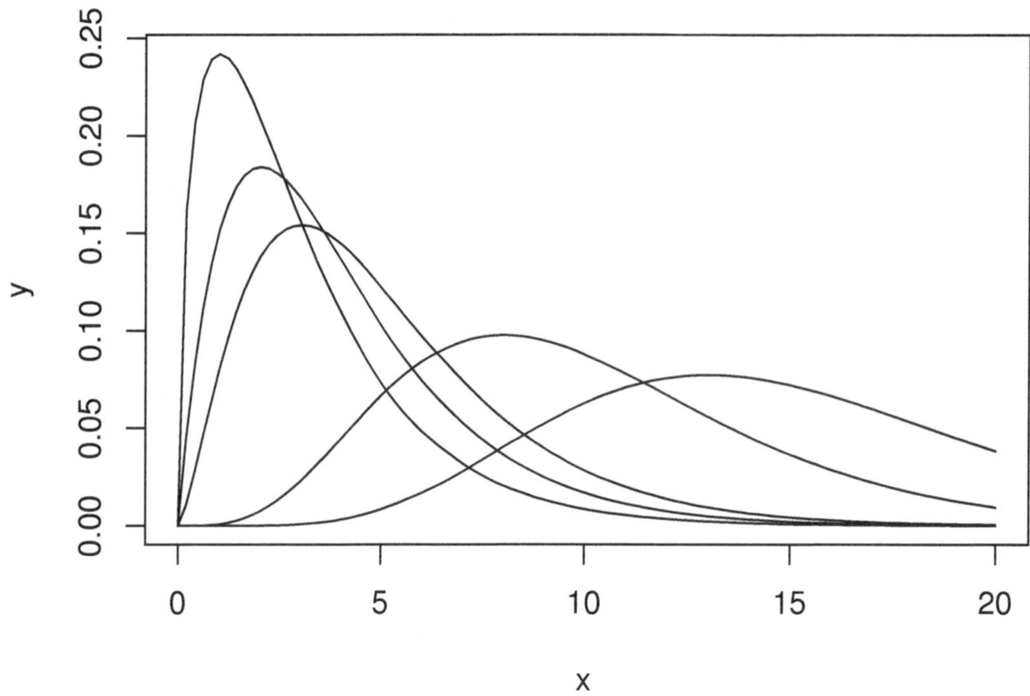

Figure 6.5.1: Chi square distribution for various degrees of freedom

Remark 6.31. Here are some useful things to know about the chi-square distribution.

1. If $Z \sim$ norm(mean $=0$, sd $=1$), then $Z^2 \sim$ chisq(df $=1$). We saw this in Example 6.29, and the fact is important when it comes time to find the distribution of the sample variance, S^2. See Theorem 8.5 in Section 8.2.2.

2. The chi-square distribution is supported on the positive x-axis, with a right-skewed distribution.

3. The chisq(df $=p$) distribution is the same as a gamma(shape $=p/2$, rate $=1/2$) distribution.

4. The MGF of $X \sim$ chisq(df $=p$) is
$$M_X(t) = (1-2t)^{-p}, \quad t < 1/2. \tag{6.5.6}$$

Student's *t* distribution

A random variable X with PDF

$$f_X(x) = \frac{\Gamma[(r+1)/2]}{\sqrt{r\pi}\,\Gamma(r/2)}\left(1+\frac{x^2}{r}\right)^{-(r+1)/2}, \quad -\infty < x < \infty \tag{6.5.7}$$

is said to have *Student's t* distribution with *r degrees of freedom*, and we write $X \sim$ t(df $=r$). The associated R functions are `dt`, `pt`, `qt`, and `rt`, which give the PDF, CDF, quantile function, and simulate random variates, respectively. See Section 8.2.

Snedecor's F distribution

A random variable X with p.d.f.

$$f_X(x) = \frac{\Gamma[(m+n)/2]}{\Gamma(m/2)\Gamma(n/2)} \left(\frac{m}{n}\right)^{m/2} x^{m/2-1} \left(1 + \frac{m}{n}x\right)^{-(m+n)/2}, \quad x > 0. \tag{6.5.8}$$

is said to have an F distribution with (m, n) degrees of freedom. We write $X \sim$ f(`df1` $= m$, `df2` $= n$). The associated R functions are `df(x, df1, df2)`, `pf`, `qf`, and `rf`, which give the PDF, CDF, quantile function, and simulate random variates, respectively. We define $F_\alpha(m, n)$ as the number on the x-axis such that there is exactly α area under the f(`df1` $= m$, `df2` $= n$) curve to its right.

Remark 6.32. Here are some notes about the F distribution.

1. If $X \sim$ f(`df1` $= m$, `df2` $= n$) and $Y = 1/X$, then $Y \sim$ f(`df1` $= n$, `df2` $= m$). Historically, this fact was especially convenient. In the old days, statisticians used printed tables for their statistical calculations. Since the F tables were symmetric in m and n, it meant that publishers could cut the size of their printed tables in half. It plays less of a role today now that personal computers are widespread.

2. If $X \sim$ t(`df` $= r$), then $X^2 \sim$ f(`df1` $= 1$, `df2` $= r$). We will see this again in Section 11.3.3.

6.5.3 Other Popular Distributions

The Cauchy Distribution

This is a special case of the Student's t distribution. It has PDF

$$f_X(x) = \frac{1}{\beta\pi} \left[1 + \left(\frac{x-m}{\beta}\right)^2\right]^{-1}, \quad -\infty < x < \infty \tag{6.5.9}$$

We write $X \sim$ cauchy(`location` $= m$, `scale` $= \beta$). The associated R function is `dcauchy(x, location = 0, scale = 1)`.

It is easy to see that a cauchy(`location` $= 0$, `scale` $= 1$) distribution is the same as a t(`df` $= 1$) distribution. The cauchy distribution looks like a norm distribution but with very heavy tails. The mean (and variance) do not exist, that is, they are infinite. The median is represented by the `location` parameter, and the `scale` parameter influences the spread of the distribution about its median.

The Beta Distribution

This is a generalization of the continuous uniform distribution.

$$f_X(x) = \frac{\Gamma(\alpha+\beta)}{\Gamma(\alpha)\Gamma(\beta)} x^{\alpha-1}(1-x)^{\beta-1}, \quad 0 < x < 1 \tag{6.5.10}$$

We write $X \sim$ beta(`shape1` $= \alpha$, `shape2` $= \beta$). The associated R function is `dbeta(x, shape1, shape2)`. The mean and variance are

$$\mu = \frac{\alpha}{\alpha+\beta} \text{ and } \sigma^2 = \frac{\alpha\beta}{(\alpha+\beta)^2(\alpha+\beta+1)}. \tag{6.5.11}$$

See Example 6.3. This distribution comes up a lot in Bayesian statistics because it is a good model for one's prior beliefs about a population proportion p, $0 \le p \le 1$.

The Logistic Distribution

$$f_X(x) = \frac{1}{\sigma}\exp\left(-\frac{x-\mu}{\sigma}\right)\left[1+\exp\left(-\frac{x-\mu}{\sigma}\right)\right]^{-2}, \quad -\infty < x < \infty. \tag{6.5.12}$$

We write $X \sim$ logis(`location` $= \mu$, `scale` $= \sigma$). The associated R function is `dlogis(x, location = 0, scale = 1)`. The logistic distribution comes up in differential equations as a model for population growth under certain assumptions. The mean is μ and the variance is $\pi^2\sigma^2/3$.

The Lognormal Distribution

This is a distribution derived from the normal distribution (hence the name). If $U \sim$ `norm(mean` $=$ μ, `sd` $= \sigma$), then $X = e^U$has PDF

$$f_X(x) = \frac{1}{\sigma x\sqrt{2\pi}}\exp\left[\frac{-(\ln x-\mu)^2}{2\sigma^2}\right], \quad 0 < x < \infty. \tag{6.5.13}$$

We write $X \sim$ lnorm(`meanlog` $= \mu$, `sdlog` $= \sigma$). The associated R function is `dlnorm(x, meanlog = 0, sdlog = 1)`. Notice that the support is concentrated on the positive x axis; the distribution is right-skewed with a heavy tail. See Example 6.22.

The Weibull Distribution

This has PDF

$$f_X(x) = \frac{\alpha}{\beta}\left(\frac{x}{\beta}\right)^{\alpha-1}\exp\left(\frac{x}{\beta}\right)^{\alpha}, \quad x > 0. \tag{6.5.14}$$

We write $X \sim$ weibull(`shape` $= \alpha$, `scale` $= \beta$). The associated R function is `dweibull(x, shape, scale = 1)`.

6.5.4 How to do it with R

There is some support of moments and moment generating functions for some continuous probability distributions included in the `actuar` package [25]. The convention is `m` in front of the distribution name for raw moments, and `mgf` in front of the distribution name for the moment generating function. At the time of this writing, the following distributions are supported: gamma, inverse Gaussian, (non-central) chi-squared, exponential, and uniform.

Example 6.33. Calculate the first four raw moments for $X \sim$ gamma(`shape` $= 13$, `rate` $= 1$) and plot the moment generating function.

We load the `actuar` package and use the functions `mgamma` and `mgfgamma`:

```
> library(actuar)
> mgamma(1:4, shape = 13, rate = 1)
[1]     13    182   2730 43680
```

For the plot we can use the function in the following form:

```
> plot(function(x) {
+     mgfgamma(x, shape = 13, rate = 1)
+ }, from = -0.1, to = 0.1, ylab = "gamma mgf")
```

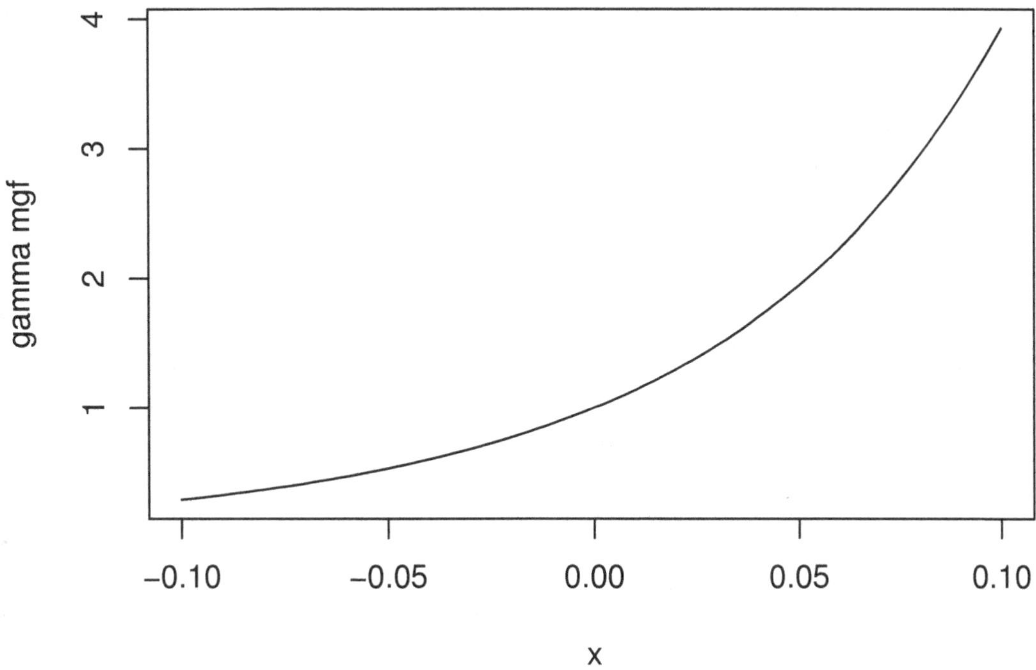

Figure 6.5.2: Plot of the gamma(shape = 13, rate = 1) MGF

Chapter Exercises

Exercise 6.1. Find the constant c so that the given function is a valid PDF of a random variable X.

1. $f(x) = Cx^n, \quad 0 < x < 1.$
2. $f(x) = Cx\mathrm{e}^{-x}, \quad 0 < x < \infty.$
3. $f(x) = \mathrm{e}^{-(x-C)}, \quad 7 < x < \infty.$
4. $f(x) = Cx^3(1-x)^2, \quad 0 < x < 1.$
5. $f(x) = C(1 + x^2/4)^{-1}, \quad -\infty < x < \infty.$

Exercise 6.2. For the following random experiments, decide what the distribution of X should be. In nearly every case, there are additional assumptions that should be made for the distribution to apply; identify those assumptions (which may or may not strictly hold in practice).

1. We throw a dart at a dart board. Let X denote the squared linear distance from the bulls-eye to the where the dart landed.
2. We randomly choose a textbook from the shelf at the bookstore and let P denote the proportion of the total pages of the book devoted to exercises.
3. We measure the time it takes for the water to completely drain out of the kitchen sink.

4. We randomly sample strangers at the grocery store and ask them how long it will take them to drive home.

Exercise 6.3. If Z is norm(mean = 0, sd = 1), find

1. $\mathbb{P}(Z > 2.64)$

```
> pnorm(2.64, lower.tail = FALSE)

[1] 0.004145301
```

2. $\mathbb{P}(0 \leq Z < 0.87)$

```
> pnorm(0.87) - 1/2

[1] 0.3078498
```

3. $\mathbb{P}(|Z| > 1.39)$ (Hint: draw a picture!)

```
> 2 * pnorm(-1.39)

[1] 0.1645289
```

Exercise 6.4. Calculate the variance of $X \sim$ unif(min $= a$, max $= b$). Hint: First calculate $\mathbb{E}\, X^2$.

type the exercise here

Exercise 6.5. Prove the memoryless property for exponential random variables. That is, for $X \sim$ exp(rate $= \lambda$) show that for any $s, t > 0$,

$$\mathbb{P}(X > s + t \,|\, X > t) = \mathbb{P}(X > s).$$

Chapter 7

Multivariate Distributions

We have built up quite a catalogue of distributions, discrete and continuous. They were all univariate, however, meaning that we only considered one random variable at a time. We can imagine nevertheless many random variables associated with a single person: their height, their weight, their wrist circumference (all continuous), or their eye/hair color, shoe size, whether they are right handed, left handed, or ambidextrous (all categorical), and we can even surmise reasonable probability distributions to associate with each of these variables.

But there is a difference: for a single person, these variables are related. For instance, a person's height betrays a lot of information about that person's weight.

The concept we are hinting at is the notion of *dependence* between random variables. It is the focus of this chapter to study this concept in some detail. Along the way, we will pick up additional models to add to our catalogue. Moreover, we will study certain classes of dependence, and clarify the special case when there is no dependence, namely, independence.

The interested reader who would like to learn more about any of the below mentioned multivariate distributions should take a look at *Discrete Multivariate Distributions* by Johnson *et al* [49] or *Continuous Multivariate Distributions* [54] by Kotz *et al.*

What do I want them to know?

- the basic notion of dependence and how it is manifested with multiple variables (two, in particular)
- joint versus marginal distributions/expectation (discrete and continuous)
- some numeric measures of dependence
- conditional distributions, in the context of independence and exchangeability
- some details of at least one multivariate model (discrete and continuous)
- what it looks like when there are more than two random variables present

7.1 Joint and Marginal Probability Distributions

Consider two discrete random variables X and Y with PMFs f_X and f_Y that are supported on the sample spaces S_X and S_Y, respectively. Let $S_{X,Y}$ denote the set of all possible observed *pairs*

(x, y), called the *joint support set* of X and Y. Then the *joint probability mass function* of X and Y is the function $f_{X,Y}$ defined by

$$f_{X,Y}(x, y) = \mathbb{P}(X = x,\ Y = y), \quad \text{for } (x, y) \in S_{X,Y}. \tag{7.1.1}$$

Every joint PMF satisfies

$$f_{X,Y}(x, y) > 0 \text{ for all } (x, y) \in S_{X,Y}, \tag{7.1.2}$$

and

$$\sum_{(x,y)\in S_{X,Y}} f_{X,Y}(x, y) = 1. \tag{7.1.3}$$

It is customary to extend the function $f_{X,Y}$ to be defined on all of $\mathbb{R}^2$ by setting $f_{X,Y}(x, y) = 0$ for $(x, y) \notin S_{X,Y}$.

In the context of this chapter, the PMFs f_X and f_Y are called the *marginal PMFs* of X and Y, respectively. If we are given only the joint PMF then we may recover each of the marginal PMFs by using the Theorem of Total Probability (see Equation4.4.5): observe

$$\begin{aligned} f_X(x) &= \mathbb{P}(X = x), && (7.1.4)\\ &= \sum_{y\in S_Y} \mathbb{P}(X = x,\ Y = y), && (7.1.5)\\ &= \sum_{y\in S_Y} f_{X,Y}(x, y). && (7.1.6) \end{aligned}$$

By interchanging the roles of X and Y it is clear that

$$f_Y(y) = \sum_{x\in S_Y} f_{X,Y}(x, y). \tag{7.1.7}$$

Given the joint PMF we may recover the marginal PMFs, but the converse is not true. Even if we have *both* marginal distributions they are not sufficient to determine the joint PMF; more information is needed[1].

Associated with the joint PMF is the *joint cumulative distribution function* $F_{X,Y}$ defined by

$$F_{X,Y}(x, y) = \mathbb{P}(X \le x,\ Y \le y), \quad \text{for } (x, y) \in \mathbb{R}^2.$$

The bivariate joint CDF is not quite as tractable as the univariate CDFs, but in principle we could calculate it by adding up quantities of the form in Equation 7.1.1. The joint CDF is typically not used in practice due to its inconvenient form; one can usually get by with the joint PMF alone.

We now introduce some examples of bivariate discrete distributions. The first we have seen before, and the second is based on the first.

Example 7.1. Roll a fair die twice. Let X be the face shown on the first roll, and let Y be the face shown on the second roll. We have already seen this example in Chapter 4, Example 4.30. For this example, it suffices to define

$$f_{X,Y}(x, y) = \frac{1}{36}, \quad x = 1, \ldots, 6,\ y = 1, \ldots, 6.$$

[1] We are not at a total loss, however. There are Frechet bounds which pose limits on how large (and small) the joint distribution must be at each point.

The marginal PMFs are given by $f_X(x) = 1/6$, $x = 1, 2, \ldots, 6$, and $f_Y(y) = 1/6$, $y = 1, 2, \ldots, 6$, since

$$f_X(x) = \sum_{y=1}^{6} \frac{1}{36} = \frac{1}{6}, \quad x = 1, \ldots, 6,$$

and the same computation with the letters switched works for Y.

In the previous example, and in many other ones, the joint support can be written as a product set of the support of X "times" the support of Y, that is, it may be represented as a cartesian product set, or rectangle, $S_{X,Y} = S_X \times S_Y$, where $S_X \times S_Y = \{(x, y) : \ x \in S_X,\ y \in S_Y\}$. As we shall see presently in Section 7.4, this form is a necessary condition for X and Y to be *independent* (or alternatively *exchangeable* when $S_X = S_Y$). But please note that in general it is not required for $S_{X,Y}$ to be of rectangle form. We next investigate just such an example.

Example 7.2. Let the random experiment again be to roll a fair die twice, except now let us define the random variables U and V by

$$\begin{aligned} U &= \text{the maximum of the two rolls, and} \\ V &= \text{the sum of the two rolls.} \end{aligned}$$

We see that the support of U is $S_U = \{1, 2, \ldots, 6\}$ and the support of V is $S_V = \{2, 3, \ldots, 12\}$. We may represent the sample space with a matrix, and for each entry in the matrix we may calculate the value that U assumes. The result is in the left half of Table 7.1.

We can use the table to calculate the marginal PMF of U, because from Example 4.30 we know that each entry in the matrix has probability $1/36$ associated with it. For instance, there is only one outcome in the matrix with $U = 1$, namely, the top left corner. This single entry has probability $1/36$, therefore, it must be that $f_U(1) = \mathbb{P}(U = 1) = 1/36$. Similarly we see that there are three entries in the matrix with $U = 2$, thus $f_U(2) = 3/36$. Continuing in this fashion we will find the marginal distribution of U may be written

$$f_U(u) = \frac{2u - 1}{36}, \quad u = 1,\ 2, \ldots, 6. \tag{7.1.8}$$

We may do a similar thing for V; see the right half of Table 7.1. Collecting all of the probability we will find that the marginal PMF of V is

$$f_V(v) = \frac{6 - |v - 7|}{36}, \quad v = 2,\ 3, \ldots, 12. \tag{7.1.9}$$

We may collapse the two matrices from Table 7.1 into one, big matrix of pairs of values (u, v). The result is shown in Table 7.2.

Again, each of these pairs has probability $1/36$ associated with it and we are looking at the joint PDF of (U, V) albeit in an unusual form. Many of the pairs are repeated, but some of them are not: $(1, 2)$ appears twice, but $(2, 3)$ appears only once. We can make more sense out of this by writing a new table with U on one side and V along the top. We will accumulate the probability just like we did in Example 7.1. See Table 7.3.

The joint support of (U, V) is concentrated along the main diagonal; note that the nonzero entries do not form a rectangle. Also notice that if we form row and column totals we are doing exactly the same thing as Equation 7.1.7, so that the marginal distribution of U is the list of totals in the right "margin" of the Table 7.3, and the marginal distribution of V is the list of totals in the bottom "margin".

U	1	2	3	4	5	6
1	1	2	3	4	5	6
2	2	2	3	4	5	6
3	3	3	3	4	5	6
4	4	4	4	4	5	6
5	5	5	5	5	5	6
6	6	6	6	6	6	6

(a) $U = \max(X, Y)$

V	1	2	3	4	5	6
1	2	3	4	5	6	7
2	3	4	5	6	7	8
3	4	5	6	7	8	9
4	5	6	7	8	9	10
5	6	7	8	9	10	11
6	7	8	9	10	11	12

(b) $V = X + Y$

Table 7.1: Maximum U and sum V of a pair of dice rolls (X, Y)

(U, V)	1	2	3	4	5	6
1	(1,2)	(2,3)	(3,4)	(4,5)	(5,6)	(6,7)
2	(2,3)	(2,4)	(3,5)	(4,6)	(5,7)	(6,8)
3	(3,4)	(3,5)	(3,6)	(4,7)	(5,8)	(6,9)
4	(4,5)	(4,6)	(4,7)	(4,8)	(5,9)	(6,10)
5	(5,6)	(5,7)	(5,8)	(5,9)	(5,10)	(6,11)
6	(6,7)	(6,8)	(6,9)	(6,10)	(6,11)	(6,12)

Table 7.2: Joint values of $U = \max(X, Y)$ and $V = X + Y$

	2	3	4	5	6	7	8	9	10	11	12	Total
1	1/36											1/36
2		2/36	1/36									3/36
3			2/36	2/36	1/36							5/36
4				2/36	2/36	2/36	1/36					7/36
5					2/36	2/36	2/36	2/36	1/36			9/36
6						2/36	2/36	2/36	2/36	2/36	1/36	11/36
Total	1/36	2/36	3/36	4/36	5/36	6/36	5/36	4/36	3/36	2/36	1/36	1

Table 7.3: The joint PMF of (U, V)

The outcomes of U are along the left and the outcomes of V are along the top. Empty entries in the table have zero probability. The row totals (on the right) and column totals (on the bottom) correspond to the marginal distribution of U and V, respectively.

Continuing the reasoning for the discrete case, given two continuous random variables X and Y there similarly exists[2] a function $f_{X,Y}(x,y)$ associated with X and Y called the *joint probability density function* of X and Y. Every joint PDF satisfies

$$f_{X,Y}(x,y) \geq 0 \text{ for all } (x,y) \in S_{X,Y}, \tag{7.1.10}$$

and

$$\iint_{S_{X,Y}} f_{X,Y}(x,y)\,\mathrm{d}x\,\mathrm{d}y = 1. \tag{7.1.11}$$

In the continuous case there is not such a simple interpretation for the joint PDF; however, we do have one for the joint CDF, namely,

$$F_{X,Y}(x,y) = \mathbb{P}(X \leq x,\ Y \leq y) = \int_{-\infty}^{x} \int_{-\infty}^{y} f_{X,Y}(u,v)\,\mathrm{d}v\,\mathrm{d}u,$$

for $(x,y) \in \mathbb{R}^2$. If X and Y have the joint PDF $f_{X,Y}$, then the marginal density of X may be recovered by

$$f_X(x) = \int_{S_Y} f_{X,Y}(x,y)\,\mathrm{d}y, \quad x \in S_X \tag{7.1.12}$$

and the marginal PDF of Y may be found with

$$f_Y(y) = \int_{S_X} f_{X,Y}(x,y)\,\mathrm{d}x, \quad y \in S_Y. \tag{7.1.13}$$

Example 7.3. Let the joint PDF of (X,Y) be given by

$$f_{X,Y}(x,y) = \frac{6}{5}\left(x + y^2\right), \quad 0 < x < 1,\ 0 < y < 1.$$

The marginal PDF of X is

$$\begin{aligned} f_X(x) &= \int_0^1 \frac{6}{5}\left(x + y^2\right)\mathrm{d}y, \\ &= \frac{6}{5}\left(xy + \frac{y^3}{3}\right)\Big|_{y=0}^{1}, \\ &= \frac{6}{5}\left(x + \frac{1}{3}\right), \end{aligned}$$

for $0 < x < 1$, and the marginal PDF of Y is

$$\begin{aligned} f_Y(y) &= \int_0^1 \frac{6}{5}\left(x + y^2\right)\mathrm{d}x, \\ &= \frac{6}{5}\left(\frac{x^2}{2} + xy^2\right)\Big|_{x=0}^{1}, \\ &= \frac{6}{5}\left(\frac{1}{2} + y^2\right), \end{aligned}$$

for $0 < y < 1$. In this example the joint support set was a rectangle $[0,1] \times [0,1]$, but it turns out that X and Y are not independent. See Section 7.4.

[2]Strictly speaking, the joint density function does not necessarily exist. But the joint CDF always exists.

7.1.1 How to do it with R

We will show how to do Example 7.2 using R; it is much simpler to do it with R than without. First we set up the sample space with the `rolldie` function. Next, we add random variables U and V with the `addrv` function. We take a look at the very top of the data frame (probability space) to make sure that everything is operating according to plan.

```
> S <- rolldie(2, makespace = TRUE)
> S <- addrv(S, FUN = max, invars = c("X1", "X2"), name = "U")
> S <- addrv(S, FUN = sum, invars = c("X1", "X2"), name = "V")
> head(S)
```

```
  X1 X2 U V      probs
1  1  1 1 2 0.02777778
2  2  1 2 3 0.02777778
3  3  1 3 4 0.02777778
4  4  1 4 5 0.02777778
5  5  1 5 6 0.02777778
6  6  1 6 7 0.02777778
```

Yes, the U and V columns have been added to the data frame and have been computed correctly. This result would be fine as it is, but the data frame has too many rows: there are repeated pairs (u, v) which show up as repeated rows in the data frame. The goal is to aggregate the rows of S such that the result has exactly one row for each unique pair (u, v) with positive probability. This sort of thing is exactly the task for which the `marginal` function was designed. We may take a look at the joint distribution of U and V (we only show the first few rows of the data frame, but the complete one has 11 rows).

```
> UV <- marginal(S, vars = c("U", "V"))
> head(UV)
```

```
  U V      probs
1 1 2 0.02777778
2 2 3 0.05555556
3 2 4 0.02777778
4 3 4 0.05555556
5 3 5 0.05555556
6 4 5 0.05555556
```

The data frame is difficult to understand. It would be better to have a tabular display like Table 7.3. We can do that with the `xtabs` function.

```
> xtabs(round(probs, 3) ~ U + V, data = UV)
```

```
   V
U       2     3     4     5     6     7     8     9    10    11    12
  1 0.028 0.000 0.000 0.000 0.000 0.000 0.000 0.000 0.000 0.000 0.000
  2 0.000 0.056 0.028 0.000 0.000 0.000 0.000 0.000 0.000 0.000 0.000
  3 0.000 0.000 0.056 0.056 0.028 0.000 0.000 0.000 0.000 0.000 0.000
  4 0.000 0.000 0.000 0.056 0.056 0.056 0.028 0.000 0.000 0.000 0.000
  5 0.000 0.000 0.000 0.000 0.056 0.056 0.056 0.056 0.028 0.000 0.000
  6 0.000 0.000 0.000 0.000 0.000 0.056 0.056 0.056 0.056 0.056 0.028
```

Compare these values to the ones shown in Table 7.3. We can repeat the process with `marginal` to get the univariate marginal distributions of U and V separately.

```
> marginal(UV, vars = "U")
  U      probs
1 1 0.02777778
2 2 0.08333333
3 3 0.13888889
4 4 0.19444444
5 5 0.25000000
6 6 0.30555556
> head(marginal(UV, vars = "V"))
  V      probs
1 2 0.02777778
2 3 0.05555556
3 4 0.08333333
4 5 0.11111111
5 6 0.13888889
6 7 0.16666667
```

Another way to do the same thing is with the `rowSums` and `colSums` of the `xtabs` object. Compare

```
> temp <- xtabs(probs ~ U + V, data = UV)
> rowSums(temp)
         1          2          3          4          5          6
0.02777778 0.08333333 0.13888889 0.19444444 0.25000000 0.30555556
> colSums(temp)
         2          3          4          5          6          7
0.02777778 0.05555556 0.08333333 0.11111111 0.13888889 0.16666667
         8          9         10         11         12
0.13888889 0.11111111 0.08333333 0.05555556 0.02777778
```

You should check that the answers that we have obtained exactly match the same (somewhat laborious) calculations that we completed in Example 7.2.

7.2 Joint and Marginal Expectation

Given a function g with arguments (x, y) we would like to know the long-run average behavior of $g(X, Y)$ and how to mathematically calculate it. Expectation in this context is computed in the pedestrian way. We simply integrate (sum) with respect to the joint probability density (mass) function.

$$\mathbb{E}\, g(X, Y) = \iint\limits_{S_{X,Y}} g(x, y)\, f_{X,Y}(x, y)\, \mathrm{d}x\, \mathrm{d}y, \tag{7.2.1}$$

or in the discrete case

$$\mathbb{E}\, g(X, Y) = \sum\sum_{(x,y)\in S_{X,Y}} g(x, y)\, f_{X,Y}(x, y). \tag{7.2.2}$$

7.2.1 Covariance and Correlation

There are two very special cases of joint expectation: the *covariance* and the *correlation*. These are measures which help us quantify the dependence between X and Y.

Definition 7.4. The *covariance* of X and Y is

$$\operatorname{Cov}(X, Y) = \mathbb{E}(X - \mathbb{E}\, X)(Y - \mathbb{E}\, Y). \tag{7.2.3}$$

By the way, there is a shortcut formula for covariance which is almost as handy as the shortcut for the variance:

$$\operatorname{Cov}(X, Y) = \mathbb{E}(XY) - (\mathbb{E}\, X)(\mathbb{E}\, Y). \tag{7.2.4}$$

The proof is left to Exercise 7.1.

The Pearson product moment correlation between X and Y is the covariance between X and Y rescaled to fall in the interval $[-1, 1]$. It is formally defined by

$$\operatorname{Corr}(X, Y) = \frac{\operatorname{Cov}(X, Y)}{\sigma_X \sigma_Y} \tag{7.2.5}$$

The correlation is usually denoted by $\rho_{X,Y}$ or simply ρ if the random variables are clear from context. There are some important facts about the correlation coefficient:

1. The range of correlation is $-1 \leq \rho_{X,Y} \leq 1$.
2. Equality holds above ($\rho_{X,Y} = \pm 1$) if and only if Y is a linear function of X with probability one.

Example 7.5. We will compute the covariance for the discrete distribution in Example 7.2. The expected value of U is

$$\mathbb{E}\, U = \sum_{u=1}^{6} u\, f_U(u) = \sum_{u=1}^{6} u\, \frac{2u-1}{36} = 1\left(\frac{1}{36}\right) + 2\left(\frac{3}{36}\right) + \cdots + 6\left(\frac{11}{36}\right) = \frac{161}{36},$$

and the expected value of V is

$$\mathbb{E}\, V = \sum_{v=2}^{12} v\, \frac{6 - |7 - v|}{36} = 2\left(\frac{1}{36}\right) + 3\left(\frac{2}{36}\right) + \cdots + 12\left(\frac{1}{36}\right) = 7,$$

and the expected value of UV is

$$\mathbb{E}\, UV = \sum_{u=1}^{6}\sum_{v=2}^{12} uv\, f_{U,V}(u, v) = 1 \cdot 2\left(\frac{1}{36}\right) + 2 \cdot 3\left(\frac{2}{36}\right) + \cdots + 6 \cdot 12\left(\frac{1}{36}\right) = \frac{308}{9}.$$

Therefore the covariance of (U, V) is

$$\operatorname{Cov}(U, V) = \mathbb{E}\, UV - (\mathbb{E}\, U)(\mathbb{E}\, V) = \frac{308}{9} - \frac{161}{36} \cdot 7 = \frac{35}{12}.$$

All we need now are the standard deviations of U and V to calculate the correlation coefficient (omitted).

We will do a continuous example so that you can see how it works.

Example 7.6. Let us find the covariance of the variables (X, Y) from Example 7.3. The expected value of X is

$$\mathbb{E} X = \int_0^1 x \cdot \frac{6}{5}\left(x + \frac{1}{3}\right) \mathrm{d}x = \frac{2}{5}x^3 + \frac{1}{5}x^2\bigg|_{x=0}^1 = \frac{3}{5},$$

and the expected value of Y is

$$\mathbb{E} Y = \int_0^1 y \cdot \frac{6}{5}\left(\frac{1}{2} + y^2\right) \mathrm{d}x = \frac{3}{10}y^2 + \frac{3}{20}y^4\bigg|_{y=0}^1 = \frac{9}{20}.$$

Finally, the expected value of XY is

$$\begin{aligned} \mathbb{E} XY &= \int_0^1 \int_0^1 xy \frac{6}{5}\left(x + y^2\right) \mathrm{d}x \, \mathrm{d}y, \\ &= \int_0^1 \left(\frac{2}{5}x^3 y + \frac{3}{10}xy^4\right)\bigg|_{x=0}^1 \mathrm{d}y, \\ &= \int_0^1 \left(\frac{2}{5}y + \frac{3}{10}y^4\right) \mathrm{d}y, \\ &= \frac{1}{5} + \frac{3}{50}, \end{aligned}$$

which is 13/50. Therefore the covariance of (X, Y) is

$$\mathrm{Cov}(X, Y) = \frac{13}{50} - \left(\frac{3}{5}\right)\left(\frac{9}{20}\right) = -\frac{1}{100}.$$

7.2.2 How to do it with R

There are not any specific functions in the `prob` package designed for multivariate expectation. This is not a problem, though, because it is easy enough to do expectation the long way – with column operations. We just need to keep the definition in mind. For instance, we may compute the covariance of (U, V) from Example 7.5.

```
> Eu <- sum(S$U * S$probs)
> Ev <- sum(S$V * S$probs)
> Euv <- sum(S$U * S$V * S$probs)
> Euv - Eu * Ev
[1] 2.916667
```

Compare this answer to what we got in Example 7.5.

To do the continuous case we could use the computer algebra utilities of `Yacas` and the associated R package `Ryacas` [35]. See Section 7.7.1 for another example where the `Ryacas` package appears.

7.3 Conditional Distributions

If $x \in S_X$ is such that $f_X(x) > 0$, then we define the *conditional density of* $Y|X = x$, denoted $f_{Y|x}$, by

$$f_{Y|x}(y|x) = \frac{f_{X,Y}(x, y)}{f_X(x)}, \quad y \in S_Y. \tag{7.3.1}$$

We define $f_{X|y}$ in a similar fashion.

Example 7.7. Let the joint PMF of X and Y be given by

$$f_{X,Y}(x, y) =$$

Example 7.8. Let the joint PDF of X and Y be given by

Bayesian Connection

Conditional distributions play a fundamental role in Bayesian probability and statistics. There is a parameter θ which is of primary interest, and about which we would like to learn. But rather than observing θ directly, we instead observe a random variable X whose probability distribution depends on θ. Using the information we provided by X, we would like to update the information that we have about θ.

Our initial beliefs about θ are represented by a probability distribution, called the *prior distribution*, denoted by π. The PDF $f_{X|\theta}$ is called the *likelihood function*, also called the *likelihood of X conditional on θ*. Given an observation $X = x$, we would like to update our beliefs π to a new distribution, called the *posterior distribution of θ given the observation $X = x$*, denoted $\pi_{\theta|x}$. It may seem a mystery how to obtain $\pi_{\theta|x}$ based only on the information provided by π and $f_{X|\theta}$, but it should not be. We have already studied this in Section 4.8 where it was called Bayes' Rule:

$$\pi(\theta|x) = \frac{\pi(\theta)\, f(x|\theta)}{\int \pi(u)\, f(x|u)\mathrm{d}u}. \tag{7.3.2}$$

Compare the above expression to Equation 4.8.1.

Example 7.9. Suppose the parameter θ is the $\mathbb{P}$(Heads) for a biased coin. It could be any value from 0 to 1. Perhaps we have some prior information about this coin, for example, maybe we have seen this coin before and we have reason to believe that it shows Heads less than half of the time. Suppose that we represent our beliefs about θ with a beta(`shape1` = 1, `shape2` = 3) prior distribution, that is, we assume

$$\theta \sim \pi(\theta) = 3(1-\theta)^2, \quad 0 < \theta < 1.$$

To learn more about θ, we will do what is natural: flip the coin. We will observe a random variable X which takes the value 1 if the coin shows Heads, and 0 if the coin shows Tails. Under these circumstances, X will have a Bernoulli distribution, and in particular, $X|\theta \sim$ binom(`size` = 1, `prob` = θ):

$$f_{X|\theta}(x|\theta) = \theta^x (1-\theta)^{1-x}, \quad x = 0, 1.$$

Based on the observation $X = x$, we will update the prior distribution to the posterior distribution, and we will do so with Bayes' Rule: it says

$$\begin{aligned}
\pi(\theta|x) &\propto \pi(\theta)\, f(x|\theta),\\
&= \theta^x (1-\theta)^{1-x} \cdot 3(1-\theta)^2,\\
&= 3\,\theta^x (1-\theta)^{3-x}, \quad 0 < \theta < 1,
\end{aligned}$$

where the constant of proportionality is given by

$$\int 3\,u^x (1-u)^{3-x}\mathrm{d}u = \int 3\,u^{(1+x)-1}(1-u)^{(4-x)-1}\mathrm{d}u = 3\,\frac{\Gamma(1+x)\Gamma(4-x)}{\Gamma[(1+x)+(4-x)]},$$

the integral being calculated by inspection of the formula for a beta(shape1 = $1+x$, shape2 = $4-x$) distribution. That is to say, our posterior distribution is precisely

$$\theta|x \sim \text{beta}(\texttt{shape1} = 1 + x,\ \texttt{shape2} = 4 - x).$$

The Bayesian statistician uses the posterior distribution for all matters concerning inference about θ.

Remark 7.10. We usually do not restrict ourselves to the observation of only one X conditional on θ. In fact, it is common to observe an entire sample $X_1, X_2, \ldots, X_n$ conditional on θ (which itself is often multidimensional). Do not be frightened, however, because the intuition is the same. There is a prior distribution $\pi(\theta)$, a likelihood $f(x_1, x_2, \ldots, x_n|\theta)$, and a posterior distribution $\pi(\theta|x_1, x_2, \ldots, x_n)$. Bayes' Rule states that the relationship between the three is

$$\pi(\theta|x_1, x_2, \ldots, x_n) \propto \pi(\theta)\, f(x_1, x_2, \ldots, x_n|\theta),$$

where the constant of proportionality is $\int \pi(u)\, f(x_1, x_2, \ldots, x_n|u)\, \mathrm{d}u$. Any good textbook on Bayesian Statistics will explain these notions in detail; to the interested reader I recommend Gelman [33] or Lee [57].

7.4 Independent Random Variables

7.4.1 Independent Random Variables

We recall from Chapter 4 that the events A and B are said to be independent when

$$\mathbb{P}(A \cap B) = \mathbb{P}(A)\,\mathbb{P}(B). \tag{7.4.1}$$

If it happens that

$$\mathbb{P}(X = x, Y = y) = \mathbb{P}(X = x)\,\mathbb{P}(Y = y), \quad \text{for every } x \in S_X,\ y \in S_Y, \tag{7.4.2}$$

then we say that X and Y are *independent random variables*. Otherwise, we say that X and Y are *dependent*. Using the PMF notation from above, we see that independent discrete random variables satisfy

$$f_{X,Y}(x, y) = f_X(x) f_Y(y) \quad \text{for every } x \in S_X,\ y \in S_Y. \tag{7.4.3}$$

Continuing the reasoning, given two continuous random variables X and Y with joint PDF $f_{X,Y}$ and respective marginal PDFs f_X and f_Y that are supported on the sets S_X and S_Y, if it happens that

$$f_{X,Y}(x, y) = f_X(x) f_Y(y) \quad \text{for every } x \in S_X,\ y \in S_Y, \tag{7.4.4}$$

then we say that X and Y are independent.

Example 7.11. In Example 7.1 we considered the random experiment of rolling a fair die twice. There we found the joint PMF to be

$$f_{X,Y}(x, y) = \frac{1}{36}, \quad x = 1, \ldots, 6,\ y = 1, \ldots, 6,$$

and we found the marginal PMFs $f_X(x) = 1/6$, $x = 1, 2, \ldots, 6$, and $f_Y(y) = 1/6$, $y = 1, 2, \ldots, 6$. Therefore in this experiment X and Y are independent since for every x and y in the joint support the joint PMF satisfies

$$f_{X,Y}(x, y) = \frac{1}{36} = \left(\frac{1}{6}\right)\left(\frac{1}{6}\right) = f_X(x)\, f_Y(y).$$

Example 7.12. In Example 7.2 we considered the same experiment but different random variables U and V. We can prove that U and V are not independent if we can find a single pair (u, v) where the independence equality does not hold. There are many such pairs. One of them is $(6, 12)$:

$$f_{U,V}(6, 12) = \frac{1}{36} \neq \left(\frac{11}{36}\right)\left(\frac{1}{36}\right) = f_U(6)\, f_V(12).$$

Independent random variables are very useful to the mathematician. They have many, many, tractable properties. We mention some of the more important ones.

Proposition 7.13. *If X and Y are independent, then for any functions u and v,*

$$\mathbb{E}\left(u(X)v(Y)\right) = \left(\mathbb{E}\, u(X)\right)\left(\mathbb{E}\, v(Y)\right). \tag{7.4.5}$$

Proof. This is straightforward from the definition.

$$\begin{aligned}
\mathbb{E}\left(u(X)v(Y)\right) &= \iint u(x)v(y)\, f_{X,Y}(x, y)\, \mathrm{d}x\mathrm{d}y \\
&= \iint u(x)v(y)\, f_X(x)\, f_Y(y)\, \mathrm{d}x\mathrm{d}y \\
&= \int u(x)\, f_X(x)\, \mathrm{d}x \int v(y)\, f_Y(y)\, \mathrm{d}y
\end{aligned}$$

and this last quantity is exactly $\left(\mathbb{E}\, u(X)\right)\left(\mathbb{E}\, v(Y)\right)$. □

Now that we have Proposition 7.13 we mention a corollary that will help us later to quickly identify those random variables which are *not* independent.

Corollary 7.14. *If X and Y are independent, then $Cov(X, Y) = 0$, and consequently, $Corr(X, Y) = 0$.*

Proof. When X and Y are independent then $\mathbb{E}\, XY = \mathbb{E}\, X\, \mathbb{E}\, Y$. And when the covariance is zero the numerator of the correlation is 0. □

Remark 7.15. Unfortunately, the converse of Corollary 7.14 is not true. That is, there are many random variables which are dependent yet their covariance and correlation is zero. For more details, see Casella and Berger [13].

Proposition 7.13 is useful to us and we will receive mileage out of it, but there is another fact which will play an even more important role. Unfortunately, the proof is beyond the techniques presented here. The inquisitive reader should consult Casella and Berger [13], Resnick [70], *etc.*

Fact 7.16. *If X and Y are independent, then $u(X)$ and $v(Y)$ are independent for any functions u and v.*

7.4.2 Combining Independent Random Variables

Another important corollary of Proposition 7.13 will allow us to find the distribution of sums of random variables.

Corollary 7.17. *If X and Y are independent, then the moment generating function of $X + Y$ is*

$$M_{X+Y}(t) = M_X(t) \cdot M_Y(t). \tag{7.4.6}$$

Proof. Choose $u(x) = \mathrm{e}^x$ and $v(y) = \mathrm{e}^y$ in Proposition 7.13, and remember the identity $\mathrm{e}^{t(x+y)} = \mathrm{e}^{tx}\,\mathrm{e}^{ty}$. □

Let us take a look at some examples of the corollary in action.

Example 7.18. Let $X \sim$ `binom(size` $= n_1$, `prob` $= p$) and $Y \sim$ `binom(size` $= n_2$, `prob` $= p$) be independent. Then $X + Y$ has MGF

$$M_{X+Y}(t) = M_X(t)\, M_Y(t) = \left(q + p\mathrm{e}^t\right)^{n_1} \left(q + p\mathrm{e}^t\right)^{n_2} = \left(q + p\mathrm{e}^t\right)^{n_1+n_2},$$

which is the MGF of a `binom(size` $= n_1 + n_2$, `prob` $= p$) distribution. Therefore, $X + Y \sim$ `binom(size` $= n_1 + n_2$, `prob` $= p$).

Example 7.19. Let $X \sim$ `norm(mean` $= \mu_1$, `sd` $= \sigma_1$) and $Y \sim$ `norm(mean` $= \mu_2$, `sd` $= \sigma_2$) be independent. Then $X + Y$ has MGF

$$M_X(t)\, M_Y(t) = \exp\left\{\mu_1 t + t^2\sigma_1^2/2\right\} \exp\left\{\mu_2 t + t^2\sigma_2^2/2\right\} = \exp\left\{(\mu_1 + \mu_2)\,t + t^2\left(\sigma_1^2 + \sigma_2^2\right)/2\right\},$$

which is the MGF of a `norm(mean` $= \mu_1 + \mu_2$, `sd` $= \sqrt{\sigma_1^2 + \sigma_2^2}$) distribution.

Even when we cannot use the MGF trick to identify the exact distribution of a linear combination of random variables, we can still say something about its mean and variance.

Proposition 7.20. *Let X_1 and X_2 be independent with respective population means μ_1 and μ_2 and population standard deviations σ_1 and σ_2. For given constants a_1 and a_2, define $Y = a_1X_1 + a_2X_2$. Then the mean and standard deviation of Y are given by the formulas*

$$\mu_Y = a_1\mu_1 + a_2\mu_2, \qquad \sigma_Y = \left(a_1^2\sigma_1^2 + a_2^2\sigma_2^2\right)^{1/2}. \tag{7.4.7}$$

Proof. We use Proposition 5.11:

$$\mathbb{E}\,Y = \mathbb{E}\left(a_1X_1 + a_2X_2\right) = a_1\,\mathbb{E}\,X_1 + a_2\,\mathbb{E}\,X_2 = a_1\mu_1 + a_2\mu_2.$$

For the standard deviation, we will find the variance and take the square root at the end. And to calculate the variance we will first compute $\mathbb{E}\,Y^2$ with an eye toward using the identity $\sigma_Y^2 = \mathbb{E}\,Y^2 - (\mathbb{E}\,Y)^2$ as a final step.

$$\mathbb{E}\,Y^2 = \mathbb{E}\left(a_1X_1 + a_2X_2\right)^2 = \mathbb{E}\left(a_1^2X_1^2 + a_2^2X_2^2 + 2a_1a_2X_1X_2\right).$$

Using linearity of expectation the $\mathbb{E}$ distributes through the sum. Now $\mathbb{E}\,X_i^2 = \sigma_i^2 + \mu_i^2$, for $i = 1$ and 2 and $\mathbb{E}\,X_1X_2 = \mathbb{E}\,X_1\,\mathbb{E}\,X_2 = \mu_1\mu_2$ because of independence. Thus

$$\begin{aligned}
\mathbb{E}\,Y^2 &= a_1^2(\sigma_1^2 + \mu_1^2) + a_2^2(\sigma_2^2 + \mu_2^2) + 2a_1a_2\mu_1\mu_2, \\
&= a_1^2\sigma_1^2 + a_2^2\sigma_2^2 + \left(a_1^2\mu_1^2 + a_2^2\mu_2^2 + 2a_1a_2\mu_1\mu_2\right).
\end{aligned}$$

But notice that the expression in the parentheses is exactly $(a_1\mu_1 + a_2\mu_2)^2 = (\mathbb{E}\,Y)^2$, so the proof is complete.. □

7.5 Exchangeable Random Variables

Two random variables X and Y are said to be *exchangeable* if their joint CDF is a symmetric function of its arguments:

$$F_{X,Y}(x,y) = F_{X,Y}(y,x), \quad \text{for all } (x,y) \in \mathbb{R}^2. \tag{7.5.1}$$

When the joint density f exists, we may equivalently say that X and Y are exchangeable if $f(x,y) = f(y,x)$ for all (x,y).

Exchangeable random variables exhibit symmetry in the sense that a person may exchange one variable for the other with no substantive changes to their joint random behavior. While independence speaks to a *lack of influence* between the two variables, exchangeability aims to capture the *symmetry* between them.

Example 7.21. Let X and Y have joint PDF

$$f_{X,Y}(x,y) = (1+\alpha)\lambda^2 e^{-\lambda(x+y)} + \alpha(2\lambda)^2 e^{-2\lambda(x+y)} - 2\alpha\lambda^2\left(e^{-\lambda(2x+y)} + e^{-\lambda(x+2y)}\right). \tag{7.5.2}$$

It is straightforward and tedious to check that $\iint f = 1$. We may see immediately that $f_{X,Y}(x,y) = f_{X,Y}(y,x)$ for all (x,y), which confirms that X and Y are exchangeable. Here, α is said to be an association parameter. This particular example is one from the Farlie-Gumbel-Morgenstern family of distributions; see [54].

Example 7.22. Suppose X and Y are i.i.d. binom(`size` = n, `prob` = p). Then their joint PMF is

$$\begin{aligned} f_{X,Y}(x,y) &= f_X(x) f_Y(y) \\ &= \binom{n}{x} p^x (1-p)^{n-x} \binom{n}{y} p^y (1-p)^{n-y}, \\ &= \binom{n}{x}\binom{n}{y} p^{x+y} (1-p)^{2n-(x+y)}, \end{aligned}$$

and the value is the same if we exchange x and y. Therefore (X,Y) are exchangeable.

Looking at Example 7.22 more closely we see that the fact that (X,Y) are exchangeable has nothing to do with the binom(`size` = n, `prob` = p) distribution; it only matters that they are independent (so that the joint PDF factors) and they are identically distributed (in which case we may swap letters to no effect). We could just have easily used any other marginal distribution. We will take this as a proof of the following proposition.

Proposition 7.23. *If X and Y are i.i.d. (with common marginal distribution F) then X and Y are exchangeable.*

Exchangeability thus contains i.i.d. as a special case.

7.6 The Bivariate Normal Distribution

The bivariate normal PDF is given by the unwieldy formula

$$f_{X,Y}(x,y) = \frac{1}{2\pi\,\sigma_X\sigma_Y\sqrt{1-\rho^2}} \exp\left\{-\frac{1}{2(1-\rho^2)}\left[\left(\frac{x-\mu_X}{\sigma_X}\right)^2 + \cdots \right.\right.$$

$$\left.\left. \cdots + 2\rho\left(\frac{x-\mu_X}{\sigma_X}\right)\left(\frac{y-\mu_Y}{\sigma_Y}\right) + \left(\frac{y-\mu_Y}{\sigma_Y}\right)^2\right]\right\}, \tag{7.6.1}$$

for $(x, y) \in \mathbb{R}^2$. We write $(X, Y) \sim$ `mvnorm(mean` $= \mu$, `sigma` $= \Sigma$), where

$$\mu = (\mu_X, \mu_Y)^T, \quad \sum = \begin{pmatrix} \sigma_X^2 & \rho\sigma_X\sigma_Y \\ \rho\sigma_X\sigma_Y & \sigma_Y^2 \end{pmatrix}. \tag{7.6.2}$$

See Appendix E. The vector notation allows for a more compact rendering of the joint PDF:

$$f_{X,Y}(\mathbf{x}) = \frac{1}{2\pi\,|\Sigma|^{1/2}} \exp\left\{-\frac{1}{2}(\mathbf{x}-\mu)^\top \Sigma^{-1} (\mathbf{x}-\mu)\right\}, \tag{7.6.3}$$

where in an abuse of notation we have written $\mathbf{x}$ for (x, y). Note that the formula only holds when $\rho \neq \pm 1$.

Remark 7.24. In Remark 7.15 we noted that just because random variables are uncorrelated it does not necessarily mean that they are independent. However, there is an important exception to this rule: the bivariate normal distribution. Indeed, $(X, Y) \sim$ `mvnorm(mean` $= \mu$, `sigma` $= \Sigma$) are independent if and only if $\rho = 0$.

Remark 7.25. Inspection of the joint PDF shows that if $\mu_X = \mu_Y$ and $\sigma_X = \sigma_Y$ then X and Y are exchangeable.

The bivariate normal MGF is

$$M_{X,Y}(\mathbf{t}) = \exp\left(\mu^\top\mathbf{t} + \frac{1}{2}\mathbf{t}^\top\Sigma\mathbf{t}\right), \tag{7.6.4}$$

where $\mathbf{t} = (t_1, t_2)$.

The bivariate normal distribution may be intimidating at first but it turns out to be very tractable compared to other multivariate distributions. An example of this is the following fact about the marginals.

Fact 7.26. *If* $(X, Y) \sim$ `mvnorm(mean` $= \mu$, `sigma` $= \Sigma$) *then*

$$X \sim \texttt{norm(mean} = \mu_X,\ \texttt{sd} = \sigma_X) \textit{ and } Y \sim \texttt{norm(mean} = \mu_Y,\ \texttt{sd} = \sigma_Y). \tag{7.6.5}$$

From this we immediately get that $\mathbb{E}X = \mu_X$ and $\mathrm{Var}(X) = \sigma_X^2$ (and the same is true for Y with the letters switched). And it should be no surprise that the correlation between X and Y is exactly $\mathrm{Corr}(X, Y) = \rho$.

Proposition 7.27. *The conditional distribution of* $Y|X = x$ *is* `norm(mean` $= \mu_{Y|x}$, `sd` $= \sigma_{Y|x}$), *where*

$$\mu_{Y|x} = \mu_Y + \rho\frac{\sigma_Y}{\sigma_X}(x - \mu_X), \textit{ and } \sigma_{Y|x} = \sigma_Y\sqrt{1-\rho^2}. \tag{7.6.6}$$

There are a few things to note about Proposition 7.27 which will be important in Chapter 11. First, the conditional mean of $Y|x$ is linear in x, with slope

$$\rho\frac{\sigma_Y}{\sigma_X}. \tag{7.6.7}$$

Second, the conditional variance of $Y|x$ is independent of x.

7.6.1 How to do it with R

The multivariate normal distribution is implemented in both the `mvtnorm` package [34] and the `mnormt` package [17]. We use the `mvtnorm` package in this book simply because it is a dependency of another package used in the book.

The `mvtnorm` package has functions `dmvnorm` and `rmvnorm` for the PDF and to generate random vectors, respectively. Let us get started with a graph of the bivariate normal PDF. We can make the plot with the following code[3], where the workhorse is the `persp` function in base R.

```
> library(mvtnorm)
> x <- y <- seq(from = -3, to = 3, length.out = 30)
> f <- function(x, y) dmvnorm(cbind(x, y), mean = c(0, 0),
+     sigma = diag(2))
> z <- outer(x, y, FUN = f)
> persp(x, y, z, theta = -30, phi = 30, ticktype = "detailed")
```

We chose the standard bivariate normal, mvnorm(mean = **0**, `sigma` = **I**), to display.

7.7 Bivariate Transformations of Random Variables

We studied in Section 6.4 how to find the PDF of $Y = g(X)$ given the PDF of X. But now we have two random variables X and Y, with joint PDF $f_{X,Y}$, and we would like to consider the joint PDF of two new random variables

$$U = g(X, Y) \quad \text{and} \quad V = h(X, Y), \tag{7.7.1}$$

where g and h are two given functions, typically "nice" in the sense of Appendix E.6.

Suppose that the transformation $(x, y) \longmapsto (u, v)$ is one-to-one. Then an inverse transformation $x = x(u, v)$ and $y = y(u, v)$ exists, so let $\partial(x, y)/\partial(u, v)$ denote the Jacobian of the inverse transformation. Then the joint PDF of (U, V) is given by

$$f_{U,V}(u, v) = f_{X,Y}\left[x(u, v),\ y(u, v)\right]\left|\frac{\partial(x, y)}{\partial(u, v)}\right|, \tag{7.7.2}$$

or we can rewrite more shortly as

$$f_{U,V}(u, v) = f_{X,Y}(x, y)\left|\frac{\partial(x, y)}{\partial(u, v)}\right|. \tag{7.7.3}$$

Take a moment and compare Equation 7.7.3 to Equation 6.4.2. Do you see the connection?

---

[3]Another way to do this is with the `curve3d` function in the `emdbook` package [9]. It looks like this:

```
library(emdbook); library(mvtnorm)   # note: the order matters
mu <- c(0,0); sigma <- diag(2)
f <- function(x,y) dmvnorm(c(x,y), mean = mu, sigma = sigma)
curve3d(f(x,y), from = c(-3,-3), to = c(3,3), theta = -30, phi = 30)
```

The code above is slightly shorter than that using `persp` and is easier to understand. One must be careful, however. If the `library` calls are swapped then the code will not work because both packages `emdbook` and `mvtnorm` have a function called "`dmvnorm`"; one must load them to the search path in the correct order or R will use the wrong one (the arguments are named differently and the underlying algorithms are different).

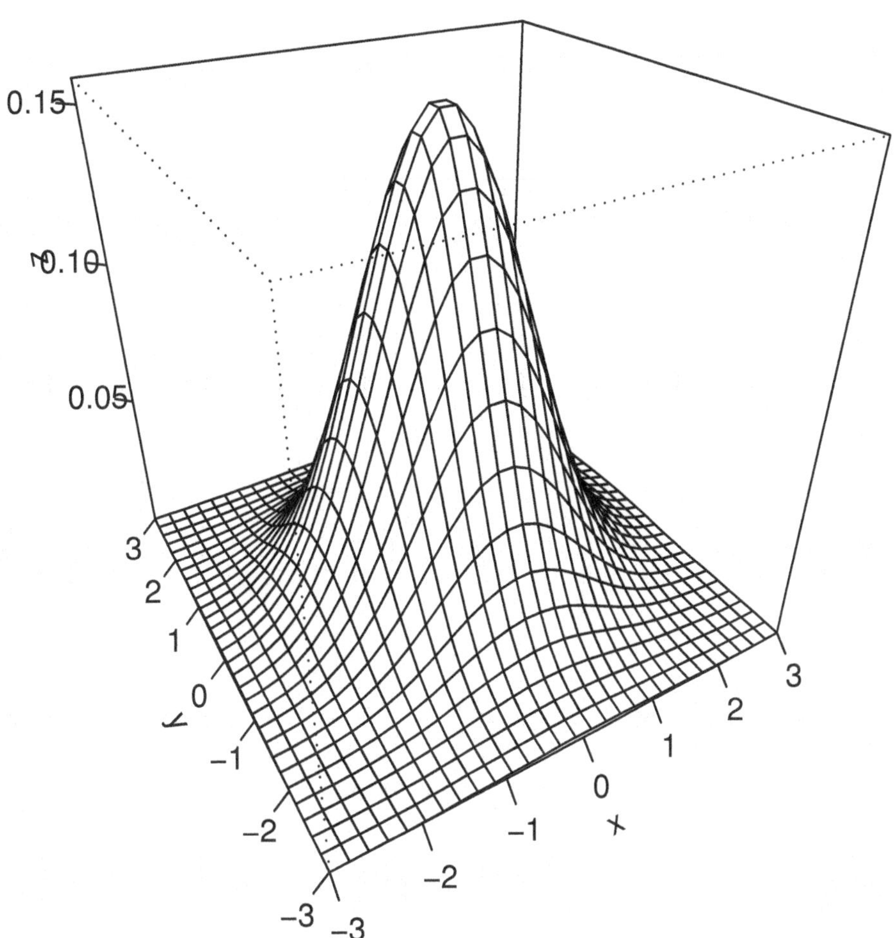

Figure 7.6.1: Graph of a bivariate normal PDF

Remark 7.28. It is sometimes easier to *postpone* solving for the inverse transformation $x = x(u, v)$ and $y = y(u, v)$. Instead, leave the transformation in the form $u = u(x, y)$ and $v = v(x, y)$ and calculate the Jacobian of the *original* transformation

$$\frac{\partial(u,v)}{\partial(x,y)} = \begin{vmatrix} \frac{\partial u}{\partial x} & \frac{\partial u}{\partial y} \\ \frac{\partial v}{\partial x} & \frac{\partial v}{\partial y} \end{vmatrix} = \frac{\partial u}{\partial x}\frac{\partial v}{\partial y} - \frac{\partial u}{\partial y}\frac{\partial v}{\partial x}. \tag{7.7.4}$$

Once this is known, we can get the PDF of (U, V) by

$$f_{U,V}(u,v) = f_{X,Y}(x,y)\left|\frac{1}{\frac{\partial(u,v)}{\partial(x,y)}}\right|. \tag{7.7.5}$$

In some cases there will be a cancellation and the work will be a lot shorter. Of course, it is not always true that

$$\frac{\partial(x,y)}{\partial(u,v)} = \frac{1}{\frac{\partial(u,v)}{\partial(x,y)}}, \tag{7.7.6}$$

but for the well-behaved examples that we will see in this book it works just fine... do you see the connection between Equations 7.7.6 and 6.4.5?

Example 7.29. Let $(X, Y) \sim$ `mvnorm(mean` $= \mathbf{0}_{2\times1}$, `sigma` $= \mathbf{I}_{2\times2}$) and consider the transformation

$$U = 3X + 4Y,$$
$$V = 5X + 6Y.$$

We can solve the system of equations to find the inverse transformations; they are

$$X = -3U + 2V,$$
$$Y = \frac{5}{2}U - \frac{3}{2}V,$$

in which case the Jacobian of the inverse transformation is

$$\begin{vmatrix} -3 & 2 \\ \frac{5}{2} & -\frac{3}{2} \end{vmatrix} = 3\left(-\frac{3}{2}\right) - 2\left(\frac{5}{2}\right) = -\frac{1}{2}.$$

As (x, y) traverses $\mathbb{R}^2$, so too does (u, v). Since the joint PDF of (X, Y) is

$$f_{X,Y}(x,y) = \frac{1}{2\pi}\exp\left\{-\frac{1}{2}\left(x^2 + y^2\right)\right\}, \quad (x,y) \in \mathbb{R}^2,$$

we get that the joint PDF of (U, V) is

$$f_{U,V}(u,v) = \frac{1}{2\pi}\exp\left\{-\frac{1}{2}\left[(-3u+2v)^2 + \left(\frac{5u-3v}{2}\right)^2\right]\right\}\cdot\frac{1}{2}, \quad (u,v) \in \mathbb{R}^2. \tag{7.7.7}$$

Remark 7.30. It may not be obvious, but Equation 7.7.7 is the PDF of a `mvnorm` distribution. For a more general result see Theorem 7.34.

7.7.1 How to do it with R

It is possible to do the computations above in R with the Ryacas package. The package is an interface to the open-source computer algebra system, "Yacas". The user installs Yacas, then employs Ryacas to submit commands to Yacas, after which the output is displayed in the R console.

There are not yet any examples of Yacas in this book, but there are online materials to help the interested reader: see http://code.google.com/p/ryacas/ to get started.

7.8 Remarks for the Multivariate Case

There is nothing spooky about $n \geq 3$ random variables. We just have a whole bunch of them: X_1, X_2,..., X_n, which we can shorten to $\mathbf{X} = (X_1, X_2, \ldots, X_n)^{\mathrm{T}}$ to make the formulas prettier (now may be a good time to check out Appendix E.5). For $\mathbf{X}$ supported on the set $S_{\mathbf{X}}$, the joint PDF $f_{\mathbf{X}}$ (if it exists) satisfies

$$f_{\mathbf{X}}(\mathbf{x}) > 0, \quad \text{for } \mathbf{x} \in S_{\mathbf{X}}, \tag{7.8.1}$$

and

$$\int\int \cdots \int f_{\mathbf{X}}(\mathbf{x})\, \mathrm{d}x_1 \mathrm{d}x_2 \cdots \mathrm{d}x_n = 1, \tag{7.8.2}$$

or even shorter: $\int f_{\mathbf{X}}(\mathbf{x})\, \mathrm{d}\mathbf{x} = 1$. The joint CDF $F_{\mathbf{X}}$ is defined by

$$F_{\mathbf{X}}(\mathbf{x}) = \mathbb{P}(X_1 \leq x_1, X_2 \leq x_2, \ldots, X_n \leq x_n), \tag{7.8.3}$$

for $\mathbf{x} \in \mathbb{R}^n$. The expectation of a function $g(\mathbf{X})$ is defined just as we would imagine:

$$\mathbb{E}\, g(\mathbf{X}) = \int g(\mathbf{x})\, f_{\mathbf{X}}(\mathbf{x})\, \mathrm{d}\mathbf{x}. \tag{7.8.4}$$

provided the integral exists and is finite. And the moment generating function in the multivariate case is defined by

$$M_{\mathbf{X}}(\mathbf{t}) = \mathbb{E} \exp\left\{\mathbf{t}^{\mathrm{T}}\mathbf{X}\right\}, \tag{7.8.5}$$

whenever the integral exists and is finite for all $\mathbf{t}$ in a neighborhood of $\mathbf{0}_{\mathrm{n}\times 1}$ (note that $\mathbf{t}^{\mathrm{T}}\mathbf{X}$ is shorthand for $t_1X_1 + t_2X_2 + \cdots + t_nX_n$). The only difference in any of the above for the discrete case is that integrals are replaced by sums.

Marginal distributions are obtained by integrating out remaining variables from the joint distribution. And even if we are given all of the univariate marginals it is not enough to determine the joint distribution uniquely.

We say that X_1, X_2, ..., X_n are *mutually independent* if their joint PDF factors into the product of the marginals

$$f_{\mathbf{X}}(\mathbf{x}) = f_{X_1}(x_1)\, f_{X_2}(x_2) \cdots f_{X_n}(x_n), \tag{7.8.6}$$

for every $\mathbf{x}$ in their joint support $S_{\mathbf{X}}$, and we say that X_1, X_2, ..., X_n are *exchangeable* if their joint PDF (or CDF) is a symmetric function of its n arguments, that is, if

$$f_{\mathbf{X}}(\mathbf{x}^*) = f_{\mathbf{X}}(\mathbf{x}), \tag{7.8.7}$$

for any reordering $\mathbf{x}^*$ of the elements of $\mathbf{x} = (x_1, x_2, \ldots, x_n)$ in the joint support.

Proposition 7.31. *Let X_1, X_2, ..., X_n be independent with respective population means μ_1, μ_2, ..., μ_n and standard deviations σ_1, σ_2, ..., σ_n. For given constants a_1, a_2, ..., a_n define $Y = \sum_{i=1}^{n} a_i X_i$. Then the mean and standard deviation of Y are given by the formulas*

$$\mu_Y = \sum_{i=1}^{n} a_i \mu_i, \quad \sigma_Y = \left(\sum_{i=1}^{n} a_i^2 \sigma_i^2 \right)^{1/2}. \tag{7.8.8}$$

Proof. The mean is easy:

$$\mathbb{E}\, Y = \mathbb{E} \left(\sum_{i=1}^{n} a_i X_i \right) = \sum_{i=1}^{n} a_i \, \mathbb{E}\, X_i = \sum_{i=1}^{n} a_i \mu_i.$$

The variance is not too difficult to compute either. As an intermediate step, we calculate $\mathbb{E}\, Y^2$.

$$\mathbb{E}\, Y^2 = \mathbb{E} \left(\sum_{i=1}^{n} a_i X_i \right)^2 = \mathbb{E} \left(\sum_{i=1}^{n} a_i^2 X_i^2 + 2 \sum_{i=1}^{n-1} \sum_{j=i+1}^{n} a_i a_j X_i X_j \right).$$

Using linearity of expectation the $\mathbb{E}$ distributes through the sums. Now $\mathbb{E}\, X_i^2 = \sigma_i^2 + \mu_i^2$ and $\mathbb{E}\, X_i X_j = \mathbb{E}\, X_i \, \mathbb{E}\, X_j = \mu_i \mu_j$ when $i \neq j$ because of independence. Thus

$$\begin{aligned} \mathbb{E}\, Y^2 &= \sum_{i=1}^{n} a_i^2 (\sigma_i^2 + \mu_i^2) + 2 \sum_{i=1}^{n-1} \sum_{j=i+1}^{n} a_i a_j \mu_i \mu_j \\ &= \sum_{i=1}^{n} a_i^2 \sigma_i^2 + \left(\sum_{i=1}^{n} a_i^2 \mu_i^2 + 2 \sum_{i=1}^{n-1} \sum_{j=i+1}^{n} a_i a_j \mu_i \mu_j \right) \end{aligned}$$

To complete the proof, note that the expression in the parentheses is exactly $(\mathbb{E}\, Y)^2$, and recall the identity $\sigma_Y^2 = \mathbb{E}\, Y^2 - (\mathbb{E}\, Y)^2$. □

There is a corresponding statement of Fact 7.16 for the multivariate case. The proof is also omitted here.

Fact 7.32. *If* **X** *and* **Y** *are mutually independent random vectors, then $u(\mathbf{X})$ and $v(\mathbf{Y})$ are independent for any functions u and v.*

Bruno de Finetti was a strong proponent of the subjective approach to probability. He proved an important theorem in 1931 which illuminates the link between exchangeable random variables and independent random variables. Here it is in one of its simplest forms.

Theorem 7.33. *De Finetti's Theorem. Let X_1, X_2, ... be a sequence of* `binom(size = 1, prob = p)` *random variables such that $(X_1, \ldots, X_k)$ are exchangeable for every k. Then there exists a random variable Θ with support* $[0, 1]$ *and PDF $f_\Theta(\theta)$ such that*

$$\mathbb{P}(X_1 = x_1, \ldots, X_k = x_k) = \int_0^1 \theta^{\sum x_i} (1 - \theta)^{k - \sum x_i} f_\Theta(\theta) \, \mathrm{d}\theta, \tag{7.8.9}$$

for all $x_i = 0, 1$, $i = 1, 2, \ldots, k$.

To get a handle on the intuitive content de Finetti's theorem, imagine that we have a *bunch* of coins in our pocket with each having its own unique value of $\theta = \mathbb{P}(\text{Heads})$. We reach into our pocket and select a coin at random according to some probability – say, $f_\Theta(\theta)$. We take the randomly selected coin and flip it k times.

Think carefully: the conditional probability of observing a sequence $X_1 = x_1, \ldots, X_k = x_k$, given a specific coin θ would just be $\theta^{\sum x_i}(1-\theta)^{k-\sum x_i}$, because the coin flips are an independent sequence of Bernoulli trials. But the coin is random, so the Theorem of Total Probability says we can get the *unconditional* probability $\mathbb{P}(X_1 = x_1, \ldots, X_k = x_k)$ by adding up terms that look like

$$\theta^{\sum x_i}(1-\theta)^{k-\sum x_i} f_\Theta(\theta), \tag{7.8.10}$$

where we sum over all possible coins. The right-hand side of Equation 7.8.9 is a sophisticated way to denote this process.

Of course, the integral's value does not change if we jumble the x_i's, so $(X_1, \ldots, X_k)$ are clearly exchangeable. The power of de Finetti's Theorem is that *every* infinite binary exchangeable sequence can be written in the above form.

The connection to subjective probability: our prior information about θ corresponds to $f_\Theta(\theta)$ and the likelihood of the sequence $X_1 = x_1, \ldots, X_k = x_k$ (conditional on θ) corresponds to $\theta^{\sum x_i}(1-\theta)^{k-\sum x_i}$. Compare Equation 7.8.9 to Section 4.8 and Section 7.3.

The multivariate normal distribution immediately generalizes from the bivariate case. If the matrix Σ is nonsingular then the joint PDF of $\mathbf{X} \sim \texttt{mvnorm(mean} = \mu\texttt{, sigma} = \Sigma)$ is

$$f_{\mathbf{X}}(\mathbf{x}) = \frac{1}{(2\pi)^{n/2}\,|\Sigma|^{1/2}} \exp\left\{-\frac{1}{2}(\mathbf{x}-\mu)^\top \Sigma^{-1}(\mathbf{x}-\mu)\right\}, \tag{7.8.11}$$

and the MGF is

$$M_{\mathbf{X}}(\mathbf{t}) = \exp\left\{\mu^\top \mathbf{t} + \frac{1}{2}\mathbf{t}^\top \Sigma \mathbf{t}\right\}. \tag{7.8.12}$$

We will need the following in Chapter 12.

Theorem 7.34. *If* $\mathbf{X} \sim \texttt{mvnorm(mean} = \mu\texttt{, sigma} = \Sigma)$ *and* $\mathbf{A}$ *is any matrix, then the random vector* $\mathbf{Y} = \mathbf{A}\mathbf{X}$ *is distributed*

$$\mathbf{Y} \sim \texttt{mvnorm(mean} = \mathbf{A}\mu\texttt{, sigma} = \mathbf{A}\Sigma\mathbf{A}^{\mathrm{T}}). \tag{7.8.13}$$

Proof. Look at the MGF of $\mathbf{Y}$:

$$\begin{aligned} M_{\mathbf{Y}}(\mathbf{t}) &= \mathbb{E}\exp\left\{\mathbf{t}^{\mathrm{T}}(\mathbf{A}\mathbf{X})\right\}, \\ &= \mathbb{E}\exp\left\{(\mathbf{A}^{\mathrm{T}}\mathbf{t})^{\mathrm{T}}\mathbf{X}\right\}, \\ &= \exp\left\{\mu^{\mathrm{T}}(\mathbf{A}^\top\mathbf{t}) + \frac{1}{2}(\mathbf{A}^{\mathrm{T}}\mathbf{t})^{\mathrm{T}}\Sigma(\mathbf{A}^{\mathrm{T}}\mathbf{t})\right\}, \\ &= \exp\left\{(\mathbf{A}\mu)^{\mathrm{T}}\mathbf{t} + \frac{1}{2}\mathbf{t}^{\mathrm{T}}\left(\mathbf{A}\Sigma\mathbf{A}^{\mathrm{T}}\right)\mathbf{t}\right\}, \end{aligned}$$

and the last expression is the MGF of an $\texttt{mvnorm(mean} = \mathbf{A}\mu\texttt{, sigma} = \mathbf{A}\Sigma\mathbf{A}^{\mathrm{T}})$ distribution.

□

7.9 The Multinomial Distribution

We sample n times, with replacement, from an urn that contains balls of k different types. Let X_1 denote the number of balls in our sample of type 1, let X_2 denote the number of balls of type 2, ... , and let X_k denote the number of balls of type k. Suppose the urn has proportion p_1 of balls of type 1, proportion p_2 of balls of type 2, ..., and proportion p_k of balls of type k. Then the joint PMF of $(X_1, \ldots, X_k)$ is

$$f_{X_1,\ldots,X_k}(x_1, \ldots, x_k) = \binom{n}{x_1\, x_2\, \cdots\, x_k} p_1^{x_1} p_2^{x_2} \cdots p_k^{x_k}, \tag{7.9.1}$$

for $(x_1, \ldots, x_k)$ in the joint support $S_{X_1,\ldots X_K}$. We write

$$(X_1, \ldots, X_k) \sim \mathsf{multinom}(\mathtt{size} = n,\ \mathtt{prob} = \mathbf{p}_{\mathrm{k}\times 1}). \tag{7.9.2}$$

Several comments are in order. First, the joint support set $S_{X_1,\ldots X_K}$ contains all nonnegative integer k-tuples $(x_1, \ldots, x_k)$ such that $x_1 + x_2 + \cdots + x_k = n$. A support set like this is called a *simplex*. Second, the proportions $p_1, p_2, \ldots, p_k$ satisfy $p_i \geq 0$ for all i and $p_1 + p_2 + \cdots + p_k = 1$. Finally, the symbol

$$\binom{n}{x_1\, x_2\, \cdots\, x_k} = \frac{n!}{x_1!\, x_2!\, \cdots x_k!} \tag{7.9.3}$$

is called a *multinomial coefficient* which generalizes the notion of a binomial coefficient we saw in Equation 4.5.1.

The form and notation we have just described matches the R usage but is not standard among other texts. Most other books use the above for a $k-1$ dimension multinomial distribution, because the linear constraint $x_1 + x_2 + \cdots + x_k = n$ means that once the values of X_1, X_2, ..., X_{k-1} are known the final value X_k is determined, not random. Another term used for this is a *singular* distribution.

For the most part we will ignore these difficulties, but the careful reader should keep them in mind. There is not much of a difference in practice, except that below we will use a two-dimensional support set for a three-dimension multinomial distribution. See Figure 7.9.1.

When $k = 2$, we have $x_1 = x$ and $x_2 = n - x$, we have $p_1 = p$ and $p_2 = 1 - p$, and the multinomial coefficient is literally a binomial coefficient. In the previous notation we have thus shown that the $\mathsf{multinom}(\mathtt{size} = n,\ \mathtt{prob} = \mathbf{p}_{2\times 1})$ distribution is the same as a $\mathsf{binom}(\mathtt{size} = n,\ \mathtt{prob} = p)$ distribution.

Example 7.35. Dinner with Barack Obama. During the 2008 U.S. presidential primary, Barack Obama offered to have dinner with three randomly selected monetary contributors to his campaign. Imagine the thousands of people in the contributor database. For the sake of argument, Suppose that the database was approximately representative of the U.S. population as a whole, Suppose Barack Obama wants to have dinner `http://pewresearch.org/pubs/773/fewer-voters-ide`
36 democrat, 27 republican , 37 independent.

Remark 7.36. Here are some facts about the multinomial distribution.

1. The expected value of $(X_1, X_2, \ldots, X_k)$ is $n\mathbf{p}_{k\times 1}$.

2. The variance-covariance matrix Σ is symmetric with diagonal entries $\sigma_i^2 = np_i(1 - p_i)$, $i = 1, 2, \ldots, k$ and off-diagonal entries $\mathrm{Cov}(X_i, X_j) = -np_ip_j$, for $i \neq j$. The correlation between X_i and X_j is therefore $\mathrm{Corr}(X_i, X_j) = -\sqrt{p_ip_j/(1 - p_i)(1 - p_j)}$.

3. The marginal distribution of $(X_1, X_2, \ldots, X_{k-1})$ is multinom(size $= n$, prob $= \mathbf{p}_{(k-1)\times 1}$) with

$$\mathbf{p}_{(k-1)\times 1} = (p_1, p_2, \ldots, p_{k-2}, p_{k-1} + p_k), \tag{7.9.4}$$

and in particular, $X_i \sim$ binom(size $= n$, prob $= p_i$).

7.9.1 How to do it with R

There is support for the multinomial distribution in base R, namely in the `stats` package. The `dmultinom` function represents the PMF and the `rmultinom` function generates random variates.

```
> library(combinat)
> tmp <- t(xsimplex(3, 6))
> p <- apply(tmp, MARGIN = 1, FUN = dmultinom, prob = c(36,
+     27, 37))
> library(prob)
> S <- probspace(tmp, probs = p)
> ProbTable <- xtabs(probs ~ X1 + X2, data = S)
> round(ProbTable, 3)
```

```
   X2
X1      0     1     2     3     4     5     6
  0 0.003 0.011 0.020 0.020 0.011 0.003 0.000
  1 0.015 0.055 0.080 0.058 0.021 0.003 0.000
  2 0.036 0.106 0.116 0.057 0.010 0.000 0.000
  3 0.047 0.103 0.076 0.018 0.000 0.000 0.000
  4 0.034 0.050 0.018 0.000 0.000 0.000 0.000
  5 0.013 0.010 0.000 0.000 0.000 0.000 0.000
  6 0.002 0.000 0.000 0.000 0.000 0.000 0.000
```

Do some examples of `rmultinom`.

Here is another way to do it[4].

[4]Another way to do the plot is with the `scatterplot3d` function in the `scatterplot3d` package [61]. It looks like this:

```
library(scatterplot3d)
X <- t(as.matrix(expand.grid(0:6, 0:6)))
X <- X[ , colSums(X) <= 6]; X <- rbind(X, 6 - colSums(X))
Z <- round(apply(X, 2, function(x) dmultinom(x, prob = 1:3)), 3)
A <- data.frame(x = X[1, ], y = X[2, ], probability = Z)
scatterplot3d(A, type = "h", lwd = 3, box = FALSE)
```

The `scatterplot3d` graph looks better in this example, but the code is clearly more difficult to understand. And with `cloud` one can easily do conditional plots of the form `cloud(z ~x + y|f)`, where `f` is a factor.

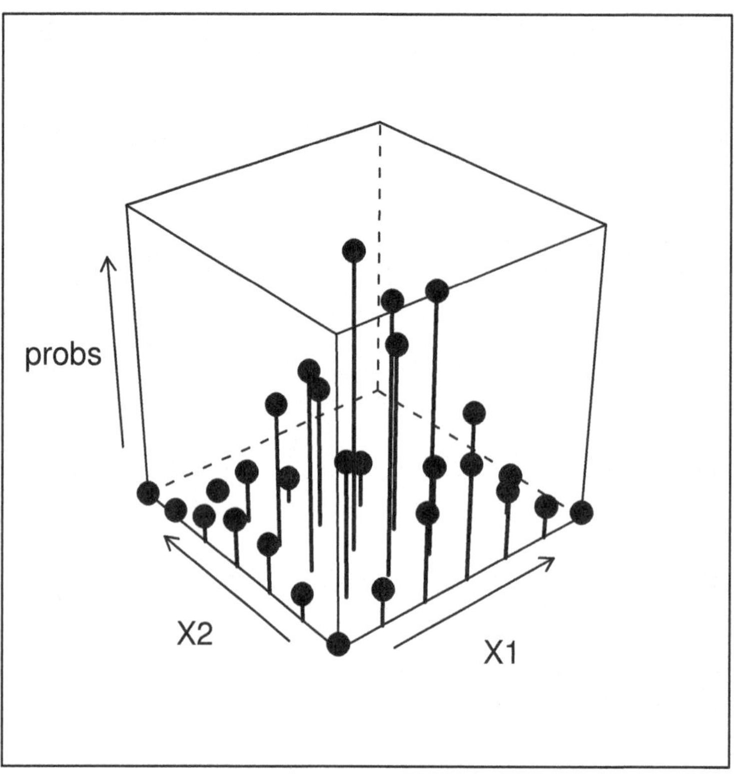

Figure 7.9.1: Plot of a multinomial PMF

Chapter Exercises

Exercise 7.1. Prove that $\mathrm{Cov}(X, Y) = \mathbb{E}(XY) - (\mathbb{E}\, X)(\mathbb{E}\, Y)$.

Exercise 7.2. Suppose $X \sim$ chisq(df $= p_1$) and $Y \sim$ chisq(df $= p_2$) are independent. Find the distribution of $X + Y$ (you may want to refer to Equation 6.5.6).

Exercise 7.3. Show that when X and Y are independent the MGF of $X - Y$ is $M_X(t)M_Y(-t)$. Use this to find the distribution of $X - Y$ when $X \sim$ norm(mean $= \mu_1$, sd $= \sigma_1$) and $Y \sim$ norm(mean $= \mu_2$, sd $= \sigma_2$) are independent.

Chapter 8

Sampling Distributions

This is an important chapter; it is the bridge from probability and descriptive statistics that we studied in Chapters 3 through 7 to inferential statistics which forms the latter part of this book.

Here is the link: we are presented with a *population* about which we would like to learn. And while it would be desirable to examine every single member of the population, we find that it is either impossible or infeasible to for us to do so, thus, we resort to collecting a *sample* instead. We do not lose heart. Our method will suffice, provided the sample is *representative* of the population. A good way to achieve this is to sample *randomly* from the population.

Supposing for the sake of argument that we have collected a random sample, the next task is to make some *sense* out of the data because the complete list of sample information is usually cumbersome, unwieldy. We summarize the data set with a descriptive *statistic*, a quantity calculated from the data (we saw many examples of these in Chapter 3). But our sample was random... therefore, it stands to reason that our statistic will be random, too. How is the statistic distributed?

The probability distribution associated with the population (from which we sample) is called the *population distribution*, and the probability distribution associated with our statistic is called its *sampling distribution*; clearly, the two are interrelated. To learn about the population distribution, it is imperative to know everything we can about the sampling distribution. Such is the goal of this chapter.

We begin by introducing the notion of simple random samples and cataloguing some of their more convenient mathematical properties. Next we focus on what happens in the special case of sampling from the normal distribution (which, again, has several convenient mathematical properties), and in particular, we meet the sampling distribution of $\overline{X}$ and S^2. Then we explore what happens to $\overline{X}$'s sampling distribution when the population is not normal and prove one of the most remarkable theorems in statistics, the Central Limit Theorem (CLT).

With the CLT in hand, we then investigate the sampling distributions of several other popular statistics, taking full advantage of those with a tractable form. We finish the chapter with an exploration of statistics whose sampling distributions are not quite so tractable, and to accomplish this goal we will use simulation methods that are grounded in all of our work in the previous four chapters.

What do I want them to know?

- the notion of population versus simple random sample, parameter versus statistic, and population distribution versus sampling distribution
- the classical sampling distributions of the standard one and two sample statistics

- how to generate a simulated sampling distribution when the statistic is crazy
- the Central Limit Theorem, period.
- some basic concepts related to sampling distribution utility, such as bias and variance

8.1 Simple Random Samples

8.1.1 Simple Random Samples

Definition 8.1. If X_1, X_2, ..., X_n are independent with $X_i \sim f$ for $i = 1, 2, \ldots, n$, then we say that X_1, X_2, ..., X_n are *independent and identically distributed* (i.i.d.) from the population f or alternatively we say that X_1, X_2, ..., X_n are a *simple random sample of size n*, denoted $SRS(n)$, from the population f.

Proposition 8.2. *Let X_1, X_2, ..., X_n be a $SRS(n)$ from a population distribution with mean μ and finite standard deviation σ. Then the mean and standard deviation of $\overline{X}$ are given by the formulas $\mu_{\overline{X}} = \mu$ and $\sigma_{\overline{X}} = \sigma/\sqrt{n}$.*

Proof. Plug in $a_1 = a_2 = \cdots = a_n = 1/n$ in Proposition 7.31. □

The next fact will be useful to us when it comes time to prove the Central Limit Theorem in Section 8.3.

Proposition 8.3. *Let X_1, X_2, ..., X_n be a $SRS(n)$ from a population distribution with MGF $M(t)$. Then the MGF of $\overline{X}$ is given by*

$$M_{\overline{X}}(t) = \left[M\left(\frac{t}{n}\right) \right]^n . \tag{8.1.1}$$

Proof. Go from the definition:

$$\begin{aligned} M_{\overline{X}}(t) &= \mathbb{E}\, \mathrm{e}^{t\overline{X}}, \\ &= \mathbb{E}\, \mathrm{e}^{t(X_1+\cdots+X_n)/n}, \\ &= \mathbb{E}\, \mathrm{e}^{tX_1/n}\mathrm{e}^{tX_2/n}\cdots\mathrm{e}^{tX_n/n}. \end{aligned}$$

And because X_1, X_2, ..., X_n are independent, Proposition 7.13 allows us to distribute the expectation among each term in the product, which is

$$\mathbb{E}\, \mathrm{e}^{tX_1/n}\, \mathbb{E}\, \mathrm{e}^{tX_2/n} \cdots \mathbb{E}\, \mathrm{e}^{tX_n/n}.$$

The last step is to recognize that each term in last product above is exactly $M(t/n)$. □

8.2 Sampling from a Normal Distribution

8.2.1 The Distribution of the Sample Mean

Proposition 8.4. *Let X_1, X_2, ..., X_n be a $SRS(n)$ from a* `norm(mean` $= \mu$, `sd` $= \sigma$) *distribution. Then the sample mean $\overline{X}$ has a* `norm(mean` $= \mu$, `sd` $= \sigma/\sqrt{n}$) *sampling distribution.*

Proof. The mean and standard deviation of $\overline{X}$ follow directly from Proposition 8.2. To address the shape, first remember from Section 6.3 that the norm(mean = μ, sd = σ) MGF is of the form

$$M(t) = \exp\left\{\mu t + \sigma^2 t^2/2\right\}.$$

Now use Proposition 8.3 to find

$$\begin{aligned} M_{\overline{X}}(t) &= \left[M\left(\frac{t}{n}\right)\right]^n, \\ &= \left[\exp\left\{\mu(t/n) + \sigma^2(t/n)^2/2\right\}\right]^n, \\ &= \exp\left\{n \cdot \left[\mu(t/n) + \sigma^2(t/n)^2/2\right]\right\}, \\ &= \exp\left\{\mu t + (\sigma/\sqrt{n})^2 t^2/2\right\}, \end{aligned}$$

and we recognize this last quantity as the MGF of a norm(mean = μ, sd = $\sigma/\sqrt{n}$) distribution. □

8.2.2 The Distribution of the Sample Variance

Theorem 8.5. *Let $X_1, X_2, \ldots, X_n$ be a SRS(n) from a* norm(mean = μ, sd = σ) *distribution, and let*

$$\overline{X} = \sum_{i=1}^{n} X_i \quad \text{and} \quad S^2 = \frac{1}{n-1}\sum_{i=1}^{n}(X_i - \overline{X})^2. \tag{8.2.1}$$

Then

1. *$\overline{X}$ and S^2 are independent, and*
2. *The rescaled sample variance*

$$\frac{(n-1)}{\sigma^2}S^2 = \frac{\sum_{i=1}^{n}(X_i - \overline{X})^2}{\sigma^2} \tag{8.2.2}$$

has a chisq(df = $n-1$) sampling distribution.

Proof. The proof is beyond the scope of the present book, but the theorem is simply too important to be omitted. The interested reader could consult Casella and Berger [13], or Hogg *et al* [43]. □

8.2.3 The Distribution of Student's T Statistic

Proposition 8.6. *Let $X_1, X_2, \ldots, X_n$ be a SRS(n) from a* norm(mean = μ, sd = σ) *distribution. Then the quantity*

$$T = \frac{\overline{X} - \mu}{S/\sqrt{n}} \tag{8.2.3}$$

has a t(df = $n-1$) *sampling distribution.*

Proof. Divide the numerator and denominator by σ and rewrite

$$T = \frac{\frac{\overline{X}-\mu}{\sigma/\sqrt{n}}}{S/\sigma} = \frac{\frac{\overline{X}-\mu}{\sigma/\sqrt{n}}}{\sqrt{\frac{(n-1)S^2}{\sigma^2}\Big/(n-1)}}.$$

Now let

$$Z = \frac{\overline{X} - \mu}{\sigma / \sqrt{n}} \quad \text{and} \quad V = \frac{(n-1)S^2}{\sigma^2},$$

so that

$$T = \frac{Z}{\sqrt{V/r}}, \tag{8.2.4}$$

where $r = n - 1$.

We know from Section 8.2.1 that $Z \sim$ norm(mean = 0, sd = 1) and we know from Section 8.2.2 that $V \sim$ chisq(df $= n - 1$). Further, since we are sampling from a normal distribution, Theorem 8.5 gives that $\overline{X}$ and S^2 are independent and by Fact 7.16 so are Z and V. In summary, the distribution of T is the same as the distribution of the quantity $Z/\sqrt{V/r}$, where $Z \sim$ norm(mean = 0, sd = 1) and $V \sim$ chisq(df $= r$) are independent. This is in fact the definition of Student's t distribution. □

This distribution was first published by W. S. Gosset (1900) under the pseudonym Student, and the distribution has consequently come to be known as Student's t distribution. The PDF of T can be derived explicitly using the techniques of Section 6.4; it takes the form

$$f_X(x) = \frac{\Gamma[(r+1)/2]}{\sqrt{r\pi}\,\Gamma(r/2)} \left(1 + \frac{x^2}{r}\right)^{-(r+1)/2}, \quad -\infty < x < \infty \tag{8.2.5}$$

Any random variable X with the preceding PDF is said to have Student's t distribution with r *degrees of freedom*, and we write $X \sim$ t(df $= r$). The shape of the PDF is similar to the normal, but the tails are considerably heavier. See Figure 8.2.1. As with the normal distribution, there are four functions in R associated with the t distribution, namely `dt`, `pt`, `qt`, and `rt`, which compute the PDF, CDF, quantile function, and generate random variates, respectively.

The code to produce Figure 8.2.1 is

```
> curve(dt(x, df = 30), from = -3, to = 3, lwd = 3, ylab = "y")
> ind <- c(1, 2, 3, 5, 10)
> for (i in ind) curve(dt(x, df = i), -3, 3, add = TRUE)
```

Similar to that done for the normal we may define t_α(df $= n - 1$) as the number on the x-axis such that there is exactly α area under the t(df $= n - 1$) curve to its right.

Example 8.7. Find $t_{0.01}$(df = 23) with the quantile function.

```
> qt(0.01, df = 23, lower.tail = FALSE)
[1] 2.499867
```

Remark 8.8. There are a few things to note about the `t(df` $= r$) distribution.

1. The `t(df` = 1) distribution is the same as the cauchy(location = 0, scale = 1) distribution. The Cauchy distribution is rather pathological and is a counterexample to many famous results.

2. The standard deviation of t(df $= r$) is undefined (that is, infinite) unless $r > 2$. When r is more than 2, the standard deviation is always bigger than one, but decreases to 1 as $r \to \infty$.

3. As $r \to \infty$, the `t(df` $= r$) distribution approaches the norm(mean = 0, sd = 1) distribution.

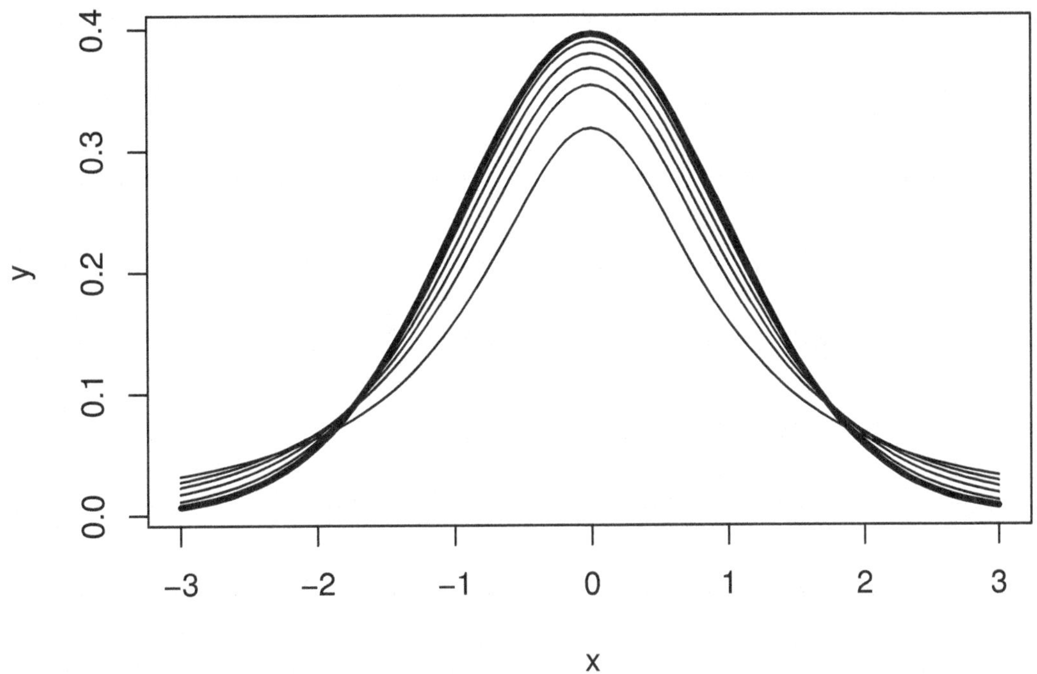

Figure 8.2.1: Student's t distribution for various degrees of freedom

8.3 The Central Limit Theorem

In this section we study the distribution of the sample mean when the underlying distribution is *not* normal. We saw in Section 8.2 that when $X_1, X_2, \ldots, X_n$ is a $SRS(n)$ from a norm(mean $= \mu$, sd $= \sigma$) distribution then $\overline{X} \sim$ norm(mean $= \mu$, sd $= \sigma/\sqrt{n}$). In other words, we may say (owing to Fact 6.24) when the underlying population is normal that the sampling distribution of Z defined by

$$Z = \frac{\overline{X} - \mu}{\sigma/\sqrt{n}} \tag{8.3.1}$$

is norm(mean $= 0$, sd $= 1$).

However, there are many populations that are *not* normal... and the statistician often finds herself sampling from such populations. What can be said in this case? The surprising answer is contained in the following theorem.

Theorem 8.9. ***The Central Limit Theorem.*** *Let $X_1, X_2, \ldots, X_n$ be a $SRS(n)$ from a population distribution with mean μ and finite standard deviation σ. Then the sampling distribution of*

$$Z = \frac{\overline{X} - \mu}{\sigma/\sqrt{n}} \tag{8.3.2}$$

approaches a norm(mean $= 0$, sd $= 1$) *distribution as $n \to \infty$.*

Remark 8.10. We suppose that $X_1, X_2, \ldots, X_n$ are i.i.d., and we learned in Section 8.1.1 that $\overline{X}$ has mean μ and standard deviation $\sigma/\sqrt{n}$, so we already knew that Z has mean 0 and standard deviation 1. The beauty of the CLT is that it addresses the *shape* of Z's distribution when the sample size is large.

Remark 8.11. Notice that the shape of the underlying population's distribution is not mentioned in Theorem 8.9; indeed, the result is true for any population that is well-behaved enough to have a finite standard deviation. In particular, if the population is normally distributed then we know from Section 8.2.1 that the distribution of $\overline{X}$ (and Z by extension) is *exactly* normal, for *every* n.

Remark 8.12. How large is "sufficiently large"? It is here that the shape of the underlying population distribution plays a role. For populations with distributions that are approximately symmetric and mound-shaped, the samples may need to be only of size four or five, while for highly skewed or heavy-tailed populations the samples may need to be much larger for the distribution of the sample means to begin to show a bell-shape. Regardless, for a given population distribution (with finite standard deviation) the approximation tends to be better for larger sample sizes.

8.3.1 How to do it with R

The `TeachingDemos` package [79] has `clt.examp` and the `distrTeach` [74] package has `illustrateCLT`. Try the following at the command line (output omitted):

```
> library(TeachingDemos)
> example(clt.examp)
```

and

```
> library(distrTeach)
> example(illustrateCLT)
```

The `IPSUR` package has the functions `clt1`, `clt2`, and `clt3` (see Exercise 8.2 at the end of this chapter). Its purpose is to investigate what happens to the sampling distribution of $\overline{X}$ when the population distribution is mound shaped, finite support, and skewed, namely t(`df` = 3), unif(a = 0, b = 10) and gamma(`shape` = 1.21, `scale` = 1/2.37), respectively.

For example, when the command `clt1()` is issued a plot window opens to show a graph of the PDF of a t(`df` = 3) distribution. On the display are shown numerical values of the population mean and variance. While the students examine the graph the computer is simulating random samples of size `sample.size = 2` from the `population = "rt"` distribution a total of `N.iter = 100000` times, and sample means are calculated of each sample. Next follows a histogram of the simulated sample means, which closely approximates the sampling distribution of $\overline{X}$, see Section 8.5. Also show are the sample mean and sample variance of all of the simulated $\overline{X}$s. As a final step, when the student clicks the second plot, a normal curve with the same mean and variance as the simulated $\overline{X}$s is superimposed over the histogram. Students should compare the population theoretical mean and variance to the simulated mean and variance of the sampling distribution. They should also compare the shape of the simulated sampling distribution to the shape of the normal distribution.

The three separate `clt1`, `clt2`, and `clt3` functions were written so that students could compare what happens overall when the shape of the population distribution changes. It would be possible to combine all three into one big function, `clt` which covers all three cases (and more).

8.4 Sampling Distributions of Two-Sample Statistics

There are often two populations under consideration, and it sometimes of interest to compare properties between groups. To do so we take independent samples from each population and calculate respective sample statistics for comparison. In some simple cases the sampling distribution of the comparison is known and easy to derive; such cases are the subject of the present section.

8.4.1 Difference of Independent Sample Means

Proposition 8.13. *Let $X_1, X_2, \ldots, X_{n_1}$ be an $SRS(n_1)$ from a* `norm(mean =` μ_X`, sd =` σ_X`)` *distribution and let $Y_1, Y_2, \ldots, Y_{n_2}$ be an $SRS(n_2)$ from a* `norm(mean =` μ_Y`, sd =` σ_Y`)` *distribution. Suppose that $X_1, X_2, \ldots, X_{n_1}$ and $Y_1, Y_2, \ldots, Y_{n_2}$ are independent samples. Then the quantity*

$$\frac{\overline{X} - \overline{Y} - (\mu_X - \mu_Y)}{\sqrt{\sigma_X^2 \big/ n_1 + \sigma_Y^2 \big/ n_2}} \tag{8.4.1}$$

has a `norm(mean = 0, sd = 1)` *sampling distribution. Equivalently, $\overline{X} - \overline{Y}$ has a* `norm(mean =` $\mu_X - \mu_Y$`, sd =` $\sqrt{\sigma_X^2 \big/ n_1 + \sigma_Y^2 \big/ n_2}$`)` *sampling distribution.*

Proof. We know that $\overline{X}$ is `norm(mean =` μ_X`, sd =` $\sigma_X / \sqrt{n_1}$`)` and we also know that $\overline{Y}$ is `norm(mean =` μ_Y`, sd =` $\sigma_Y / \sqrt{n_2}$`)`. And since the samples $X_1, X_2, \ldots, X_{n_1}$ and $Y_1, Y_2, \ldots, Y_{n_2}$ are independent, so too are $\overline{X}$ and $\overline{Y}$. The distribution of their difference is thus normal as well, and the mean and standard deviation are given by Proposition 7.20. □

Remark 8.14. Even if the distribution of one or both of the samples is not normal, the quantity in Equation 8.4.1 will be approximately normal provided both sample sizes are large.

Remark 8.15. For the special case of $\mu_X = \mu_Y$ we have shown that

$$\frac{\overline{X} - \overline{Y}}{\sqrt{\sigma_X^2 / n_1 + \sigma_Y^2 / n_2}} \tag{8.4.2}$$

has a `norm(mean = 0, sd = 1)` sampling distribution, or in other words, $\overline{X} - \overline{Y}$ has a `norm(mean = 0, sd =` $\sqrt{\sigma_X^2 / n_1 + \sigma_Y^2 / n_2}$`)` sampling distribution. This will be important when it comes time to do hypothesis tests; see Section 9.3.

8.4.2 Difference of Independent Sample Proportions

Proposition 8.16. *Let $X_1, X_2, \ldots, X_{n_1}$ be an $SRS(n_1)$ from a* `binom(size = 1, prob =` p_1`)` *distribution and let $Y_1, Y_2, \ldots, Y_{n_2}$ be an $SRS(n_2)$ from a* `binom(size = 1, prob =` p_2`)` *distribution. Suppose that $X_1, X_2, \ldots, X_{n_1}$ and $Y_1, Y_2, \ldots, Y_{n_2}$ are independent samples. Define*

$$\hat{p}_1 = \frac{1}{n_1} \sum_{i=1}^{n_1} X_i \quad \textit{and} \quad \hat{p}_2 = \frac{1}{n_2} \sum_{j=1}^{n_2} Y_j. \tag{8.4.3}$$

Then the sampling distribution of

$$\frac{\hat{p}_1 - \hat{p}_2 - (p_1 - p_2)}{\sqrt{\frac{p_1(1-p_1)}{n_1} + \frac{p_2(1-p_2)}{n_2}}} \tag{8.4.4}$$

approaches a norm(mean $= 0$, sd $= 1$) *distribution as both* $n_1, n_2 \to \infty$. *In other words, the sampling distribution of* $\hat{p}_1 - \hat{p}_2$ *is approximately*

$$\text{norm}\left(\text{mean} = p_1 - p_2,\ \text{sd} = \sqrt{\frac{p_1(1-p_1)}{n_1} + \frac{p_2(1-p_2)}{n_2}}\right), \tag{8.4.5}$$

provided both n_1 *and* n_2 *are sufficiently large.*

Proof. We know that $\hat{p}_1$ is approximately normal for n_1 sufficiently large by the CLT, and we know that $\hat{p}_2$ is approximately normal for n_2 sufficiently large, also by the CLT. Further, $\hat{p}_1$ and $\hat{p}_2$ are independent since they are derived from independent samples. And a difference of independent (approximately) normal distributions is (approximately) normal, by Exercise 7.3[1]. The expressions for the mean and standard deviation follow immediately from Proposition 7.20 combined with the formulas for the binom(size $= 1$, prob $= p$) distribution from Chapter 5. □

8.4.3 Ratio of Independent Sample Variances

Proposition 8.18. *Let* $X_1, X_2, \ldots, X_{n_1}$ *be an* $SRS(n_1)$ *from a* norm(mean $= \mu_X$, sd $= \sigma_X$) *distribution and let* $Y_1, Y_2, \ldots, Y_{n_2}$ *be an* $SRS(n_2)$ *from a* norm(mean $= \mu_Y$, sd $= \sigma_Y$) *distribution. Suppose that* $X_1, X_2, \ldots, X_{n_1}$ *and* $Y_1, Y_2, \ldots, Y_{n_2}$ *are independent samples. Then the ratio*

$$F = \frac{\sigma_Y^2 S_X^2}{\sigma_X^2 S_Y^2} \tag{8.4.6}$$

has an f(df1 $= n_1 - 1$, df2 $= n_2 - 1$) *sampling distribution.*

Proof. We know from Theorem 8.5 that $(n_1 - 1)S_X^2/\sigma_X^2$ is distributed chisq(df $= n_1 - 1$) and $(n_2 - 1)S_Y^2/\sigma_Y^2$ is distributed chisq(df $= n_2 - 1$). Now write

$$F = \frac{\sigma_Y^2 S_X^2}{\sigma_X^2 S_Y^2} = \frac{(n_1 - 1)S_Y^2 \big/ (n_1 - 1)}{(n_2 - 1)S_Y^2 \big/ (n_2 - 1)} \cdot \frac{1/\sigma_X^2}{1/\sigma_Y^2},$$

by multiplying and dividing the numerator with $n_1 - 1$ and doing likewise for the denominator with $n_2 - 1$. Now we may regroup the terms into

$$F = \frac{\frac{(n_1-1)S_X^2}{\sigma_X^2} \Big/ (n_1 - 1)}{\frac{(n_2-1)S_Y^2}{\sigma_Y^2} \Big/ (n_2 - 1)},$$

and we recognize F to be the ratio of independent chisq distributions, each divided by its respective numerator df $= n_1 - 1$ and denominator df $= n_1 - 1$ degrees of freedom. This is, indeed, the definition of Snedecor's F distribution. □

1

Remark 8.17. This does not explicitly follow, because of our cavalier use of "approximately" in too many places. To be more thorough, however, would require more concepts than we can afford at the moment. The interested reader may consult a more advanced text, specifically the topic of weak convergence, that is, convergence in distribution.

Remark 8.19. For the special case of $\sigma_X = \sigma_Y$ we have shown that

$$F = \frac{S_X^2}{S_Y^2} \tag{8.4.7}$$

has an f(`df1` $= n_1 - 1$, `df2` $= n_2 - 1$) sampling distribution. This will be important in Chapters 9 onward.

8.5 Simulated Sampling Distributions

Some comparisons are meaningful, but their sampling distribution is not quite so tidy to describe analytically. What do we do then?

As it turns out, we do not need to know the exact analytical form of the sampling distribution; sometimes it is enough to approximate it with a simulated distribution. In this section we will show you how. Note that R is particularly well suited to compute simulated sampling distributions, much more so than, say, SPSS or SAS.

8.5.1 The Interquartile Range

```
> iqrs <- replicate(100, IQR(rnorm(100)))
```

We can look at the mean of the simulated values

```
> mean(iqrs)    # close to 1
[1] 1.322562
```

and we can see the standard deviation

```
> sd(iqrs)
[1] 0.1694132
```

Now let's take a look at a plot of the simulated values

8.5.2 The Median Absolute Deviation

```
> mads <- replicate(100, mad(rnorm(100)))
```

We can look at the mean of the simulated values

```
> mean(mads)    # close to 1.349
[1] 0.9833985
```

and we can see the standard deviation

```
> sd(mads)
[1] 0.1139002
```

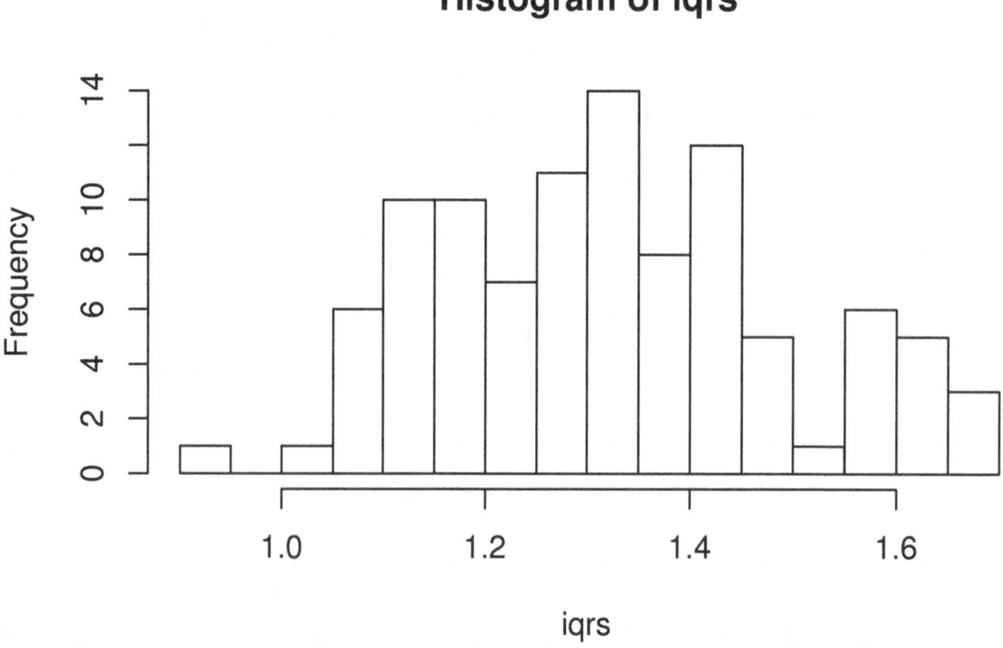

Figure 8.5.1: Plot of simulated IQRs

Now let's take a look at a plot of the simulated values

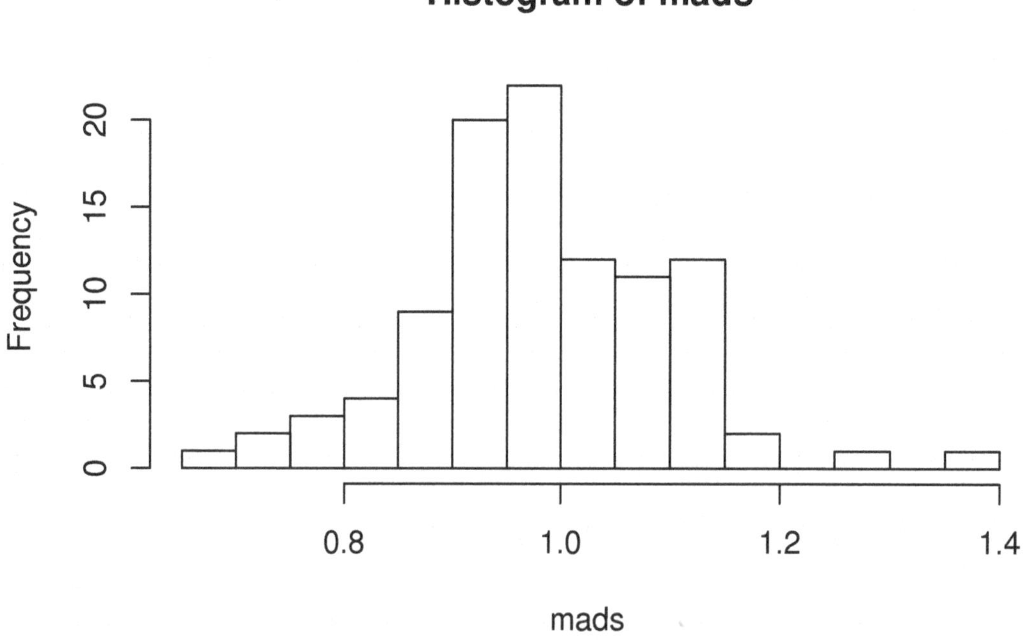

Figure 8.5.2: Plot of simulated MADs

Chapter Exercises

Exercise 8.1. Suppose that we observe a random sample $X_1, X_2, \ldots, X_n$ of size $SRS(n = 19)$ from a norm(mean =20) distribution.

1. What is the mean of $\overline{X}$?
2. What is the standard deviation of $\overline{X}$?
3. What is the distribution of $\overline{X}$? (approximately)
4. Find $\mathbb{P}(a < \overline{X} \leq b)$
5. Find $\mathbb{P}(\overline{X} > c)$.

Exercise 8.2. In this exercise we will investigate how the shape of the population distribution affects the time until the distribution of $\overline{X}$ is acceptably normal.

Answer the questions and write a report about what you have learned. Use plots and histograms to support your conclusions. See Appendix F for instructions about writing reports with R. For these problems, the discussion/interpretation parts are the most important, so be sure to ANSWER THE WHOLE QUESTION.

The Central Limit Theorem

For Questions 1-3, we assume that we have observed random variables $X_1, X_2, \ldots, X_n$ that are an $SRS(n)$ from a given population (depending on the problem) and we want to investigate the distribution of $\overline{X}$ as the sample size n increases.

1. The population of interest in this problem has a Student's t distribution with $r = 3$ degrees of freedom. We begin our investigation with a sample size of $n = 2$. Open an R session, make sure to type `library(IPSUR)` and then follow that with `clt1()`.

   (a) Look closely and thoughtfully at the first graph. How would you describe the population distribution? Think back to the different properties of distributions in Chapter 3. Is the graph symmetric? Skewed? Does it have heavy tails or thin tails? What else can you say?

   (b) What is the population mean μ and the population variance σ^2? (Read these from the first graph.)

   (c) The second graph shows (after a few seconds) a relative frequency histogram which closely approximates the distribution of $\overline{X}$. Record the values of `mean(xbar)` and `var(xbar)`, where `xbar` denotes the vector that contains the simulated sample means. Use the answers from part (b) to calculate what these estimates *should* be, based on what you know about the theoretical mean and variance of $\overline{X}$. How well do your answers to parts (b) and (c) agree?

   (d) Click on the histogram to superimpose a red normal curve, which is the theoretical limit of the distribution of $\overline{X}$ as $n \to \infty$. How well do the histogram and the normal curve match? Describe the differences between the two distributions. When judging between the two, do not worry so much about the scale (the graphs are being rescaled automatically, anyway). Rather, look at the peak: does the histogram poke through the top of the normal curve? How about on the sides: are there patches of white space between the histogram and line on either side (or both)? How do the curvature of the histogram and the line compare? Check down by the tails: does the red line drop off visibly below the level of the histogram, or do they taper off at the same height?

(e) We can increase our sample size from 2 to 11 with the command `clt1(sample.size = 11)`. Return to the command prompt to do this. Answer parts (b) and (c) for this new sample size.

(f) Go back to `clt1` and increase the `sample.size` from 11 to 31. Answer parts (b) and (c) for this new sample size.

(g) Comment on whether it appears that the histogram and the red curve are "noticeably different" or whether they are "essentially the same" for the largest sample size $n = 31$. If they are still "noticeably different" at $n = 31$, how large does n need to be until they are "essentially the same"? (Experiment with different values of n).

2. Repeat Question 1 for the function `clt2`. In this problem, the population of interest has a unif(`min` = 0, `max` = 10) distribution.

3. Repeat Question 1 for the function `clt3`. In this problem, the population of interest has a gamma(`shape` = 1.21, `rate` = 1/2.37) distribution.

4. Summarize what you have learned. In your own words, what is the general trend that is being displayed in these histograms, as the sample size n increases from 2 to 11, on to 31, and onward?

5. How would you describe the relationship between the ***shape*** of the population distribution and the ***speed*** at which $\overline{X}$'s distribution converges to normal? In particular, consider a population which is highly **skewed**. Will we need a relatively *large* sample size or a relatively *small* sample size in order for $\overline{X}$'s distribution to be approximately bell shaped?

Exercise 8.3. Let $X_1, \ldots, X_{25}$ be a random sample from a norm(`mean` = 37, `sd` = 45) distribution, and let $\overline{X}$ be the sample mean of these $n = 25$ observations. Find the following probabilities.

1. How is $\overline{X}$ distributed?

   norm(`mean` = 37, `sd` = $45/\sqrt{25}$)

2. Find $\mathbb{P}(\overline{X} > 43.1)$.

```
> pnorm(43.1, mean = 37, sd = 9, lower.tail = FALSE)

[1] 0.2489563
```

Chapter 9

Estimation

We will discuss two branches of estimation procedures: point estimation and interval estimation. We briefly discuss point estimation first and then spend the rest of the chapter on interval estimation.

We find an estimator with the methods of Section 9.1. We make some assumptions about the underlying population distribution and use what we know from Chapter 8 about sampling distributions both to study how the estimator will perform, and to find intervals of confidence for underlying parameters associated with the population distribution. Once we have confidence intervals we can do inference in the form of hypothesis tests in the next chapter.

What do I want them to know?

- how to look at a problem, identify a reasonable model, and estimate a parameter associated with the model
- about maximum likelihood, and in particular, how to
  - eyeball a likelihood to get a maximum
  - use calculus to find an MLE for one-parameter families
- about properties of the estimators they find, such as bias, minimum variance, MSE
- point versus interval estimation, and how to find and interpret confidence intervals for basic experimental designs
- the concept of margin of error and its relationship to sample size

9.1 Point Estimation

The following example is how I was introduced to maximum likelihood.

Example 9.1. Suppose we have a small pond in our backyard, and in the pond there live some fish. We would like to know how many fish live in the pond. How can we estimate this? One procedure developed by researchers is the capture-recapture method. Here is how it works.

We will fish from the pond and suppose that we capture $M = 7$ fish. On each caught fish we attach an unobtrusive tag to the fish's tail, and release it back into the water.

Next, we wait a few days for the fish to remix and become accustomed to their new tag. Then we go fishing again. On the second trip some of the fish we catch may be tagged; some may not be. Let X denote the number of caught fish which are tagged[1], and suppose for the sake of argument that we catch $K = 4$ fish and we find that 3 of them are tagged.

Now let F denote the (unknown) total number of fish in the pond. We know that $F \geq 7$, because we tagged that many on the first trip. In fact, if we let N denote the number of untagged fish in the pond, then $F = M + N$. We have sampled $K = 4$ times, without replacement, from an urn which has $M = 7$ white balls and $N = F - M$ black balls, and we have observed $x = 3$ of them to be white. What is the probability of this?

Looking back to Section 5.6, we see that the random variable X has a hyper(m $= M$, n $= F - M$, k $= K$) distribution. Therefore, for an observed value $X = x$ the probability would be

$$\mathbb{P}(X = x) = \frac{\binom{M}{x}\binom{F-M}{K-x}}{\binom{F}{K}}.$$

First we notice that F must be at least 7. Could F be equal to seven? If $F = 7$ then all of the fish would have been tagged on the first run, and there would be no untagged fish in the pond, thus, $\mathbb{P}(3 \text{ successes in } 4 \text{ trials}) = 0$.

What about $F = 8$; what would be the probability of observing $X = 3$ tagged fish?

$$\mathbb{P}(3 \text{ successes in } 4 \text{ trials}) = \frac{\binom{7}{3}\binom{1}{1}}{\binom{8}{4}} = \frac{35}{70} = 0.5.$$

Similarly, if $F = 9$ then the probability of observing $X = 3$ tagged fish would be

$$\mathbb{P}(3 \text{ successes in } 4 \text{ trials}) = \frac{\binom{7}{3}\binom{2}{1}}{\binom{9}{4}} = \frac{70}{126} \approx 0.556.$$

We can see already that the observed data $X = 3$ is more likely when $F = 9$ than it is when $F = 8$. And here lies the genius of Sir Ronald Aylmer Fisher: he asks, "What is the value of F which has the highest likelihood?" In other words, for all of the different possible values of F, which one makes the above probability the biggest? We can answer this question with a plot of $\mathbb{P}(X = x)$ versus F. See Figure 9.1.1.

Example 9.2. In the last example we were only concerned with how many fish were in the pond, but now, we will ask a different question. Suppose it is known that there are only two species of fish in the pond: smallmouth bass (*Micropterus dolomieu*) and bluegill (*Lepomis macrochirus*); perhaps we built the pond some years ago and stocked it with only these two species. We would like to estimate the proportion of fish in the pond which are bass.

Let $p =$ the proportion of bass. Without any other information, it is conceivable for p to be any value in the interval $[0, 1]$, but for the sake of argument we will suppose that p falls strictly between 0 and 1. How can we learn about the true value of p? Go fishing! As before, we will use catch-and-release, but unlike before, we will not tag the fish. We will simply note the species of any caught fish before returning it to the pond.

[1]It is theoretically possible that we could catch the same tagged fish more than once, which would inflate our count of tagged fish. To avoid this difficulty, suppose that on the second trip we use a tank on the boat to hold the caught fish until data collection is completed.

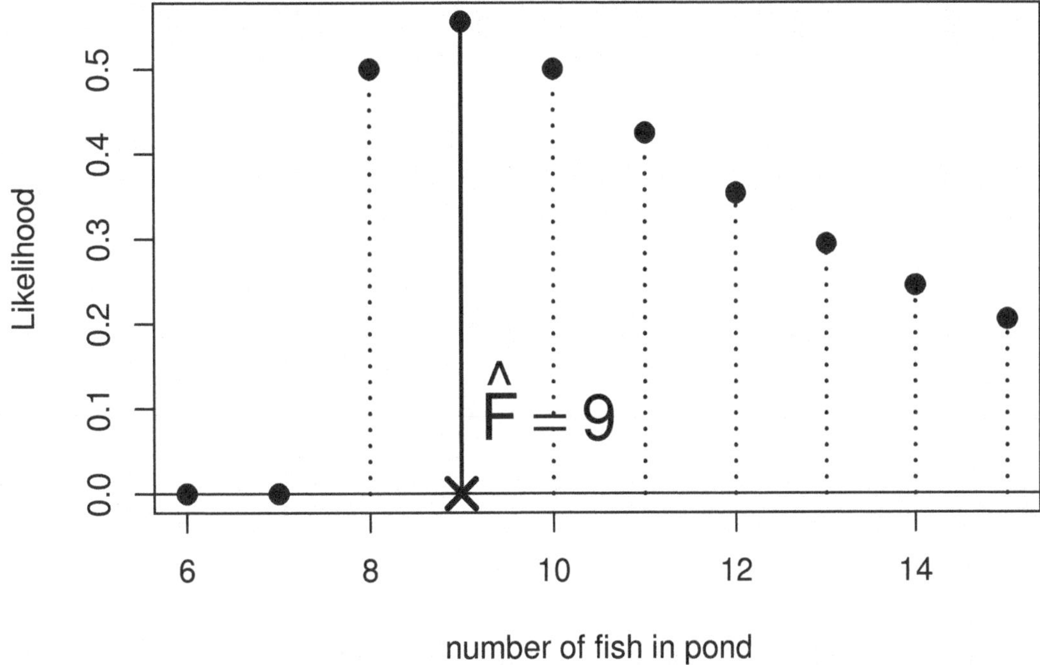

Figure 9.1.1: Capture-recapture experiment

Suppose we catch n fish. Let

$$X_i = \begin{cases} 1, & \text{if the ith fish is a bass,} \\ 0, & \text{if the ith fish is a bluegill.} \end{cases}$$

Since we are returning the fish to the pond once caught, we may think of this as a sampling scheme with replacement where the proportion of bass p does not change. Given that we allow the fish sufficient time to "mix" once returned, it is not completely unreasonable to model our fishing experiment as a sequence of Bernoulli trials, so that the X_i's would be i.i.d. binom(`size` = 1, `prob` = p). Under those assumptions we would have

$$\begin{aligned} \mathbb{P}(X_1 = x_1, X_2 = x_2, \ldots, X_n = x_n) &= \mathbb{P}(X_1 = x_1)\, \mathbb{P}(X_2 = x_2) \cdots \mathbb{P}(X_n = x_n), \\ &= p^{x_1}(1-p)^{x_1}\, p^{x_2}(1-p)^{x_2} \cdots p^{x_n}(1-p)^{x_n}, \\ &= p^{\sum x_i}(1-p)^{n-\sum x_i}. \end{aligned}$$

That is,

$$\mathbb{P}(X_1 = x_1, X_2 = x_2, \ldots, X_n = x_n) = p^{\sum x_i}(1-p)^{n-\sum x_i}.$$

This last quantity is a function of p, called the *likelihood function* $L(p)$:

$$L(p) = p^{\sum x_i}(1-p)^{n-\sum x_i}.$$

A graph of L for values of $\sum x_i = 3,\ 4$, and 5 when $n = 7$ is shown in Figure 9.1.2.

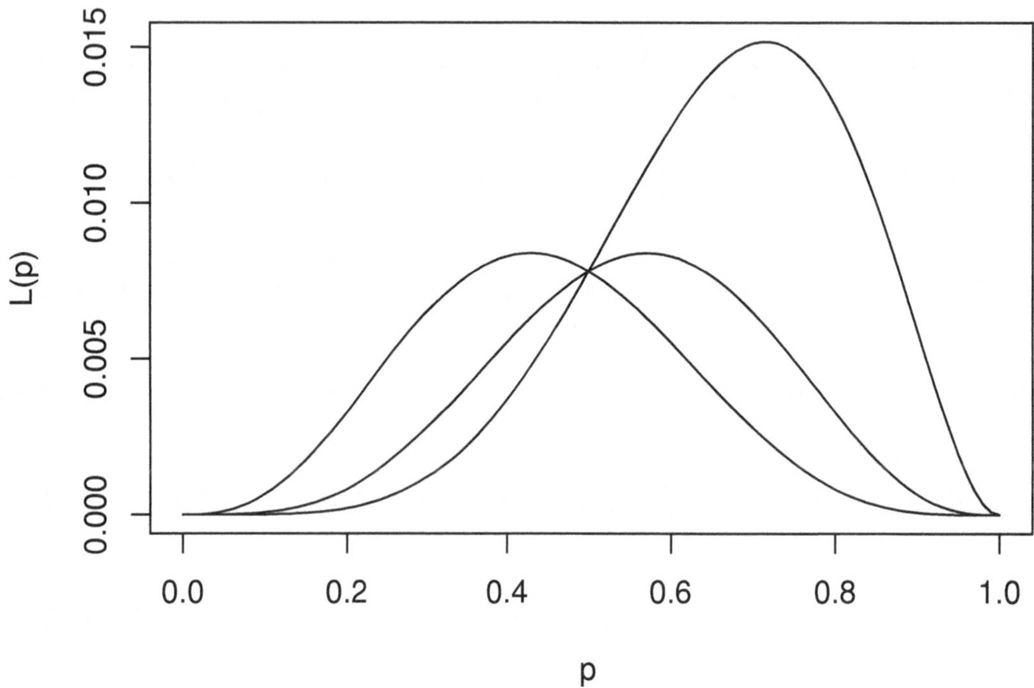

Figure 9.1.2: Assorted likelihood functions for fishing, part two

Three graphs are shown of L when $\sum x_i$ equals 3, 4, and 5, respectively, from left to right. We pick an L that matches the observed data and then maximize L as a function of p. If $\sum x_i = 4$, then the maximum appears to occur somewhere around $p \approx 0.6$.

```
> curve(x^5 * (1 - x)^2, from = 0, to = 1, xlab = "p", ylab = "L(p)")
> curve(x^4 * (1 - x)^3, from = 0, to = 1, add = TRUE)
> curve(x^3 * (1 - x)^4, 0, 1, add = TRUE)
```

We want the value of p which has the highest likelihood, that is, we again wish to maximize the likelihood. We know from calculus (see Appendix E.2) to differentiate L and set $L' = 0$ to find a maximum.

$$L'(p) = \left(\sum x_i\right) p^{\sum x_i - 1}(1-p)^{n-\sum x_i} + p^{\sum x_i}\left(n - \sum x_i\right)(1-p)^{n-\sum x_i - 1}(-1).$$

The derivative vanishes ($L' = 0$) when

$$\begin{aligned}
\left(\sum x_i\right) p^{\sum x_i - 1}(1-p)^{n-\sum x_i} &= p^{\sum x_i}\left(n - \sum x_i\right)(1-p)^{n-\sum x_i - 1}, \\
\sum x_i(1-p) &= \left(n - \sum x_i\right)p, \\
\sum x_i - p\sum x_i &= np - p\sum x_i, \\
\frac{1}{n}\sum_{i=1}^{n} x_i &= p.
\end{aligned}$$

This "best" p, the one which maximizes the likelihood, is called the maximum likelihood estimator (MLE) of p and is denoted $\hat{p}$. That is,

$$\hat{p} = \frac{\sum_{i=1}^{n} x_i}{n} = \overline{x}. \tag{9.1.1}$$

Remark 9.3. Strictly speaking we have only shown that the derivative equals zero at $\hat{p}$, so it is theoretically possible that the critical value $\hat{p} = \overline{x}$ is located at a minimum[2] instead of a maximum! We should be thorough and check that $L' > 0$ when $p < \overline{x}$ and $L' < 0$ when $p > \overline{x}$. Then by the First Derivative Test (Theorem E.6) we could be certain that $\hat{p} = \overline{x}$ is indeed a maximum likelihood estimator, and not a minimum likelihood estimator.

The result is shown in Figure 9.1.3.

In general, we have a family of PDFs $f(x|\theta)$ indexed by a parameter θ in some parameter space Θ. We want to learn about θ. We take a $SRS(n)$:

$$X_1, X_2, \ldots, X_n \text{ which are i.i.d. f(x}|\theta). \tag{9.1.2}$$

Definition 9.4. Given the observed data $x_1, x_2, \ldots, x_n$, the *likelihood function* L is defined by

$$L(\theta) = \prod_{i=1}^{n} f(x_i|\theta), \quad \theta \in \Theta.$$

The next step is to maximize L. The method we will use in this book is to find the derivative L' and solve the equation $L'(\theta) = 0$. Call a solution $\hat{\theta}$. We will check that L is maximized at $\hat{\theta}$ using the First Derivative Test or the Second Derivative Test $\left(L''(\hat{\theta}) < 0\right)$.

Definition 9.5. A value θ that maximizes L is called a *maximum likelihood estimator* (MLE) and is denoted $\hat{\theta}$. It is a function of the sample, $\hat{\theta} = \hat{\theta}(X_1, X_2, \ldots, X_n)$, and is called a *point estimator* of θ.

[2]We can tell from the graph that our value of $\hat{p}$ is a maximum instead of a minimum so we do not really need to worry for this example. Other examples are not so easy, however, and we should be careful to be cognizant of this extra step.

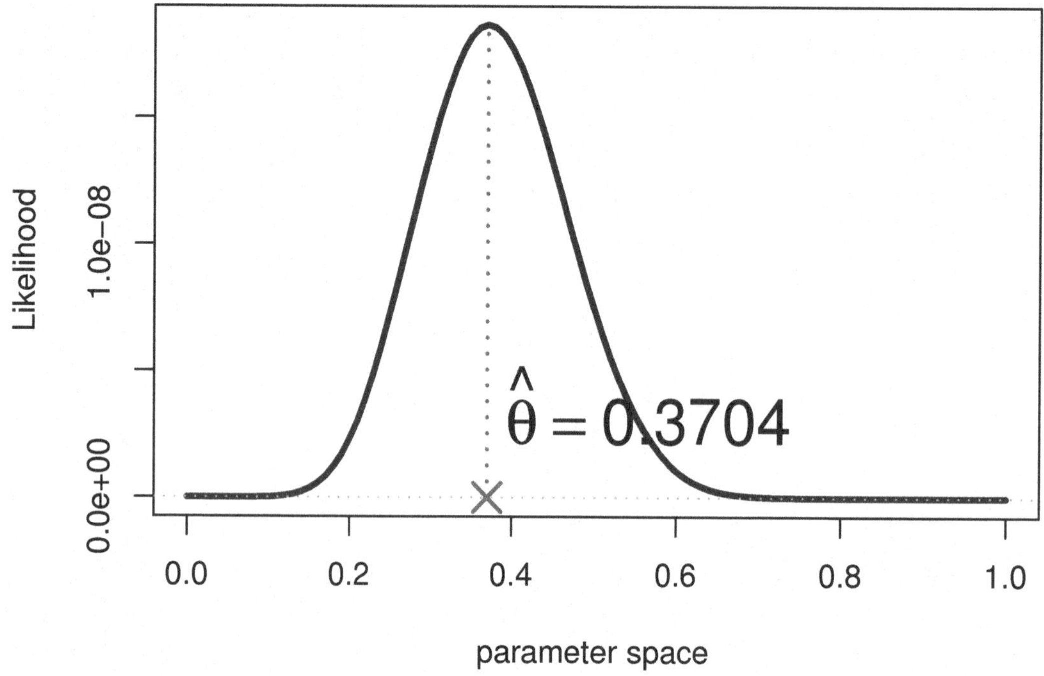

Figure 9.1.3: Species maximum likelihood

Remark 9.6. Some comments about maximum likelihood estimators:

- Often it is easier to maximize the *log-likelihood* $l(\theta) = \ln L(\theta)$ instead of the likelihood L. Since the logarithmic function $y = \ln x$ is a monotone transformation, the solutions to both problems are the same.
- MLEs do not always exist (for instance, sometimes the likelihood has a vertical asymptote), and even when they do exist, they are not always unique (imagine a function with a bunch of humps of equal height). For any given problem, there could be zero, one, or any number of values of θ for which $L(\theta)$ is a maximum.
- The problems we encounter in this book are all very nice with likelihood functions that have closed form representations and which are optimized by some calculus acrobatics. In practice, however, likelihood functions are sometimes nasty in which case we are obliged to use numerical methods to find maxima (if there are any).
- MLEs are just one of <u>many</u> possible estimators. One of the more popular alternatives are the *method of moments estimators*; see Casella and Berger [13] for more.

Notice, in Example 9.2 we had X_i i.i.d. `binom(size` $= 1$, `prob` $= p)$, and we saw that the

MLE was $\hat{p} = \overline{X}$. But further

$$\begin{aligned} \mathbb{E}\,\overline{X} &= \mathbb{E}\,\frac{X_1 + X_2 + \cdots + X_n}{n}, \\ &= \frac{1}{n}\left(\mathbb{E}\,X_1 + \mathbb{E}\,X_2 + \cdots + \mathbb{E}\,X_n\right), \\ &= \frac{1}{n}(np), \\ &= p, \end{aligned}$$

which is exactly the same as the parameter which we estimated. More concisely, $\mathbb{E}\,\hat{p} = p$, that is, on the average, the estimator is exactly right.

Definition 9.7. Let $s(X_1, X_2, \ldots, X_n)$ be a statistic which estimates θ. If

$$\mathbb{E}\,s(X_1, X_2, \ldots, X_n) = \theta,$$

then the statistic $s(X_1, X_2, \ldots, X_n)$ is said to be an *unbiased estimator* of θ. Otherwise, it is *biased*.

Example 9.8. Let X_1, X_2, ..., X_n be an $SRS(n)$ from a norm(mean $= \mu$, sd $= \sigma$) distribution. It can be shown (in Exercise 9.1) that if $\theta = (\mu, \sigma^2)$ then the MLE of θ is

$$\hat{\theta} = (\hat{\mu}, \hat{\sigma}^2), \tag{9.1.3}$$

where $\hat{\mu} = \overline{X}$ and

$$\hat{\sigma^2} = \frac{1}{n}\sum_{i=1}^{n}\left(X_i - \overline{X}\right)^2 = \frac{n-1}{n}S^2. \tag{9.1.4}$$

We of course know from 8.2 that $\hat{\mu}$ is unbiased. What about $\hat{\sigma^2}$? Let us check:

$$\begin{aligned} \mathbb{E}\,\hat{\sigma^2} &= \mathbb{E}\,\frac{n-1}{n}S^2 \\ &= \mathbb{E}\left(\frac{\sigma^2}{n}\frac{(n-1)S^2}{\sigma^2}\right) \\ &= \frac{\sigma^2}{n}\,\mathbb{E}\;\mathrm{chisq}(\mathrm{df} = n-1) \\ &= \frac{\sigma^2}{n}(n-1), \end{aligned}$$

from which we may conclude two things:

1. $\hat{\sigma^2}$ is a biased estimator of σ^2, and
2. $S^2 = n\hat{\sigma^2}/(n-1)$ is an unbiased estimator of σ^2.

One of the most common questions in an introductory statistics class is, "Why do we divide by $n-1$ when we compute the sample variance? Why do we not divide by n?" We see now that division by n amounts to the use of a *biased* estimator for σ^2, that is, if we divided by n then on the average we would *underestimate* the true value of σ^2. We use $n-1$ so that, on the average, our estimator of σ^2 will be exactly right.

9.1.1 How to do it with R

R can be used to find maximum likelihood estimators in a lot of diverse settings. We will discuss only the most basic here and will leave the rest to more sophisticated texts.

For one parameter estimation problems we may use the `optimize` function to find MLEs. The arguments are the function to be maximized (the likelihood function), the range over which the optimization is to take place, and optionally any other arguments to be passed to the likelihood if needed.

Let us see how to do Example 9.2. Recall that our likelihood function was given by

$$L(p) = p^{\sum x_i}(1-p)^{n-\sum x_i}. \tag{9.1.5}$$

Notice that the likelihood is just a product of binom(`size` = 1, `prob` = p) PMFs. We first give some sample data (in the vector `datavals`), next we define the likelihood function `L`, and finally we `optimize` `L` over the range `c(0,1)`.

```
> x <- mtcars$am
> L <- function(p, x) prod(dbinom(x, size = 1, prob = p))
> optimize(L, interval = c(0, 1), x = x, maximum = TRUE)

$maximum
[1] 0.4062458

$objective
[1] 4.099989e-10
```

Note that the `optimize` function by default minimizes the function `L`, so we have to set `maximum = TRUE` to get an MLE. The returned value of `$maximum` gives an approximate value of the MLE to be 0.406 and `$objective` gives `L` evaluated at the MLE which is approximately 0.

We previously remarked that it is usually more numerically convenient to maximize the log-likelihood (or minimize the negative log-likelihood), and we can just as easily do this with R. We just need to calculate the log-likelihood beforehand which (for this example) is

$$-l(p) = -\sum x_i \ln p - \left(n - \sum x_i\right) \ln(1-p).$$

It is done in R with

```
> minuslogL <- function(p, x) -sum(dbinom(x, size = 1, prob = p,
+      log = TRUE))
> optimize(minuslogL, interval = c(0, 1), x = x)

$minimum
[1] 0.4062525

$objective
[1] 21.61487
```

Note that we did not need `maximum = TRUE` because we minimized the negative log-likelihood. The answer for the MLE is essentially the same as before, but the `$objective` value was different, of course.

For multiparameter problems we may use a similar approach by way of the `mle` function in the `stats4` package.

Example 9.9. Plant Growth. We will investigate the `weight` variable of the `PlantGrowth` data. We will suppose that the weights constitute a random observations $X_1, X_2, \ldots, X_n$ that are i.i.d. norm(mean $= \mu$, sd $= \sigma$) which is not unreasonable based on a histogram and other exploratory measures. We will find the MLE of $\theta = (\mu, \sigma^2)$. We claimed in Example 9.8 that $\hat{\theta} = (\hat{\mu}, \hat{\sigma}^2)$ had the form given above. Let us check whether this is plausible numerically. The negative log-likelihood function is

```
> minuslogL <- function(mu, sigma2){
+   -sum(dnorm(x, mean = mu, sd = sqrt(sigma2), log = TRUE))
+ }
```

Note that we omitted the data as an argument to the log-likelihood function; the only arguments were the parameters over which the maximization is to take place. Now we will simulate some data and find the MLE. The optimization algorithm requires starting values (intelligent guesses) for the parameters. We choose values close to the sample mean and variance (which turn out to be approximately 5 and 0.5, respectively) to illustrate the procedure.

```
> x <- PlantGrowth$weight
> library(stats4)
> MaxLikeEst <- mle(minuslogL, start = list(mu = 5, sigma2 = 0.5))
> summary(MaxLikeEst)
Maximum likelihood estimation

Call:
mle(minuslogl = minuslogL, start = list(mu = 5, sigma2 = 0.5))

Coefficients:
        Estimate Std. Error
mu     5.0729848  0.1258666
sigma2 0.4752721  0.1227108

-2 log L: 62.82084
```

The outputted MLEs are shown above, and `mle` even gives us estimates for the standard errors of $\hat{\mu}$ and $\hat{\sigma}^2$ (which were obtained by inverting the numerical Hessian matrix at the optima; see Appendix E.6). Let us check how close the numerical MLEs came to the theoretical MLEs:

```
> mean(x)
[1] 5.073
> var(x) * 29/30
[1] 0.475281
> sd(x)/sqrt(30)
[1] 0.1280195
```

The numerical MLEs were very close to the theoretical MLEs. We already knew that the standard error of $\hat{\mu} = \overline{X}$ is $\sigma/\sqrt{n}$, and the numerical estimate of this was very close too.

There is functionality in the `distrTest` package [74] to calculate theoretical MLEs; we will skip examples of these for the time being.

9.2 Confidence Intervals for Means

We are given $X_1, X_2, \ldots, X_n$ that are an $SRS(n)$ from a $\mathtt{norm}(\mathtt{mean} = \mu,\ \mathtt{sd} = \sigma)$ distribution, where μ is unknown. We know that we may estimate μ with $\overline{X}$, and we have seen that this estimator is the MLE. But how good is our estimate? We know that

$$\frac{\overline{X} - \mu}{\sigma/\sqrt{n}} \sim \mathtt{norm}(\mathtt{mean} = 0,\ \mathtt{sd} = 1). \tag{9.2.1}$$

For a big probability $1 - \alpha$, for instance, 95%, we can calculate the quantile $z_{\alpha/2}$. Then

$$\mathbb{P}\left(-z_{\alpha/2} \leq \frac{\overline{X} - \mu}{\sigma/\sqrt{n}} \leq z_{\alpha/2}\right) = 1 - \alpha. \tag{9.2.2}$$

But now consider the following string of equivalent inequalities:

$$-z_{\alpha/2} \leq \frac{\overline{X} - \mu}{\sigma/\sqrt{n}} \leq z_{\alpha/2},$$

$$-z_{\alpha/2}\left(\frac{\sigma}{\sqrt{n}}\right) \leq \overline{X} - \mu \leq z_{\alpha/2}\left(\frac{\sigma}{\sqrt{n}}\right),$$

$$-\overline{X} - z_{\alpha/2}\left(\frac{\sigma}{\sqrt{n}}\right) \leq -\mu \leq -\overline{X} + z_{\alpha/2}\left(\frac{\sigma}{\sqrt{n}}\right),$$

$$\overline{X} - z_{\alpha/2}\left(\frac{\sigma}{\sqrt{n}}\right) \leq \mu \leq \overline{X} + z_{\alpha/2}\left(\frac{\sigma}{\sqrt{n}}\right).$$

That is,

$$\mathbb{P}\left(\overline{X} - z_{\alpha/2}\frac{\sigma}{\sqrt{n}} \leq \mu \leq \overline{X} + z_{\alpha/2}\frac{\sigma}{\sqrt{n}}\right) = 1 - \alpha. \tag{9.2.3}$$

Definition 9.10. The interval

$$\left[\overline{X} - z_{\alpha/2}\frac{\sigma}{\sqrt{n}},\ \overline{X} + z_{\alpha/2}\frac{\sigma}{\sqrt{n}}\right] \tag{9.2.4}$$

is a $100(1-\alpha)\%$ *confidence interval for* μ. The quantity $1-\alpha$ is called the *confidence coefficient*.

Remark 9.11. The interval is also sometimes written more compactly as

$$\overline{X} \pm z_{\alpha/2}\frac{\sigma}{\sqrt{n}}. \tag{9.2.5}$$

The interpretation of confidence intervals is tricky and often mistaken by novices. When I am teaching the concept "live" during class, I usually ask the students to imagine that my piece of chalk represents the "unknown" parameter, and I lay it down on the desk in front of me. Once the chalk has been lain, it is *fixed*; it does not move. Our goal is to estimate the parameter. For the estimator I pick up a sheet of loose paper lying nearby. The estimation procedure is to randomly drop the piece of paper from above, and observe where it lands. If the piece of paper covers the piece of chalk, then we are successful – our estimator covers the parameter. If it falls off to one side or the other, then we are unsuccessful; our interval fails to cover the parameter.

Then I ask them: suppose we were to repeat this procedure hundreds, thousands, millions of times. Suppose we kept track of how many times we covered and how many times we did not. What percentage of the time would we be successful?

In the demonstration, the parameter corresponds to the chalk, the sheet of paper corresponds to the confidence interval, and the random experiment corresponds to dropping the sheet of paper. The percentage of the time that we are successful *exactly* corresponds to the *confidence coefficient*. That is, if we use a 95% confidence interval, then we can say that, in the long run, approximately 95% of our intervals will cover the true parameter (which is fixed, but unknown).

See Figure 9.2.1, which is a graphical display of these ideas.

Under the above framework, we can reason that an "interval" with a *larger* confidence coefficient corresponds to a *wider* sheet of paper. Furthermore, the width of the confidence interval (sheet of paper) should be *somehow* related to the amount of information contained in the random sample, $X_1, X_2, \ldots, X_n$. The following remarks makes these notions precise.

Remark 9.12. For a fixed confidence coefficient $1 - \alpha$,

$$\text{if } n \text{ increases, then the confidence interval gets } \textit{SHORTER}. \tag{9.2.6}$$

Remark 9.13. For a fixed sample size n,

$$\text{if } 1 - \alpha \text{ increases, then the confidence interval gets } \textit{WIDER}. \tag{9.2.7}$$

Example 9.14. Results from an Experiment on Plant Growth. The `PlantGrowth` data frame gives the results of an experiment to measure plant yield (as measured by the weight of the plant). We would like to a 95% confidence interval for the mean weight of the plants. Suppose that we know from prior research that the true population standard deviation of the plant weights is 0.7 g.

The parameter of interest is μ, which represents the true mean weight of the population of all plants of the particular species in the study. We will first take a look at a stemplot of the data:

```
> library(aplpack)
> with(PlantGrowth, stem.leaf(weight))
1 | 2: represents 1.2
 leaf unit: 0.1
            n: 30
   1     f | 5
         s |
   2    3. | 8
   4    4* | 11
   5     t | 3
   8     f | 455
  10     s | 66
  13    4. | 889
  (4)   5* | 1111
  13     t | 2233
   9     f | 555
         s |
   6    5. | 88
   4    6* | 011
   1     t | 3
```

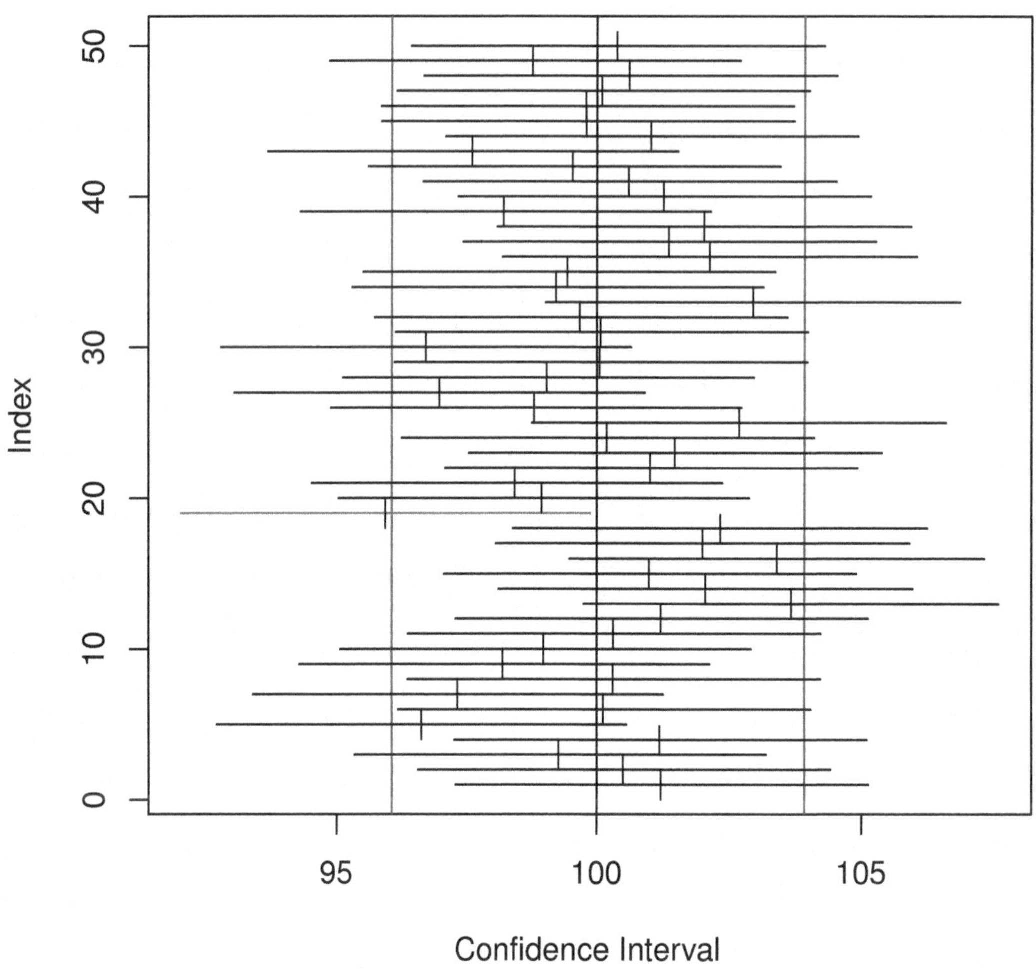

Figure 9.2.1: Simulated confidence intervals

The graph was generated by the `ci.examp` function from the `TeachingDemos` package. Fifty (50) samples of size twenty five (25) were generated from a `norm(mean = 100, sd = 10)` distribution, and each sample was used to find a 95% confidence interval for the population mean using Equation 9.2.5. The 50 confidence intervals are represented above by horizontal lines, and the respective sample means are denoted by vertical slashes. Confidence intervals that "cover" the true mean value of 100 are plotted in black; those that fail to cover are plotted in a lighter color. In the plot we see that only one (1) of the simulated intervals out of the 50 failed to cover $\mu = 100$, which is a success rate of 98%. If the number of generated samples were to increase from 50 to 500 to 50000, ..., then we would expect our success rate to approach the exact value of 95%.

The data appear to be approximately normal with no extreme values. The data come from a designed experiment, so it is reasonable to suppose that the observations constitute a simple random sample of weights[3]. We know the population standard deviation $\sigma = 0.70$ from prior research. We are going to use the one-sample z-interval.

```
> dim(PlantGrowth)   # sample size is first entry
[1] 30  2
> with(PlantGrowth, mean(weight))
[1] 5.073
> qnorm(0.975)
[1] 1.959964
```

We find the sample mean of the data to be $\overline{x} = 5.073$ and $z_{\alpha/2} = z_{0.025} \approx 1.96$. Our interval is therefore

$$\overline{x} \pm z_{\alpha/2}\frac{\sigma}{\sqrt{n}} = 5.073 \pm 1.96 \cdot \frac{0.70}{\sqrt{30}},$$

which comes out to approximately [4.823, 5.323]. In conclusion, we are 95% confident that the true mean weight μ of all plants of this species lies somewhere between 4.823 g and 5.323 g, that is, we are 95% confident that the interval [4.823, 5.323] covers μ. See Figure

Example 9.15. Give some data with $X_1, X_2, \ldots, X_n$ an $SRS(n)$ from a norm(mean $= \mu$, sd $= \sigma$) distribution. Maybe small sample?

1. What is the parameter of interest? in the context of the problem. Give a point estimate for μ.
2. What are the assumptions being made in the problem? Do they meet the conditions of the interval?
3. Calculate the interval.
4. Draw the conclusion.

Remark 9.16. What if σ is unknown? We instead use the interval

$$\overline{X} \pm z_{\alpha/2}\frac{S}{\sqrt{n}}, \tag{9.2.8}$$

where S is the sample standard deviation.

- If n is large, then $\overline{X}$ will have an approximately normal distribution regardless of the underlying population (by the CLT) and S will be very close to the parameter σ (by the SLLN); thus the above interval will have approximately $100(1-\alpha)\%$ confidence of covering μ.
- If n is small, then

[3] Actually we will see later that there is reason to believe that the observations are simple random samples from three distinct populations. See Section 10.6.

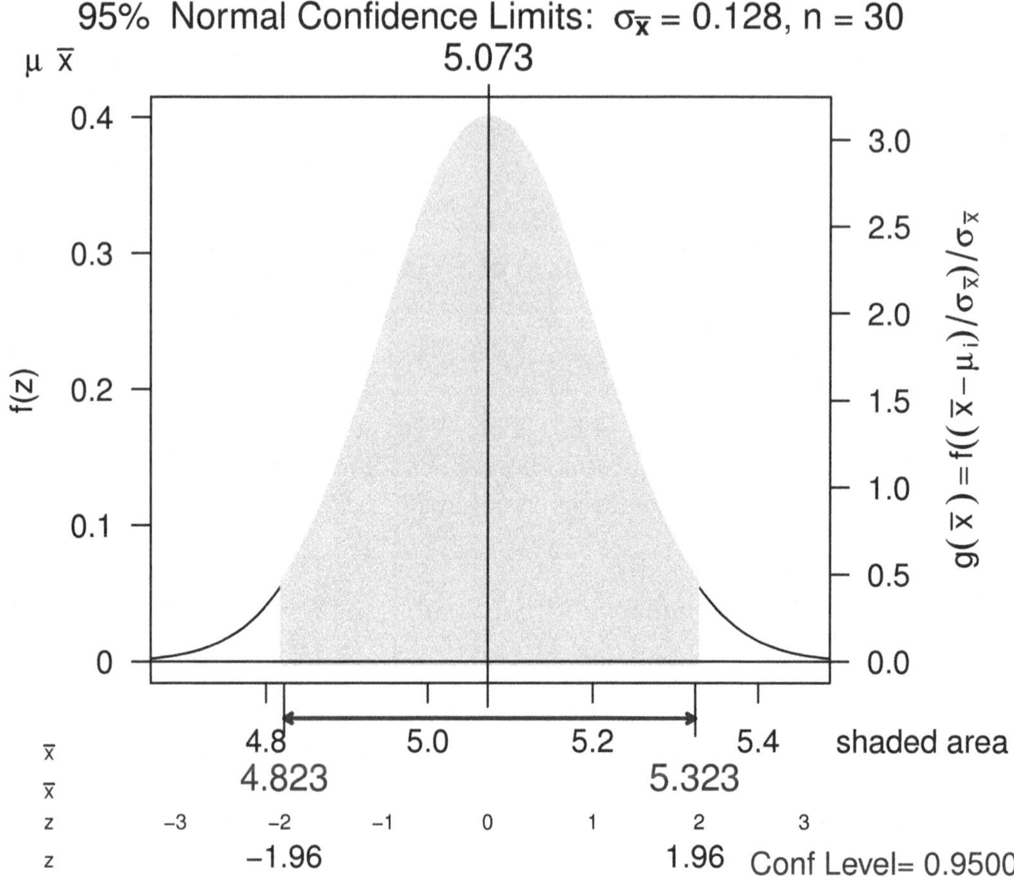

Figure 9.2.2: Confidence interval plot for the `PlantGrowth` data

The shaded portion represents 95% of the total area under the curve, and the upper and lower bounds are the limits of the one-sample 95% confidence interval. The graph is centered at the observed sample mean. It was generated by computing a `z.test` from the `TeachingDemos` package, storing the resulting `htest` object, and plotting it with the `normal.and.t.dist` function from the `HH` package. See the remarks in the "How to do it with R" discussion later in this section.

- If the underlying population is normal then we may replace $z_{\alpha/2}$ with $t_{\alpha/2}(\mathtt{df} = n-1)$. The resulting $100(1-\alpha)\%$ confidence interval is

$$\overline{X} \pm t_{\alpha/2}(\mathtt{df} = n-1)\frac{S}{\sqrt{n}} \tag{9.2.9}$$

- if the underlying population is not normal, but approximately normal, then we may use the t interval, Equation 9.2.9. The interval will have approximately $100(1-\alpha)\%$ confidence of covering μ. However, if the population is highly skewed or the data have outliers, then we should ask a professional statistician for advice.

The author learned of a handy acronym from AP Statistics Exam graders that summarizes the important parts of confidence interval estimation, which is PANIC: *P*arameter, *A*ssumptions, *N*ame, *I*nterval, and *C*onclusion.

Parameter: identify the parameter of interest with the proper symbols. Write down what the parameter means in the context of the problem.

Assumptions: list any assumptions made in the experiment. If there are any other assumptions needed or that were not checked, state what they are and why they are important.

Name: choose a statistical procedure from your bag of tricks based on the answers to the previous two parts. The assumptions of the procedure you choose should match those of the problem; if they do not match then either pick a different procedure or openly admit that the results may not be reliable. Write down any underlying formulas used.

Interval: calculate the interval from the sample data. This can be done by hand but will more often be done with the aid of a computer. Regardless of the method, all calculations or code should be shown so that the entire process is repeatable by a subsequent reader.

Conclusion: state the final results, using language in the context of the problem. Include the appropriate interpretation of the interval, making reference to the confidence coefficient.

Remark 9.17. All of the above intervals for μ were two-sided, but there are also one-sided intervals for μ. They look like

$$\left[\overline{X} - z_{\alpha}\frac{\sigma}{\sqrt{n}},\ \infty\right) \quad \text{or} \quad \left(-\infty,\ \overline{X} + z_{\alpha}\frac{\sigma}{\sqrt{n}}\right] \tag{9.2.10}$$

and satisfy

$$\mathbb{P}\left(\overline{X} - z_{\alpha}\frac{\sigma}{\sqrt{n}} \leq \mu\right) = 1-\alpha \quad \text{and} \quad \mathbb{P}\left(\overline{X} + z_{\alpha}\frac{\sigma}{\sqrt{n}} \geq \mu\right) = 1-\alpha. \tag{9.2.11}$$

Example 9.18. Small sample, some data with $X_1, X_2, \ldots, X_n$ an $SRS(n)$ from a $\mathsf{norm}(\mathtt{mean} = \mu,\ \mathtt{sd} = \sigma)$ distribution.

1. PANIC

9.2.1 How to do it with R

We can do Example 9.14 with the following code.

```
> library(TeachingDemos)
> temp <- with(PlantGrowth, z.test(weight, stdev = 0.7))
> temp

        One Sample z-test

data:  weight
z = 39.6942, n = 30.000, Std. Dev. = 0.700, Std. Dev. of the
sample mean = 0.128, p-value < 2.2e-16
alternative hypothesis: true mean is not equal to 0
95 percent confidence interval:
 4.822513 5.323487
sample estimates:
mean of weight
         5.073
```

The confidence interval bounds are shown in the sixth line down of the output (please disregard all of the additional output information for now – we will use it in Chapter 10). We can make the plot for Figure 9.2.2 with

```
> library(IPSUR)
> plot(temp, "Conf")
```

9.3 Confidence Intervals for Differences of Means

Let $X_1, X_2, \ldots, X_n$ be a $SRS(n)$ from a $\mathsf{norm}(\mathtt{mean} = \mu_X,\ \mathtt{sd} = \sigma_X)$ distribution and let $Y_1, Y_2, \ldots, Y_m$ be a $SRS(m)$ from a $\mathsf{norm}(\mathtt{mean} = \mu_Y,\ \mathtt{sd} = \sigma_Y)$ distribution. Further, assume that the $X_1, X_2, \ldots, X_n$ sample is independent of the $Y_1, Y_2, \ldots, Y_m$ sample.

Suppose that σ_X and σ_Y are known. We would like a confidence interval for $\mu_X - \mu_Y$. We know that

$$\overline{X} - \overline{Y} \sim \mathsf{norm}\left(\mathtt{mean} = \mu_X - \mu_Y,\ \mathtt{sd} = \sqrt{\frac{\sigma_X^2}{n} + \frac{\sigma_Y^2}{m}}\right). \tag{9.3.1}$$

Therefore, a $100(1-\alpha)\%$ confidence interval for $\mu_X - \mu_Y$ is given by

$$\left(\overline{X} - \overline{Y}\right) \pm z_{\alpha/2}\sqrt{\frac{\sigma_X^2}{n} + \frac{\sigma_Y^2}{m}}. \tag{9.3.2}$$

Unfortunately, most of the time the values of σ_X and σ_Y are unknown. This leads us to the following:

- If both sample sizes are large, then we may appeal to the CLT/SLLN (see 8.3) and substitute S_X^2 and S_Y^2 for σ_X^2 and σ_Y^2 in the interval 9.3.2. The resulting confidence interval will have approximately $100(1-\alpha)\%$ confidence.

- If one or more of the sample sizes is small then we are in trouble, unless
  - the underlying populations are both normal and $\sigma_X = \sigma_Y$. In this case (setting $\sigma = \sigma_X = \sigma_Y$),

$$\overline{X} - \overline{Y} \sim \mathsf{norm}\left(\mathtt{mean} = \mu_X - \mu_Y,\ \mathsf{sd} = \sigma\sqrt{\frac{1}{n} + \frac{1}{m}}\right). \tag{9.3.3}$$

Now let

$$U = \frac{n-1}{\sigma^2} S_X^2 + \frac{m-1}{\sigma^2} S_Y^2. \tag{9.3.4}$$

Then by Exercise 7.2 we know that $U \sim \mathsf{chisq}(\mathtt{df} = n + m - 2)$ and is not a large leap to believe that U is independent of $\overline{X} - \overline{Y}$; thus

$$T = \frac{Z}{\sqrt{U/(n+m-2)}} \sim \mathsf{t}(\mathtt{df} = n + m - 2). \tag{9.3.5}$$

But

$$\begin{aligned} T &= \frac{\frac{\overline{X}-\overline{Y}-(\mu_X-\mu_Y)}{\sigma\sqrt{\frac{1}{n}+\frac{1}{m}}}}{\sqrt{\frac{n-1}{\sigma^2}S_X^2 + \frac{m-1}{\sigma^2}S_Y^2 \Big/ (n+m-2)}}, \\ &= \frac{\overline{X} - \overline{Y} - (\mu_X - \mu_Y)}{\sqrt{\left(\frac{1}{n} + \frac{1}{m}\right)\left(\frac{(n-1)S_X^2 + (m-1)S_Y^2}{n+m-2}\right)}}, \\ &\sim \mathsf{t}(\mathtt{df} = n + m - 2). \end{aligned}$$

Therefore a $100(1-\alpha)\%$ confidence interval for $\mu_X - \mu_Y$ is given by

$$\left(\overline{X} - \overline{Y}\right) \pm t_{\alpha/2}(\mathtt{df} = n + m - 2)\, S_p \sqrt{\frac{1}{n} + \frac{1}{m}}, \tag{9.3.6}$$

where

$$S_p = \sqrt{\frac{(n-1)S_X^2 + (m-1)S_Y^2}{n+m-2}} \tag{9.3.7}$$

is called the "pooled" estimator of σ.

  - if one of the samples is small, and both underlying populations are normal, but $\sigma_X \neq \sigma_Y$, then we may use a Welch (or Satterthwaite) approximation to the degrees of freedom. See Welch [88], Satterthwaite [76], or Neter *et al* [67]. The idea is to use an interval of the form

$$\left(\overline{X} - \overline{Y}\right) \pm \mathsf{t}_{\alpha/2}(\mathtt{df} = r)\sqrt{\frac{S_X^2}{n} + \frac{S_Y^2}{m}}, \tag{9.3.8}$$

where the degrees of freedom r is chosen so that the interval has nice statistical properties. It turns out that a good choice for r is given by

$$r = \frac{\left(S_X^2/n + S_Y^2/m\right)^2}{\frac{1}{n-1}\left(S_X^2/n\right)^2 + \frac{1}{m-1}\left(S_Y^2/m\right)^2}, \tag{9.3.9}$$

where we understand that r is rounded down to the nearest integer. The resulting interval has approximately $100(1-\alpha)\%$ confidence.

9.3.1 How to do it with R

The basic function is `t.test` which has a `var.equal` argument that may be set to `TRUE` or `FALSE`. The confidence interval is shown as part of the output, although there is a lot of additional information that is not needed until Chapter 10.

There is not any specific functionality to handle the z-interval for small samples, but if the samples are large then `t.test` with `var.equal = FALSE` will be essentially the same thing. The standard deviations are never (?) known in advance anyway so it does not really matter in practice.

9.4 Confidence Intervals for Proportions

We would like to know p which is the "proportion of successes". For instance, p could be:

- the proportion of U.S. citizens that support Obama,
- the proportion of smokers among adults age 18 or over,
- the proportion of people worldwide infected by the H1N1 virus.

We are given an $SRS(n)$ $X_1, X_2, \ldots, X_n$ distributed binom(`size` = 1, `prob` = p). Recall from Section 5.3 that the common mean of these variables is $\mathbb{E}\, X = p$ and the variance is $\mathbb{E}(X-p)^2 = p(1-p)$. If we let $Y = \sum X_i$, then from Section 5.3 we know that $Y \sim$ binom(`size` = n, `prob` = p) and that

$$\overline{X} = \frac{Y}{n} \text{ has } \mathbb{E}\,\overline{X} = p \text{ and } \mathrm{Var}(\overline{X}) = \frac{p(1-p)}{n}.$$

Thus if n is large (here is the CLT) then an approximate $100(1-\alpha)\%$ confidence interval for p would be given by

$$\overline{X} \pm z_{\alpha/2}\sqrt{\frac{p(1-p)}{n}}. \tag{9.4.1}$$

OOPS...! Equation 9.4.1 is of no use to us because the <u>unknown</u> parameter p is in the formula! (If we knew what p was to plug in the formula then we would not need a confidence interval in the first place.) There are two solutions to this problem.

1. Replace p with $\hat{p} = \overline{X}$. Then an approximate $100(1-\alpha)\%$ confidence interval for p is given by

   $$\hat{p} \pm z_{\alpha/2}\sqrt{\frac{\hat{p}(1-\hat{p})}{n}}. \tag{9.4.2}$$

   This approach is called the *Wald interval* and is also known as the *asymptotic interval* because it appeals to the CLT for large sample sizes.

2. Go back to first principles. Note that

   $$-z_{\alpha/2} \leq \frac{Y/n - p}{\sqrt{p(1-p)/n}} \leq z_{\alpha/2}$$

   exactly when the function f defined by

   $$f(p) = (Y/n - p)^2 - z_{\alpha/2}^2\frac{p(1-p)}{n}$$

satisfies $f(p) \leq 0$. But f is quadratic in p so its graph is a parabola; it has two roots, and these roots form the limits of the confidence interval. We can find them with the quadratic formula (see Exercise 9.2):

$$\left[\left(\hat{p} + \frac{z_{\alpha/2}^2}{2n}\right) \pm z_{\alpha/2}\sqrt{\frac{\hat{p}(1-\hat{p})}{n} + \frac{z_{\alpha/2}^2}{(2n)^2}}\right] \Bigg/ \left(1 + \frac{z_{\alpha/2}^2}{n}\right) \tag{9.4.3}$$

This approach is called the *score interval* because it is based on the inversion of the "Score test". See Chapter 14. It is also known as the *Wilson interval*; see Agresti [3].

For two proportions p_1 and p_2, we may collect independent $\mathsf{binom}(\mathtt{size} = 1, \mathtt{prob} = p)$ samples of size n_1 and n_2, respectively. Let Y_1 and Y_2 denote the number of successes in the respective samples.

We know that

$$\frac{Y_1}{n_1} \approx \mathsf{norm}\left(\mathtt{mean} = p_1,\ \mathtt{sd} = \sqrt{\frac{p_1(1-p_1)}{n_1}}\right)$$

and

$$\frac{Y_2}{n_2} \approx \mathsf{norm}\left(\mathtt{mean} = p_2,\ \mathtt{sd} = \sqrt{\frac{p_2(1-p_2)}{n_2}}\right)$$

so it stands to reason that an approximate $100(1-\alpha)\%$ confidence interval for $p_1 - p_2$ is given by

$$(\hat{p}_1 - \hat{p}_2) \pm z_{\alpha/2}\sqrt{\frac{\hat{p}_1(1-\hat{p}_1)}{n_1} + \frac{\hat{p}_2(1-\hat{p}_2)}{n_2}}, \tag{9.4.4}$$

where $\hat{p}_1 = Y_1/n_1$ and $\hat{p}_2 = Y_2/n_2$.

Remark 9.19. When estimating a single proportion, one-sided intervals are sometimes needed. They take the form

$$\left[0,\ \hat{p} + z_{\alpha/2}\sqrt{\frac{\hat{p}(1-\hat{p})}{n}}\right] \tag{9.4.5}$$

or

$$\left[\hat{p} - z_{\alpha/2}\sqrt{\frac{\hat{p}(1-\hat{p})}{n}},\ 1\right] \tag{9.4.6}$$

or in other words, we know in advance that the true proportion is restricted to the interval [0, 1], so we can truncate our confidence interval to those values on either side.

9.4.1 How to do it with R

```
> library(Hmisc)
> binconf(x = 7, n = 25, method = "asymptotic")

 PointEst     Lower     Upper
     0.28 0.1039957 0.4560043

> binconf(x = 7, n = 25, method = "wilson")

 PointEst     Lower     Upper
     0.28 0.1428385 0.4757661
```

The default value of the `method` argument is `wilson`.
An alternate way is

```
> tab <- xtabs(~gender, data = RcmdrTestDrive)
> prop.test(rbind(tab), conf.level = 0.95, correct = FALSE)

        1-sample proportions test without continuity correction

data:  rbind(tab), null probability 0.5
X-squared = 2.881, df = 1, p-value = 0.08963
alternative hypothesis: true p is not equal to 0.5
95 percent confidence interval:
 0.4898844 0.6381406
sample estimates:
        p
0.5654762
```

```
> A <- as.data.frame(Titanic)
> library(reshape)
> B <- with(A, untable(A, Freq))
```

9.5 Confidence Intervals for Variances

I am thinking one and two sample problems here.

9.5.1 How to do it with R

I am thinking about sigma.test in the TeachingDemos package and var.test in base R here.

9.6 Fitting Distributions

9.6.1 How to do it with R

I am thinking about fitdistr from the MASS package [84].

9.7 Sample Size and Margin of Error

Sections 9.2 through 9.5 all began the same way: we were given the sample size n and the confidence coefficient $1-\alpha$, and our task was to find a margin of error E so that

$$\hat{\theta} \pm E \text{ is a } 100(1-\alpha)\% \text{ confidence interval for } \theta.$$

Some examples we saw were:

- $E = z_{\alpha/2}\sigma/\sqrt{n}$, in the one-sample z-interval,
- $E = t_{\alpha/2}(\mathtt{df} = n+m-2)S_p\sqrt{n^{-1}+m^{-1}}$, in the two-sample pooled t-interval.

We already know (we can see in the formulas above) that E decreases as n increases. Now we would like to use this information to our advantage: suppose that we have a fixed margin of error E, say $E = 3$, and we want a $100(1-\alpha)\%$ confidence interval for μ. The question is: how big does n have to be?

For the case of a population mean the answer is easy: we set up an equation and solve for n.

Example 9.20. Given a situation, given σ, given E, we would like to know how big n has to be to ensure that $\overline{X} \pm 5$ is a 95% confidence interval for μ.

Remark 9.21.

1. Always round up any decimal values of n, no matter how small the decimal is.
2. Another name for E is the "maximum error of the estimate".

For proportions, recall that the asymptotic formula to estimate p was

$$\hat{p} \pm z_{\alpha/2}\sqrt{\frac{\hat{p}(1-\hat{p})}{n}}.$$

Reasoning as above we would want

$$E = z_{\alpha/2}\sqrt{\frac{\hat{p}(1-\hat{p})}{n}}, \quad \text{or} \tag{9.7.1}$$

$$n = z_{\alpha/2}^2\frac{\hat{p}(1-\hat{p})}{E^2}. \tag{9.7.2}$$

OOPS! Recall that $\hat{p} = Y/n$, which would put the variable n on both sides of Equation 9.7.2. Again, there are two solutions to the problem.

1. If we have a good idea of what p is, say p^* then we can plug it in to get

$$n = z_{\alpha/2}^2\frac{p^*(1-p^*)}{E^2}. \tag{9.7.3}$$

2. Even if we have no idea what p is, we do know from calculus that $p(1-p) \leq 1/4$ because the function $f(x) = x(1-x)$ is quadratic (so its graph is a parabola which opens downward) with maximum value attained at $x = 1/2$. Therefore, regardless of our choice for p^* the sample size must satisfy

$$n = z_{\alpha/2}^2\frac{p^*(1-p^*)}{E^2} \leq \frac{z_{\alpha/2}^2}{4E^2}. \tag{9.7.4}$$

The quantity $z_{\alpha/2}^2/4E^2$ is large enough to guarantee $100(1-\alpha)\%$ confidence.

Example 9.22. Proportion example

Remark 9.23. For very small populations sometimes the value of n obtained from the formula is too big. In this case we should use the hypergeometric distribution for a sampling model rather than the binomial model. With this modification the formulas change to the following: if N denotes the population size then let

$$m = z_{\alpha/2}^2\frac{p^*(1-p^*)}{E^2} \tag{9.7.5}$$

and the sample size needed to ensure $100(1-\alpha)\%$ confidence is achieved is

$$n = \frac{m}{1 + \frac{m-1}{N}}. \tag{9.7.6}$$

If we do not have a good value for the estimate p^* then we may use $p^* = 1/2$.

9.7.1 How to do it with R

I am thinking about power.t.test, power.prop.test, power.anova.test, and I am also thinking about replicate.

9.8 Other Topics

Mention mle from the stats4 package.

Chapter Exercises

Exercise 9.1. Let $X_1, X_2, \ldots, X_n$ be an $SRS(n)$ from a `norm(mean` $= \mu$, `sd` $= \sigma$) distribution. Find a two-dimensional MLE for $\theta = (\mu, \sigma)$.

Exercise 9.2. Find the upper and lower limits for the confidence interval procedure by finding the roots of f defined by

$$f(p) = (Y/n - p)^2 - z_{\alpha/2}^2 \frac{p(1-p)}{n}.$$

You are going to need the quadratic formula.

Chapter 10

Hypothesis Testing

What do I want them to know?

- basic terminology and philosophy of the Neyman-Pearson paradigm
- classical hypothesis tests for the standard one and two sample problems with means, variances, and proportions
- the notion of between versus within group variation and how it plays out with one-way ANOVA
- the concept of statistical power and its relation to sample size

10.1 Introduction

I spent a week during the summer of 2005 at the University of Nebraska at Lincoln grading Advanced Placement Statistics exams, and while I was there I attended a presentation by Dr. Roxy Peck. At the end of her talk she described an activity she had used with students to introduce the basic concepts of hypothesis testing. I was impressed by the activity and have used it in my own classes several times since.

The instructor (with a box of cookies in hand) enters a class of fifteen or more students and produces a brand-new, sealed deck of ordinary playing cards. The instructor asks for a student volunteer to break the seal, and then the instructor prominently shuffles the deck[1] several times in front of the class, after which time the students are asked to line up in a row. They are going to play a game. Each student will draw a card from the top of the deck, in turn. If the card is black, then the lucky student will get a cookie. If the card is red, then the unlucky student will sit down empty-handed. Let the game begin.

The first student draws a card: red. There are jeers and outbursts, and the student slinks off to his/her chair. (S)he is disappointed, of course, but not really. After all, (s)he had a 50-50 chance of getting black, and it did not happen. Oh well.

The second student draws a card: red, again. There are more jeers, and the second student slips away. This student is also disappointed, but again, not so much, because it is probably his/her unlucky day. On to the next student.

The student draws: red again! There are a few wiseguys who yell (happy to make noise, more than anything else), but there are a few other students who are not yelling any more – they are thinking. This is the third red in a row, which is possible, of course, but what is going

[1] The jokers are removed before shuffling.

on, here? They are not quite sure. They are now concentrating on the next card... it is bound to be black, right?

The fourth student draws: red. Hmmm... now there are groans instead of outbursts. A few of the students at the end of the line shrug their shoulders and start to make their way back to their desk, complaining that the teacher does not want to give away any cookies. There are still some students in line though, salivating, waiting for the inevitable black to appear.

The fifth student draws red. Now it isn't funny any more. As the remaining students make their way back to their seats an uproar ensues, from an entire classroom demanding cookies.

Keep the preceding experiment in the back of your mind as you read the following sections. When you have finished the entire chapter, come back and read this introduction again. All of the mathematical jargon that follows is connected to the above paragraphs. In the meantime, I will get you started:

Null hypothesis: it is an ordinary deck of playing cards, shuffled thoroughly.

Alternative hypothesis: either it is a trick deck of cards, or the instructor did some fancy shufflework.

Observed data: a sequence of draws from the deck, five reds in a row.

If it were truly an ordinary, well-shuffled deck of cards, the probability of observing zero blacks out of a sample of size five (without replacement) from a deck with 26 black cards and 26 red cards would be

```
> dhyper(0, m = 26, n = 26, k = 5)
[1] 0.02531012
```

There are two very important final thoughts. First, everybody gets a cookie in the end. Second, the students invariably (and aggressively) attempt to get me to open up the deck and reveal the true nature of the cards. I never do.

10.2 Tests for Proportions

Example 10.1. We have a machine that makes widgets.

- Under normal operation, about 0.10 of the widgets produced are defective.
- Go out and purchase a torque converter.
- Install the torque converter, and observe $n = 100$ widgets from the machine.
- Let Y = number of defective widgets observed.

If

- $Y = 0$, then the torque converter is great!
- $Y = 4$, then the torque converter seems to be helping.
- $Y = 9$, then there is not much evidence that the torque converter helps.

- $Y = 17$, then throw away the torque converter.

Let p denote the proportion of defectives produced by the machine. Before the installation of the torque converter p was 0.10. Then we installed the torque converter. Did p change? Did it go up or down? We use statistics to decide. Our method is to observe data and construct a 95% confidence interval for p,

$$\hat{p} \pm z_{\alpha/2} \sqrt{\frac{\hat{p}(1-\hat{p})}{n}}. \tag{10.2.1}$$

If the confidence interval is

- [0.01, 0.05], then we are 95% confident that $0.01 \leq p \leq 0.05$, so there is evidence that the torque converter is helping.
- [0.15, 0.19], then we are 95% confident that $0.15 \leq p \leq 0.19$, so there is evidence that the torque converter is hurting.
- [0.07, 0.11], then there is not enough evidence to conclude that the torque converter is doing anything at all, positive or negative.

10.2.1 Terminology

The *null hypothesis* H_0 is a "nothing" hypothesis, whose interpretation could be that nothing has changed, there is no difference, there is nothing special taking place, *etc.*. In Example 10.1 the null hypothesis would be $H_0 : p = 0.10$. The *alternative hypothesis* H_1 is the hypothesis that something has changed, in this case, $H_1 : p \neq 0.10$. Our goal is to statistically *test* the hypothesis $H_0 : p = 0.10$ versus the alternative $H_1 : p \neq 0.10$. Our procedure will be:

1. Go out and collect some data, in particular, a simple random sample of observations from the machine.
2. Suppose that H_0 is true and construct a $100(1-\alpha)\%$ confidence interval for p.
3. If the confidence interval does not cover $p = 0.10$, then we *reject*H_0. Otherwise, we *fail to reject*H_0.

Remark 10.2. Every time we make a decision it is possible to be wrong, and there are two possible mistakes that we could make. We have committed a

Type I Error if we reject H_0 when in fact H_0 is true. This would be akin to convicting an innocent person for a crime (s)he did not commit.

Type II Error if we fail to reject H_0 when in fact H_1 is true. This is analogous to a guilty person escaping conviction.

Type I Errors are usually considered worse[2], and we design our statistical procedures to control the probability of making such a mistake. We define the

$$\text{significance level of the test} = \mathbb{P}(\text{Type I Error}) = \alpha. \tag{10.2.2}$$

We want α to be small which conventionally means, say, $\alpha = 0.05$, $\alpha = 0.01$, or $\alpha = 0.005$ (but could mean anything, in principle).

[2]There is no mathematical difference between the errors, however. The bottom line is that we choose one type of error to control with an iron fist, and we try to minimize the probability of making the other type. That being said, null hypotheses are often by design to correspond to the "simpler" model, so it is often easier to analyze (and thereby control) the probabilities associated with Type I Errors.

- The *rejection region* (also known as the *critical region*) for the test is the set of sample values which would result in the rejection of H_0. For Example 10.1, the rejection region would be all possible samples that result in a 95% confidence interval that does not cover $p = 0.10$.
- The above example with $H_1 : p \neq 0.10$ is called a *two-sided* test. Many times we are interested in a *one-sided* test, which would look like $H_1 : p < 0.10$ or $H_1 : p > 0.10$.

We are ready for tests of hypotheses for one proportion.

Table here.

Don't forget the assumptions.

Example 10.3. Find

1. The null and alternative hypotheses
2. Check your assumptions.
3. Define a critical region with an $\alpha = 0.05$ significance level.
4. Calculate the value of the test statistic and state your conclusion.

Example 10.4. Suppose p = the proportion of students who are admitted to the graduate school of the University of California at Berkeley, and suppose that a public relations officer boasts that UCB has historically had a 40% acceptance rate for its graduate school. Consider the data stored in the table `UCBAdmissions` from 1973. Assuming these observations constituted a simple random sample, are they consistent with the officer's claim, or do they provide evidence that the acceptance rate was significantly less than 40%? Use an $\alpha = 0.01$ significance level.

Our null hypothesis in this problem is $H_0 : p = 0.4$ and the alternative hypothesis is $H_1 : p < 0.4$. We reject the null hypothesis if $\hat{p}$ is too small, that is, if

$$\frac{\hat{p} - 0.4}{\sqrt{0.4(1 - 0.4)/n}} < -z_{\alpha}, \tag{10.2.3}$$

where $\alpha = 0.01$ and $-z_{0.01}$ is

```
> -qnorm(0.99)
[1] -2.326348
```

Our only remaining task is to find the value of the test statistic and see where it falls relative to the critical value. We can find the number of people admitted and not admitted to the UCB graduate school with the following.

```
> A <- as.data.frame(UCBAdmissions)
> head(A)
     Admit Gender Dept Freq
1 Admitted   Male    A  512
2 Rejected   Male    A  313
3 Admitted Female    A   89
4 Rejected Female    A   19
5 Admitted   Male    B  353
6 Rejected   Male    B  207
```

```
> xtabs(Freq ~ Admit, data = A)
```

```
Admit
Admitted Rejected
    1755     2771
```

Now we calculate the value of the test statistic.

```
> phat <- 1755/(1755 + 2771)
> (phat - 0.4)/sqrt(0.4 * 0.6/(1755 + 2771))
```

```
[1] -1.680919
```

Our test statistic is not less than -2.32, so it does not fall into the critical region. Therefore, we *fail* to reject the null hypothesis that the true proportion of students admitted to graduate school is less than 40% and say that the observed data are consistent with the officer's claim at the $\alpha = 0.01$ significance level.

Example 10.5. We are going to do Example 10.4 all over again. Everything will be exactly the same except for one change. Suppose we choose significance level $\alpha = 0.05$ instead of $\alpha = 0.01$. Are the 1973 data consistent with the officer's claim?

Our null and alternative hypotheses are the same. Our observed test statistic is the same: it was approximately -1.68. But notice that our critical value has changed: $\alpha = 0.05$ and $-z_{0.05}$ is

```
> -qnorm(0.95)
```

```
[1] -1.644854
```

Our test statistic is less than -1.64 so it now falls into the critical region! We now *reject* the null hypothesis and conclude that the 1973 data provide evidence that the true proportion of students admitted to the graduate school of UCB in 1973 was significantly less than 40%. The data are *not* consistent with the officer's claim at the $\alpha = 0.05$ significance level.

What is going on, here? If we choose $\alpha = 0.05$ then we reject the null hypothesis, but if we choose $\alpha = 0.01$ then we fail to reject the null hypothesis. Our final conclusion seems to depend on our selection of the significance level. This is bad; for a particular test, we never know whether our conclusion would have been different if we had chosen a different significance level.

Or do we?

Clearly, for some significance levels we reject, and for some significance levels we do not. Where is the boundary? That is, what is the significance level for which we would *reject* at any significance level *bigger*, and we would *fail to reject* at any significance level *smaller*? This boundary value has a special name: it is called the *p-value* of the test.

Definition 10.6. The *p-value*, or *observed significance level*, of a hypothesis test is the probability when the null hypothesis is true of obtaining the observed value of the test statistic (such as $\hat{p}$) or values more extreme – meaning, in the direction of the alternative hypothesis[3].

[3]Bickel and Doksum [7] state the definition particularly well: the p-value is "the smallest level of significance α at which an experimenter using [the test statistic] T would reject [H_0] on the basis of the observed [sample] outcome x".

Example 10.7. Calculate the p-value for the test in Examples 10.4 and 10.5.

The p-value for this test is the probability of obtaining a z-score equal to our observed test statistic (which had z-score ≈ -1.680919) or more extreme, which in this example is less than the observed test statistic. In other words, we want to know the area under a standard normal curve on the interval $(-\infty, -1.680919]$. We can get this easily with

```
> pnorm(-1.680919)
[1] 0.04638932
```

We see that the p-value is strictly between the significance levels $\alpha = 0.01$ and $\alpha = 0.05$. This makes sense: it has to be bigger than $\alpha = 0.01$ (otherwise we would have rejected H_0 in Example 10.4) and it must also be smaller than $\alpha = 0.05$ (otherwise we would not have rejected H_0 in Example 10.5). Indeed, p-values are a characteristic indicator of whether or not we would have rejected at assorted significance levels, and for this reason a statistician will often skip the calculation of critical regions and critical values entirely. If (s)he knows the p-value, then (s)he knows immediately whether or not (s)he would have rejected at *any* given significance level.

Thus, another way to phrase our significance test procedure is: we will reject H_0 at the α-level of significance if the p-value is less than α.

Remark 10.8. If we have two populations with proportions p_1 and p_2 then we can test the null hypothesis $H_0 : p_1 = p_2$.

Table Here.

Example 10.9. Example.

10.2.2 How to do it with R

The following does the test.

```
> prop.test(1755, 1755 + 2771, p = 0.4, alternative = "less",
+      conf.level = 0.99, correct = FALSE)
        1-sample proportions test without continuity correction

data:  1755 out of 1755 + 2771, null probability 0.4
X-squared = 2.8255, df = 1, p-value = 0.04639
alternative hypothesis: true p is less than 0.4
99 percent confidence interval:
 0.0000000 0.4047326
sample estimates:
        p
0.3877596
```

Do the following to make the plot.

```
> library(IPSUR)
> library(HH)
> temp <- prop.test(1755, 1755 + 2771, p = 0.4, alternative = "less",
+      conf.level = 0.99, correct = FALSE)
> plot(temp, "Hypoth")
```

Use Yates' continuity correction when the expected frequency of successes is less than 10. You can use it all of the time, but you will have a decrease in power. For large samples the correction does not matter.

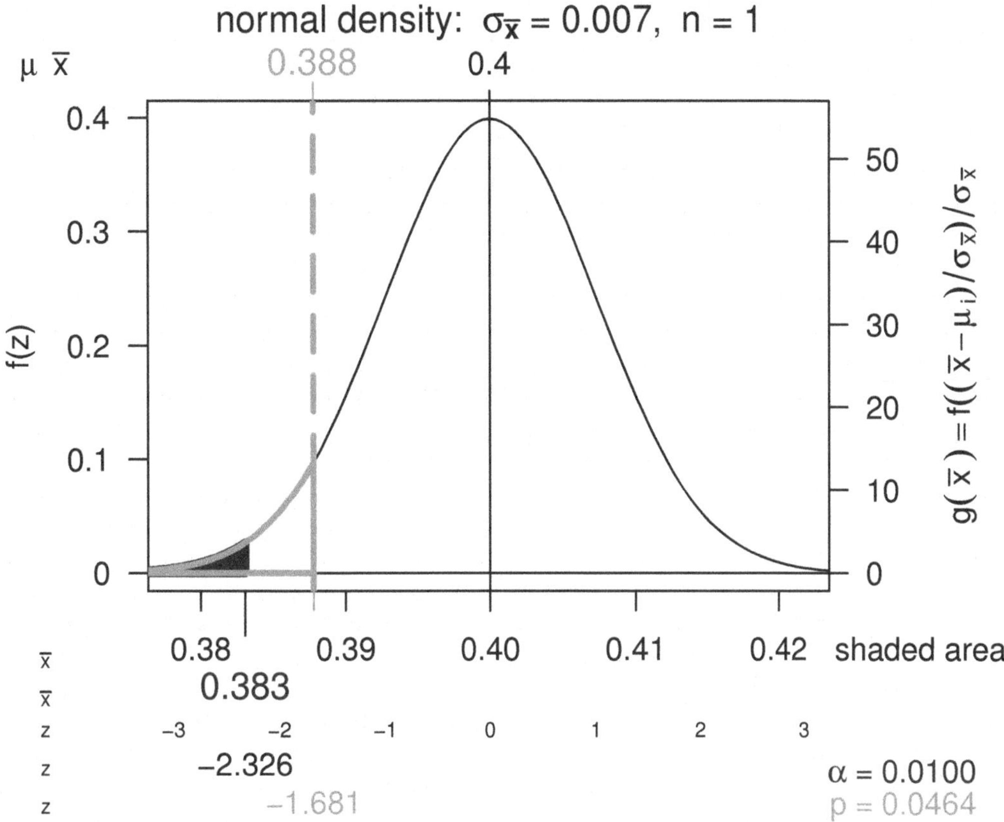

Figure 10.2.1: Hypothesis test plot based on `normal.and.t.dist` from the `HH` package

This plot shows all of the important features of hypothesis tests in one magnificent display. The (asymptotic) distribution of the test statistic (under the null hypothesis) is standard normal, represented by the bell curve, above. We see the critical region to the left, and the blue shaded area is the significance level, which for this example is $\alpha = 0.05$. The area outlined in green is the p-value, and the observed test statistic determines the upper bound of this region. We can see clearly that the p-value is larger than the significance level, thus, we would not reject the null hypothesis. There are all sorts of tick marks shown below the graph which detail how the different pieces are measured on different scales (the original data scale, the standardized scale, *etc.*). The workhorse behind the plot is the `normal.and.t.dist` function from the `HH` package. See the discussion in "How to do it with R" for the exact sequence of commands to generate the plot.

With the R Commander If you already know the number of successes and failures, then you can use the menu Statistics ▹ Proportions ▹ IPSUR Enter table for single sample...

Otherwise, your data – the raw successes and failures – should be in a column of the Active Data Set. Furthermore, the data must be stored as a "factor" internally. If the data are not a factor but are numeric then you can use the menu Data ▹ Manage variables in active data set ▹ Convert numeric variables to factors... to convert the variable to a factor. Or, you can always use the `factor` function.

Once your unsummarized data is a column, then you can use the menu Statistics ▹ Proportions ▹ Single-sample proportion test...

10.3 One Sample Tests for Means and Variances

10.3.1 For Means

Here, $X_1, X_2, \ldots, X_n$ are a $SRS(n)$ from a $\mathsf{norm}(\mathtt{mean} = \mu,\ \mathtt{sd} = \sigma)$ distribution. We would like to test $H_0 : \mu = \mu_0$.

Case A: Suppose σ is known. Then under H_0,

$$Z = \frac{\overline{X} - \mu_0}{\sigma / \sqrt{n}} \sim \mathsf{norm}(\mathtt{mean} = 0,\ \mathtt{sd} = 1).$$

Table here.

Case B: When σ is unknown, under H_0

$$T = \frac{\overline{X} - \mu_0}{S / \sqrt{n}} \sim \mathsf{t}(\mathtt{df} = n - 1).$$

Table here.

Remark 10.10. If σ is unknown but n is large then we can use the z-test.

Example 10.11. In this example we

1. Find the null and alternative hypotheses.

2. Choose a test and find the critical region.

3. Calculate the value of the test statistic and state the conclusion.

4. Find the p-value.

Remark 10.12. Remarks

- p-values are also known as tail end probabilities. We reject H_0 when the p-value is small.

- $\sigma / \sqrt{n}$ when σ is known, is called the standard error of the sample mean. In general, if we have an estimator $\hat{\theta}$ then $\sigma_{\hat{\theta}}$ is called the standard error of $\hat{\theta}$. We usually need to estimate $\sigma_{\hat{\theta}}$ with $\hat{\sigma}\theta$.

10.3.2 How to do it with R

I am thinking `z.test` in `TeachingDemos`, `t.test` in base R.

```
> x <- rnorm(37, mean = 2, sd = 3)
> library(TeachingDemos)
> z.test(x, mu = 1, sd = 3, conf.level = 0.9)
        One Sample z-test

data:  x
z = 2.8126, n = 37.000, Std. Dev. = 3.000, Std. Dev. of the sample
mean = 0.493, p-value = 0.004914
alternative hypothesis: true mean is not equal to 1
90 percent confidence interval:
 1.575948 3.198422
sample estimates:
mean of x
 2.387185
```

The `RcmdrPlugin.IPSUR` package does not have a menu for `z.test` yet.

```
> x <- rnorm(13, mean = 2, sd = 3)
> t.test(x, mu = 0, conf.level = 0.9, alternative = "greater")
        One Sample t-test

data:  x
t = 1.2949, df = 12, p-value = 0.1099
alternative hypothesis: true mean is greater than 0
90 percent confidence interval:
 -0.05064006         Inf
sample estimates:
mean of x
 1.068850
```

With the R Commander Your data should be in a single numeric column (a variable) of the Active Data Set. Use the menu Statistics ▹ Means ▹ Single-sample t-test...

10.3.3 Tests for a Variance

Here, $X_1, X_2, \ldots, X_n$ are a $SRS(n)$ from a norm(mean $= \mu$, sd $= \sigma$) distribution. We would like to test $H_0 : \sigma^2 = \sigma_0$. We know that under H_0,

$$X^2 = \frac{(n-1)S^2}{\sigma^2} \sim \mathsf{chisq}(\mathtt{df} = n-1).$$

Table here.

Example 10.13. Give some data and a hypothesis.

1. Give an α-level and test the critical region way.

2. Find the p-value for the test.

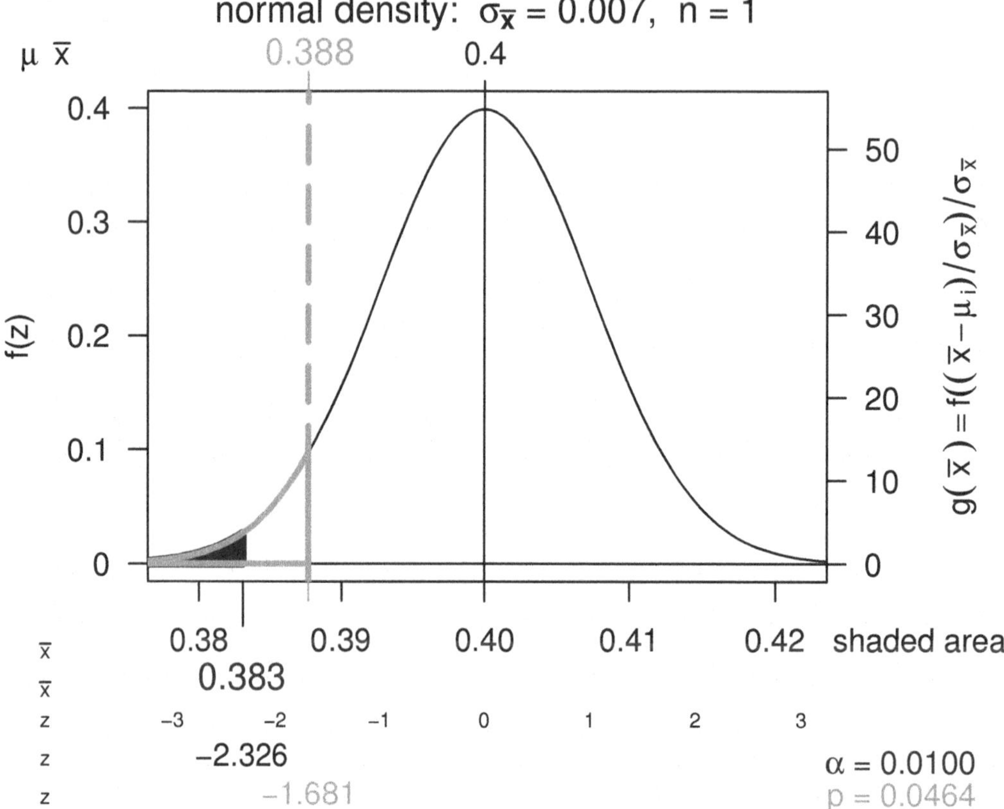

Figure 10.3.1: Hypothesis test plot based on `normal.and.t.dist` from the `HH` package

This plot shows the important features of hypothesis tests.

10.3.4 How to do it with R

I am thinking about `sigma.test` in the `TeachingDemos` package.

```
> library(TeachingDemos)
> sigma.test(women$height, sigma = 8)

        One sample Chi-squared test for variance

data:  women$height
X-squared = 4.375, df = 14, p-value = 0.01449
alternative hypothesis: true variance is not equal to 64
95 percent confidence interval:
 10.72019 49.74483
sample estimates:
var of women$height
                 20
```

10.4 Two-Sample Tests for Means and Variances

The basic idea for this section is the following. We have $X \sim \mathsf{norm}(\mathtt{mean} = \mu_X,\ \mathtt{sd} = \sigma_X)$ and $Y \sim \mathsf{norm}(\mathtt{mean} = \mu_Y,\ \mathtt{sd} = \sigma_Y)$. distributed independently. We would like to know whether X and Y come from the same population distribution, that is, we would like to know:

$$\text{Does } X \overset{\text{d}}{=} Y? \tag{10.4.1}$$

where the symbol $\overset{\text{d}}{=}$ means equality of probability distributions.

Since both X and Y are normal, we may rephrase the question:

$$\text{Does } \mu_X = \mu_Y \text{ and } \sigma_X = \sigma_Y? \tag{10.4.2}$$

Suppose first that we do not know the values of σ_X and σ_Y, but we know that they are equal, $\sigma_X = \sigma_Y$. Our test would then simplify to $H_0 : \mu_X = \mu_Y$. We collect data $X_1, X_2, \ldots, X_n$ and $Y_1, Y_2, \ldots, Y_m$, both simple random samples of size n and m from their respective normal distributions. Then under H_0 (that is, assuming H_0 is true) we have $\mu_X = \mu_Y$ or rewriting, $\mu_X - \mu_Y = 0$, so

$$T = \frac{\overline{X} - \overline{Y}}{S_p\sqrt{\frac{1}{n} + \frac{1}{m}}} = \frac{\overline{X} - \overline{Y} - (\mu_X - \mu_Y)}{S_p\sqrt{\frac{1}{n} + \frac{1}{m}}} \sim \mathsf{t}(\mathtt{df} = n + m - 2). \tag{10.4.3}$$

10.4.1 Independent Samples

Remark 10.14. If the values of σ_X and σ_Y are known, then we can plug them in to our statistic:

$$Z = \frac{\overline{X} - \overline{Y}}{\sqrt{\sigma_X^2/n + \sigma_Y^2/m}}; \tag{10.4.4}$$

the result will have a $\mathsf{norm}(\mathtt{mean} = 0,\ \mathtt{sd} = 1)$ distribution when $H_0 : \mu_X = \mu_Y$ is true.

Remark 10.15. Even if the values of σ_X and σ_Y are not known, if both n and m are large then we can plug in the sample estimates and the result will have approximately a norm(mean = 0, sd = 1) distribution when $H_0 : \mu_X = \mu_Y$ is true.

$$Z = \frac{\overline{X} - \overline{Y}}{\sqrt{S_X^2/n + S_Y^2/m}}. \tag{10.4.5}$$

Remark 10.16. It is usually important to construct side-by-side boxplots and other visual displays in concert with the hypothesis test. This gives a visual comparison of the samples and helps to identify departures from the test's assumptions – such as outliers.

Remark 10.17. WATCH YOUR ASSUMPTIONS.

- The normality assumption can be relaxed as long as the population distributions are not highly skewed.
- The equal variance assumption can be relaxed as long as both sample sizes n and m are large. However, if one (or both) samples is small, then the test does not perform well; we should instead use the methods of Chapter 13.

For a nonparametric alternative to the two-sample F test see Chapter 15.

10.4.2 Paired Samples

10.4.3 How to do it with R

```
> t.test(extra ~ group, data = sleep, paired = TRUE)
        Paired t-test

data:  extra by group
t = -4.0621, df = 9, p-value = 0.002833
alternative hypothesis: true difference in means is not equal to 0
95 percent confidence interval:
 -2.4598858 -0.7001142
sample estimates:
mean of the differences
                  -1.58
```

10.5 Other Hypothesis Tests

10.5.1 Kolmogorov-Smirnov Goodness-of-Fit Test

10.5.2 How to do it with R

```
> ks.test(randu$x, "punif")
        One-sample Kolmogorov-Smirnov test

data:  randu$x
D = 0.0555, p-value = 0.1697
alternative hypothesis: two-sided
```

10.5.3 Shapiro-Wilk Normality Test

10.5.4 How to do it with R

```
> shapiro.test(women$height)

        Shapiro-Wilk normality test

data:  women$height
W = 0.9636, p-value = 0.7545
```

10.6 Analysis of Variance

10.6.1 How to do it with R

I am thinking

```
> with(chickwts, by(weight, feed, shapiro.test))
feed: casein

        Shapiro-Wilk normality test

data:  dd[x, ]
W = 0.9166, p-value = 0.2592

--------------------------------------------------------
feed: horsebean

        Shapiro-Wilk normality test

data:  dd[x, ]
W = 0.9376, p-value = 0.5265

--------------------------------------------------------
feed: linseed

        Shapiro-Wilk normality test

data:  dd[x, ]
W = 0.9693, p-value = 0.9035

--------------------------------------------------------
feed: meatmeal

        Shapiro-Wilk normality test

data:  dd[x, ]
```

```
W = 0.9791, p-value = 0.9612

--------------------------------------------------------
feed: soybean

        Shapiro-Wilk normality test

data:  dd[x, ]
W = 0.9464, p-value = 0.5064

--------------------------------------------------------
feed: sunflower

        Shapiro-Wilk normality test

data:  dd[x, ]
W = 0.9281, p-value = 0.3603
```

and

```
> temp <- lm(weight ~ feed, data = chickwts)
```

and

```
> anova(temp)
Analysis of Variance Table

Response: weight
          Df Sum Sq Mean Sq F value    Pr(>F)
feed       5 231129   46226  15.365 5.936e-10 ***
Residuals 65 195556    3009
---
Signif. codes:  0 '***' 0.001 '**' 0.01 '*' 0.05 '.' 0.1 ' ' 1
```

Plot for the intuition of between versus within group variation.

Plots for the hypothesis tests:

10.7 Sample Size and Power

The power function of a test for a parameter θ is

$$\beta(\theta) = \underset{\theta}{\mathbb{P}}(\text{Reject } H_0), \quad -\infty < \theta < \infty.$$

Here are some properties of power functions:

1. $\beta(\theta) \leq \alpha$ for any $\theta \in \Theta_0$, and $\beta(\theta_0) = \alpha$. We interpret this by saying that no matter what value θ takes inside the null parameter space, there is never more than a chance of α of rejecting the null hypothesis. We have controlled the Type I error rate to be no greater than α.

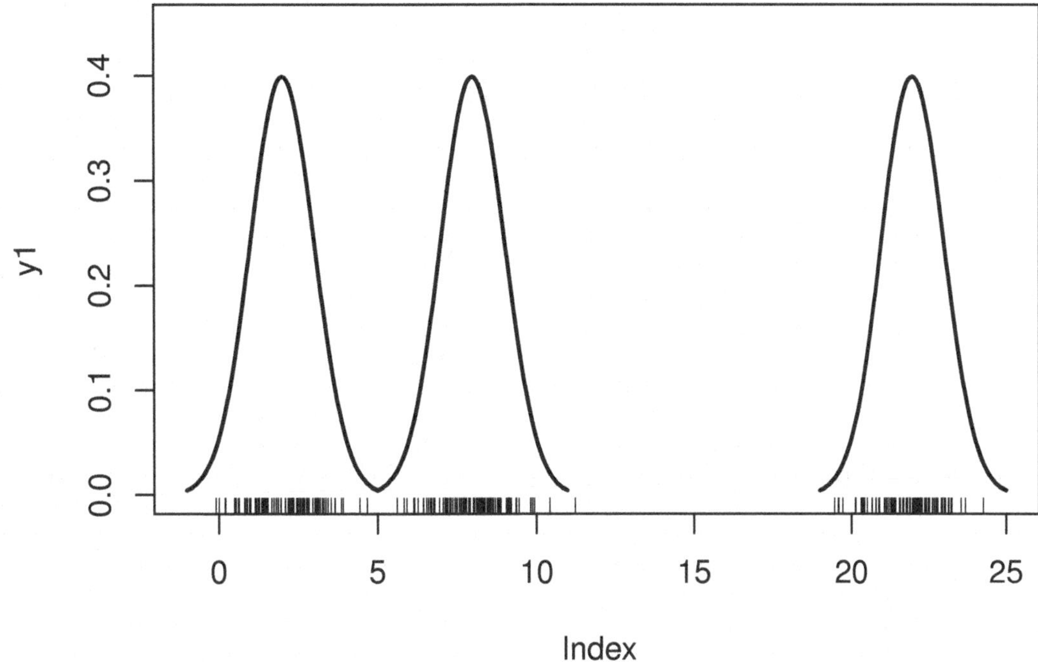

Figure 10.6.1: Between group versus within group variation

2. $\lim_{n\to\infty}\beta(\theta) = 1$ for any fixed $\theta \in \Theta_1$. In other words, as the sample size grows without bound we are able to detect a nonnull value of θ with increasing accuracy, no matter how close it lies to the null parameter space. This may appear to be a good thing at first glance, but it often turns out to be a curse. For another interpretation is that our Type II error rate grows as the sample size increases.

10.7.1 How to do it with R

I am thinking about `replicate` here, and also `power.examp` from the `TeachingDemos` package. There is an even better plot in upcoming work from the HH package.

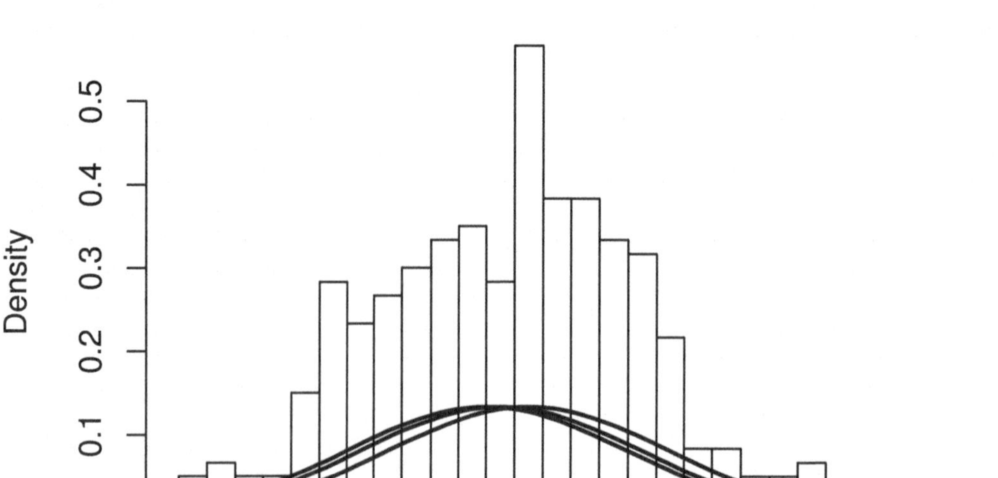

Figure 10.6.2: Between group versus within group variation

Chapter Exercises

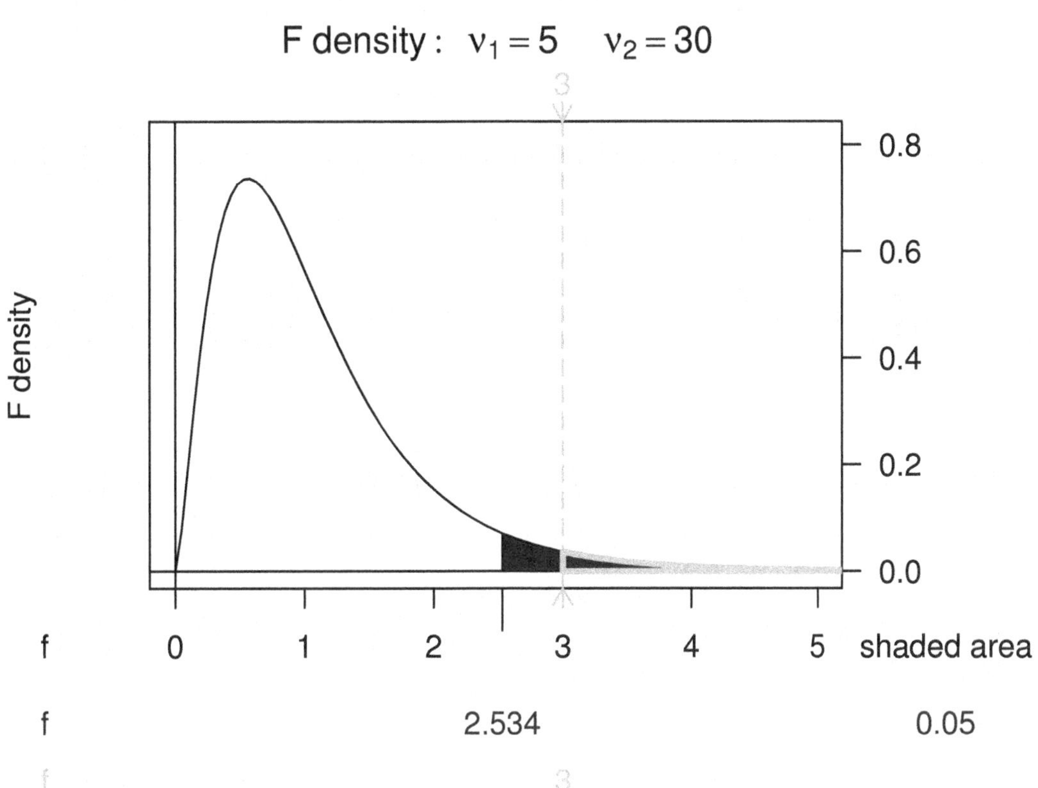

Figure 10.6.3: Some F plots from the HH package

se = 1.00   z* = 1.64   power = 0.26
n = 1   sd = 1.00   diff = 1.00   alpha = 0.050

Null Distribution

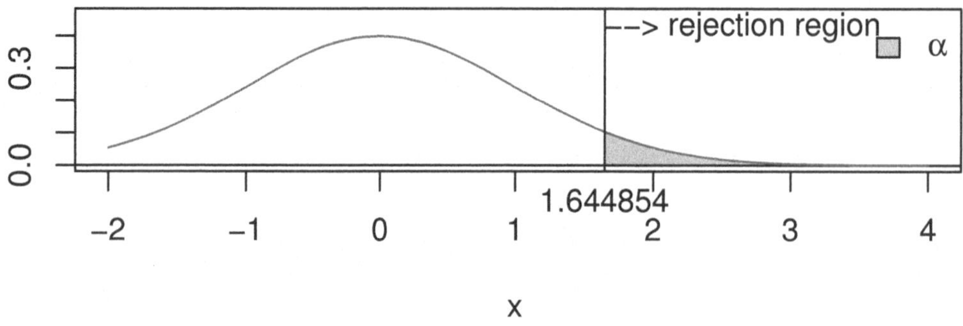

Alternative Distribution

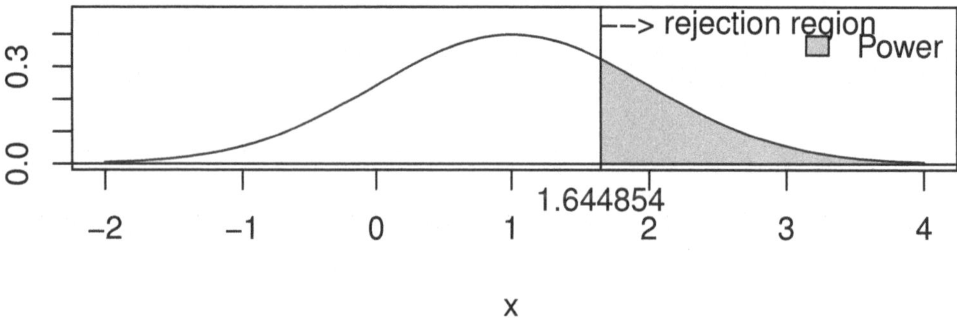

Figure 10.7.1: Plot of significance level and power

This graph was generated by the `power.examp` function from the `TeachingDemos` package. The plot corresponds to the hypothesis test $H_0 : \mu = \mu_0$ versus $H_1 : \mu = \mu_1$ (where $\mu_0 = 0$ and $\mu_1 = 1$, by default) based on a single observation $X \sim$ norm(`mean` $= \mu$, `sd` $= \sigma$). The top graph is of the H_0 density while the bottom is of the H_1 density. The significance level is set at $\alpha = 0.05$, the sample size is $n = 1$, and the standard deviation is $\sigma = 1$. The pink area is the significance level, and the critical value $z_{0.05} \approx 1.645$ is marked at the left boundary – this defines the rejection region. When H_0 is true, the probability of falling in the rejection region is exactly $\alpha = 0.05$. The same rejection region is marked on the bottom graph, and the probability of falling in it (when H_1 is true) is the blue area shown at the top of the display to be approximately 0.26. This probability represents the *power* to detect a non-null mean value of $\mu = 1$. With the command the `run.power.examp()` at the command line the same plot opens, but in addition, there are sliders available that allow the user to interactively change the sample size n, the standard deviation σ, the true difference between the means $\mu_1 - \mu_0$, and the significance level α. By playing around the student can investigate the effect each of the aforementioned parameters has on the statistical power. Note that you need the `tkrplot` package for `run.power.examp`.

Chapter 11

Simple Linear Regression

What do I want them to know?

- basic philosophy of SLR and the regression assumptions
- point and interval estimation of the model parameters, and how to use it to make predictions
- point and interval estimation of future observations from the model
- regression diagnostics, including R^2 and basic residual analysis
- the concept of influential versus outlying observations, and how to tell the difference

11.1 Basic Philosophy

Here we have two variables X and Y. For our purposes, X is not random (so we will write x), but Y is random. We believe that Y depends in *some* way on x. Some typical examples of (x, Y) pairs are

- x = study time and Y = score on a test.
- x = height and Y = weight.
- x = smoking frequency and Y = age of first heart attack.

Given information about the relationship between x and Y, we would like to *predict* future values of Y for particular values of x. This turns out to be a difficult problem[1], so instead we first tackle an easier problem: we estimate $\mathbb{E}\,Y$. How can we accomplish this? Well, we know that Y depends somehow on x, so it stands to reason that

$$\mathbb{E}\,Y = \mu(x),\ \text{a function of } x. \tag{11.1.1}$$

But we should be able to say more than that. To focus our efforts we impose some structure on the functional form of μ. For instance,

- if $\mu(x) = \beta_0 + \beta_1 x$, we try to estimate β_0 and β_1.
- if $\mu(x) = \beta_0 + \beta_1 x + \beta_2 x^2$, we try to estimate β_0, β_1, and β_2.

[1] Yogi Berra once said, "It is always difficult to make predictions, especially about the future."

- if $\mu(x) = \beta_0 e^{\beta_1 x}$, we try to estimate β_0 and β_1.

This helps us in the sense that we concentrate on the estimation of just a few parameters, β_0 and β_1, say, rather than some nebulous function. Our *modus operandi* is simply to perform the random experiment n times and observe the n ordered pairs of data (x_1, Y_1), (x_2, Y_2), $\ldots, (x_n, Y_n)$. We use these n data points to estimate the parameters.

More to the point, there are *three simple linear regression (SLR) assumptions* that will form the basis for the rest of this chapter:

Assumption 11.1. *We assume that μ is a linear function of x, that is,*

$$\mu(x) = \beta_0 + \beta_1 x, \tag{11.1.2}$$

where β_0 and β_1 are unknown constants to be estimated.

Assumption 11.2. *We further assume that Y_i is $\mu(x_i)$ – the "signal" – plus some "error" (represented by the symbol ϵ_i):*

$$Y_i = \beta_0 + \beta_1 x_i + \epsilon_i, \quad i = 1, 2, \ldots, n. \tag{11.1.3}$$

Assumption 11.3. *We lastly assume that the errors are i.i.d. normal with mean 0 and variance σ^2:*

$$\epsilon_1, \epsilon_2, \ldots, \epsilon_n \sim \mathtt{norm}(\mathtt{mean} = 0,\ \mathtt{sd} = \sigma). \tag{11.1.4}$$

Remark 11.4. We assume both the normality of the errors ϵ and the linearity of the mean function μ. Recall from Proposition 7.27 of Chapter 7 that if $(X, Y) \sim$ mvnorm then the mean of $Y|x$ is a linear function of x. This is not a coincidence. In more advanced classes we study the case that both X and Y are random, and in particular, when they are jointly normally distributed.

What does it all mean?

See Figure 11.1.1. Shown in the figure is a solid line, the regression line μ, which in this display has slope 0.5 and y-intercept 2.5, that is, $\mu(x) = 2.5 + 0.5x$. The intuition is that for each given value of x, we observe a random value of Y which is normally distributed with a mean equal to the height of the regression line at that x value. Normal densities are superimposed on the plot to drive this point home; in principle, the densities stand outside of the page, perpendicular to the plane of the paper. The figure shows three such values of x, namely, $x = 1$, $x = 2.5$, and $x = 4$. Not only do we assume that the observations at the three locations are independent, but we also assume that their distributions have the same spread. In mathematical terms this means that the normal densities all along the line have identical standard deviations – there is no "fanning out" or "scrunching in" of the normal densities as x increases[2].

Example 11.5. Speed and stopping distance of cars. We will use the data frame `cars` from the `datasets` package. It has two variables: `speed` and `dist`. We can take a look at some of the values in the data frame:

[2]In practical terms, this constant variance assumption is often violated, in that we often observe scatterplots that fan out from the line as x gets large or small. We say under those circumstances that the data show *heteroscedasticity*. There are methods to address it, but they fall outside the realm of SLR.

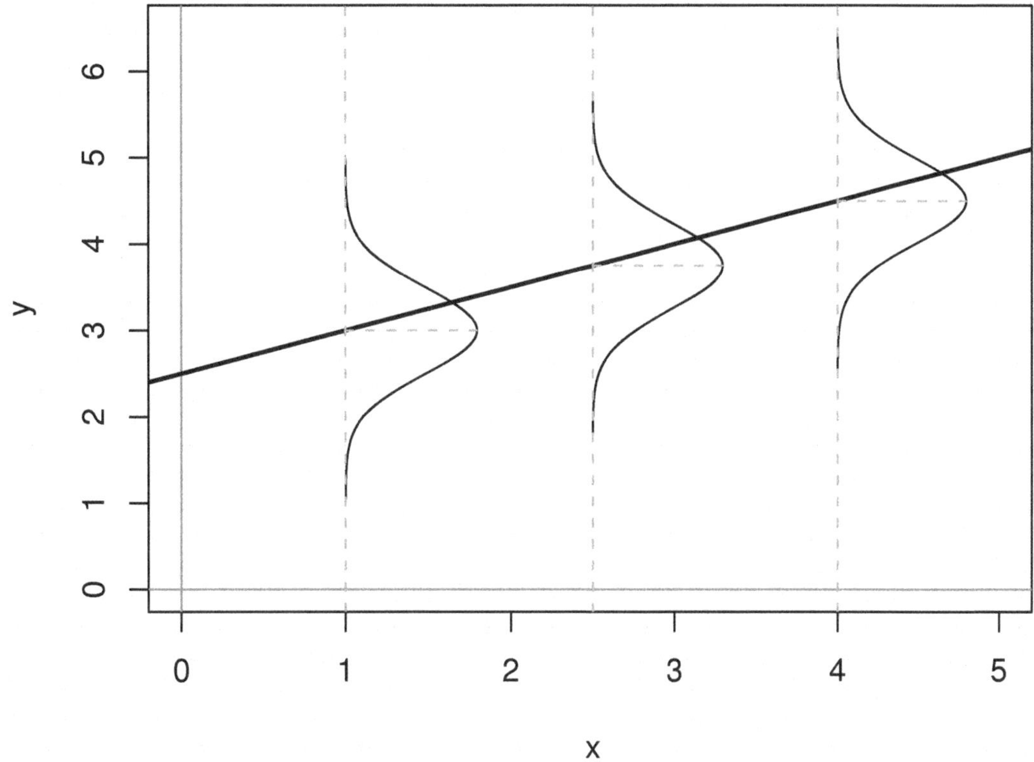

Figure 11.1.1: Philosophical foundations of SLR

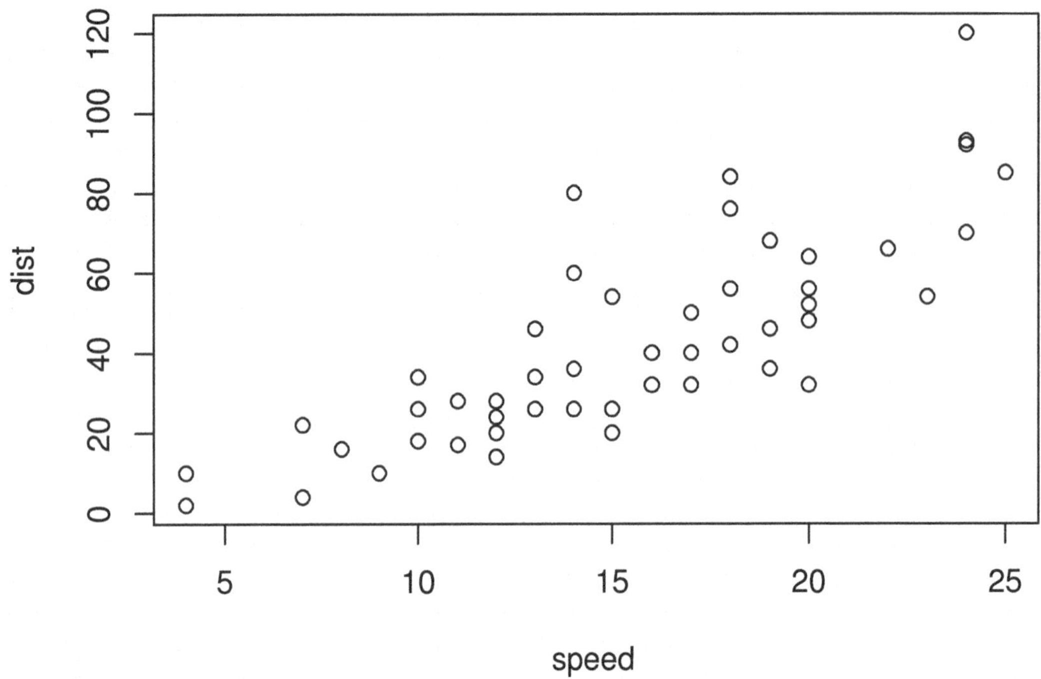

Figure 11.1.2: Scatterplot of `dist` versus `speed` for the `cars` data

```
> head(cars)

  speed dist
1     4    2
2     4   10
3     7    4
4     7   22
5     8   16
6     9   10
```

The `speed` represents how fast the car was going (x) in miles per hour and `dist` (Y) measures how far it took the car to stop, in feet. We can make a simple scatterplot of the data with the command `plot(dist ~speed, data = cars)`.

You can see the output in Figure 11.1.2, which was produced by the following code.

```
> plot(dist ~ speed, data = cars)
```

There is a pronounced upward trend to the data points, and the pattern looks approximately linear. There does not appear to be substantial fanning out of the points or extreme values.

11.2 Estimation

11.2.1 Point Estimates of the Parameters

Where is $\mu(x)$? In essence, we would like to "fit" a line to the points. But how do we determine a "good" line? Is there a *best* line? We will use maximum likelihood to find it. We know:

$$Y_i = \beta_0 + \beta_1 x_i + \epsilon_i, \quad i = 1, \ldots, n, \tag{11.2.1}$$

where the ϵ_i's are i.i.d. $\mathtt{norm(mean} = 0,\ \mathtt{sd} = \sigma)$. Thus $Y_i \sim \mathtt{norm(mean} = \beta_0 + \beta_1 x_i,\ \mathtt{sd} = \sigma)$, $i = 1, \ldots, n$. Furthermore, $Y_1, \ldots, Y_n$ are independent – but not identically distributed. The likelihood function is:

$$\begin{aligned} L(\beta_0, \beta_1, \sigma) &= \prod_{i=1}^{n} f_{Y_i}(y_i), & (11.2.2)\\ &= \prod_{i=1}^{n} (2\pi\sigma^2)^{-1/2} \exp\left\{ \frac{-(y_i - \beta_0 - \beta_1 x_i)^2}{2\sigma^2} \right\}, & (11.2.3)\\ &= (2\pi\sigma^2)^{-n/2} \exp\left\{ \frac{-\sum_{i=1}^{n}(y_i - \beta_0 - \beta_1 x_i)^2}{2\sigma^2} \right\}. & (11.2.4) \end{aligned}$$

We take the natural logarithm to get

$$\ln L(\beta_0, \beta_1, \sigma) = -\frac{n}{2} \ln(2\pi\sigma^2) - \frac{\sum_{i=1}^{n}(y_i - \beta_0 - \beta_1 x_i)^2}{2\sigma^2}. \tag{11.2.5}$$

We would like to maximize this function of β_0 and β_1. See Appendix E.6 which tells us that we should find critical points by means of the partial derivatives. Let us start by differentiating with respect to β_0:

$$\frac{\partial}{\partial \beta_0} \ln L = 0 - \frac{1}{2\sigma^2} \sum_{i=1}^{n} 2(y_i - \beta_0 - \beta_1 x_i)(-1), \tag{11.2.6}$$

and the partial derivative equals zero when $\sum_{i=1}^{n}(y_i - \beta_0 - \beta_1 x_i) = 0$, that is, when

$$n\beta_0 + \beta_1 \sum_{i=1}^{n} x_i = \sum_{i=1}^{n} y_i. \tag{11.2.7}$$

Moving on, we next take the partial derivative of $\ln L$ (Equation 11.2.5) with respect to β_1 to get

$$\begin{aligned} \frac{\partial}{\partial \beta_1} \ln L &= 0 - \frac{1}{2\sigma^2} \sum_{i=1}^{n} 2(y_i - \beta_0 - \beta_1 x_i)(-x_i), & (11.2.8)\\ &= \frac{1}{\sigma^2} \sum_{i=1}^{n} \left(x_i y_i - \beta_0 x_i - \beta_1 x_i^2 \right), & (11.2.9) \end{aligned}$$

and this equals zero when the last sum equals zero, that is, when

$$\beta_0 \sum_{i=1}^{n} x_i + \beta_1 \sum_{i=1}^{n} x_i^2 = \sum_{i=1}^{n} x_i y_i. \tag{11.2.10}$$

Solving the system of equations 11.2.7 and 11.2.10

$$n\beta_0 + \beta_1 \sum_{i=1}^{n} x_i = \sum_{i=1}^{n} y_i \tag{11.2.11}$$

$$\beta_0 \sum_{i=1}^{n} x_i + \beta_1 \sum_{i=1}^{n} x_i^2 = \sum_{i=1}^{n} x_i y_i \tag{11.2.12}$$

for β_0 and β_1 (in Exercise 11.2) gives

$$\hat{\beta}_1 = \frac{\sum_{i=1}^{n} x_i y_i - \left(\sum_{i=1}^{n} x_i\right)\left(\sum_{i=1}^{n} y_i\right)/n}{\sum_{i=1}^{n} x_i^2 - \left(\sum_{i=1}^{n} x_i\right)^2 \big/ n} \tag{11.2.13}$$

and

$$\hat{\beta}_0 = \overline{y} - \hat{\beta}_1 \overline{x}. \tag{11.2.14}$$

The conclusion? To estimate the mean line

$$\mu(x) = \beta_0 + \beta_1 x, \tag{11.2.15}$$

we use the "line of best fit"

$$\hat{\mu}(x) = \hat{\beta}_0 + \hat{\beta}_1 x, \tag{11.2.16}$$

where $\hat{\beta}_0$ and $\hat{\beta}_1$ are given as above. For notation we will usually write $b_0 = \hat{\beta}_0$ and $b_1 = \hat{\beta}_1$ so that $\hat{\mu}(x) = b_0 + b_1 x$.

Remark 11.6. The formula for b_1 in Equation 11.2.13 gets the job done but does not really make any sense. There are many equivalent formulas for b_1 that are more intuitive, or at the least are easier to remember. One of the author's favorites is

$$b_1 = r\frac{s_y}{s_x}, \tag{11.2.17}$$

where r, s_y, and s_x are the sample correlation coefficient and the sample standard deviations of the Y and x data, respectively. See Exercise 11.3. Also, notice the similarity between Equation 11.2.17 and Equation 7.6.7.

How to do it with R

Here we go. R will calculate the linear regression line with the `lm` function. We will store the result in an object which we will call `cars.lm`. Here is how it works:

```
> cars.lm <- lm(dist ~ speed, data = cars)
```

The first part of the input to the `lm` function, `dist~speed`, is a *model formula*, read as "`dist` is described by `speed`". The `data = cars` argument tells R where to look for the variables quoted in the model formula. The output object `cars.lm` contains a multitude of information. Let's first take a look at the coefficients of the fitted regression line, which are extracted by the `coef` function[3]:

```
> coef(cars.lm)
```

[3]Alternatively, we could just type `cars.lm` to see the same thing.

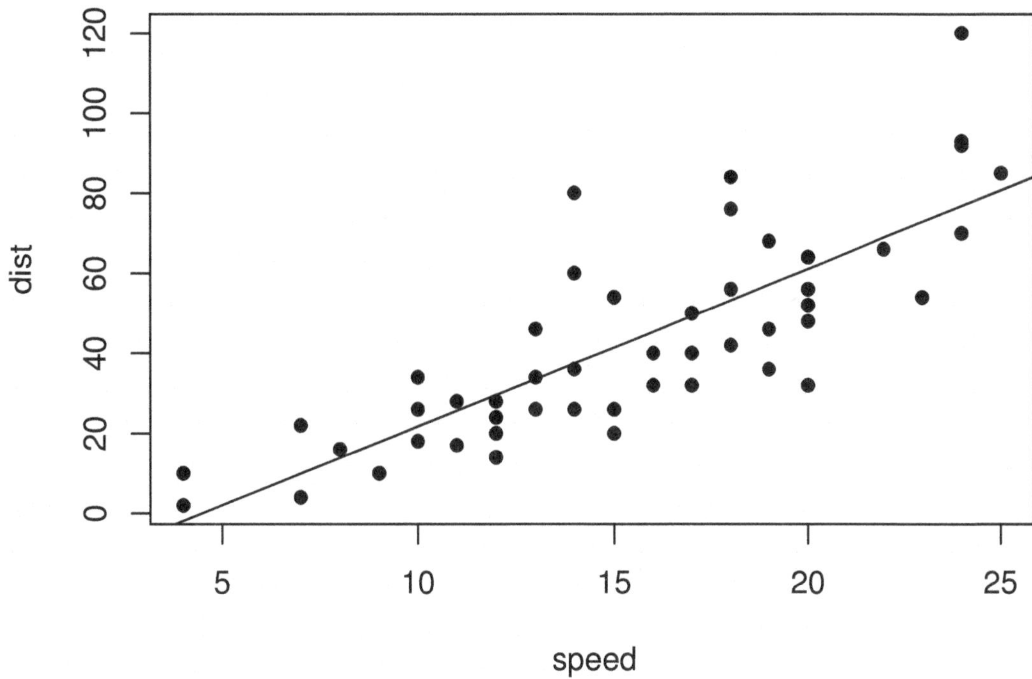

Figure 11.2.1: Scatterplot with added regression line for the `cars` data

```
(Intercept)       speed
 -17.579095    3.932409
```

The parameter estimates b_0 and b_1 for the intercept and slope, respectively, are shown above. The regression line is thus given by $\hat{\mu}$(`speed`) = -17.58 + 3.93`speed`.

It is good practice to visually inspect the data with the regression line added to the plot. To do this we first scatterplot the original data and then follow with a call to the `abline` function. The inputs to `abline` are the coefficients of `cars.lm` (see Figure 11.2.1):

```
> plot(dist ~ speed, data = cars, pch = 16)
> abline(coef(cars))
```

To calculate points on the regression line we may simply plug the desired x value(s) into $\hat{\mu}$, either by hand, or with the `predict` function. The inputs to `predict` are the fitted linear model object, `cars.lm`, and the desired x value(s) represented by a data frame. See the example below.

Example 11.7. Using the regression line for the `cars` data:

1. What is the meaning of $\mu(60) = \beta_0 + \beta_1(8)$?

   This represents the average stopping distance (in feet) for a car going 8 mph.

2. Interpret the slope β_1.

The true slope β_1 represents the increase in average stopping distance for each mile per hour faster that the car drives. In this case, we estimate the car to take approximately 3.93 additional feet to stop for each additional mph increase in speed.

3. Interpret the intercept β_0.

   This would represent the mean stopping distance for a car traveling 0 mph (which our regression line estimates to be -17.58). Of course, this interpretation does not make any sense for this example, because a car travelling 0 mph takes 0 ft to stop (it was not moving in the first place)! What went wrong? Looking at the data, we notice that the smallest speed for which we have measured data is 4 mph. Therefore, if we predict what would happen for slower speeds then we would be *extrapolating*, a dangerous practice which often gives nonsensical results.

11.2.2 Point Estimates of the Regression Line

We said at the beginning of the chapter that our goal was to estimate $\mu = \mathbb{E}\, Y$, and the arguments in Section 11.2.1 showed how to obtain an estimate $\hat{\mu}$ of μ when the regression assumptions hold. Now we will reap the benefits of our work in more ways than we previously disclosed. Given a particular value x_0, there are two values we would like to estimate:

1. the mean value of Y at x_0, and

2. a future value of Y at x_0.

The first is a number, $\mu(x_0)$, and the second is a random variable, $Y(x_0)$, but our point estimate is the same for both: $\hat{\mu}(x_0)$.

Example 11.8. We may use the regression line to obtain a point estimate of the mean stopping distance for a car traveling 8 mph: $\hat{\mu}(15) = b_0 + 8b_1 \approx$ -17.58 +(8) (3.93)$\approx$ 13.88. We would also use 13.88 as a point estimate for the stopping distance of a future car traveling 8 mph.

Note that we actually have observed data for a car traveling 8 mph; its stopping distance was 16 ft as listed in the fifth row of the `cars` data:

```
> cars[5, ]

  speed dist
5     8   16
```

There is a special name for estimates $\hat{\mu}(x_0)$ when x_0 matches an observed value x_i from the data set. They are called *fitted values*, they are denoted by $\hat{Y}_1, \hat{Y}_2, \ldots, \hat{Y}_n$ (ignoring repetition), and they play an important role in the sections that follow.

In an abuse of notation we will sometimes write $\hat{Y}$ or $\hat{Y}(x_0)$ to denote a point on the regression line even when x_0 does not belong to the original data if the context of the statement obviates any danger of confusion.

We saw in Example 11.7 that spooky things can happen when we are cavalier about point estimation. While it is usually acceptable to predict/estimate at values of x_0 that fall within the range of the original x data, it is reckless to use $\hat{\mu}$ for point estimates at locations outside that range. Such estimates are usually worthless. *Do not extrapolate* unless there are compelling external reasons, and even then, temper it with a good deal of caution.

How to do it with R

The fitted values are automatically computed as a byproduct of the model fitting procedure and are already stored as a component of the `cars.lm` object. We may access them with the `fitted` function (we only show the first five entries):

```
> fitted(cars.lm)[1:5]
```

```
        1         2         3         4         5
-1.849460 -1.849460  9.947766  9.947766 13.880175
```

Predictions at x values that are not necessarily part of the original data are done with the `predict` function. The first argument is the original `cars.lm` object and the second argument `newdata` accepts a dataframe (in the same form that was used to fit `cars.lm`) that contains the locations at which we are seeking predictions.

Let us predict the average stopping distances of cars traveling 6 mph, 8 mph, and 21 mph:

```
> predict(cars.lm, newdata = data.frame(speed = c(6, 8, 21)))
```

```
        1         2         3
 6.015358 13.880175 65.001489
```

Note that there were no observed cars that traveled 6 mph or 21 mph. Also note that our estimate for a car traveling 8 mph matches the value we computed by hand in Example 11.8.

11.2.3 Mean Square Error and Standard Error

To find the MLE of σ^2 we consider the partial derivative

$$\frac{\partial}{\partial\sigma^2}\ln L = \frac{n}{2\sigma^2} - \frac{1}{2(\sigma^2)^2}\sum_{i=1}^{n}(y_i - \beta_0 - \beta_1 x_i)^2, \tag{11.2.18}$$

and after plugging in $\hat{\beta}_0$ and $\hat{\beta}_1$ and setting equal to zero we get

$$\hat{\sigma^2} = \frac{1}{n}\sum_{i=1}^{n}(y_i - \hat{\beta}_0 - \hat{\beta}_1 x_i)^2 = \frac{1}{n}\sum_{i=1}^{n}[y_i - \hat{\mu}(x_i)]^2. \tag{11.2.19}$$

We write $\hat{Y}i = \hat{\mu}(x_i)$, and we let $E_i = Y_i - \hat{Y}_i$ be the ith *residual*. We see

$$n\hat{\sigma^2} = \sum_{i=1}^{n} E_i^2 = SSE = \text{ the sum of squared errors.} \tag{11.2.20}$$

For a point estimate of σ^2 we use the *mean square error* S^2 defined by

$$S^2 = \frac{SSE}{n-2}, \tag{11.2.21}$$

and we estimate σ with the *standard error* $S = \sqrt{S^2}$.[4]

[4]Be careful not to confuse the mean square error S^2 with the sample variance S^2 in Chapter 3. Other notation the reader may encounter is the lowercase s^2 or the bulky MSE.

How to do it with R

The residuals for the model may be obtained with the `residuals` function; we only show the first few entries in the interest of space:

```
> residuals(cars.lm)[1:5]

        1         2         3         4         5
 3.849460 11.849460 -5.947766 12.052234  2.119825
```

In the last section, we calculated the fitted value for $x = 8$ and found it to be approximately $\hat{\mu}(8) \approx 13.88$. Now, it turns out that there was only one recorded observation at $x = 8$, and we have seen this value in the output of `head(cars)` in Example 11.5; it was `dist` = 16 ft for a car with `speed` = 8 mph. Therefore, the residual should be $E = Y - \hat{Y}$ which is $E \approx 16-13.88$. Now take a look at the last entry of `residuals(cars.lm)`, above. It is not a coincidence.

The estimate S for σ is called the `Residual standard error` and for the `cars` data is shown a few lines up on the `summary(cars.lm)` output (see How to do it with R in Section 11.2.4). We may read it from there to be $S \approx 15.38$, or we can access it directly from the `summary` object.

```
> carsumry <- summary(cars.lm)
> carsumry$sigma

[1] 15.37959
```

11.2.4 Interval Estimates of the Parameters

We discussed general interval estimation in Chapter 9. There we found that we could use what we know about the sampling distribution of certain statistics to construct confidence intervals for the parameter being estimated. We will continue in that vein, and to get started we will determine the sampling distributions of the parameter estimates, b_1 and b_0.

To that end, we can see from Equation 11.2.13 (and it is made clear in Chapter 12) that b_1 is just a linear combination of normally distributed random variables, so b_1 is normally distributed too. Further, it can be shown that

$$b_1 \sim \mathsf{norm}\left(\mathtt{mean} = \beta_1,\ \mathtt{sd} = \sigma_{b_1}\right) \tag{11.2.22}$$

where

$$\sigma_{b_1} = \frac{\sigma}{\sqrt{\sum_{i=1}^{n}(x_i - \overline{x})^2}} \tag{11.2.23}$$

is called *the standard error of* b_1 which unfortunately depends on the unknown value of σ. We do not lose heart, though, because we can estimate σ with the standard error S from the last section. This gives us an estimate S_{b_1} for σ_{b_1} defined by

$$S_{b_1} = \frac{S}{\sqrt{\sum_{i=1}^{n}(x_i - \overline{x})^2}}. \tag{11.2.24}$$

Now, it turns out that b_0, b_1, and S are mutually independent (see the footnote in Section 12.2.7). Therefore, the quantity

$$T = \frac{b_1 - \beta_1}{S_{b_1}} \tag{11.2.25}$$

has a t(df $= n-2$) distribution. Therefore, a $100(1-\alpha)\%$ confidence interval for β_1 is given by

$$b_1 \pm \mathsf{t}_{\alpha/2}(\mathtt{df} = n-1)\, S_{b_1} \tag{11.2.26}$$

It is also sometimes of interest to construct a confidence interval for β_0 in which case we will need the sampling distribution of b_0. It is shown in Chapter 12 that

$$b_0 \sim \mathsf{norm}\left(\mathtt{mean} = \beta_0,\ \mathtt{sd} = \sigma_{b_0}\right), \tag{11.2.27}$$

where σ_{b_0} is given by

$$\sigma_{b_0} = \sigma \sqrt{\frac{1}{n} + \frac{\overline{x}^2}{\sum_{i=1}^{n}(x_i - \overline{x})^2}}, \tag{11.2.28}$$

and which we estimate with the S_{b_0} defined by

$$S_{b_0} = S \sqrt{\frac{1}{n} + \frac{\overline{x}^2}{\sum_{i=1}^{n}(x_i - \overline{x})^2}}. \tag{11.2.29}$$

Thus the quantity

$$T = \frac{b_0 - \beta_0}{S_{b_0}} \tag{11.2.30}$$

has a t(df $= n-2$) distribution and a $100(1-\alpha)\%$ confidence interval for β_0 is given by

$$b_0 \pm \mathsf{t}_{\alpha/2}(\mathtt{df} = n-1)\, S_{b_0} \tag{11.2.31}$$

How to do it with R

Let us take a look at the output from `summary(cars.lm)`:

```
> summary(cars.lm)

Call:
lm(formula = dist ~ speed, data = cars)

Residuals:
    Min      1Q  Median      3Q     Max 
-29.069  -9.525  -2.272   9.215  43.201 

Coefficients:
            Estimate Std. Error t value Pr(>|t|)    
(Intercept) -17.5791     6.7584  -2.601   0.0123 *  
speed         3.9324     0.4155   9.464 1.49e-12 ***
---
Signif. codes:  0 '***' 0.001 '**' 0.01 '*' 0.05 '.' 0.1 ' ' 1 

Residual standard error: 15.38 on 48 degrees of freedom
Multiple R-squared: 0.6511,	Adjusted R-squared: 0.6438 
F-statistic: 89.57 on 1 and 48 DF,  p-value: 1.490e-12
```

In the `Coefficients` section we find the parameter estimates and their respective standard errors in the second and third columns; the other columns are discussed in Section 11.3. If we wanted, say, a 95% confidence interval for β_1 we could use $b_1 = 3.932$ and $S_{b_1} = 0.416$ together with a $t_{0.025}(\mathtt{df} = 23)$ critical value to calculate $b_1 \pm t_{0.025}(\mathtt{df} = 23) S_{b_1}$.

Or, we could use the `confint` function.

```
> confint(cars.lm)
                 2.5 %    97.5 %
(Intercept) -31.167850 -3.990340
speed         3.096964  4.767853
```

With 95% confidence, the random interval [3.097, 4.768] covers the parameter β_1.

11.2.5 Interval Estimates of the Regression Line

We have seen how to estimate the coefficients of regression line with both point estimates and confidence intervals. We even saw how to estimate a value $\hat{\mu}(x)$ on the regression line for a given value of x, such as $x = 15$.

But how good is our estimate $\hat{\mu}(15)$? How much confidence do we have in *this* estimate? Furthermore, suppose we were going to observe another value of Y at $x = 15$. What could we say?

Intuitively, it should be easier to get bounds on the mean (average) value of Y at x_0 (called a *confidence interval for the mean value of* Y *at* x_0) than it is to get bounds on a future observation of Y (called a *prediction interval for* Y *at* x_0). As we shall see, the intuition serves us well and confidence intervals are shorter for the mean value, longer for the individual value.

Our point estimate of $\mu(x_0)$ is of course $\hat{Y} = \hat{Y}(x_0)$, so for a confidence interval we will need to know $\hat{Y}$'s sampling distribution. It turns out (see Section) that $\hat{Y} = \hat{\mu}(x_0)$ is distributed

$$\hat{Y} \sim \mathsf{norm}\left(\mathtt{mean} = \mu(x_0),\ \mathtt{sd} = \sigma\sqrt{\frac{1}{n} + \frac{(x_0 - \overline{x})^2}{\sum_{i=1}^{n}(x_i - \overline{x})^2}}\right). \tag{11.2.32}$$

Since σ is unknown we estimate it with S (we should expect the appearance of a $\mathsf{t}(\mathtt{df} = n - 2)$ distribution in the near future).

A $100(1 - \alpha)\%$ *confidence interval (CI) for* $\mu(x_0)$ is given by

$$\hat{Y} \pm t_{\alpha/2}(\mathtt{df} = n - 2)\, S\sqrt{\frac{1}{n} + \frac{(x_0 - \overline{x}^2)}{\sum_{i=1}^{n}(x_i - \overline{x})^2}}. \tag{11.2.33}$$

It is time for prediction intervals, which are slightly different. In order to find confidence bounds for a new observation of Y (we will denote it Y_{new}) we use the fact that

$$Y_{\text{new}} \sim \mathtt{norm}\left(\mathtt{mean} = \mu(x_0),\ \mathtt{sd} = \sigma\sqrt{1 + \frac{1}{n} + \frac{(x_0 - \overline{x})^2}{\sum_{i=1}^{n}(x_i - \overline{x})^2}}\right). \tag{11.2.34}$$

Of course σ is unknown and we estimate it with S. Thus, a $100(1 - \alpha)\%$ prediction interval (PI) for a future value of Y at x_0 is given by

$$\hat{Y}(x_0) \pm t_{\alpha/2}(\mathtt{df} = n - 1)\, S\sqrt{1 + \frac{1}{n} + \frac{(x_0 - \overline{x})^2}{\sum_{i=1}^{n}(x_i - \overline{x})^2}}. \tag{11.2.35}$$

We notice that the prediction interval in Equation 11.2.35 is wider than the confidence interval in Equation 11.2.33, as we expected at the beginning of the section.

How to do it with R

Confidence and prediction intervals are calculated in R with the `predict` function, which we encountered in Section 11.2.2. There we neglected to take advantage of its additional `interval` argument. The general syntax follows.

Example 11.9. We will find confidence and prediction intervals for the stopping distance of a car travelling 5, 6, and 21 mph (note from the graph that there are no collected data for these speeds). We have computed `cars.lm` earlier, and we will use this for input to the `predict` function. Also, we need to tell R the values of x_0 at which we want the predictions made, and store the x_0 values in a data frame whose variable is labeled with the correct name. *This is important.*

```
> new <- data.frame(speed = c(5, 6, 21))
```

Next we instruct R to calculate the intervals. Confidence intervals are given by

```
> predict(cars.lm, newdata = new, interval = "confidence")
        fit       lwr      upr
1  2.082949 -7.644150 11.81005
2  6.015358 -2.973341 15.00406
3 65.001489 58.597384 71.40559
```

Prediction intervals are given by

```
> predict(cars.lm, newdata = new, interval = "prediction")
        fit       lwr      upr
1  2.082949 -30.33359 34.49948
2  6.015358 -26.18731 38.21803
3 65.001489  33.42257 96.58040
```

The type of interval is dictated by the `interval` argument (which is `none` by default), and the default confidence level is 95% (which can be changed with the `level` argument).

Example 11.10. Using the `cars` data,

1. Report a point estimate of and a 95% confidence interval for the mean stopping distance for a car travelling 5 mph.

   The fitted value for $x = 5$ is 2.08, so a point estimate would be 2.08 ft. The 95% CI is given by [-7.64, 11.81], so with 95% confidence the mean stopping distance lies somewhere between -7.64 ft and 11.81 ft.

2. Report a point prediction for and a 95% prediction interval for the stopping distance of a hypothetical car travelling 21 mph.

   The fitted value for $x = 21$ is 65, so a point prediction for the stopping distance is 65 ft. The 95% PI is given by [33.42, 96.58], so with 95% confidence we may assert that the hypothetical stopping distance for a car travelling 21 mph would lie somewhere between 33.42 ft and 96.58 ft.

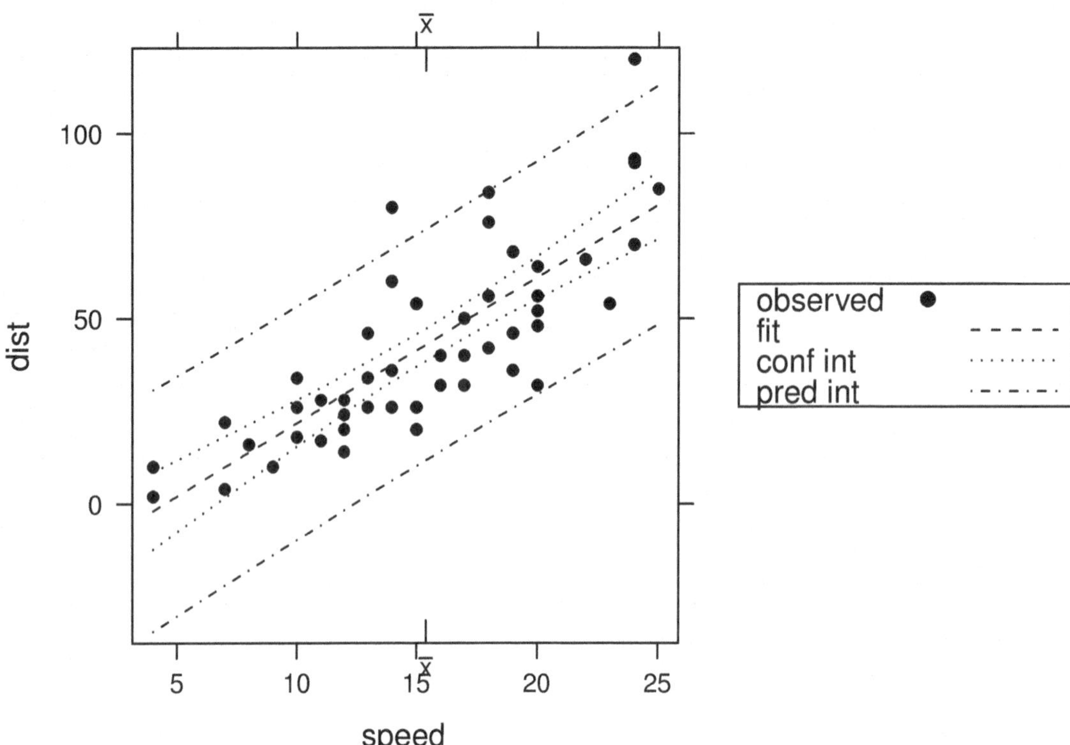

Figure 11.2.2: Scatterplot with confidence/prediction bands for the `cars` data

Graphing the Confidence and Prediction Bands

We earlier guessed that a bound on the value of a single new observation would be inherently less certain than a bound for an average (mean) value; therefore, we expect the CIs for the mean to be tighter than the PIs for a new observation. A close look at the standard deviations in Equations 11.2.33 and 11.2.35 confirms our guess, but we would like to see a picture to drive the point home.

We may plot the confidence and prediction intervals with one fell swoop using the `ci.plot` function from the `HH` package [40]. The graph is displayed in Figure 11.2.2.

```
> library(HH)
> ci.plot(cars.lm)
```

Notice that the bands curve outward away from the regression line as the x values move away from the center. This is expected once we notice the $(x_0 - \overline{x})^2$ term in the standard deviation formulas in Equations 11.2.33 and 11.2.35.

11.3 Model Utility and Inference

11.3.1 Hypothesis Tests for the Parameters

Much of the attention of SLR is directed toward β_1 because when $\beta_1 \neq 0$ the mean value of Y increases (or decreases) as x increases. Further, if $\beta_1 = 0$ then the mean value of Y remains the same, regardless of the value of x (when the regression assumptions hold, of course). It is thus very important to decide whether or not $\beta_1 = 0$. We address the question with a statistical test of the null hypothesis $H_0 : \beta_1 = 0$ versus the alternative hypothesis $H_1 : \beta_1 \neq 0$, and to do that we need to know the sampling distribution of b_1 when the null hypothesis is true.

To this end we already know from Section 11.2.4 that the quantity

$$T = \frac{b_1 - \beta_1}{S_{b_1}} \tag{11.3.1}$$

has a t(`df` $= n - 2$) distribution; therefore, when $\beta_1 = 0$ the quantity b_1/S_{b_1} has a t(`df` $= n - 2$) distribution and we can compute a p-value by comparing the observed value of b_1/S_{b_1} with values under a t(`df` $= n - 2$) curve.

Similarly, we may test the hypothesis $H_0 : \beta_0 = 0$ versus the alternative $H_1 : \beta_0 \neq 0$ with the statistic $T = b_0/S_{b_0}$, where S_{b_0} is given in Section 11.2.4. The test is conducted the same way as for β_1.

How to do it with R

Let us take another look at the output from `summary(cars.lm)`:

```
> summary(cars.lm)

Call:
lm(formula = dist ~ speed, data = cars)

Residuals:
    Min      1Q  Median      3Q     Max 
-29.069  -9.525  -2.272   9.215  43.201 

Coefficients:
            Estimate Std. Error t value Pr(>|t|)    
(Intercept) -17.5791     6.7584  -2.601   0.0123 *  
speed         3.9324     0.4155   9.464 1.49e-12 ***
---
Signif. codes:  0 '***' 0.001 '**' 0.01 '*' 0.05 '.' 0.1 ' ' 1

Residual standard error: 15.38 on 48 degrees of freedom
Multiple R-squared: 0.6511,	Adjusted R-squared: 0.6438 
F-statistic: 89.57 on 1 and 48 DF,  p-value: 1.490e-12
```

In the `Coefficients` section we find the t statistics and the p-values associated with the tests that the respective parameters are zero in the fourth and fifth columns. Since the p-values are (much) less than 0.05, we conclude that there is strong evidence that the parameters $\beta_1 \neq 0$ and $\beta_0 \neq 0$, and as such, we say that there is a statistically significant linear relationship between `dist` and `speed`.

11.3.2 Simple Coefficient of Determination

It would be nice to have a single number that indicates how well our linear regression model is doing, and the *simple coefficient of determination* is designed for that purpose. In what follows, we observe the values Y_1, Y_2, ..., Y_n, and the goal is to estimate $\mu(x_0)$, the mean value of Y at the location x_0.

If we disregard the dependence of Y and x and base our estimate only on the Y values then a reasonable choice for an estimator is just the MLE of μ, which is $\overline{Y}$. Then the errors incurred by the estimate are just $Y_i - \overline{Y}$ and the variation about the estimate as measured by the sample variance is proportional to

$$SSTO = \sum_{i=1}^{n} (Y_i - \overline{Y})^2. \tag{11.3.2}$$

Here, $SSTO$ is an acronym for the *total sum of squares*.

But we do have additional information, namely, we have values x_i associated with each value of Y_i. We have seen that this information leads us to the estimate $\hat{Y}_i$ and the errors incurred are just the residuals, $E_i = Y_i - \hat{Y}_i$. The variation associated with these errors can be measured with

$$SSE = \sum_{i=1}^{n} (Y_i - \hat{Y}_i)^2. \tag{11.3.3}$$

We have seen the SSE before, which stands for the *sum of squared errors* or *error sum of squares*. Of course, we would expect the error to be less in the latter case, since we have used more information. The improvement in our estimation as a result of the linear regression model can be measured with the difference

$$(Y_i - \overline{Y}) - (Y_i - \hat{Y}_i) = \hat{Y}_i - \overline{Y},$$

and we measure the variation in these errors with

$$SSR = \sum_{i=1}^{n} (\hat{Y}_i - \overline{Y})^2, \tag{11.3.4}$$

also known as the *regression sum of squares*. It is not obvious, but some algebra proved a famous result known as the **ANOVA Equality**:

$$\sum_{i=1}^{n} (Y_i - \overline{Y})^2 = \sum_{i=1}^{n} (\hat{Y}_i - \overline{Y})^2 + \sum_{i=1}^{n} (Y_i - \hat{Y}_i)^2 \tag{11.3.5}$$

or in other words,

$$SSTO = SSR + SSE. \tag{11.3.6}$$

This equality has a nice interpretation. Consider $SSTO$ to be the *total variation* of the errors. Think of a decomposition of the total variation into pieces: one piece measuring the reduction of error from using the linear regression model, or *explained variation* (SSR), while the other represents what is left over, that is, the errors that the linear regression model doesn't explain, or *unexplained variation* (SSE). In this way we see that the ANOVA equality merely partitions the variation into

total variation = explained variation + unexplained variation.

For a single number to summarize how well our model is doing we use the simple coefficient of determination r^2, defined by

$$r^2 = 1 - \frac{SSE}{SSTO}. \tag{11.3.7}$$

We interpret r^2 as the proportion of total variation that is explained by the simple linear regression model. When r^2 is large, the model is doing a good job; when r^2 is small, the model is not doing a good job.

Related to the simple coefficient of determination is the sample correlation coefficient, r. As you can guess, the way we get r is by the formula $|r| = \sqrt{r^2}$. But how do we get the sign? It is equal the sign of the slope estimate b_1. That is, if the regression line $\hat{\mu}(x)$ has positive slope, then $r = \sqrt{r^2}$. Likewise, if the slope of $\hat{\mu}(x)$ is negative, then $r = -\sqrt{r^2}$.

How to do it with R

The primary method to display partitioned sums of squared errors is with an *ANOVA table*. The command in R to produce such a table is `anova`. The input to `anova` is the result of an `lm` call which for the `cars` data is `cars.lm`.

```
> anova(cars.lm)

Analysis of Variance Table

Response: dist
          Df Sum Sq Mean Sq F value    Pr(>F)
speed      1  21186 21185.5  89.567 1.490e-12 ***
Residuals 48  11354   236.5
---
Signif. codes:  0 '***' 0.001 '**' 0.01 '*' 0.05 '.' 0.1 ' ' 1
```

The output gives

$$r^2 = 1 - \frac{SSE}{SSR + SSE} = 1 - \frac{11353.5}{21185.5 + 11353.5} \approx 0.65.$$

The interpretation should be: "The linear regression line accounts for approximately 65% of the variation of `dist` as explained by `speed`".

The value of r^2 is stored in the `r.squared` component of `summary(cars.lm)`, which we called `carsumry`.

```
> carsumry$r.squared

[1] 0.6510794
```

We already knew this. We saw it in the next to the last line of the `summary(cars.lm)` output where it was called "`Multiple R-squared`". Listed right beside it is the `Adjusted R-squared` which we will discuss in Chapter 12.

For the `cars` data, we find r to be

```
> sqrt(carsumry$r.squared)

[1] 0.8068949
```

We choose the principal square root because the slope of the regression line is positive.

11.3.3 Overall F statistic

There is another way to test the significance of the linear regression model. In SLR, the new way also tests the hypothesis $H_0 : \beta_1 = 0$ versus $H_1 : \beta_1 \neq 0$, but it is done with a new test statistic called the *overall F statistic*. It is defined by

$$F = \frac{SSR}{SSE/(n-2)}. \tag{11.3.8}$$

Under the regression assumptions and when H_0 is true, the F statistic has an `f(df1` $= 1$, `df2` $= n - 2$) distribution. We reject H_0 when F is large – that is, when the explained variation is large relative to the unexplained variation.

All this being said, we have not yet gained much from the overall F statistic because we already knew from Section 11.3.1 how to test $H_0 : \beta_1 = 0\ldots$ we use the Student's t statistic. What is worse is that (in the simple linear regression model) it can be proved that the F in Equation 11.3.8 is exactly the Student's t statistic for β_1 squared,

$$F = \left(\frac{b_1}{S_{b_1}}\right)^2. \tag{11.3.9}$$

So why bother to define the F statistic? Why not just square the t statistic and be done with it? The answer is that the F statistic has a more complicated interpretation and plays a more important role in the multiple linear regression model which we will study in Chapter 12. See Section 12.3.3 for details.

11.3.4 How to do it with R

The overall F statistic and p-value are displayed in the bottom line of the `summary(cars.lm)` output. It is also shown in the final columns of `anova(cars.lm)`:

```
> anova(cars.lm)

Analysis of Variance Table

Response: dist
          Df Sum Sq Mean Sq F value    Pr(>F)
speed      1  21186 21185.5  89.567 1.490e-12 ***
Residuals 48  11354   236.5
---
Signif. codes:  0 '***' 0.001 '**' 0.01 '*' 0.05 '.' 0.1 ' ' 1
```

Here we see that the F statistic is 89.57 with a p-value very close to zero. The conclusion: there is very strong evidence that $H_0 : \beta_1 = 0$ is false, that is, there is strong evidence that $\beta_1 \neq 0$. Moreover, we conclude that the regression relationship between `dist` and `speed` is significant.

Note that the value of the F statistic is the same as the Student's t statistic for `speed` squared.

11.4 Residual Analysis

We know from our model that $Y = \mu(x) + \epsilon$, or in other words, $\epsilon = Y - \mu(x)$. Further, we know that $\epsilon \sim$ norm(mean $= 0$, sd $= \sigma$). We may estimate ϵ_i with the *residual* $E_i = Y_i - \hat{Y}_i$,

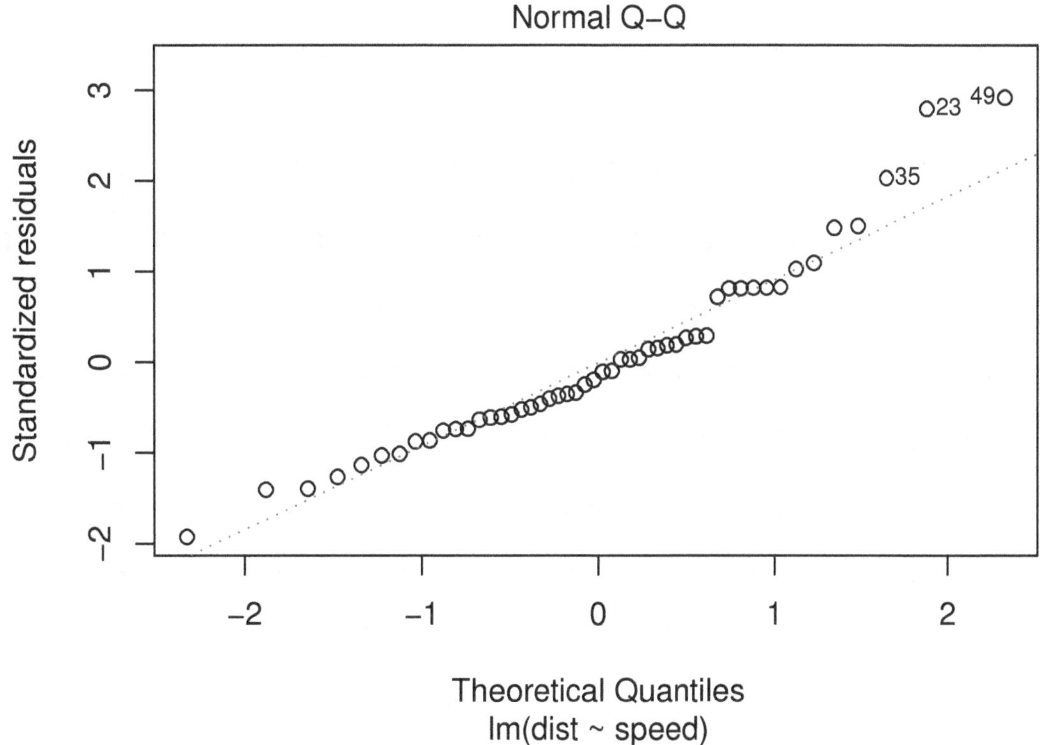

Figure 11.4.1: Normal q-q plot of the residuals for the `cars` data
Used for checking the normality assumption. Look out for any curvature or substantial departures from the straight line; hopefully the dots hug the line closely.

where $\hat{Y}_i = \hat{\mu}(x_i)$. If the regression assumptions hold, then the residuals should be normally distributed. We check this in Section 11.4.1. Further, the residuals should have mean zero with constant variance σ^2, and we check this in Section 11.4.2. Last, the residuals should be independent, and we check this in Section 11.4.3.

In every case, we will begin by looking at residual plots – that is, scatterplots of the residuals E_i versus index or predicted values $\hat{Y}_i$ – and follow up with hypothesis tests.

11.4.1 Normality Assumption

We can assess the normality of the residuals with graphical methods and hypothesis tests. To check graphically whether the residuals are normally distributed we may look at histograms or *q-q* plots. We first examine a histogram in Figure 11.4.1. There we see that the distribution of the residuals appears to be mound shaped, for the most part. We can plot the order statistics of the sample versus quantiles from a `norm(mean = 0, sd = 1)` distribution with the command `plot(cars.lm, which = 2)`, and the results are in Figure 11.4.1. If the assumption of normality were true, then we would expect points randomly scattered about the dotted straight line displayed in the figure. In this case, we see a slight departure from normality in that the dots show systematic clustering on one side or the other of the line. The points on the upper end of the plot also appear begin to stray from the line. We would say there is some evidence that the residuals are not perfectly normal.

Testing the Normality Assumption

Even though we may be concerned about the plots, we can use tests to determine if the evidence present is statistically significant, or if it could have happened merely by chance. There are many statistical tests of normality. We will use the Shapiro-Wilk test, since it is known to be a good test and to be quite powerful. However, there are many other fine tests of normality including the Anderson-Darling test and the Lillefors test, just to mention two of them.

The Shapiro-Wilk test is based on the statistic

$$W = \frac{\left(\sum_{i=1}^{n} a_i E_{(i)}\right)^2}{\sum_{j=1}^{n} E_j^2}, \tag{11.4.1}$$

where the $E_{(i)}$ are the ordered residuals and the a_i are constants derived from the order statistics of a sample of size n from a normal distribution. See Section 10.5.3.

We perform the Shapiro-Wilk test below, using the `shapiro.test` function from the `stats` package. The hypotheses are

$$H_0: \text{ the residuals are normally distributed}$$

versus

$$H_1: \text{ the residuals are not normally distributed.}$$

The results from R are

```
> shapiro.test(residuals(cars.lm))
        Shapiro-Wilk normality test

data:  residuals(cars.lm)
W = 0.9451, p-value = 0.02153
```

For these data we would reject the assumption of normality of the residuals at the $\alpha = 0.05$ significance level, but do not lose heart, because the regression model is reasonably robust to departures from the normality assumption. As long as the residual distribution is not highly skewed, then the regression estimators will perform reasonably well. Moreover, departures from constant variance and independence will sometimes affect the quantile plots and histograms, therefore it is wise to delay final decisions regarding normality until all diagnostic measures have been investigated.

11.4.2 Constant Variance Assumption

We will again go to residual plots to try and determine if the spread of the residuals is changing over time (or index). However, it is unfortunately not that easy because the residuals do not have constant variance! In fact, it can be shown that the variance of the residual E_i is

$$\mathrm{Var}(E_i) = \sigma^2(1 - h_{ii}), \quad i = 1, 2, \ldots, n, \tag{11.4.2}$$

where h_{ii} is a quantity called the *leverage* which is defined below. Consequently, in order to check the constant variance assumption we must standardize the residuals before plotting. We estimate the standard error of E_i with $s_{E_i} = s\sqrt{(1 - h_{ii})}$ and define the *standardized residuals* R_i, $i = 1, 2, \ldots, n$, by

$$R_i = \frac{E_i}{s\sqrt{1 - h_{ii}}}, \quad i = 1, 2, \ldots, n. \tag{11.4.3}$$

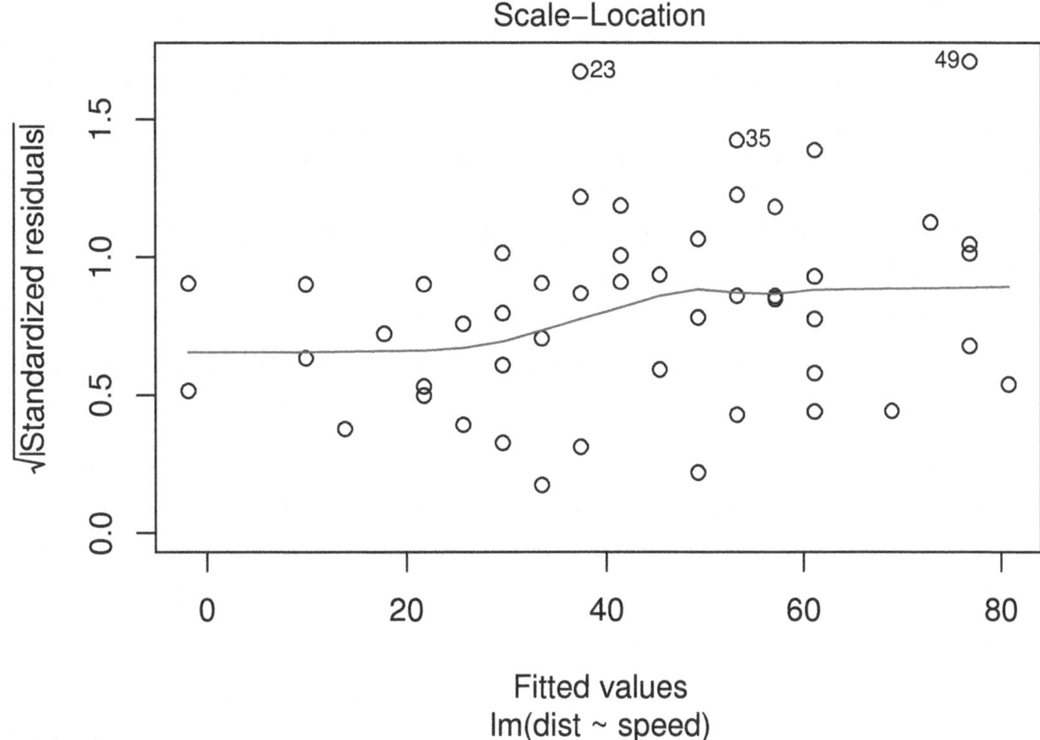

Figure 11.4.2: Plot of standardized residuals against the fitted values for the `cars` data
Used for checking the constant variance assumption. Watch out for any fanning out (or in) of the dots; hopefully they fall in a constant band.

For the constant variance assumption we do not need the sign of the residual so we will plot $\sqrt{|R_i|}$ versus the fitted values. As we look at a scatterplot of $\sqrt{|R_i|}$ versus $\hat{Y}_i$ we would expect under the regression assumptions to see a constant band of observations, indicating no change in the magnitude of the observed distance from the line. We want to watch out for a fanning-out of the residuals, or a less common funneling-in of the residuals. Both patterns indicate a change in the residual variance and a consequent departure from the regression assumptions, the first an increase, the second a decrease.

In this case, we plot the standardized residuals versus the fitted values. The graph may be seen in Figure 11.4.2. For these data there does appear to be somewhat of a slight fanning-out of the residuals.

Testing the Constant Variance Assumption

We will use the Breusch-Pagan test to decide whether the variance of the residuals is nonconstant. The null hypothesis is that the variance is the same for all observations, and the alternative hypothesis is that the variance is not the same for all observations. The test statistic is found by fitting a linear model to the centered squared residuals

$$W_i = E_i^2 - \frac{SSE}{n}, \quad i = 1, 2, \ldots, n. \tag{11.4.4}$$

By default the same explanatory variables are used in the new model which produces fitted values $\hat{W}_i$, $i = 1, 2, \ldots, n$. The Breusch-Pagan test statistic in R is then calculated with

$$BP = n \sum_{i=1}^{n} \hat{W}_i^2 \div \sum_{i=1}^{n} W_i^2. \tag{11.4.5}$$

We reject the null hypothesis if BP is too large, which happens when the explained variation in the new model is large relative to the unexplained variation in the original model.

We do it in R with the `bptest` function from the `lmtest` package [93].

```
> library(lmtest)
> bptest(cars.lm)

        studentized Breusch-Pagan test

data:  cars.lm
BP = 3.2149, df = 1, p-value = 0.07297
```

For these data we would not reject the null hypothesis at the $\alpha = 0.05$ level. There is relatively weak evidence against the assumption of constant variance.

11.4.3 Independence Assumption

One of the strongest of the regression assumptions is the one regarding independence. Departures from the independence assumption are often exhibited by correlation (or autocorrelation, literally, self-correlation) present in the residuals. There can be positive or negative correlation.

Positive correlation is displayed by positive residuals followed by positive residuals, and negative residuals followed by negative residuals. Looking from left to right, this is exhibited by a cyclical feature in the residual plots, with long sequences of positive residuals being followed by long sequences of negative ones.

On the other hand, negative correlation implies positive residuals followed by negative residuals, which are then followed by positive residuals, *etc.* Consequently, negatively correlated residuals are often associated with an alternating pattern in the residual plots. We examine the residual plot in Figure 11.4.3. There is no obvious cyclical wave pattern or structure to the residual plot.

Testing the Independence Assumption

We may statistically test whether there is evidence of autocorrelation in the residuals with the Durbin-Watson test. The test is based on the statistic

$$D = \frac{\sum_{i=2}^{n} (E_i - E_{i-1})^2}{\sum_{j=1}^{n} E_j^2}. \tag{11.4.6}$$

Exact critical values are difficult to obtain, but R will calculate the p-value to great accuracy. It is performed with the `dwtest` function from the `lmtest` package. We will conduct a two sided test that the correlation is not zero, which is not the default (the default is to test that the autocorrelation is positive).

```
> library(lmtest)
> dwtest(cars.lm, alternative = "two.sided")
```

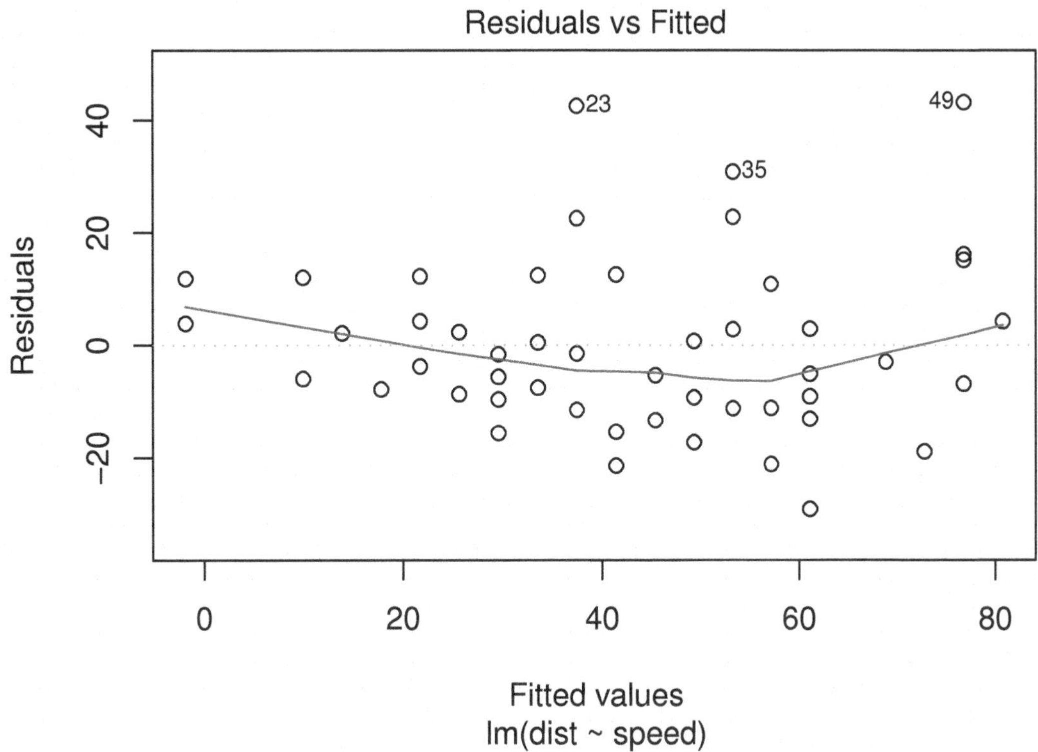

Figure 11.4.3: Plot of the residuals versus the fitted values for the `cars` data
Used for checking the independence assumption. Watch out for any patterns or structure; hopefully the points are randomly scattered on the plot.

```
        Durbin-Watson test

data:  cars.lm
DW = 1.6762, p-value = 0.1904
alternative hypothesis: true autocorelation is not 0
```

In this case we do not reject the null hypothesis at the $\alpha = 0.05$ significance level; there is very little evidence of nonzero autocorrelation in the residuals.

11.4.4 Remedial Measures

We often find problems with our model that suggest that at least one of the three regression assumptions is violated. What do we do then? There are many measures at the statistician's disposal, and we mention specific steps one can take to improve the model under certain types of violation.

Mean response is not linear. We can directly modify the model to better approximate the mean response. In particular, perhaps a polynomial regression function of the form

$$\mu(x) = \beta_0 + \beta_1 x_1 + \beta_2 x_1^2$$

would be appropriate. Alternatively, we could have a function of the form

$$\mu(x) = \beta_0 e^{\beta_1 x}.$$

Models like these are studied in nonlinear regression courses.

Error variance is not constant. Sometimes a transformation of the dependent variable will take care of the problem. There is a large class of them called *Box-Cox transformations*. They take the form

$$Y^* = Y^{\lambda}, \tag{11.4.7}$$

where λ is a constant. (The method proposed by Box and Cox will determine a suitable value of λ automatically by maximum likelihood). The class contains the transformations

$$\begin{aligned} \lambda = 2, &\quad Y^* = Y^2 \\ \lambda = 0.5, &\quad Y^* = \sqrt{Y} \\ \lambda = 0, &\quad Y^* = \ln\, Y \\ \lambda = -1, &\quad Y^* = 1/Y \end{aligned}$$

Alternatively, we can use the method of *weighted least squares*. This is studied in more detail in later classes.

Error distribution is not normal. The same transformations for stabilizing the variance are equally appropriate for smoothing the residuals to a more Gaussian form. In fact, often we will kill two birds with one stone.

Errors are not independent. There is a large class of autoregressive models to be used in this situation which occupy the latter part of Chapter 16.

11.5 Other Diagnostic Tools

There are two types of observations with which we must be especially careful:

Influential observations are those that have a substantial effect on our estimates, predictions, or inferences. A small change in an influential observation is followed by a large change in the parameter estimates or inferences.

Outlying observations are those that fall fall far from the rest of the data. They may be indicating a lack of fit for our regression model, or they may just be a mistake or typographical error that should be corrected. Regardless, special attention should be given to these observations. An outlying observation may or may not be influential.

We will discuss outliers first because the notation builds sequentially in that order.

11.5.1 Outliers

There are three ways that an observation (x_i, y_i) may be an outlier: it can have an x_i value which falls far from the other x values, it can have a y_i value which falls far from the other y values, or it can have both its x_i and y_i values falling far from the other x and y values.

Leverage

Leverage statistics are designed to identify observations which have x values that are far away from the rest of the data. In the simple linear regression model the leverage of x_i is denoted by h_{ii} and defined by

$$h_{ii} = \frac{1}{n} + \frac{(x_i - \overline{x})^2}{\sum_{k=1}^{n}(x_k - \overline{x})^2}, \quad i = 1, 2, \ldots, n. \tag{11.5.1}$$

The formula has a nice interpretation in the SLR model: if the distance from x_i to $\overline{x}$ is large relative to the other x's then h_{ii} will be close to 1.

Leverages have nice mathematical properties; for example, they satisfy

$$0 \leq h_{ii} \leq 1, \tag{11.5.2}$$

and their sum is

$$\begin{aligned} \sum_{i=1}^{n} h_{ii} &= \sum_{i=1}^{n}\left[\frac{1}{n} + \frac{(x_i - \overline{x})^2}{\sum_{k=1}^{n}(x_k - \overline{x})^2}\right], && (11.5.3)\\ &= \frac{n}{n} + \frac{\sum_i (x_i - \overline{x})^2}{\sum_k (x_k - \overline{x})^2}, && (11.5.4)\\ &= 2. && (11.5.5) \end{aligned}$$

A rule of thumb is to consider leverage values to be large if they are more than double their average size (which is $2/n$ according to Equation 11.5.5). So leverages larger than $4/n$ are suspect. Another rule of thumb is to say that values bigger than 0.5 indicate high leverage, while values between 0.3 and 0.5 indicate moderate leverage.

Standardized and Studentized Deleted Residuals

We have already encountered the *standardized residuals* r_i in Section 11.4.2; they are merely residuals that have been divided by their respective standard deviations:

$$R_i = \frac{E_i}{S\sqrt{1 - h_{ii}}}, \quad i = 1, 2, \ldots, n. \tag{11.5.6}$$

Values of $|R_i| > 2$ are extreme and suggest that the observation has an outlying y-value.

Now delete the ith case and fit the regression function to the remaining $n-1$ cases, producing a fitted value $\hat{Y}_{(i)}$ with *deleted residual* $D_i = Y_i - \hat{Y}_{(i)}$. It is shown in later classes that

$$\text{Var}(D_i) = \frac{S^2_{(i)}}{1 - h_{ii}}, \quad i = 1, 2, \ldots, n, \tag{11.5.7}$$

so that the *studentized deleted residuals* t_i defined by

$$t_i = \frac{D_i}{S_{(i)}/(1 - h_{ii})}, \quad i = 1, 2, \ldots, n, \tag{11.5.8}$$

have a $\mathtt{t}(\mathtt{df} = n - 3)$ distribution and we compare observed values of t_i to this distribution to decide whether or not an observation is extreme.

The folklore in regression classes is that a test based on the statistic in Equation 11.5.8 can be too liberal. A rule of thumb is if we suspect an observation to be an outlier *before* seeing the data then we say it is significantly outlying if its two-tailed p-value is less than α, but if we suspect an observation to be an outlier *after* seeing the data then we should only say it is significantly outlying if its two-tailed p-value is less than α/n. The latter rule of thumb is called the *Bonferroni approach* and can be overly conservative for large data sets. The responsible statistician should look at the data and use his/her best judgement, in every case.

11.5.2 How to do it with R

We can calculate the standardized residuals with the `rstandard` function. The input is the `lm` object, which is `cars.lm`.

```
> sres <- rstandard(cars.lm)
> sres[1:5]
```

```
         1          2          3          4          5 
 0.2660415  0.8189327 -0.4013462  0.8132663  0.1421624 
```

We can find out which observations have studentized residuals larger than two with the command

```
> sres[which(abs(sres) > 2)]
```

```
      23       35       49 
2.795166 2.027818 2.919060 
```

In this case, we see that observations 23, 35, and 49 are potential outliers with respect to their y-value.

We can compute the studentized deleted residuals with `rstudent`:

```
> sdelres <- rstudent(cars.lm)
> sdelres[1:5]
```

```
        1         2          3         4         5
0.2634500 0.8160784 -0.3978115 0.8103526 0.1407033
```

We should compare these values with critical values from a t(df $= n-3$) distribution, which in this case is t(df $= 50 - 3 = 47$). We can calculate a 0.005 quantile and check with

```
> t0.005 <- qt(0.005, df = 47, lower.tail = FALSE)
> sdelres[which(abs(sdelres) > t0.005)]
```

```
      23       49
3.022829 3.184993
```

This means that observations 23 and 49 have a large studentized deleted residual. The leverages can be found with the hatvalues function:

```
> leverage <- hatvalues(cars.lm)
> leverage[1:5]
```

```
         1          2          3          4          5
0.11486131 0.11486131 0.07150365 0.07150365 0.05997080
```

```
> leverage[which(leverage > 4/50)]
```

```
         1          2         50
0.11486131 0.11486131 0.08727007
```

Here we see that observations 1, 2, and 50 have leverages bigger than double their mean value. These observations would be considered outlying with respect to their x value (although they may or may not be influential).

11.5.3 Influential Observations

DFBETAS and *DFFITS*

Anytime we do a statistical analysis, we are confronted with the variability of data. It is always a concern when an observation plays too large a role in our regression model, and we would not like or procedures to be overly influenced by the value of a single observation. Hence, it becomes desirable to check to see how much our estimates and predictions would change if one of the observations were not included in the analysis. If an observation changes the estimates/predictions a large amount, then the observation is influential and should be subjected to a higher level of scrutiny.

We measure the change in the parameter estimates as a result of deleting an observation with *DFBETAS*. The *DFBETAS* for the intercept b_0 are given by

$$(DFBETAS)_{0(i)} = \frac{b_0 - b_{0(i)}}{S_{(i)}\sqrt{\frac{1}{n} + \frac{\overline{x}^2}{\sum_{i=1}^{n}(x_i - \overline{x})^2}}}, \quad i = 1, 2, \ldots, n. \tag{11.5.9}$$

and the *DFBETAS* for the slope b_1 are given by

$$(DFBETAS)_{1(i)} = \frac{b_1 - b_{1(i)}}{S_{(i)}\left[\sum_{i=1}^{n}(x_i - \overline{x})^2\right]^{-1/2}}, \quad i = 1, 2, \ldots, n. \tag{11.5.10}$$

See Section 12.8 for a better way to write these. The signs of the $DFBETAS$ indicate whether the coefficients would increase or decrease as a result of including the observation. If the $DFBETAS$ are large, then the observation has a large impact on those regression coefficients. We label observations as suspicious if their $DFBETAS$ have magnitude greater 1 for small data or $2/\sqrt{n}$ for large data sets.

We can calculate the $DFBETAS$ with the `dfbetas` function (some output has been omitted):

```
> dfb <- dfbetas(cars.lm)
> head(dfb)

  (Intercept)       speed
1  0.09440188 -0.08624563
2  0.29242487 -0.26715961
3 -0.10749794  0.09369281
4  0.21897614 -0.19085472
5  0.03407516 -0.02901384
6 -0.11100703  0.09174024
```

We see that the inclusion of the first observation slightly increases the `Intercept` and slightly decreases the coefficient on `speed`.

We can measure the influence that an observation has on its fitted value with $DFFITS$. These are calculated by deleting an observation, refitting the model, recalculating the fit, then standardizing. The formula is

$$(DFFITS)_i = \frac{\hat{Y}_i - \hat{Y}_{(i)}}{S_{(i)}\sqrt{h_{ii}}}, \quad i = 1, 2, \ldots, n. \tag{11.5.11}$$

The value represents the number of standard deviations of $\hat{Y}_i$ that the fitted value $\hat{Y}_i$ increases or decreases with the inclusion of the ith observation. We can compute them with the `dffits` function.

```
> dff <- dffits(cars.lm)
> dff[1:5]

         1          2           3          4          5
0.09490289 0.29397684 -0.11039550 0.22487854 0.03553887
```

A rule of thumb is to flag observations whose $DFFIT$ exceeds one in absolute value, but there are none of those in this data set.

Cook's Distance

The $DFFITS$ are good for measuring the influence on a single fitted value, but we may want to measure the influence an observation has on all of the fitted values simultaneously. The statistics used for measuring this are Cook's distances which may be calculated[5] by the formula

$$D_i = \frac{E_i^2}{(p+1)S^2} \cdot \frac{h_{ii}}{(1-h_{ii})^2}, \quad i = 1, 2, \ldots, n. \tag{11.5.12}$$

[5]Cook's distances are actually defined by a different formula than the one shown. The formula in Equation 11.5.12 is algebraically equivalent to the defining formula and is, in the author's opinion, more transparent.

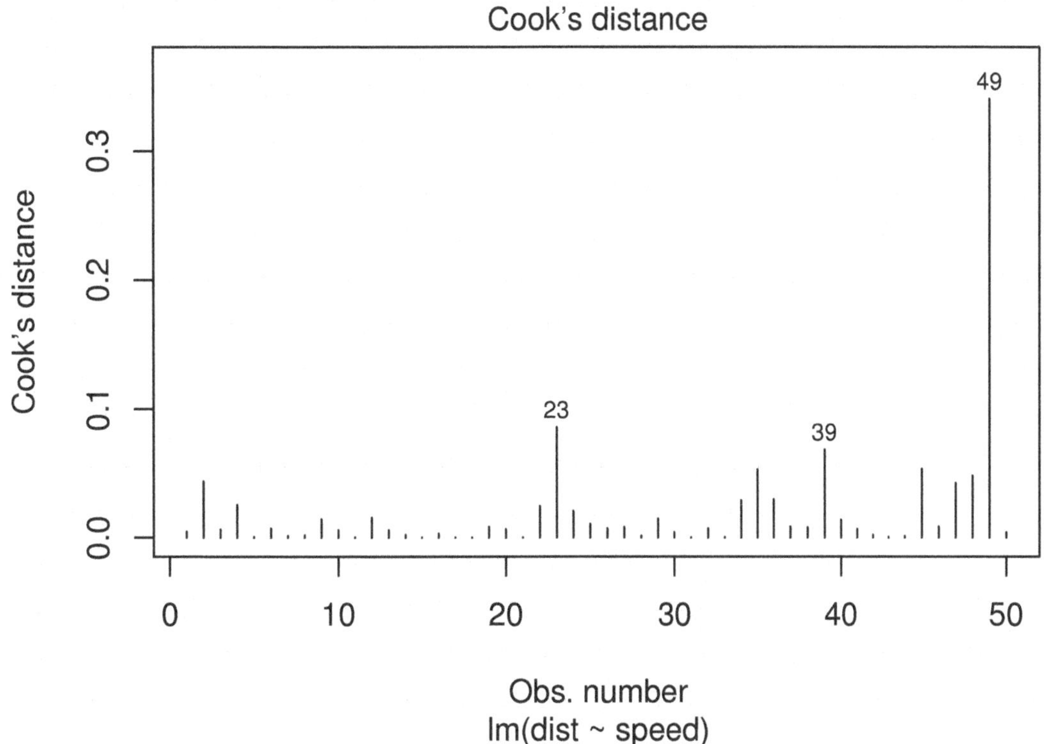

Figure 11.5.1: Cook's distances for the `cars` data
Used for checking for influential and/our outlying observations. Values with large Cook's distance merit further investigation.

It shows that Cook's distance depends both on the residual E_i and the leverage h_{ii} and in this way D_i contains information about outlying x and y values.

To assess the significance of D, we compare to quantiles of an f(`df1` = 2, `df2` = $n - 2$) distribution. A rule of thumb is to classify observations falling higher than the 50th percentile as being extreme.

11.5.4 How to do it with R

We can calculate the Cook's Distances with the `cooks.distance` function.

```
> cooksD <- cooks.distance(cars.lm)
> cooksD[1:5]
```

```
           1            2            3            4            5
0.0045923121 0.0435139907 0.0062023503 0.0254673384 0.0006446705
```

We can look at a plot of the Cook's distances with the command `plot(cars.lm, which = 4)`.

Observations with the largest Cook's D values are labeled, hence we see that observations 23, 39, and 49 are suspicious. However, we need to compare to the quantiles of an f(`df1` = 2, `df2` = 48) distribution:

```
> F0.50 <- qf(0.5, df1 = 2, df2 = 48)
> cooksD[which(cooksD > F0.50)]
```

```
named numeric(0)
```

We see that with this data set there are no observations with extreme Cook's distance, after all.

11.5.5 All Influence Measures Simultaneously

We can display the result of diagnostic checking all at once in one table, with potentially influential points displayed. We do it with the command `influence.measures(cars.lm)`:

```
> influence.measures(cars.lm)
```

The output is a huge matrix display, which we have omitted in the interest of brevity. A point is identified if it is classified to be influential with respect to any of the diagnostic measures. Here we see that observations 2, 11, 15, and 18 merit further investigation.

We can also look at all diagnostic plots at once with the commands

```
> par(mfrow = c(2, 2))
> plot(cars.lm)
> par(mfrow = c(1, 1))
```

The `par` command is used so that $2 \times 2 = 4$ plots will be shown on the same display. The diagnostic plots for the `cars` data are shown in Figure 11.5.2:

We have discussed all of the plots except the last, which is possibly the most interesting. It shows Residuals vs. Leverage, which will identify outlying y values versus outlying x values. Here we see that observation 23 has a high residual, but low leverage, and it turns out that observations 1 and 2 have relatively high leverage but low/moderate leverage (they are on the right side of the plot, just above the horizontal line). Observation 49 has a large residual with a comparatively large leverage.

We can identify the observations with the `identify` command; it allows us to display the observation number of dots on the plot. First, we plot the graph, then we call `identify`:

```
> plot(cars.lm, which = 5)   # std'd resids vs lev plot
> identify(leverage, sres, n = 4)   # identify 4 points
```

The graph with the identified points is omitted (but the plain plot is shown in the bottom right corner of Figure 11.5.2). Observations 1 and 2 fall on the far right side of the plot, near the horizontal axis.

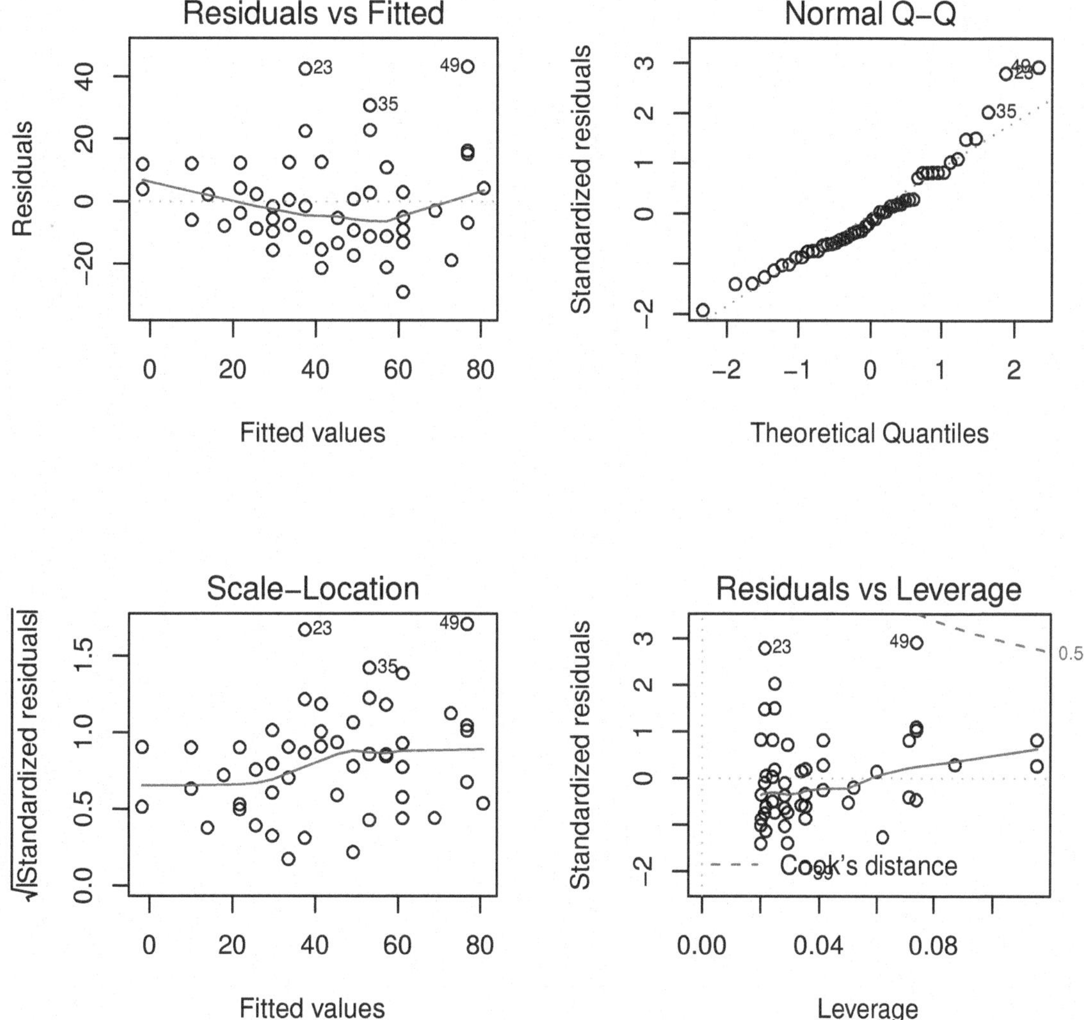

Figure 11.5.2: Diagnostic plots for the `cars` data

Chapter Exercises

Exercise 11.1. Prove the ANOVA equality, Equation 11.3.5. *Hint*: show that

$$\sum_{i=1}^{n}(Y_i - \hat{Y}_i)(\hat{Y}_i - \overline{Y}) = 0.$$

Exercise 11.2. Solve the following system of equations for β_1 and β_0 to find the MLEs for slope and intercept in the simple linear regression model.

$$\begin{aligned} n\beta_0 + \beta_1 \sum_{i=1}^{n} x_i &= \sum_{i=1}^{n} y_i \\ \beta_0 \sum_{i=1}^{n} x_i + \beta_1 \sum_{i=1}^{n} x_i^2 &= \sum_{i=1}^{n} x_i y_i \end{aligned}$$

Exercise 11.3. Show that the formula given in Equation 11.2.17 is equivalent to

$$\hat{\beta}_1 = \frac{\sum_{i=1}^{n} x_i y_i - \left(\sum_{i=1}^{n} x_i\right)\left(\sum_{i=1}^{n} y_i\right)\big/ n}{\sum_{i=1}^{n} x_i^2 - \left(\sum_{i=1}^{n} x_i\right)^2\big/ n}.$$

Chapter 12

Multiple Linear Regression

We know a lot about simple linear regression models, and a next step is to study multiple regression models that have more than one independent (explanatory) variable. In the discussion that follows we will assume that we have p explanatory variables, where $p > 1$.

The language is phrased in matrix terms – for two reasons. First, it is quicker to write and (arguably) more pleasant to read. Second, the matrix approach will be required for later study of the subject; the reader might as well be introduced to it now.

Most of the results are stated without proof or with only a cursory justification. Those yearning for more should consult an advanced text in linear regression for details, such as *Applied Linear Regression Models* [67]or *Linear Models: Least Squares and Alternatives* [69].

What do I want them to know?

- the basic MLR model, and how it relates to the SLR
- how to estimate the parameters and use those estimates to make predictions
- basic strategies to determine whether or not the model is doing a good job
- a few thoughts about selected applications of the MLR, such as polynomial, interaction, and dummy variable models
- some of the uses of residuals to diagnose problems
- hints about what will be coming later

12.1 The Multiple Linear Regression Model

The first thing to do is get some better notation. We will write

$$\mathbf{Y}_{\mathrm{n}\times 1} = \begin{bmatrix} y_1 \\ y_2 \\ \vdots \\ y_n \end{bmatrix}, \quad \text{and} \quad \mathbf{X}_{\mathrm{n}\times(\mathrm{p}+1)} = \begin{bmatrix} 1 & x_{11} & x_{21} & \cdots & x_{p1} \\ 1 & x_{12} & x_{22} & \cdots & x_{p2} \\ \vdots & \vdots & \vdots & \ddots & \vdots \\ 1 & x_{1n} & x_{2n} & \cdots & x_{pn} \end{bmatrix}. \tag{12.1.1}$$

The vector $\mathbf{Y}$ is called the *response vector* and the matrix $\mathbf{X}$ is called the *model matrix*. As in Chapter 11, the most general assumption that relates $\mathbf{Y}$ to $\mathbf{X}$ is

$$\mathbf{Y} = \mu(\mathbf{X}) + \epsilon, \tag{12.1.2}$$

where μ is some function (the *signal*) and ϵ is the *noise* (everything else). We usually impose some structure on μ and ϵ. In particular, the standard multiple linear regression model assumes

$$\mathbf{Y} = \mathbf{X}\beta + \epsilon, \tag{12.1.3}$$

where the parameter vector β looks like

$$\beta_{(p+1)\times 1} = \begin{bmatrix}\beta_0 & \beta_1 & \cdots & \beta_p\end{bmatrix}^{\mathrm{T}}, \tag{12.1.4}$$

and the random vector $\epsilon_{n\times 1} = \begin{bmatrix}\epsilon_1 & \epsilon_2 & \cdots & \epsilon_n\end{bmatrix}^{\mathrm{T}}$ is assumed to be distributed

$$\epsilon \sim \mathsf{mvnorm}\left(\mathtt{mean} = \mathbf{0}_{n\times 1},\ \mathtt{sigma} = \sigma^2\mathbf{I}_{n\times n}\right). \tag{12.1.5}$$

The assumption on ϵ is equivalent to the assumption that $\epsilon_1, \epsilon_2, \ldots, \epsilon_n$ are i.i.d. norm(mean = 0, sd = σ). It is a linear model because the quantity $\mu(\mathbf{X}) = \mathbf{X}\beta$ is linear in the parameters β_0, $\beta_1, \ldots, \beta_p$. It may be helpful to see the model in expanded form; the above matrix formulation is equivalent to the more lengthy

$$Y_i = \beta_0 + \beta_1 x_{1i} + \beta_2 x_{2i} + \cdots + \beta_p x_{pi} + \epsilon_i, \quad i = 1, 2, \ldots, n. \tag{12.1.6}$$

Example 12.1. Girth, Height, and Volume for Black Cherry trees. Measurements were made of the girth, height, and volume of timber in 31 felled black cherry trees. Note that girth is the diameter of the tree (in inches) measured at 4 ft 6 in above the ground. The variables are

1. `Girth`: tree diameter in inches (denoted x_1)
2. `Height`: tree height in feet (x_2).
3. `Volume`: volume of the tree in cubic feet. (y)

The data are in the `datasets` package and are already on the search path; they can be viewed with

```
> head(trees)
  Girth Height Volume
1   8.3     70   10.3
2   8.6     65   10.3
3   8.8     63   10.2
4  10.5     72   16.4
5  10.7     81   18.8
6  10.8     83   19.7
```

Let us take a look at a visual display of the data. For multiple variables, instead of a simple scatterplot we use a scatterplot matrix which is made with the `splom` function in the `lattice` package [75] as shown below. The plot is shown in Figure 12.1.1.

```
> library(lattice)
> splom(trees)
```

The dependent (response) variable `Volume` is listed in the first row of the scatterplot matrix. Moving from left to right, we see an approximately linear relationship between `Volume` and the independent (explanatory) variables `Height` and `Girth`. A first guess at a model for these data might be

$$Y = \beta_0 + \beta_1 x_1 + \beta_2 x_2 + \epsilon, \tag{12.1.7}$$

in which case the quantity $\mu(x_1, x_2) = \beta_0 + \beta_1 x_1 + \beta_2 x_2$ would represent the mean value of Y at the point (x_1, x_2).

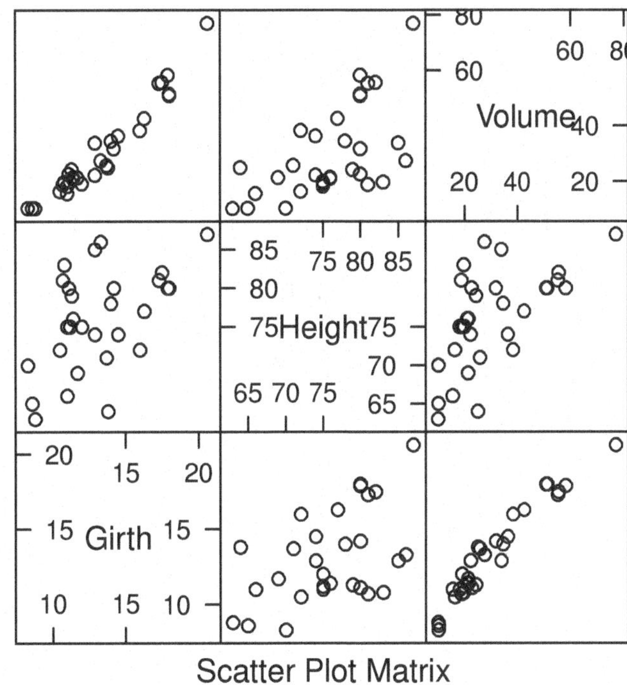

Figure 12.1.1: Scatterplot matrix of `trees` data

What does it mean?

The interpretation is simple. The intercept β_0 represents the mean `Volume` when all other independent variables are zero. The parameter β_i represents the change in mean `Volume` when there is a unit increase in x_i, while the other independent variable is held constant. For the `trees` data, β_1 represents the change in average `Volume` as `Girth` increases by one unit when the `Height` is held constant, and β_2 represents the change in average `Volume` as `Height` increases by one unit when the `Girth` is held constant.

In simple linear regression, we had one independent variable and our linear regression surface was 1D, simply a line. In multiple regression there are many independent variables and so our linear regression surface will be many-D... in general, a hyperplane. But when there are only two explanatory variables the hyperplane is just an ordinary plane and we can look at it with a 3D scatterplot.

One way to do this is with the R Commander in the `Rcmdr` package [31]. It has a 3D scatterplot option under the Graphs menu. It is especially great because the resulting graph is dynamic; it can be moved around with the mouse, zoomed, *etc.* But that particular display does not translate well to a printed book.

Another way to do it is with the `scatterplot3d` function in the `scatterplot3d` package. The code follows, and the result is shown in Figure 12.1.2.

```
> library(scatterplot3d)
> s3d <- with(trees, scatterplot3d(Girth, Height, Volume, pch = 16,
+      highlight.3d = TRUE, angle = 60))
> fit <- lm(Volume ~ Girth + Height, data = trees)
> s3d$plane3d(fit)
```

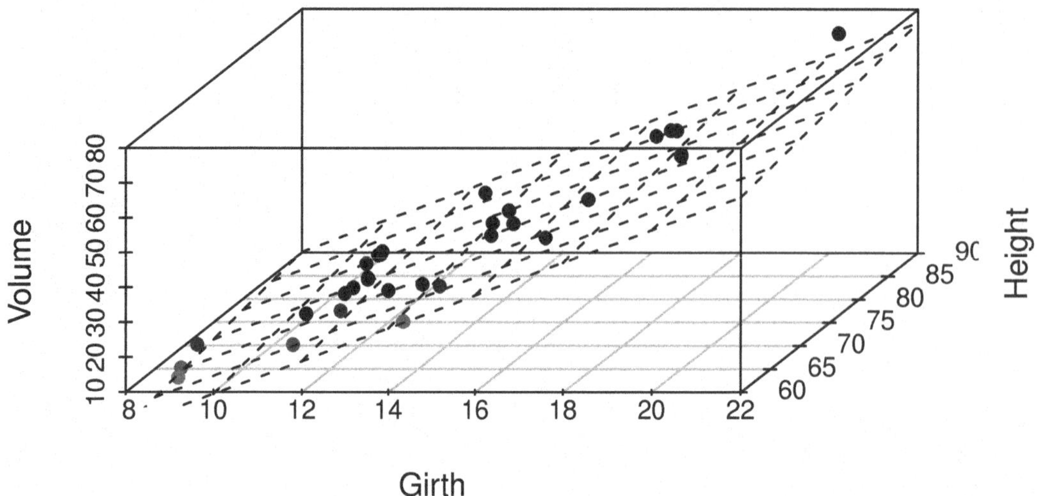

Figure 12.1.2: 3D scatterplot with regression plane for the `trees` data

Looking at the graph we see that the data points fall close to a plane in three dimensional space. (The plot looks remarkably good. In the author's experience it is rare to see points fit so well to the plane without some additional work.)

12.2 Estimation and Prediction

12.2.1 Parameter estimates

We will proceed exactly like we did in Section 11.2. We know

$$\epsilon \sim \mathsf{mvnorm}\left(\mathtt{mean} = \mathbf{0}_{\mathrm{n}\times 1},\ \mathtt{sigma} = \sigma^2\mathbf{I}_{\mathrm{n}\times\mathrm{n}}\right), \tag{12.2.1}$$

which means that $\mathbf{Y} = \mathbf{X}\beta + \epsilon$ has an $\mathsf{mvnorm}\left(\mathtt{mean} = \mathbf{X}\beta,\ \mathtt{sigma} = \sigma^2\mathbf{I}_{\mathrm{n}\times\mathrm{n}}\right)$ distribution. Therefore, the likelihood function is

$$L(\beta, \sigma) = \frac{1}{2\pi^{n/2}\sigma}\exp\left\{-\frac{1}{2\sigma^2}\left(\mathbf{Y} - \mathbf{X}\beta\right)^{\mathrm{T}}\left(\mathbf{Y} - \mathbf{X}\beta\right)\right\}. \tag{12.2.2}$$

To *maximize* the likelihood in β, we need to *minimize* the quantity $g(\beta) = \left(\mathbf{Y} - \mathbf{X}\beta\right)^{\mathrm{T}}\left(\mathbf{Y} - \mathbf{X}\beta\right)$. We do this by differentiating g with respect to β. (It may be a good idea to brush up on the material in Appendices E.5 and E.6.) First we will rewrite g:

$$g(\beta) = \mathbf{Y}^{\mathrm{T}}\mathbf{Y} - \mathbf{Y}^{\mathrm{T}}\mathbf{X}\beta - \beta^{\mathrm{T}}\mathbf{X}^{\mathrm{T}}\mathbf{Y} + \beta^{\mathrm{T}}\mathbf{X}^{\mathrm{T}}\mathbf{X}\beta, \tag{12.2.3}$$

which can be further simplified to $g(\beta) = \mathbf{Y}^{\mathrm{T}}\mathbf{Y} - 2\beta^{\mathrm{T}}\mathbf{X}^{\mathrm{T}}\mathbf{Y} + \beta^{\mathrm{T}}\mathbf{X}^{\mathrm{T}}\mathbf{X}\beta$ since $\beta^{\mathrm{T}}\mathbf{X}^{\mathrm{T}}\mathbf{Y}$ is 1×1 and thus equal to its transpose. Now we differentiate to get

$$\frac{\partial g}{\partial \beta} = \mathbf{0} - 2\mathbf{X}^{\mathrm{T}}\mathbf{Y} + 2\mathbf{X}^{\mathrm{T}}\mathbf{X}\beta, \tag{12.2.4}$$

since $\mathbf{X}^{\mathrm{T}}\mathbf{X}$ is symmetric. Setting the derivative equal to the zero vector yields the so called "normal equations"

$$\mathbf{X}^{\mathrm{T}}\mathbf{X}\beta = \mathbf{X}^{\mathrm{T}}\mathbf{Y}. \tag{12.2.5}$$

In the case that $\mathbf{X}^{\mathrm{T}}\mathbf{X}$ is invertible[1], we may solve the equation for β to get the maximum likelihood estimator of β which we denote by $\mathbf{b}$:

$$\mathbf{b} = \left(\mathbf{X}^{\mathrm{T}}\mathbf{X}\right)^{-1}\mathbf{X}^{\mathrm{T}}\mathbf{Y}. \tag{12.2.6}$$

Remark 12.2. The formula in Equation 12.2.6 is convenient for mathematical study but is inconvenient for numerical computation. Researchers have devised much more efficient algorithms for the actual calculation of the parameter estimates, and we do not explore them here.

Remark 12.3. We have only found a critical value, and have not actually shown that the critical value is a minimum. We omit the details and refer the interested reader to [69].

12.2.2 How to do it with R

We do all of the above just as we would in simple linear regression. The powerhouse is the `lm` function. Everything else is based on it. We separate explanatory variables in the model formula by a plus sign.

```
> trees.lm <- lm(Volume ~ Girth + Height, data = trees)
> trees.lm

Call:
lm(formula = Volume ~ Girth + Height, data = trees)

Coefficients:
(Intercept)        Girth       Height
   -57.9877       4.7082       0.3393
```

We see from the output that for the `trees` data our parameter estimates are $\mathbf{b} = \begin{bmatrix}-58.0 & 4.7 & 0.3\end{bmatrix}$, and consequently our estimate of the mean response is $\hat{\mu}$ given by

$$\hat{\mu}(x_1, x_2) = b_0 + b_1 x_1 + b_2 x_2, \tag{12.2.7}$$
$$\approx -58.0 + 4.7 x_1 + 0.3 x_2. \tag{12.2.8}$$

We could see the entire model matrix $\mathbf{X}$ with the `model.matrix` function, but in the interest of brevity we only show the first few rows.

```
> head(model.matrix(trees.lm))

  (Intercept) Girth Height
1           1   8.3     70
2           1   8.6     65
3           1   8.8     63
4           1  10.5     72
5           1  10.7     81
6           1  10.8     83
```

[1]We can find solutions of the normal equations even when $\mathbf{X}^{\mathrm{T}}\mathbf{X}$ is not of full rank, but the topic falls outside the scope of this book. The interested reader can consult an advanced text such as Rao [69].

12.2.3 Point Estimates of the Regression Surface

The parameter estimates **b** make it easy to find the fitted values, $\hat{\mathbf{Y}}$. We write them individually as $\hat{Y}_i$, $i = 1, 2, \ldots, n$, and recall that they are defined by

$$\begin{aligned} \hat{Y}_i &= \hat{\mu}(x_{1i}, x_{2i}), && (12.2.9) \\ &= b_0 + b_1 x_{1i} + b_2 x_{2i}, \quad i = 1, 2, \ldots, n. && (12.2.10) \end{aligned}$$

They are expressed more compactly by the matrix equation

$$\hat{\mathbf{Y}} = \mathbf{X}\mathbf{b}. \qquad (12.2.11)$$

From Equation 12.2.6 we know that $\mathbf{b} = \left(\mathbf{X}^{\mathrm{T}}\mathbf{X}\right)^{-1}\mathbf{X}^{\mathrm{T}}\mathbf{Y}$, so we can rewrite

$$\begin{aligned} \hat{\mathbf{Y}} &= \mathbf{X}\left[\left(\mathbf{X}^{\mathrm{T}}\mathbf{X}\right)^{-1}\mathbf{X}^{\mathrm{T}}\mathbf{Y}\right], && (12.2.12) \\ &= \mathbf{H}\mathbf{Y}, && (12.2.13) \end{aligned}$$

where $\mathbf{H} = \mathbf{X}\left(\mathbf{X}^{\mathrm{T}}\mathbf{X}\right)^{-1}\mathbf{X}^{\mathrm{T}}$ is appropriately named *the hat matrix* because it "puts the hat on **Y**". The hat matrix is very important in later courses. Some facts about **H** are

- **H** is a symmetric square matrix, of dimension $\mathrm{n} \times \mathrm{n}$.
- The diagonal entries h_{ii} satisfy $0 \leq h_{ii} \leq 1$ (compare to Equation 11.5.2).
- The trace is $\mathrm{tr}(\mathbf{H}) = p$.
- **H** is *idempotent* (also known as a *projection matrix*) which means that $\mathbf{H}^2 = \mathbf{H}$. The same is true of $\mathbf{I} - \mathbf{H}$.

Now let us write a column vector $\mathbf{x}_0 = (x_{10}, x_{20})^{\mathrm{T}}$ to denote given values of the explanatory variables `Girth` $= x_{10}$ and `Height` $= x_{20}$. These values may match those of the collected data, or they may be completely new values not observed in the original data set. We may use the parameter estimates to find $\hat{Y}(\mathbf{x}_0)$, which will give us

1. an estimate of $\mu(\mathbf{x}_0)$, the mean value of a future observation at $\mathbf{x}_0$, and
2. a prediction for $Y(\mathbf{x}_0)$, the actual value of a future observation at $\mathbf{x}_0$.

We can represent $\hat{Y}(\mathbf{x}_0)$ by the matrix equation

$$\hat{Y}(\mathbf{x}_0) = \mathbf{x}_0^{\mathrm{T}}\mathbf{b}, \qquad (12.2.14)$$

which is just a fancy way to write

$$\hat{Y}(x_{10}, x_{20}) = b_0 + b_1 x_{10} + b_2 x_{20}. \qquad (12.2.15)$$

Example 12.4. If we wanted to predict the average volume of black cherry trees that have `Girth = 15` in and are `Height = 77` ft tall then we would use the estimate

$$\begin{aligned} \hat{\mu}(15,\ 77) &= -\ 58 + 4.7(15) + 0.3(77), \\ &\approx 35.6\ \mathrm{ft}^3. \end{aligned}$$

We would use the same estimate $\hat{Y} = 35.6$ to predict the measured `Volume` of another black cherry tree – yet to be observed – that has `Girth = 15` in and is `Height = 77` ft tall.

12.2.4 How to do it with R

The fitted values are stored inside `trees.lm` and may be accessed with the `fitted` function. We only show the first five fitted values.

```
> fitted(trees.lm)[1:5]

        1         2         3         4         5
 4.837660  4.553852  4.816981 15.874115 19.869008
```

The syntax for general prediction does not change much from simple linear regression. The computations are done with the `predict` function as described below.

The only difference from SLR is in the way we tell R the values of the explanatory variables for which we want predictions. In SLR we had only one independent variable but in MLR we have many (for the `trees` data we have two). We will store values for the independent variables in the data frame `new`, which has two columns (one for each independent variable) and three rows (we shall make predictions at three different locations).

```
> new <- data.frame(Girth = c(9.1, 11.6, 12.5), Height = c(69,
+     74, 87))
```

We can view the locations at which we will predict:

```
> new

  Girth Height
1   9.1     69
2  11.6     74
3  12.5     87
```

We continue just like we would have done in SLR.

```
> predict(trees.lm, newdata = new)

        1         2         3
 8.264937 21.731594 30.379205
```

Example 12.5. Using the `trees` data,

1. Report a point estimate of the mean `Volume` of a tree of `Girth` 9.1 in and `Height` 69 ft.

   The fitted value for $x_1 = 9.1$ and $x_2 = 69$ is 8.3, so a point estimate would be 8.3 cubic feet.

2. Report a point prediction for and a 95% prediction interval for the `Volume` of a hypothetical tree of `Girth` 12.5 in and `Height` 87 ft.

   The fitted value for $x_1 = 12.5$ and $x_2 = 87$ is 30.4, so a point prediction for the `Volume` is 30.4 cubic feet.

12.2.5 Mean Square Error and Standard Error

The residuals are given by

$$\mathbf{E} = \mathbf{Y} - \hat{\mathbf{Y}} = \mathbf{Y} - \mathbf{H}\mathbf{Y} = (\mathbf{I} - \mathbf{H})\mathbf{Y}. \tag{12.2.16}$$

Now we can use Theorem 7.34 to see that the residuals are distributed

$$\mathbf{E} \sim \mathsf{mvnorm}(\mathtt{mean} = \mathbf{0},\ \mathtt{sigma} = \sigma^2(\mathbf{I} - \mathbf{H})), \tag{12.2.17}$$

since $(\mathbf{I} - \mathbf{H})\mathbf{X}\beta = \mathbf{X}\beta - \mathbf{X}\beta = \mathbf{0}$ and $(\mathbf{I} - \mathbf{H})\,(\sigma^2\mathbf{I})\,(\mathbf{I} - \mathbf{H})^{\mathrm{T}} = \sigma^2(\mathbf{I} - \mathbf{H})^2 = \sigma^2(\mathbf{I} - \mathbf{H})$. The sum of squared errors SSE is just

$$SSE = \mathbf{E}^{\mathrm{T}}\mathbf{E} = \mathbf{Y}^{\mathrm{T}}(\mathbf{I} - \mathbf{H})(\mathbf{I} - \mathbf{H})\mathbf{Y} = \mathbf{Y}^{\mathrm{T}}(\mathbf{I} - \mathbf{H})\mathbf{Y}. \tag{12.2.18}$$

Recall that in SLR we had two parameters (β_0 and β_1) in our regression model and we estimated σ^2 with $s^2 = SSE/(n-2)$. In MLR, we have $p+1$ parameters in our regression model and we might guess that to estimate σ^2 we would use the *mean square error* S^2 defined by

$$S^2 = \frac{SSE}{n - (p+1)}. \tag{12.2.19}$$

That would be a good guess. The *residual standard error* is $S = \sqrt{S^2}$.

12.2.6 How to do it with R

The residuals are also stored with `trees.lm` and may be accessed with the `residuals` function. We only show the first five residuals.

```
> residuals(trees.lm)[1:5]
```

```
        1         2         3         4         5 
5.4623403 5.7461484 5.3830187 0.5258848 -1.0690084 
```

The `summary` function output (shown later) lists the `Residual Standard Error` which is just $S = \sqrt{S^2}$. It is stored in the `sigma` component of the `summary` object.

```
> treesumry <- summary(trees.lm)
> treesumry$sigma
```

```
[1] 3.881832
```

For the `trees` data we find $s \approx 3.882$.

12.2.7 Interval Estimates of the Parameters

We showed in Section 12.2.1 that $\mathbf{b} = \left(\mathbf{X}^{\mathrm{T}}\mathbf{X}\right)^{-1}\mathbf{X}^{\mathrm{T}}\mathbf{Y}$, which is really just a big matrix – namely $\left(\mathbf{X}^{\mathrm{T}}\mathbf{X}\right)^{-1}\mathbf{X}^{\mathrm{T}}$ – multiplied by $\mathbf{Y}$. It stands to reason that the sampling distribution of $\mathbf{b}$ would be intimately related to the distribution of $\mathbf{Y}$, which we assumed to be

$$\mathbf{Y} \sim \mathsf{mvnorm}\left(\mathtt{mean} = \mathbf{X}\beta,\ \mathtt{sigma} = \sigma^2\mathbf{I}\right). \tag{12.2.20}$$

Now recall Theorem 7.34 that we said we were going to need eventually (the time is now). That proposition guarantees that

$$\mathbf{b} \sim \mathsf{mvnorm}\left(\mathtt{mean} = \beta,\ \mathtt{sigma} = \sigma^2\left(\mathbf{X}^{\mathrm{T}}\mathbf{X}\right)^{-1}\right), \tag{12.2.21}$$

since

$$\mathbb{E}\,\mathbf{b} = \left(\mathbf{X}^{\mathrm{T}}\mathbf{X}\right)^{-1}\mathbf{X}^{\mathrm{T}}(\mathbf{X}\beta) = \beta, \tag{12.2.22}$$

and

$$\mathrm{Var}(\mathbf{b}) = \left(\mathbf{X}^{\mathrm{T}}\mathbf{X}\right)^{-1}\mathbf{X}^{\mathrm{T}}(\sigma^2\mathbf{I})\mathbf{X}\left(\mathbf{X}^{\mathrm{T}}\mathbf{X}\right)^{-1} = \sigma^2\left(\mathbf{X}^{\mathrm{T}}\mathbf{X}\right)^{-1}, \tag{12.2.23}$$

the first equality following because the matrix $\left(\mathbf{X}^{\mathrm{T}}\mathbf{X}\right)^{-1}$ is symmetric.

There is a lot that we can glean from Equation 12.2.21. First, it follows that the estimator $\mathbf{b}$ is unbiased (see Section 9.1). Second, the variances of $b_0, b_1, \ldots, b_n$ are exactly the diagonal elements of $\sigma^2\left(\mathbf{X}^{\mathrm{T}}\mathbf{X}\right)^{-1}$, which is completely known except for that pesky parameter σ^2. Third, we can estimate the standard error of b_i (denoted S_{b_i}) with the mean square error S (defined in the previous section) multiplied by the corresponding diagonal element of $\left(\mathbf{X}^{\mathrm{T}}\mathbf{X}\right)^{-1}$. Finally, given estimates of the standard errors we may construct confidence intervals for β_i with an interval that looks like

$$b_i \pm \mathsf{t}_{\alpha/2}(\mathtt{df} = n - p - 1)S_{b_i}. \tag{12.2.24}$$

The degrees of freedom for the Student's t distribution[2] are the same as the denominator of S^2.

12.2.8 How to do it with R

To get confidence intervals for the parameters we need only use `confint`:

```
> confint(trees.lm)
                   2.5 %      97.5 %
(Intercept) -75.68226247 -40.2930554
Girth         4.16683899   5.2494820
Height        0.07264863   0.6058538
```

For example, using the calculations above we say that for the regression model `Volume ~Girth + Height` we are 95% confident that the parameter β_1 lies somewhere in the interval [4.2, 5.2].

12.2.9 Confidence and Prediction Intervals

We saw in Section 12.2.3 how to make point estimates of the mean value of additional observations and predict values of future observations, but how good are our estimates? We need confidence and prediction intervals to gauge their accuracy, and lucky for us the formulas look similar to the ones we saw in SLR.

In Equation 12.2.14 we wrote $\hat{Y}(\mathbf{x}_0) = \mathbf{x}_0^{\mathrm{T}}\mathbf{b}$, and in Equation 12.2.21 we saw that

$$\mathbf{b} \sim \mathsf{mvnorm}\left(\mathtt{mean} = \beta,\ \mathtt{sigma} = \sigma^2\left(\mathbf{X}^{\mathrm{T}}\mathbf{X}\right)^{-1}\right), \tag{12.2.25}$$

[2]We are taking great leaps over the mathematical details. In particular, we have yet to show that s^2 has a chi-square distribution and we have not even come close to showing that b_i and s_{b_i} are independent. But these are entirely outside the scope of the present book and the reader may rest assured that the proofs await in later classes. See C.R. Rao for more.

The following is therefore immediate from Theorem 7.34:

$$\hat{Y}(\mathbf{x}_0) \sim \mathsf{mvnorm}\left(\mathtt{mean} = \mathbf{x}_0^{\mathrm{T}}\beta,\ \mathtt{sigma} = \sigma^2 \mathbf{x}_0^{\mathrm{T}} \left(\mathbf{X}^{\mathrm{T}}\mathbf{X}\right)^{-1} \mathbf{x}_0\right). \tag{12.2.26}$$

It should be no surprise that confidence intervals for the mean value of a future observation at the location $\mathbf{x}_0 = \begin{bmatrix} x_{10} & x_{20} & \ldots & x_{p0} \end{bmatrix}^{\mathrm{T}}$ are given by

$$\hat{Y}(\mathbf{x}_0) \pm \mathsf{t}_{\alpha/2}(\mathtt{df} = n - p - 1)\, S\, \sqrt{\mathbf{x}_0^{\mathrm{T}} (\mathbf{X}^{\mathrm{T}}\mathbf{X})^{-1} \mathbf{x}_0}. \tag{12.2.27}$$

Intuitively, $\mathbf{x}_0^{\mathrm{T}} \left(\mathbf{X}^{\mathrm{T}}\mathbf{X}\right)^{-1} \mathbf{x}_0$ measures the distance of $\mathbf{x}_0$ from the center of the data. The degrees of freedom in the Student's t critical value are $n - (p + 1)$ because we need to estimate $p + 1$ parameters.

Prediction intervals for a new observation at $\mathbf{x}_0$ are given by

$$\hat{Y}(\mathbf{x}_0) \pm \mathsf{t}_{\alpha/2}(\mathtt{df} = n - p - 1)\, S\, \sqrt{1 + \mathbf{x}_0^{\mathrm{T}} (\mathbf{X}^{\mathrm{T}}\mathbf{X})^{-1} \mathbf{x}_0}. \tag{12.2.28}$$

The prediction intervals are wider than the confidence intervals, just as in Section 11.2.5.

12.2.10 How to do it with R

The syntax is identical to that used in SLR, with the proviso that we need to specify values of the independent variables in the data frame new as we did in Section 11.2.5 (which we repeat here for illustration).

```
> new <- data.frame(Girth = c(9.1, 11.6, 12.5), Height = c(69,
+     74, 87))
```

Confidence intervals are given by

```
> predict(trees.lm, newdata = new, interval = "confidence")

        fit      lwr      upr
1  8.264937  5.77240 10.75747
2 21.731594 20.11110 23.35208
3 30.379205 26.90964 33.84877
```

Prediction intervals are given by

```
> predict(trees.lm, newdata = new, interval = "prediction")

        fit         lwr      upr
1  8.264937 -0.06814444 16.59802
2 21.731594 13.61657775 29.84661
3 30.379205 21.70364103 39.05477
```

As before, the interval type is decided by the `interval` argument and the default confidence level is 95% (which can be changed with the `level` argument).

Example 12.6. Using the `trees` data,

1. Report a 95% confidence interval for the mean `Volume` of a tree of `Girth` 9.1 in and `Height` 69 ft.

   The 95% CI is given by [5.8, 10.8], so with 95% confidence the mean `Volume` lies somewhere between 5.8 cubic feet and 10.8 cubic feet.

2. Report a 95% prediction interval for the `Volume` of a hypothetical tree of `Girth` 12.5 in and `Height` 87 ft.

   The 95% prediction interval is given by [26.9, 33.8], so with 95% confidence we may assert that the hypothetical `Volume` of a tree of `Girth` 12.5 in and `Height` 87 ft would lie somewhere between 26.9 cubic feet and 33.8 feet.

12.3 Model Utility and Inference

12.3.1 Multiple Coefficient of Determination

We saw in Section 12.2.5 that the error sum of squares SSE can be conveniently written in MLR as

$$SSE = \mathbf{Y}^{\mathrm{T}}(\mathbf{I} - \mathbf{H})\mathbf{Y}. \tag{12.3.1}$$

It turns out that there are equally convenient formulas for the total sum of squares $SSTO$ and the regression sum of squares SSR. They are :

$$SSTO = \mathbf{Y}^{\mathrm{T}}\left(\mathbf{I} - \frac{1}{n}\mathbf{J}\right)\mathbf{Y} \tag{12.3.2}$$

and

$$SSR = \mathbf{Y}^{\mathrm{T}}\left(\mathbf{H} - \frac{1}{n}\mathbf{J}\right)\mathbf{Y}. \tag{12.3.3}$$

(The matrix $\mathbf{J}$ is defined in Appendix E.5.) Immediately from Equations 12.3.1, 12.3.2, and 12.3.3 we get the *Anova Equality*

$$SSTO = SSE + SSR. \tag{12.3.4}$$

(See Exercise 12.1.) We define the *multiple coefficient of determination* by the formula

$$R^2 = 1 - \frac{SSE}{SSTO}. \tag{12.3.5}$$

We interpret R^2 as the proportion of total variation that is explained by the multiple regression model. In MLR we must be careful, however, because the value of R^2 can be artificially inflated by the addition of explanatory variables to the model, regardless of whether or not the added variables are useful with respect to prediction of the response variable. In fact, it can be proved that the addition of a single explanatory variable to a regression model will increase the value of R^2, *no matter how worthless* the explanatory variable is. We could model the height of the ocean tides, then add a variable for the length of cheetah tongues on the Serengeti plain, and our R^2 would inevitably increase.

This is a problem, because as the philosopher, Occam, once said: "causes should not be multiplied beyond necessity". We address the problem by penalizing R^2 when parameters are added to the model. The result is an *adjusted* R^2 which we denote by $\overline{R}^2$.

$$\overline{R}^2 = \left(R^2 - \frac{p}{n-1}\right)\left(\frac{n-1}{n-p-1}\right). \tag{12.3.6}$$

It is good practice for the statistician to weigh both R^2 and $\overline{R}^2$ during assessment of model utility. In many cases their values will be very close to each other. If their values differ substantially, or if one changes dramatically when an explanatory variable is added, then (s)he should take a closer look at the explanatory variables in the model.

12.3.2 How to do it with R

For the `trees` data, we can get R^2 and $\overline{R}^2$ from the `summary` output or access the values directly by name as shown (recall that we stored the `summary` object in `treesumry`).

```
> treesumry$r.squared
[1] 0.94795
> treesumry$adj.r.squared
[1] 0.9442322
```

High values of R^2 and $\overline{R}^2$ such as these indicate that the model fits very well, which agrees with what we saw in Figure 12.1.2.

12.3.3 Overall F-Test

Another way to assess the model's utility is to to test the hypothesis

$$H_0 : \beta_1 = \beta_2 = \cdots = \beta_p = 0 \text{ versus } H_1 : \text{ at least one } \beta_i \neq 0.$$

The idea is that if all β_i's were zero, then the explanatory variables $X_1, \ldots, X_p$ would be worthless predictors for the response variable Y. We can test the above hypothesis with the overall F statistic, which in MLR is defined by

$$F = \frac{SSR/p}{SSE/(n-p-1)}. \tag{12.3.7}$$

When the regression assumptions hold and under H_0, it can be shown that $F \sim$ `f(df1` $= p$, `df2` $= n - p - 1$). We reject H_0 when F is large, that is, when the explained variation is large relative to the unexplained variation.

12.3.4 How to do it with R

The overall F statistic and its associated p-value is listed at the bottom of the `summary` output, or we can access it directly by name; it is stored in the `fstatistic` component of the `summary` object.

```
> treesumry$fstatistic
   value    numdf    dendf
254.9723   2.0000  28.0000
```

For the `trees` data, we see that F = 254.972337410669 with a p-value < `2.2e-16`. Consequently we reject H_0, that is, the data provide strong evidence that not all β_i's are zero.

12.3.5 Student's t Tests

We know that

$$\mathbf{b} \sim \texttt{mvnorm}\left(\texttt{mean} = \beta,\ \texttt{sigma} = \sigma^2\left(\mathbf{X}^{\mathrm{T}}\mathbf{X}\right)^{-1}\right) \tag{12.3.8}$$

and we have seen how to test the hypothesis $H_0 : \beta_1 = \beta_2 = \cdots = \beta_p = 0$, but let us now consider the test

$$H_0 : \beta_i = 0 \text{ versus } H_1 : \beta_i \neq 0, \tag{12.3.9}$$

where β_i is the coefficient for the ith independent variable. We test the hypothesis by calculating a statistic, examining it's null distribution, and rejecting H_0 if the p-value is small. If H_0 is rejected, then we conclude that there is a significant relationship between Y and x_i *in the regression model* $Y \sim (x_1, \ldots, x_p)$. This last part of the sentence is very important because the significance of the variable x_i sometimes depends on the presence of other independent variables in the model[3].

To test the hypothesis we go to find the sampling distribution of b_i, the estimator of the corresponding parameter β_i, when the null hypothesis is true. We saw in Section 12.2.7 that

$$T_i = \frac{b_i - \beta_i}{S_{b_i}} \tag{12.3.10}$$

has a Student's t distribution with $n-(p+1)$ degrees of freedom. (Remember, we are estimating $p+1$ parameters.) Consequently, under the null hypothesis $H_0 : \beta_i = 0$ the statistic $t_i = b_i / S_{b_i}$ has a $\mathsf{t}(\texttt{df} = n - p - 1)$ distribution.

12.3.6 How to do it with R

The Student's t tests for significance of the individual explanatory variables are shown in the `summary` output.

```
> treesumry

Call:
lm(formula = Volume ~ Girth + Height, data = trees)

Residuals:
    Min      1Q  Median      3Q     Max
-6.4065 -2.6493 -0.2876  2.2003  8.4847

Coefficients:
            Estimate Std. Error t value Pr(>|t|)
(Intercept) -57.9877     8.6382  -6.713 2.75e-07 ***
Girth         4.7082     0.2643  17.816  < 2e-16 ***
Height        0.3393     0.1302   2.607   0.0145 *
---
Signif. codes:  0 '***' 0.001 '**' 0.01 '*' 0.05 '.' 0.1 ' ' 1

Residual standard error: 3.882 on 28 degrees of freedom
```

[3]In other words, a variable might be highly significant one moment but then fail to be significant when another variable is added to the model. When this happens it often indicates a problem with the explanatory variables, such as *multicollinearity*. See Section 12.9.3.

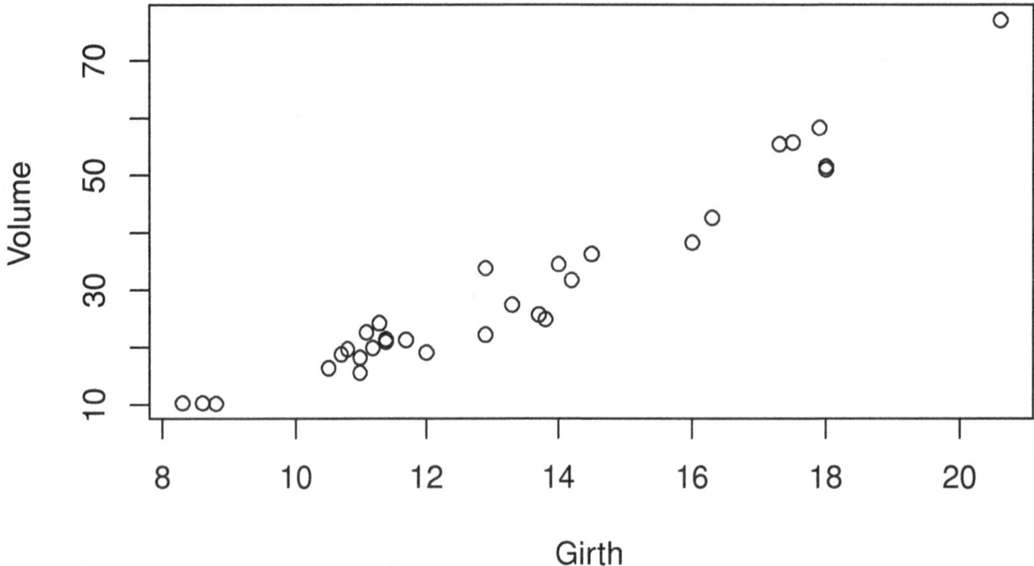

Figure 12.4.1: Scatterplot of `Volume` versus `Girth` for the `trees` data

```
Multiple R-squared: 0.948,       Adjusted R-squared: 0.9442
F-statistic:   255 on 2 and 28 DF,  p-value: < 2.2e-16
```

We see from the p-values that there is a significant linear relationship between `Volume` and `Girth` and between `Volume` and `Height` in the regression model `Volume ~Girth + Height`. Further, it appears that the `Intercept` is significant in the aforementioned model.

12.4 Polynomial Regression

12.4.1 Quadratic Regression Model

In each of the previous sections we assumed that μ was a linear function of the explanatory variables. For example, in SLR we assumed that $\mu(x) = \beta_0 + \beta_1 x$, and in our previous MLR examples we assumed $\mu(x_1, x_2) = \beta_0 + \beta_1 x_1 + \beta_2 x_2$. In every case the scatterplots indicated that our assumption was reasonable. Sometimes, however, plots of the data suggest that the linear model is incomplete and should be modified.

For example, let us examine a scatterplot of `Volume` versus `Girth` a little more closely. See Figure 12.4.1. There might be a slight curvature to the data; the volume curves ever so slightly upward as the girth increases. After looking at the plot we might try to capture the curvature with a mean response such as

$$\mu(x_1) = \beta_0 + \beta_1 x_1 + \beta_2 x_1^2. \tag{12.4.1}$$

The model associated with this choice of μ is

$$Y = \beta_0 + \beta_1 x_1 + \beta_2 x_1^2 + \epsilon. \tag{12.4.2}$$

The regression assumptions are the same. Almost everything indeed is the same. In fact, it is still called a "linear regression model", since the mean response μ is linear *in the parameters* β_0, β_1, and β_2.

However, there is one important difference. When we introduce the squared variable in the model we inadvertently also introduce strong dependence between the terms which can cause significant numerical problems when it comes time to calculate the parameter estimates. Therefore, we should usually rescale the independent variable to have mean zero (and even variance one if we wish) BEFORE fitting the model. That is, we replace the x_i's with $x_i - \overline{x}$ (or $(x_i - \overline{x})/s$) before fitting the model[4].

How to do it with R

There are multiple ways to fit a quadratic model to the variables `Volume` and `Girth` using R.

1. One way would be to square the values for `Girth` and save them in a vector `Girthsq`. Next, fit the linear model `Volume ~Girth + Girthsq`.

2. A second way would be to use the *insulate* function in R, denoted by `I`:

   `Volume ~ Girth + I(Girth^2)`

   The second method is shorter than the first but the end result is the same. And once we calculate and store the fitted model (in, say, `treesquad.lm`) all of the previous comments regarding R apply.

3. A third and "right" way to do it is with orthogonal polynomials:

   `Volume ~ poly(Girth, degree = 2)`

   See `?poly` and `?cars` for more information. Note that we can recover the approach in 2 with `poly(Girth, degree = 2, raw = TRUE)`.

Example 12.7. We will fit the quadratic model to the `trees` data and display the results with `summary`, being careful to rescale the data before fitting the model. We may rescale the `Girth` variable to have zero mean and unit variance on-the-fly with the `scale` function.

```
> treesquad.lm <- lm(Volume ~ scale(Girth) + I(scale(Girth)^2),
+       data = trees)
> summary(treesquad.lm)
```

```
Call:
lm(formula = Volume ~ scale(Girth) + I(scale(Girth)^2), data = trees)

Residuals:
    Min      1Q  Median      3Q     Max
-5.4889 -2.4293 -0.3718  2.0764  7.6447
```

[4]Rescaling the data gets the job done but a better way to avoid the multicollinearity introduced by the higher order terms is with *orthogonal polynomials*, whose coefficients are chosen just right so that the polynomials are not correlated with each other. This is beginning to linger outside the scope of this book, however, so we will content ourselves with a brief mention and then stick with the rescaling approach in the discussion that follows. A nice example of orthogonal polynomials in action can be run with `example(cars)`.

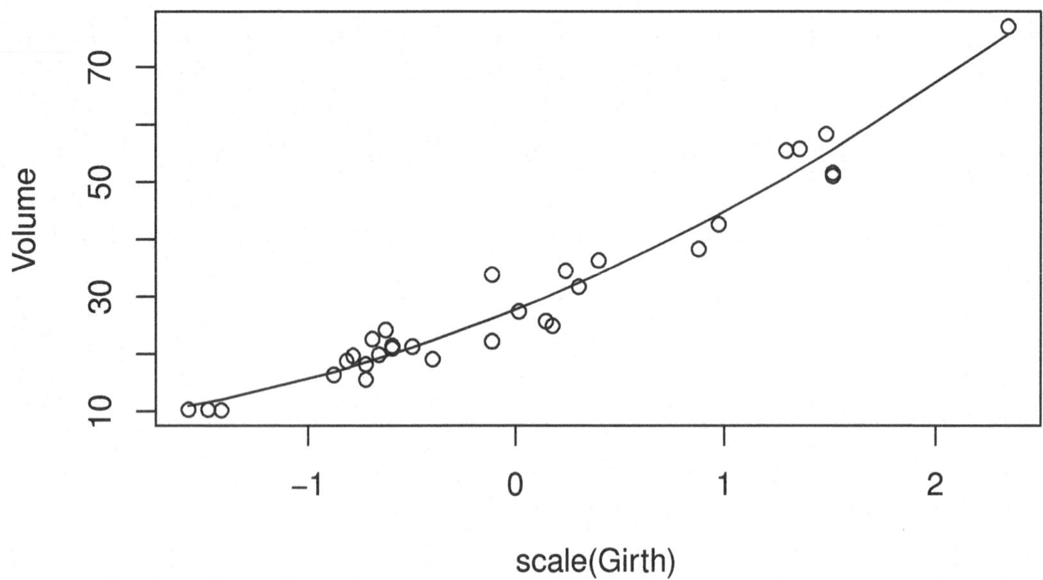

Figure 12.4.2: A quadratic model for the `trees` data

```
Coefficients:
                  Estimate Std. Error t value Pr(>|t|)
(Intercept)        27.7452     0.8161  33.996  < 2e-16 ***
scale(Girth)       14.5995     0.6773  21.557  < 2e-16 ***
I(scale(Girth)^2)   2.5067     0.5729   4.376 0.000152 ***
---
Signif. codes:  0 '***' 0.001 '**' 0.01 '*' 0.05 '.' 0.1 ' ' 1

Residual standard error: 3.335 on 28 degrees of freedom
Multiple R-squared: 0.9616,     Adjusted R-squared: 0.9588
F-statistic: 350.5 on 2 and 28 DF,  p-value: < 2.2e-16
```

We see that the F statistic indicates the overall model including `Girth` and `Girth^2` is significant. Further, there is strong evidence that both `Girth` and `Girth^2` are significantly related to `Volume`. We may examine a scatterplot together with the fitted quadratic function using the `lines` function, which adds a line to the plot tracing the estimated mean response.

```
> plot(Volume ~ scale(Girth), data = trees)
> lines(fitted(treesquad.lm) ~ scale(Girth), data = trees)
```

The plot is shown in Figure 12.4.2. Pay attention to the scale on the x-axis: it is on the scale of the transformed `Girth` data and not on the original scale.

Remark 12.8. When a model includes a quadratic term for an independent variable, it is customary to also include the linear term in the model. The principle is called *parsimony*. More generally, if the researcher decides to include x^m as a term in the model, then (s)he should also include all lower order terms $x, x^2, \ldots, x^{m-1}$ in the model.

We do estimation/prediction the same way that we did in Section 12.2.3, except we do not need a `Height` column in the dataframe `new` since the variable is not included in the quadratic model.

```
> new <- data.frame(Girth = c(9.1, 11.6, 12.5))
> predict(treesquad.lm, newdata = new, interval = "prediction")
       fit       lwr      upr
1 11.56982  4.347426 18.79221
2 20.30615 13.299050 27.31325
3 25.92290 18.972934 32.87286
```

The predictions and intervals are slightly different from what they were previously. Notice that it was not necessary to rescale the `Girth` prediction data before input to the `predict` function; the model did the rescaling for us automatically.

Remark 12.9. We have mentioned on several occasions that it is important to rescale the explanatory variables for polynomial regression. Watch what happens if we ignore this advice:

```
> summary(lm(Volume ~ Girth + I(Girth^2), data = trees))
Call:
lm(formula = Volume ~ Girth + I(Girth^2), data = trees)

Residuals:
    Min      1Q  Median      3Q     Max
-5.4889 -2.4293 -0.3718  2.0764  7.6447

Coefficients:
            Estimate Std. Error t value Pr(>|t|)
(Intercept) 10.78627   11.22282   0.961 0.344728
Girth       -2.09214    1.64734  -1.270 0.214534
I(Girth^2)   0.25454    0.05817   4.376 0.000152 ***
---
Signif. codes:  0 '***' 0.001 '**' 0.01 '*' 0.05 '.' 0.1 ' ' 1

Residual standard error: 3.335 on 28 degrees of freedom
Multiple R-squared: 0.9616,      Adjusted R-squared: 0.9588
F-statistic: 350.5 on 2 and 28 DF,  p-value: < 2.2e-16
```

Now nothing is significant in the model except `Girth^2`. We could delete the `Intercept` and `Girth` from the model, but the model would no longer be *parsimonious*. A novice may see the output and be confused about how to proceed, while the seasoned statistician recognizes immediately that `Girth` and `Girth^2` are highly correlated (see Section 12.9.3). The only remedy to this ailment is to rescale `Girth`, which we should have done in the first place.

In Example 12.14 of Section 12.7 we investigate this issue further.

12.5 Interaction

In our model for tree volume there have been two independent variables: `Girth` and `Height`. We may suspect that the independent variables are related, that is, values of one variable may tend to influence values of the other. It may be desirable to include an additional term in our model to try and capture the dependence between the variables. Interaction terms are formed by multiplying one (or more) explanatory variable(s) by another.

Example 12.10. Perhaps the `Girth` and `Height` of the tree interact to influence the its `Volume`; we would like to investigate whether the model (`Girth` = x_1 and `Height` = x_2)

$$Y = \beta_0 + \beta_1 x_1 + \beta_2 x_2 + \epsilon \tag{12.5.1}$$

would be significantly improved by the model

$$Y = \beta_0 + \beta_1 x_1 + \beta_2 x_2 + \beta_{1:2} x_1 x_2 + \epsilon, \tag{12.5.2}$$

where the subscript $1:2$ denotes that $\beta_{1:2}$ is a coefficient of an interaction term between x_1 and x_2.

What does it mean? Consider the mean response $\mu(x_1, x_2)$ as a function of x_2:

$$\mu(x_2) = (\beta_0 + \beta_1 x_1) + \beta_2 x_2. \tag{12.5.3}$$

This is a linear function of x_2 with slope β_2. As x_1 changes, the y-intercept of the mean response in x_2 changes, but the slope remains the same. Therefore, the mean response in x_2 is represented by a collection of parallel lines all with common slope β_2.

Now think about what happens when the interaction term $\beta_{1:2} x_1 x_2$ is included. The mean response in x_2 now looks like

$$\mu(x_2) = (\beta_0 + \beta_1 x_1) + (\beta_2 + \beta_{1:2} x_1) x_2. \tag{12.5.4}$$

In this case we see that not only the y-intercept changes when x_1 varies, but the slope also changes in x_1. Thus, the interaction term allows the slope of the mean response in x_2 to increase and decrease as x_1 varies.

How to do it with R

There are several ways to introduce an interaction term into the model.

1. Make a new variable `prod <-Girth *Height`, then include `prod` in the model formula `Volume ~Girth + Height + prod`. This method is perhaps the most transparent, but it also reserves memory space unnecessarily.

2. Once can construct an interaction term directly in R with a colon "`:`". For this example, the model formula would look like `Volume ~Girth + Height + Girth:Height`.

For the `trees` data, we fit the model with the interaction using method two and see if it is significant:

```
> treesint.lm <- lm(Volume ~ Girth + Height + Girth:Height,
+      data = trees)
> summary(treesint.lm)
```

```
Call:
lm(formula = Volume ~ Girth + Height + Girth:Height, data = trees)

Residuals:
    Min      1Q  Median      3Q     Max 
-6.5821 -1.0673  0.3026  1.5641  4.6649 

Coefficients:
             Estimate Std. Error t value Pr(>|t|)    
(Intercept)  69.39632   23.83575   2.911  0.00713 ** 
Girth        -5.85585    1.92134  -3.048  0.00511 ** 
Height       -1.29708    0.30984  -4.186  0.00027 ***
Girth:Height  0.13465    0.02438   5.524 7.48e-06 ***
---
Signif. codes:  0 '***' 0.001 '**' 0.01 '*' 0.05 '.' 0.1 ' ' 1

Residual standard error: 2.709 on 27 degrees of freedom
Multiple R-squared: 0.9756,	Adjusted R-squared: 0.9728 
F-statistic: 359.3 on 3 and 27 DF,  p-value: < 2.2e-16
```

We can see from the output that the interaction term is highly significant. Further, the estimate $b_{1:2}$ is positive. This means that the slope of $\mu(x_2)$ is steeper for bigger values of `Girth`. Keep in mind: the same interpretation holds for $\mu(x_1)$; that is, the slope of $\mu(x_1)$ is steeper for bigger values of `Height`.

For the sake of completeness we calculate confidence intervals for the parameters and do prediction as before.

```
> confint(treesint.lm)

                   2.5 %      97.5 %
(Intercept)  20.48938699 118.3032441
Girth        -9.79810354  -1.9135923
Height       -1.93282845  -0.6613383
Girth:Height  0.08463628   0.1846725

> new <- data.frame(Girth = c(9.1, 11.6, 12.5), Height = c(69,
+     74, 87))
> predict(treesint.lm, newdata = new, interval = "prediction")

       fit       lwr      upr
1 11.15884  5.236341 17.08134
2 21.07164 15.394628 26.74866
3 29.78862 23.721155 35.85608
```

Remark 12.11. There are two other ways to include interaction terms in model formulas. For example, we could have written `Girth *Height` or even `(Girth + Height)^2` and both would be the same as `Girth + Height + Girth:Height`.

These examples can be generalized to more than two independent variables, say three, four, or even more. We may be interested in seeing whether any pairwise interactions are significant. We do this with a model formula that looks something like `y ~ (x1 + x2 + x3 + x4)^2`.

12.6 Qualitative Explanatory Variables

We have so far been concerned with numerical independent variables taking values in a subset of real numbers. In this section, we extend our treatment to include the case in which one of the explanatory variables is qualitative, that is, a *factor*. Qualitative variables take values in a set of *levels*, which may or may not be ordered. See Section 3.1.2.

Note. The `trees` data do not have any qualitative explanatory variables, so we will construct one for illustrative purposes[5]. We will leave the `Girth` variable alone, but we will replace the variable `Height` by a new variable `Tall` which indicates whether or not the cherry tree is taller than a certain threshold (which for the sake of argument will be the sample median height of 76 ft). That is, `Tall` will be defined by

$$\texttt{Tall} = \begin{cases} \texttt{yes}, & \text{if } \texttt{Height} > 76, \\ \texttt{no}, & \text{if } \texttt{Height} \leq 76. \end{cases} \tag{12.6.1}$$

We can construct `Tall` very quickly in R with the `cut` function:

```
> trees$Tall <- cut(trees$Height, breaks = c(-Inf, 76, Inf),
+      labels = c("no", "yes"))
> trees$Tall[1:5]
```

```
[1] no  no  no  no  yes
Levels: no yes
```

Note that `Tall` is automatically generated to be a factor with the labels in the correct order. See `?cut` for more.

Once we have `Tall`, we include it in the regression model just like we would any other variable. It is handled internally in a special way. Define a "dummy variable" `Tallyes` that takes values

$$\texttt{Tallyes} = \begin{cases} 1, & \text{if } \texttt{Tall} = \texttt{yes}, \\ 0, & \text{otherwise.} \end{cases} \tag{12.6.2}$$

That is, `Tallyes` is an *indicator variable* which indicates when a respective tree is tall. The model may now be written as

$$\texttt{Volume} = \beta_0 + \beta_1 \texttt{Girth} + \beta_2 \texttt{Tallyes} + \epsilon. \tag{12.6.3}$$

Let us take a look at what this definition does to the mean response. Trees with `Tall = yes` will have the mean response

$$\mu(\texttt{Girth}) = (\beta_0 + \beta_2) + \beta_1 \texttt{Girth}, \tag{12.6.4}$$

while trees with `Tall = no` will have the mean response

$$\mu(\texttt{Girth}) = \beta_0 + \beta_1 \texttt{Girth}. \tag{12.6.5}$$

In essence, we are fitting two regression lines: one for tall trees, and one for short trees. The regression lines have the same slope but they have different y intercepts (which are exactly $|\beta_2|$ far apart).

---

[5]This procedure of replacing a continuous variable by a discrete/qualitative one is called *binning*, and is almost *never* the right thing to do. We are in a bind at this point, however, because we have invested this chapter in the `trees` data and I do not want to switch mid-discussion. I am currently searching for a data set with pre-existing qualitative variables that also conveys the same points present in the trees data, and when I find it I will update this chapter accordingly.

How to do it with R

The important thing is to double check that the qualitative variable in question is stored as a factor. The way to check is with the `class` command. For example,

```
> class(trees$Tall)
[1] "factor"
```

If the qualitative variable is not yet stored as a factor then we may convert it to one with the `factor` command. See Section 3.1.2. Other than this we perform MLR as we normally would.

```
> treesdummy.lm <- lm(Volume ~ Girth + Tall, data = trees)
> summary(treesdummy.lm)
Call:
lm(formula = Volume ~ Girth + Tall, data = trees)

Residuals:
    Min      1Q  Median      3Q     Max
-5.7788 -3.1710  0.4888  2.6737 10.0619

Coefficients:
            Estimate Std. Error t value Pr(>|t|)
(Intercept) -34.1652     3.2438  -10.53 3.02e-11 ***
Girth         4.6988     0.2652   17.72  < 2e-16 ***
Tallyes       4.3072     1.6380    2.63   0.0137 *
---
Signif. codes:  0 '***' 0.001 '**' 0.01 '*' 0.05 '.' 0.1 ' ' 1

Residual standard error: 3.875 on 28 degrees of freedom
Multiple R-squared: 0.9481,     Adjusted R-squared: 0.9444
F-statistic: 255.9 on 2 and 28 DF,  p-value: < 2.2e-16
```

From the output we see that all parameter estimates are statistically significant and we conclude that the mean response differs for trees with `Tall = yes` and trees with `Tall = no`.

Remark 12.12. We were somewhat disingenuous when we defined the dummy variable `Tallyes` because, in truth, R defines `Tallyes` automatically without input from the user[6]. Indeed, the author fit the model beforehand and wrote the discussion afterward with the knowledge of what R would do so that the output the reader saw would match what (s)he had previously read. The way that R handles factors internally is part of a much larger topic concerning *contrasts*, which falls outside the scope of this book. The interested reader should see Neter et al [67] or Fox [28] for more.

Remark 12.13. In general, if an explanatory variable `foo` is qualitative with n levels `bar1`, `bar2`, ..., `barn` then R will by default automatically define $n - 1$ indicator variables in the following way:

$$\texttt{foobar2} = \begin{cases} 1, & \text{if } \texttt{foo} = \text{"}\texttt{bar2}\text{"}, \\ 0, & \text{otherwise.} \end{cases}, \ldots, \texttt{foobarn} = \begin{cases} 1, & \text{if } \texttt{foo} = \text{"}\texttt{barn}\text{"}, \\ 0, & \text{otherwise.} \end{cases}$$

[6]That is, R by default handles contrasts according to its internal settings which may be customized by the user for fine control. Given that we will not investigate contrasts further in this book it does not serve the discussion to delve into those settings, either. The interested reader should check ?contrasts for details.

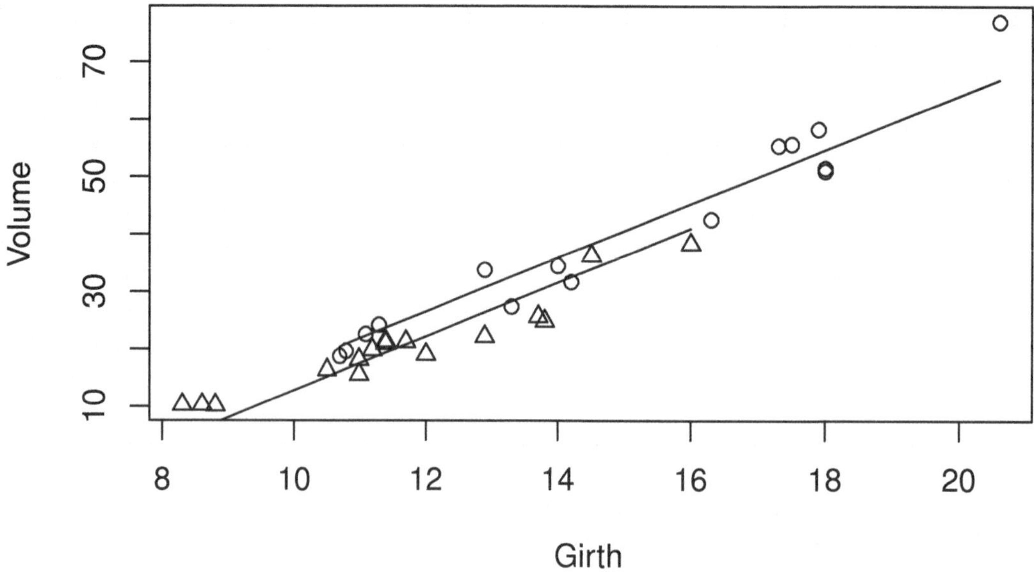

Figure 12.6.1: A dummy variable model for the `trees` data

The level `bar1` is represented by `foobar2` $= \cdots =$ `foobarn` $= 0$. We just need to make sure that `foo` is stored as a factor and R will take care of the rest.

Graphing the Regression Lines

We can see a plot of the two regression lines with the following mouthful of code.

```
> treesTall <- split(trees, trees$Tall)
> treesTall[["yes"]]$Fit <- predict(treesdummy.lm, treesTall[["yes"]])
> treesTall[["no"]]$Fit <- predict(treesdummy.lm, treesTall[["no"]])
> plot(Volume ~ Girth, data = trees, type = "n")
> points(Volume ~ Girth, data = treesTall[["yes"]], pch = 1)
> points(Volume ~ Girth, data = treesTall[["no"]], pch = 2)
> lines(Fit ~ Girth, data = treesTall[["yes"]])
> lines(Fit ~ Girth, data = treesTall[["no"]])
```

It may look intimidating but there is reason to the madness. First we `split` the `trees` data into two pieces, with groups determined by the `Tall` variable. Next we add the `Fit`ted values to each piece via `predict`. Then we set up a `plot` for the variables `Volume` versus `Girth`, but we do not plot anything yet (`type = n`) because we want to use different symbols for the two groups. Next we add `points` to the plot for the `Tall = yes` trees and use an open circle for a plot character (`pch = 1`), followed by `points` for the `Tall = no` trees with a triangle character (`pch = 2`). Finally, we add regression `lines` to the plot, one for each group.

There are other – shorter – ways to plot regression lines by groups, namely the `scatterplot` function in the `car` [30] package and the `xyplot` function in the `lattice` package. We elected to introduce the reader to the above approach since many advanced plots in R are done in a similar, consecutive fashion.

12.7 Partial *F* Statistic

We saw in Section 12.3.3 how to test $H_0 : \beta_0 = \beta_1 = \cdots = \beta_p = 0$ with the overall F statistic and we saw in Section 12.3.5 how to test $H_0 : \beta_i = 0$ that a particular coefficient β_i is zero. Sometimes, however, we would like to test whether a certain part of the model is significant. Consider the regression model

$$Y = \beta_0 + \beta_1 x_1 + \cdots + \beta_j x_j + \beta_{j+1} x_{j+1} + \cdots + \beta_p x_p + \epsilon, \tag{12.7.1}$$

where $j \geq 1$ and $p \geq 2$. Now we wish to test the hypothesis

$$H_0 : \beta_{j+1} = \beta_{j+2} = \cdots = \beta_p = 0 \tag{12.7.2}$$

versus the alternative

$$H_1 : \text{at least one of } \beta_{j+1},\ \beta_{j+2},\ \ldots, \beta_p \neq 0. \tag{12.7.3}$$

The interpretation of H_0 is that none of the variables $x_{j+1}, \ldots, x_p$ is significantly related to Y and the interpretation of H_1 is that at least one of $x_{j+1}, \ldots, x_p$ is significantly related to Y. In essence, for this hypothesis test there are two competing models under consideration:

$$\text{the full model:} \quad y = \beta_0 + \beta_1 x_1 + \cdots + \beta_p x_p + \epsilon, \tag{12.7.4}$$

$$\text{the reduced model:} \quad y = \beta_0 + \beta_1 x_1 + \cdots + \beta_j x_j + \epsilon, \tag{12.7.5}$$

Of course, the full model will always explain the data *better* than the reduced model, but does the full model explain the data *significantly better* than the reduced model? This question is exactly what the partial F statistic is designed to answer.

We first calculate SSE_f, the unexplained variation in the full model, and SSE_r, the unexplained variation in the reduced model. We base our test on the difference $SSE_r - SSE_f$ which measures the reduction in unexplained variation attributable to the variables $x_{j+1}, \ldots, x_p$. In the full model there are $p+1$ parameters and in the reduced model there are $j+1$ parameters, which gives a difference of $p-j$ parameters (hence degrees of freedom). The partial F statistic is

$$F = \frac{(SSE_r - SSE_f)/(p-j)}{SSE_f/(n-p-1)}. \tag{12.7.6}$$

It can be shown when the regression assumptions hold under H_0 that the partial F statistic has an f(`df1` $= p - j$, `df2` $= n - p - 1$) distribution. We calculate the p-value of the observed partial F statistic and reject H_0 if the p-value is small.

How to do it with R

The key ingredient above is that the two competing models are *nested* in the sense that the reduced model is entirely contained within the complete model. The way to test whether the improvement is significant is to compute `lm` objects both for the complete model and the reduced model then compare the answers with the anova function.

Example 12.14. For the `trees` data, let us fit a polynomial regression model and for the sake of argument we will ignore our own good advice and fail to rescale the explanatory variables.

```
> treesfull.lm <- lm(Volume ~ Girth + I(Girth^2) + Height +
+      I(Height^2), data = trees)
> summary(treesfull.lm)
```

```
Call:
lm(formula = Volume ~ Girth + I(Girth^2) + Height + I(Height^2),
    data = trees)

Residuals:
    Min      1Q  Median      3Q     Max
-4.3679 -1.6698 -0.1580  1.7915  4.3581

Coefficients:
             Estimate Std. Error t value Pr(>|t|)
(Intercept) -0.955101  63.013630  -0.015    0.988
Girth       -2.796569   1.468677  -1.904    0.068 .
I(Girth^2)   0.265446   0.051689   5.135 2.35e-05 ***
Height       0.119372   1.784588   0.067    0.947
I(Height^2)  0.001717   0.011905   0.144    0.886
---
Signif. codes:  0 '***' 0.001 '**' 0.01 '*' 0.05 '.' 0.1 ' ' 1

Residual standard error: 2.674 on 26 degrees of freedom
Multiple R-squared: 0.9771,      Adjusted R-squared: 0.9735
F-statistic:   277 on 4 and 26 DF,  p-value: < 2.2e-16
```

In this ill-formed model nothing is significant except `Girth` and `Girth^2`. Let us continue down this path and suppose that we would like to try a reduced model which contains nothing but `Girth` and `Girth^2` (not even an `Intercept`). Our two models are now

$$\text{the full model:} \quad Y = \beta_0 + \beta_1 x_1 + \beta_2 x_1^2 + \beta_3 x_2 + \beta_4 x_2^2 + \epsilon,$$
$$\text{the reduced model:} \quad Y = \beta_1 x_1 + \beta_2 x_1^2 + \epsilon,$$

We fit the reduced model with `lm` and store the results:

```
> treesreduced.lm <- lm(Volume ~ -1 + Girth + I(Girth^2), data = trees)
```

To delete the intercept from the model we used `-1` in the model formula. Next we compare the two models with the `anova` function. The convention is to list the models from smallest to largest.

```
> anova(treesreduced.lm, treesfull.lm)
```

```
Analysis of Variance Table

Model 1: Volume ~ -1 + Girth + I(Girth^2)
Model 2: Volume ~ Girth + I(Girth^2) + Height + I(Height^2)
```

```
  Res.Df    RSS Df Sum of Sq      F   Pr(>F)
1     29 321.65
2     26 185.86  3    135.79 6.3319 0.002279 **
---
Signif. codes:  0 '***' 0.001 '**' 0.01 '*' 0.05 '.' 0.1 ' ' 1
```

We see from the output that the complete model is highly significant compared to the model that does not incorporate `Height` or the `Intercept`. We wonder (with our tongue in our cheek) if the `Height^2` term in the full model is causing all of the trouble. We will fit an alternative reduced model that only deletes `Height^2`.

```
> treesreduced2.lm <- lm(Volume ~ Girth + I(Girth^2) + Height,
+     data = trees)
> anova(treesreduced2.lm, treesfull.lm)
Analysis of Variance Table

Model 1: Volume ~ Girth + I(Girth^2) + Height
Model 2: Volume ~ Girth + I(Girth^2) + Height + I(Height^2)
  Res.Df    RSS Df Sum of Sq      F Pr(>F)
1     27 186.01
2     26 185.86  1   0.14865 0.0208 0.8865
```

In this case, the improvement to the reduced model that is attributable to `Height^2` is not significant, so we can delete `Height^2` from the model with a clear conscience. We notice that the p-value for this latest partial F test is 0.8865, which seems to be remarkably close to the p-value we saw for the univariate t test of `Height^2` at the beginning of this example. In fact, the p-values are *exactly* the same. Perhaps now we gain some insight into the true meaning of the univariate tests.

12.8 Residual Analysis and Diagnostic Tools

We encountered many, many diagnostic measures for simple linear regression in Sections 11.4 and 11.5. All of these are valid in multiple linear regression, too, but there are some slight changes that we need to make for the multivariate case. We list these below, and apply them to the trees example.

Shapiro-Wilk, Breusch-Pagan, Durbin-Watson: unchanged from SLR, but we are now equipped to talk about the Shapiro-Wilk test statistic for the residuals. It is defined by the formula

$$W = \frac{\mathbf{a}^{\mathrm{T}}\mathbf{E}^{*}}{\mathbf{E}^{\mathrm{T}}\mathbf{E}}, \tag{12.8.1}$$

where $\mathbf{E}^{*}$ is the sorted residuals and $\mathbf{a}_{1\times n}$ is defined by

$$\mathbf{a} = \frac{\mathbf{m}^{\mathrm{T}}\mathbf{V}^{-1}}{\sqrt{\mathbf{m}^{\mathrm{T}}\mathbf{V}^{-1}\mathbf{V}^{-1}\mathbf{m}}}, \tag{12.8.2}$$

where $\mathbf{m}_{n\times 1}$ and $\mathbf{V}_{n\times n}$ are the mean and covariance matrix, respectively, of the order statistics from an mvnorm (`mean` = $\mathbf{0}$, `sigma` = $\mathbf{I}$) distribution.

Leverages: are defined to be the diagonal entries of the hat matrix $\mathbf{H}$ (which is why we called them h_{ii} in Section 12.2.3). The sum of the leverages is $\mathrm{tr}(\mathbf{H}) = p + 1$. One rule of thumb considers a leverage extreme if it is larger than double the mean leverage value, which is $2(p+1)/n$, and another rule of thumb considers leverages bigger than 0.5 to indicate high leverage, while values between 0.3 and 0.5 indicate moderate leverage.

Standardized residuals: unchanged. Considered extreme if $|R_i| > 2$.

Studentized residuals: compared to a $\mathsf{t}(\mathtt{df} = n - p - 2)$ distribution.

DFBETAS: The formula is generalized to

$$(DFBETAS)_{j(i)} = \frac{b_j - b_{j(i)}}{S_{(i)}\sqrt{c_{jj}}}, \quad j = 0, \ldots p,\ i = 1, \ldots, n, \tag{12.8.3}$$

where c_{jj} is the jth diagonal entry of $(\mathbf{X}^{\mathrm{T}}\mathbf{X})^{-1}$. Values larger than one for small data sets or $2/\sqrt{n}$ for large data sets should be investigated.

DFFITS: unchanged. Larger than one in absolute value is considered extreme.

Cook's D: compared to an $\mathsf{f}(\mathtt{df1} = p + 1, \mathtt{df2} = n - p - 1)$ distribution. Observations falling higher than the 50th percentile are extreme.

Note that plugging the value $p = 1$ into the formulas will recover all of the ones we saw in Chapter 11.

12.9 Additional Topics

12.9.1 Nonlinear Regression

We spent the entire chapter talking about the `trees` data, and all of our models looked like `Volume ~Girth + Height` or a variant of this model. But let us think again: we know from elementary school that the volume of a rectangle is $V = lwh$ and the volume of a cylinder (which is closer to what a black cherry tree looks like) is

$$V = \pi r^2 h \quad \text{or} \quad V = 4\pi dh, \tag{12.9.1}$$

where r and d represent the radius and diameter of the tree, respectively. With this in mind, it would seem that a more appropriate model for μ might be

$$\mu(x_1, x_2) = \beta_0 x_1^{\beta_1} x_2^{\beta_2}, \tag{12.9.2}$$

where β_1 and β_2 are parameters to adjust for the fact that a black cherry tree is not a perfect cylinder.

How can we fit this model? The model is not linear in the parameters any more, so our linear regression methods will not work... or will they? In the `trees` example we may take the logarithm of both sides of Equation 12.9.2 to get

$$\mu^*(x_1, x_2) = \ln\left[\mu(x_1, x_2)\right] = \ln\beta_0 + \beta_1 \ln x_1 + \beta_2 \ln x_2, \tag{12.9.3}$$

and this new model μ^* is linear in the parameters $\beta_0^* = \ln\beta_0$, $\beta_1^* = \beta_1$ and $\beta_2^* = \beta_2$. We can use what we have learned to fit a linear model `log(Volume)~log(Girth)+ log(Height)`, and everything will proceed as before, with one exception: we will need to be mindful when it comes time to make predictions because the model will have been fit on the log scale, and we will need to transform our predictions back to the original scale (by exponentiating with exp) to make sense.

```
> treesNonlin.lm <- lm(log(Volume) ~ log(Girth) + log(Height),
+     data = trees)
> summary(treesNonlin.lm)

Call:
lm(formula = log(Volume) ~ log(Girth) + log(Height), data = trees)

Residuals:
      Min        1Q    Median        3Q       Max
-0.168561 -0.048488  0.002431  0.063637  0.129223

Coefficients:
            Estimate Std. Error t value Pr(>|t|)
(Intercept) -6.63162    0.79979  -8.292 5.06e-09 ***
log(Girth)   1.98265    0.07501  26.432  < 2e-16 ***
log(Height)  1.11712    0.20444   5.464 7.81e-06 ***
---
Signif. codes:  0 '***' 0.001 '**' 0.01 '*' 0.05 '.' 0.1 ' ' 1

Residual standard error: 0.08139 on 28 degrees of freedom
Multiple R-squared: 0.9777,     Adjusted R-squared: 0.9761
F-statistic: 613.2 on 2 and 28 DF,  p-value: < 2.2e-16
```

This is our best model yet (judging by R^2 and $\overline{R}^2$), all of the parameters are significant, it is simpler than the quadratic or interaction models, and it even makes theoretical sense. It rarely gets any better than that.

We may get confidence intervals for the parameters, but remember that it is usually better to transform back to the original scale for interpretation purposes :

```
> exp(confint(treesNonlin.lm))

                   2.5 %      97.5 %
(Intercept) 0.0002561078 0.006783093
log(Girth)  6.2276411645 8.468066317
log(Height) 2.0104387829 4.645475188
```

(Note that we did not update the row labels of the matrix to show that we exponentiated and so they are misleading as written.) We do predictions just as before. Remember to transform the response variable back to the original scale after prediction.

```
> new <- data.frame(Girth = c(9.1, 11.6, 12.5), Height = c(69,
+     74, 87))
> exp(predict(treesNonlin.lm, newdata = new, interval = "confidence"))
```

```
       fit      lwr      upr
1 11.90117 11.25908 12.57989
2 20.82261 20.14652 21.52139
3 28.93317 27.03755 30.96169
```

The predictions and intervals are slightly different from those calculated earlier, but they are close. Note that we did not need to transform the `Girth` and `Height` arguments in the dataframe `new`. All transformations are done for us automatically.

12.9.2 Real Nonlinear Regression

We saw with the `trees` data that a nonlinear model might be more appropriate for the data based on theoretical considerations, and we were lucky because the functional form of μ allowed us to take logarithms to transform the nonlinear model to a linear one. The same trick will not work in other circumstances, however. We need techniques to fit general models of the form

$$\mathbf{Y} = \mu(\mathbf{X}) + \epsilon, \tag{12.9.4}$$

where μ is some crazy function that does not lend itself to linear transformations.

There are a host of methods to address problems like these which are studied in advanced regression classes. The interested reader should see Neter *et al* [67] or Tabachnick and Fidell [83].

It turns out that John Fox has posted an Appendix to his book [29] which discusses some of the methods and issues associated with nonlinear regression; see

`http://cran.r-project.org/doc/contrib/Fox-Companion/appendix.html`

12.9.3 Multicollinearity

A multiple regression model exhibits *multicollinearity* when two or more of the explanatory variables are substantially correlated with each other. We can measure multicollinearity by having one of the explanatory play the role of "dependent variable" and regress it on the remaining explanatory variables. The the R^2 of the resulting model is near one, then we say that the model is multicollinear or shows multicollinearity.

Multicollinearity is a problem because it causes instability in the regression model. The instability is a consequence of redundancy in the explanatory variables: a high R^2 indicates a strong dependence between the selected independent variable and the others. The redundant information inflates the variance of the parameter estimates which can cause them to be statistically insignificant when they would have been significant otherwise. To wit, multicollinearity is usually measured by what are called *variance inflation factors*.

Once multicollinearity has been diagnosed there are several approaches to remediate it. Here are a couple of important ones.

Principal Components Analysis. This approach casts out two or more of the original explanatory variables and replaces them with new variables, derived from the original ones, that are by design uncorrelated with one another. The redundancy is thus eliminated and we may proceed as usual with the new variables in hand. Principal Components Analysis is important for other reasons, too, not just for fixing multicollinearity problems.

Ridge Regression. The idea of this approach is to replace the original parameter estimates with a different type of parameter estimate which is more stable under multicollinearity. The estimators are not found by ordinary least squares but rather a different optimization procedure which incorporates the variance inflation factor information.

We decided to omit a thorough discussion of multicollinearity because we are not equipped to handle the mathematical details. Perhaps the topic will receive more attention in a later edition.

- What to do when data are not normal
    - Bootstrap (see Chapter 13).

12.9.4 Akaike's Information Criterion

$$AIC = -2 \ln L + 2(p + 1)$$

Chapter Exercises

Exercise 12.1. Use Equations 12.3.1, 12.3.2, and 12.3.3 to prove the Anova Equality:

$$SSTO = SSE + SSR.$$

Chapter 13

Resampling Methods

Computers have changed the face of statistics. Their quick computational speed and flawless accuracy, coupled with large data sets acquired by the researcher, make them indispensable for many modern analyses. In particular, resampling methods (due in large part to Bradley Efron) have gained prominence in the modern statistician's repertoire. We first look at a classical problem to get some insight why.

I have seen *Statistical Computing with R* by Rizzo [71] and I recommend it to those looking for a more advanced treatment with additional topics. I believe that *Monte Carlo Statistical Methods* by Robert and Casella [72] has a new edition that integrates R into the narrative.

What do I want them to know?

- basic philosophy of resampling and why it is important
- resampling for standard errors and confidence intervals
- resampling for hypothesis tests (permutation tests)

13.1 Introduction

Classical question Given a population of interest, how may we effectively learn some of its salient features, *e.g.*, the population's mean? One way is through representative random sampling. Given a random sample, we summarize the information contained therein by calculating a reasonable statistic, *e.g.*, the sample mean. Given a value of a statistic, how do we know whether that value is significantly different from that which was expected? We don't; we look at the *sampling distribution* of the statistic, and we try to make probabilistic assertions based on a confidence level or other consideration. For example, we may find ourselves saying things like, "With 95% confidence, the true population mean is greater than zero."

Problem Unfortunately, in most cases the sampling distribution is *unknown*. Thus, in the past, in efforts to say something useful, statisticians have been obligated to place some restrictive assumptions on the underlying population. For example, if we suppose that the population has a normal distribution, then we can say that the distribution of $\overline{X}$ is normal, too, with the same mean (and a smaller standard deviation). It is then easy to draw conclusions, make inferences, and go on about our business.

Alternative We don't know what the underlying population distributions is, so let us *estimate* it, just like we would with any other parameter. The statistic we use is the *empirical CDF*, that is, the function that places mass $1/n$ at each of the observed data points $x_1, \ldots, x_n$ (see Section 5.5). As the sample size increases, we would expect the approximation to get better and better (with i.i.d. observations, it does, and there is a wonderful theorem by Glivenko and Cantelli that proves it). And now that we have an (estimated) population distribution, it is easy to find the sampling distribution of any statistic we like: just **sample** from the empirical CDF many, many times, calculate the statistic each time, and make a histogram. Done! Of course, the number of samples needed to get a representative histogram is prohibitively large... human beings are simply too slow (and clumsy) to do this tedious procedure.

Fortunately, computers are very skilled at doing simple, repetitive tasks very quickly and accurately. So we employ them to give us a reasonable idea about the sampling distribution of our statistic, and we use the generated sampling distribution to guide our inferences and draw our conclusions. If we would like to have a better approximation for the sampling distribution (within the confines of the information contained in the original sample), we merely tell the computer to sample more. In this (restricted) sense, we are limited only by our current computational speed and pocket book.

In short, here are some of the benefits that the advent of resampling methods has given us:

Fewer assumptions. We are no longer required to assume the population is normal or the sample size is large (though, as before, the larger the sample the better).

Greater accuracy. Many classical methods are based on rough upper bounds or Taylor expansions. The bootstrap procedures can be iterated long enough to give results accurate to several decimal places, often beating classical approximations.

Generality. Resampling methods are easy to understand and apply to a large class of seemingly unrelated procedures. One no longer needs to memorize long complicated formulas and algorithms.

Remark 13.1. Due to the special structure of the empirical CDF, to get an i.i.d. sample we just need to take a random sample of size n, with replacement, from the observed data $x_1, \ldots, x_n$. Repeats are expected and acceptable. Since we already sampled to get the original data, the term *resampling* is used to describe the procedure.

General bootstrap procedure. The above discussion leads us to the following general procedure to approximate the sampling distribution of a statistic $S = S(x_1, x_2, \ldots, x_n)$ based on an observed simple random sample $\mathbf{x} = (x_1, x_2, \ldots, x_n)$ of size n:

1. Create many many samples $\mathbf{x}_1^*, \ldots, \mathbf{x}_M^*$, called *resamples*, by sampling with replacement from the data.

2. Calculate the statistic of interest $S(\mathbf{x}_1^*), \ldots, S(\mathbf{x}_M^*)$ for each resample. The distribution of the resample statistics is called a *bootstrap distribution*.

3. The bootstrap distribution gives information about the sampling distribution of the original statistic S. In particular, the bootstrap distribution gives us some idea about the center, spread, and shape of the sampling distribution of S.

13.2 Bootstrap Standard Errors

Since the bootstrap distribution gives us information about a statistic's sampling distribution, we can use the bootstrap distribution to estimate properties of the statistic. We will illustrate the bootstrap procedure in the special case that the statistic S is a standard error.

Example 13.2. Standard error of the mean. In this example we illustrate the bootstrap by estimating the standard error of the sample meanand we will do it in the special case that the underlying population is norm(mean = 3, sd = 1).

Of course, we do not really need a bootstrap distribution here because from Section 8.2 we know that $\overline{X} \sim$ norm(mean = 3, sd = $1/\sqrt{n}$), but we proceed anyway to investigate how the bootstrap performs when we know what the answer should be ahead of time.

We will take a random sample of size $n = 25$ from the population. Then we will *resample* the data 1000 times to get 1000 resamples of size 25. We will calculate the sample mean of each of the resamples, and will study the data distribution of the 1000 values of $\overline{x}$.

```
> srs <- rnorm(25, mean = 3)
> resamps <- replicate(1000, sample(srs, 25, TRUE), simplify = FALSE)
> xbarstar <- sapply(resamps, mean, simplify = TRUE)
```

A histogram of the 1000 values of $\overline{x}$ is shown in Figure 13.2.1, and was produced by the following code.

```
> hist(xbarstar, breaks = 40, prob = TRUE)
> curve(dnorm(x, 3, 0.2), add = TRUE)  # overlay true normal density
```

We have overlain what we know to be the true sampling distribution of $\overline{X}$, namely, a norm(mean = 3, sd = $1/\sqrt{25}$) distribution. The histogram matches the true sampling distribution pretty well with respect to shape and spread... but notice how the histogram is off-center a little bit. This is not a coincidence – in fact, it can be shown that the mean of the bootstrap distribution is exactly the mean of the original sample, that is, the value of the statistic that we originally observed. Let us calculate the mean of the bootstrap distribution and compare it to the mean of the original sample:

```
> mean(xbarstar)
[1] 2.711477
> mean(srs)
[1] 2.712087
> mean(xbarstar) - mean(srs)
[1] -0.0006096438
```

Notice how close the two values are. The difference between them is an estimate of how biased the original statistic is, the so-called *bootstrap estimate of bias*. Since the estimate is so small we would expect our original statistic ($\overline{X}$) to have small bias, but this is no surprise to us because we already knew from Section 8.1.1 that $\overline{X}$ is an unbiased estimator of the population mean.

Now back to our original problem, we would like to estimate the standard error of $\overline{X}$. Looking at the histogram, we see that the spread of the bootstrap distribution is similar to the spread of the sampling distribution. Therefore, it stands to reason that we could estimate the standard error of $\overline{X}$ with the sample standard deviation of the resample statistics. Let us try and see.

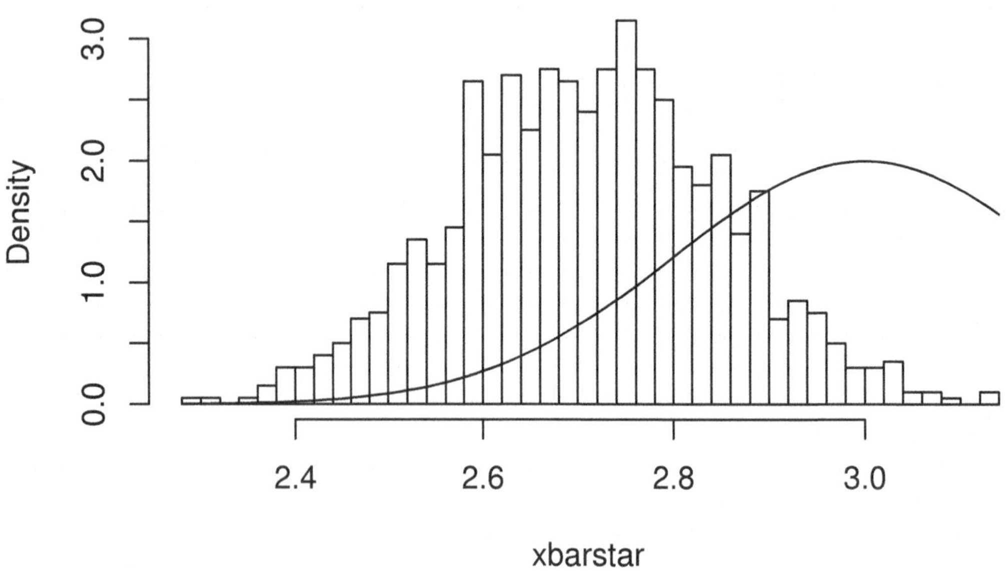

Figure 13.2.1: Bootstrapping the standard error of the mean, simulated data

The original data were 25 observations generated from a `norm(mean = 3, sd = 1)` distribution. We next resampled to get 1000 resamples, each of size 25, and calculated the sample mean for each resample. A histogram of the 1000 values of $\overline{x}$ is shown above. Also shown (with a solid line) is the true sampling distribution of $\overline{X}$, which is a `norm(mean = 3, sd = 0.2)` distribution. Note that the histogram is centered at the sample mean of the original data, while the true sampling distribution is centered at the true value of $\mu = 3$. The shape and spread of the histogram is similar to the shape and spread of the true sampling distribution.

```
> sd(xbarstar)
[1] 0.1390366
```

We know from theory that the true standard error is $1/\sqrt{25} = 0.20$. Our bootstrap estimate is not very far from the theoretical value.

Remark 13.3. What would happen if we take more resamples? Instead of 1000 resamples, we could increase to, say, 2000, 3000, or even 4000... would it help? The answer is both yes and no. Keep in mind that with resampling methods there are two sources of randomness: that from the original sample, and that from the subsequent resampling procedure. An increased number of resamples would reduce the variation due to the second part, but would do nothing to reduce the variation due to the first part. We only took an original sample of size $n = 25$, and resampling more and more would never generate more information about the population than was already there. In this sense, the statistician is limited by the information contained in the original sample.

Example 13.4. Standard error of the median. We look at one where we do not know the answer ahead of time. This example uses the `rivers` data set. Recall the stemplot on page on page 41 that we made for these data which shows them to be markedly right-skewed, so a natural estimate of center would be the sample median. Unfortunately, its sampling distribution falls out of our reach. We use the bootstrap to help us with this problem, and the modifications to the last example are trivial.

```
> resamps <- replicate(1000, sample(rivers, 141, TRUE), simplify = FALSE)
> medstar <- sapply(resamps, median, simplify = TRUE)
> sd(medstar)
[1] 27.21154
```

The graph is shown in Figure 13.2.2, and was produced by the following code.

```
> hist(medstar, breaks = 40, prob = TRUE)
```

```
> median(rivers)
[1] 425
> mean(medstar)
[1] 427.88
> mean(medstar) - median(rivers)
[1] 2.88
```

Example 13.5. The boot package in R. It turns out that there are many bootstrap procedures and commands already built into base R, in the `boot` package. Further, inside the `boot` package there is even a function called `boot`. The basic syntax is of the form:

```
boot(data, statistic, R)
```

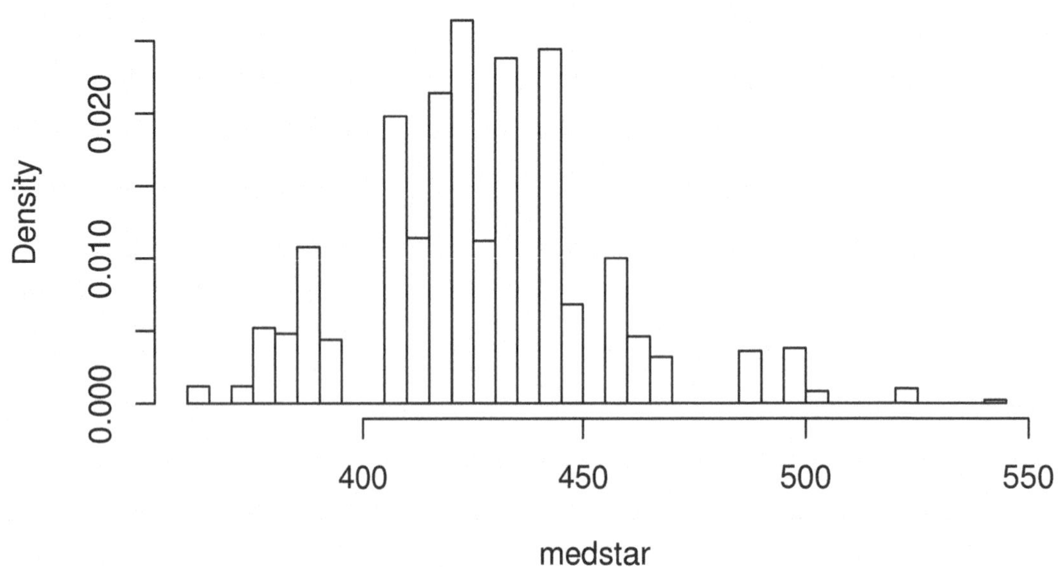

Figure 13.2.2: Bootstrapping the standard error of the median for the `rivers` data

Here, `data` is a vector (or matrix) containing the data to be resampled, `statistic` is a defined function, *of two arguments*, that tells which statistic should be computed, and the parameter R specifies how many resamples should be taken.

For the standard error of the mean (Example 13.2):

```
> library(boot)
> mean_fun <- function(x, indices) mean(x[indices])
> boot(data = srs, statistic = mean_fun, R = 1000)

ORDINARY NONPARAMETRIC BOOTSTRAP


Call:
boot(data = srs, statistic = mean_fun, R = 1000)


Bootstrap Statistics :
    original        bias    std. error
t1* 2.712087 -0.007877409   0.1391195
```

For the standard error of the median (Example 13.4):

```
> median_fun <- function(x, indices) median(x[indices])
> boot(data = rivers, statistic = median_fun, R = 1000)

ORDINARY NONPARAMETRIC BOOTSTRAP
```

```
Call:
boot(data = rivers, statistic = median_fun, R = 1000)


Bootstrap Statistics :
    original  bias    std. error
t1*      425   2.456    25.63723
```

We notice that the output from both methods of estimating the standard errors produced similar results. In fact, the `boot` procedure is to be preferred since it invisibly returns much more information (which we will use later) than our naive script and it is much quicker in its computations.

Remark 13.6. Some things to keep in mind about the bootstrap:

- For many statistics, the bootstrap distribution closely resembles the sampling distribution with respect to spread and shape. However, the bootstrap will not have the same center as the true sampling distribution. While the sampling distribution is centered at the population mean (plus any bias), the bootstrap distribution is centered at the original value of the statistic (plus any bias). The `boot` function gives an empirical estimate of the bias of the statistic as part of its output.

- We tried to estimate the standard error, but we could have (in principle) tried to estimate something else. Note from the previous remark, however, that it would be useless to estimate the population mean μ using the bootstrap since the mean of the bootstrap distribution is the observed $\overline{x}$.

- You don't get something from nothing. We have seen that we can take a random sample from a population and use bootstrap methods to get a very good idea about standard errors, bias, and the like. However, one must not get lured into believing that by doing some random resampling somehow one gets more information about the parameters than that which was contained in the original sample. Indeed, there is some uncertainty about the parameter due to the randomness of the original sample, and there is even more uncertainty introduced by resampling. One should think of the bootstrap as just another estimation method, nothing more, nothing less.

13.3 Bootstrap Confidence Intervals

13.3.1 Percentile Confidence Intervals

As a first try, we want to obtain a 95% confidence interval for a parameter. Typically the statistic we use to estimate the parameter is centered at (or at least close by) the parameter; in such cases a 95% confidence interval for the parameter is nothing more than a 95% confidence interval for the statistic. And to find a 95% confidence interval for the statistic we need only go to its sampling distribution to find an interval that contains 95% of the area. (The most popular choice is the equal-tailed interval with 2.5% in each tail.)

This is incredibly easy to accomplish with the bootstrap. We need only to take a bunch of bootstrap resamples, order them, and choose the $\alpha/2$th and $(1-\alpha)$th percentiles. There is a function `boot.ci` in R already created to do just this. Note that in order to use the function boot.ci we must first run the boot function and save the output in a variable, for example, data.boot. We then plug data.boot into the function boot.ci.

Example 13.7. Percentile interval for the expected value of the median. Wee will try the naive approach where we generate the resamples and calculate the percentile interval by hand.

```
> btsamps <- replicate(2000, sample(stack.loss, 21, TRUE),
+      simplify = FALSE)
> thetast <- sapply(btsamps, median, simplify = TRUE)
> mean(thetast)

[1] 14.794

> median(stack.loss)

[1] 15

> quantile(thetast, c(0.025, 0.975))

 2.5% 97.5%
   12    18
```

Example 13.8. Confidence interval for expected value of the median, 2nd try. Now we will do it the right way with the boot function.

```
> library(boot)
> med_fun <- function(x, ind) median(x[ind])
> med_boot <- boot(stack.loss, med_fun, R = 2000)
> boot.ci(med_boot, type = c("perc", "norm", "bca"))

BOOTSTRAP CONFIDENCE INTERVAL CALCULATIONS
Based on 2000 bootstrap replicates

CALL :
boot.ci(boot.out = med_boot, type = c("perc", "norm", "bca"))

Intervals :
Level      Normal              Percentile            BCa
95%   (12.11, 18.34 )   (12.00, 18.00 )   (11.00, 18.00 )
Calculations and Intervals on Original Scale
```

13.3.2 Student's *t* intervals ("normal intervals")

The idea is to use confidence intervals that we already know and let the bootstrap help us when we get into trouble. We know that a $100(1-\alpha)\%$ confidence interval for the mean of a $SRS(n)$ from a normal distribution is

$$\overline{X} \pm \mathrm{t}_{\alpha/2}(\mathtt{df} = n-1)\frac{S}{\sqrt{n}}, \tag{13.3.1}$$

where $\mathrm{t}_{\alpha/2}(\mathtt{df} = n-1)$ is the appropriate critical value from Student's t distribution, and we remember that an estimate for the standard error of $\overline{X}$ is $S/\sqrt{n}$. Of course, the estimate for the standard error will change when the underlying population distribution is not normal, or when we use a statistic more complicated than $\overline{X}$. In those situations the bootstrap will give us quite reasonable estimates for the standard error. And as long as the sampling distribution of our statistic is approximately bell-shaped with small bias, the interval

$$\text{statistic} \pm \mathtt{t}_{\alpha/2}(\mathtt{df} = n-1) * \mathrm{SE}(\text{statistic}) \tag{13.3.2}$$

will have approximately $100(1-\alpha)\%$ confidence of containing $\mathbb{E}(\text{statistic})$.

Example 13.9. We will use the t-interval method to find the bootstrap CI for the median. We have looked at the bootstrap distribution; it appears to be symmetric and approximately mound shaped. Further, we may check that the bias is approximately 40, which on the scale of these data is practically negligible. Thus, we may consider looking at the t-intervals. Note that, since our sample is so large, instead of t-intervals we will essentially be using z-intervals.

Please see the handout, "Bootstrapping Confidence Intervals for the Median, 3rd try."

We see that, considering the scale of the data, the confidence intervals compare with each other quite well.

Remark 13.10. We have seen two methods for bootstrapping confidence intervals for a statistic. Which method should we use? If the bias of the bootstrap distribution is small and if the distribution is close to normal, then the percentile and t-intervals will closely agree. If the intervals are noticeably different, then it should be considered evidence that the normality and bias conditions are not met. In this case, *neither* interval should be used.

- BC_a: bias-corrected and accelerated
  - transformation invariant
  - more correct and accurate
  - not monotone in coverage level?
- t - intervals
  - more natural
  - numerically unstable
- Can do things like transform scales, compute confidence intervals, and then transform back.
- Studentized bootstrap confidence intervals where is the Studentized version of is the order statistic of the simulation

13.4 Resampling in Hypothesis Tests

The classical two-sample problem can be stated as follows: given two groups of interest, we would like to know whether these two groups are significantly different from one another or whether the groups are reasonably similar. The standard way to decide is to

1. Go collect some information from the two groups and calculate an associated statistic, for example, $\overline{X}_1 - \overline{X}_2$.

2. Suppose that there is no difference in the groups, and find the distribution of the statistic in 1.

3. Locate the observed value of the statistic with respect to the distribution found in 2. A value in the main body of the distribution is not spectacular, it could reasonably have occurred by chance. A value in the tail of the distribution is unlikely, and hence provides evidence *against* the null hypothesis that the population distributions are the same.

Of course, we usually compute a p-value, defined to be the probability of the observed value of the statistic or more extreme when the null hypothesis is true. Small p-values are evidence against the null hypothesis. It is not immediately obvious how to use resampling methods here, so we discuss an example.

Example 13.11. A study concerned differing dosages of the antiretroviral drug AZT. The common dosage is 300mg daily. Higher doses cause more side affects, but are they significantly higher? We examine for a 600mg dose. The data are as follows: We compare the scores from the two groups by computing the difference in their sample means. The 300mg data were entered in x1 and the 600mg data were entered into x2. The observed difference was

300 mg	284	279	289	292	287	295	285	279	306	298
600 mg	298	307	297	279	291	335	299	300	306	291

The average amounts can be found:

```
> mean(x1)
[1] 289.4
> mean(x2)
[1] 300.3
```

with an observed difference of `mean(x2) - mean(x1) = 10.9`. As expected, the 600 mg measurements seem to have a higher average, and we might be interested in trying to decide if the average amounts are *significantly* different. The null hypothesis should be that there is no difference in the amounts, that is, the groups are more or less the same. If the null hypothesis were true, then the two groups would indeed be the same, or just one big group. In that case, the observed difference in the sample means just reflects the random assignment into the arbitrary `x1` and `x2` categories. It is now clear how we may resample, consistent with the null hypothesis.

Procedure:

1. Randomly resample 10 scores from the combined scores of `x1` and `x2`, and assign then to the "`x1`" group. The rest will then be in the "`x2`" group. Calculate the difference in (re)sampled means, and store that value.

2. Repeat this procedure many, many times and draw a histogram of the resampled statistics, called the *permutation distribution*. Locate the observed difference 10.9 on the histogram to get the p-value. If the p-value is small, then we consider that evidence against the hypothesis that the groups are the same.

Remark 13.12. In calculating the permutation test p-value, the formula is essentially the proportion of resample statistics that are greater than or equal to the observed value. Of course, this is merely an *estimate* of the true p-value. As it turns out, an adjustment of +1 to both the numerator and denominator of the proportion improves the performance of the estimated p-value, and this adjustment is implemented in the `ts.perm` function.

```
> library(coin)
> oneway_test(len ~ supp, data = ToothGrowth)
        Asymptotic 2-Sample Permutation Test

data:  len by supp (OJ, VC)
Z = 1.8734, p-value = 0.06102
alternative hypothesis: true mu is not equal to 0
```

13.4.1 Comparison with the Two Sample t test

We know from Chapter 10 to use the two-sample t-test to tell whether there is an improvement as a result of taking the intervention class. Note that the t-test assumes normal underlying populations, with unknown variance, and small sample $n = 10$. What does the t-test say? Below is the output.

```
> t.test(len ~ supp, data = ToothGrowth, alt = "greater", var.equal = TRUE)
        Two Sample t-test

data:  len by supp
t = 1.9153, df = 58, p-value = 0.03020
alternative hypothesis: true difference in means is greater than 0
95 percent confidence interval:
 0.4708204       Inf
sample estimates:
mean in group OJ mean in group VC
        20.66333         16.96333
```

The p-value for the t-test was 0.03, while the permutation test p-value was 0.061. Note that there is an underlying normality assumption for the t-test, which isn't present in the permutation test. If the normality assumption may be questionable, then the permutation test would be more reasonable. We see what can happen when using a test in a situation where the assumptions are not met: smaller p-values. In situations where the normality assumptions are not met, for example, small sample scenarios, the permutation test is to be preferred. In particular, if accuracy is very important then we should use the permutation test.

Remark 13.13. Here are some things about permutation tests to keep in mind.

- While the permutation test does not require normality of the populations (as contrasted with the t-test), nevertheless it still requires that the two groups are exchangeable; see Section 7.5. In particular, this means that they must be identically distributed under the null hypothesis. They must have not only the same means, but they must also have the same spread, shape, and everything else. This assumption may or may not be true in a given example, but it will rarely cause the t-test to outperform the permutation test, because even if the sample standard deviations are markedly different it does not mean that the population standard deviations are different. In many situations the permutation test will also carry over to the t-test.

- If the distribution of the groups is close to normal, then the t-test p-value and the bootstrap p-value will be approximately equal. If they differ markedly, then this should be considered evidence that the normality assumptions do not hold.

- The generality of the permutation test is such that one can use all kinds of statistics to compare the two groups. One could compare the difference in variances or the difference in (just about anything). Alternatively, one could compare the ratio of sample means, $\overline{X}_1/\overline{X}_2$. Of course, under the null hypothesis this last quantity should be near 1.

- Just as with the bootstrap, the answer we get is subject to variability due to the inherent randomness of resampling from the data. We can make the variability as small as we like by taking sufficiently many resamples. How many? If the conclusion is very important (that is, if lots of money is at stake), then take thousands. For point estimation problems typically, $R = 1000$ resamples, or so, is enough. In general, if the true p-value is p then the standard error of the estimated p-value is $\sqrt{p(1-p)/R}$. You can choose R to get whatever accuracy desired.

- Other possible testing designs:

  - Matched Pairs Designs.
  - Relationship between two variables.

Chapter Exercises

Chapter 14

Categorical Data Analysis

This chapter is still under substantial revision. At any time you can preview any released drafts with the development version of the IPSUR package which is available from R-Forge:

```
> install.packages("IPSUR", repos = "http://R-Forge.R-project.org")
> library(IPSUR)
> read(IPSUR)
```

Chapter 15

Nonparametric Statistics

This chapter is still under substantial revision. At any time you can preview any released drafts with the development version of the IPSUR package which is available from R-Forge:

```
> install.packages("IPSUR", repos = "http://R-Forge.R-project.org")
> library(IPSUR)
> read(IPSUR)
```

Chapter 16

Time Series

This chapter is still under substantial revision. At any time you can preview any released drafts with the development version of the IPSUR package which is available from R-Forge:

```
> install.packages("IPSUR", repos = "http://R-Forge.R-project.org")
> library(IPSUR)
> read(IPSUR)
```

Appendix A

R Session Information

If you ever write the R help mailing list with a question, then you should include your session information in the email; it makes the reader's job easier and is requested by the Posting Guide. Here is how to do that, and below is what the output looks like.

```
> sessionInfo()
```

```
R version 2.11.1 (2010-05-31)
x86_64-pc-linux-gnu

locale:
 [1] LC_CTYPE=en_US.UTF-8       LC_NUMERIC=C
 [3] LC_TIME=en_US.UTF-8        LC_COLLATE=en_US.UTF-8
 [5] LC_MONETARY=C              LC_MESSAGES=en_US.UTF-8
 [7] LC_PAPER=en_US.UTF-8       LC_NAME=C
 [9] LC_ADDRESS=C               LC_TELEPHONE=C
[11] LC_MEASUREMENT=en_US.UTF-8 LC_IDENTIFICATION=C

attached base packages:
 [1] splines   grid      stats4    tcltk     stats     graphics  grDevices
 [8] utils     datasets  methods   base

other attached packages:
 [1] coin_1.0-12             modeltools_0.2-16
 [3] boot_1.2-42             scatterplot3d_0.3-30
 [5] lmtest_0.9-26           zoo_1.6-4
 [7] reshape_0.8.3           plyr_1.0.3
 [9] Hmisc_3.8-2             HH_2.1-32
[11] leaps_2.9               multcomp_1.1-7
[13] survival_2.35-8         TeachingDemos_2.6
[15] mvtnorm_0.9-92          distrEx_2.2
[17] actuar_1.1-0            evd_2.2-4
[19] distr_2.2.3             sfsmisc_1.0-11
[21] startupmsg_0.7          combinat_0.0-7
[23] prob_0.9-2              lattice_0.18-8
[25] e1071_1.5-24            class_7.3-2
[27] qcc_2.0.1               aplpack_1.2.3
```

```
[29] RcmdrPlugin.IPSUR_0.1-7 Rcmdr_1.5-6
[31] car_1.2-16

loaded via a namespace (and not attached):
[1] cluster_1.13.1 tools_2.11.1
```

Appendix B

GNU Free Documentation License

Version 1.3, 3 November 2008

0. PREAMBLE

The purpose of this License is to make a manual, textbook, or other functional and useful document "free" in the sense of freedom: to assure everyone the effective freedom to copy and redistribute it, with or without modifying it, either commercially or noncommercially. Secondarily, this License preserves for the author and publisher a way to get credit for their work, while not being considered responsible for modifications made by others.

This License is a kind of "copyleft", which means that derivative works of the document must themselves be free in the same sense. It complements the GNU General Public License, which is a copyleft license designed for free software.

We have designed this License in order to use it for manuals for free software, because free software needs free documentation: a free program should come with manuals providing the same freedoms that the software does. But this License is not limited to software manuals; it can be used for any textual work, regardless of subject matter or whether it is published as a printed book. We recommend this License principally for works whose purpose is instruction or reference.

1. APPLICABILITY AND DEFINITIONS

This License applies to any manual or other work, in any medium, that contains a notice placed by the copyright holder saying it can be distributed under the terms of this License. Such a notice grants a world-wide, royalty-free license, unlimited in duration, to use that work under the conditions stated herein. The "Document", below, refers to any such manual or work. Any member of the public is a licensee, and is addressed as "you". You accept the license if you copy, modify or distribute the work in a way requiring permission under copyright law.

A "Modified Version" of the Document means any work containing the Document or a portion of it, either copied verbatim, or with modifications and/or translated into another language.

A "Secondary Section" is a named appendix or a front-matter section of the Document that deals exclusively with the relationship of the publishers or authors of the Document to the Document's overall subject (or to related matters) and contains nothing that could fall directly within that overall subject. (Thus, if the Document is in part a textbook of mathematics, a Secondary Section may not explain any mathematics.) The relationship could be a matter of historical connection with the subject or with related matters, or of legal, commercial, philosophical, ethical or political position regarding them.

The "Invariant Sections" are certain Secondary Sections whose titles are designated, as being those of Invariant Sections, in the notice that says that the Document is released under this License. If a section does not fit the above definition of Secondary then it is not allowed to be designated as Invariant. The Document may contain zero Invariant Sections. If the Document does not identify any Invariant Sections then there are none.

The "Cover Texts" are certain short passages of text that are listed, as Front-Cover Texts or Back-Cover Texts, in the notice that says that the Document is released under this License. A Front-Cover Text may be at most 5 words, and a Back-Cover Text may be at most 25 words.

A "Transparent" copy of the Document means a machine-readable copy, represented in a format whose specification is available to the general public, that is suitable for revising the document straightforwardly with generic text editors or (for images composed of pixels) generic paint programs or (for drawings) some widely available drawing editor, and that is suitable for input to text formatters or for automatic translation to a variety of formats suitable for input to text formatters. A copy made in an otherwise Transparent file format whose markup, or absence of markup, has been arranged to thwart or discourage subsequent modification by readers is not Transparent. An image format is not Transparent if used for any substantial amount of text. A copy that is not "Transparent" is called "Opaque".

Examples of suitable formats for Transparent copies include plain ASCII without markup, Texinfo input format, LaTeX input format, SGML or XML using a publicly available DTD, and standard-conforming simple HTML, PostScript or PDF designed for human modification. Examples of transparent image formats include PNG, XCF and JPG. Opaque formats include proprietary formats that can be read and edited only by proprietary word processors, SGML or XML for which the DTD and/or processing tools are not generally available, and the machine-generated HTML, PostScript or PDF produced by some word processors for output purposes only.

The "Title Page" means, for a printed book, the title page itself, plus such following pages as are needed to hold, legibly, the material this License requires to appear in the title page. For works in formats which do not have any title page as such, "Title Page" means the text near the most prominent appearance of the work's title, preceding the beginning of the body of the text.

The "publisher" means any person or entity that distributes copies of the Document to the public.

A section "Entitled XYZ" means a named subunit of the Document whose title either is precisely XYZ or contains XYZ in parentheses following text that translates XYZ in another language. (Here XYZ stands for a specific section name mentioned below, such as "Acknowledgements", "Dedications", "Endorsements", or "History".) To "Preserve the Title" of such a section when you modify the Document means that it remains a section "Entitled XYZ" according to this definition.

The Document may include Warranty Disclaimers next to the notice which states that this License applies to the Document. These Warranty Disclaimers are considered to be included by reference in this License, but only as regards disclaiming warranties: any other implication that these Warranty Disclaimers may have is void and has no effect on the meaning of this License.

2. VERBATIM COPYING

You may copy and distribute the Document in any medium, either commercially or noncommercially, provided that this License, the copyright notices, and the license notice saying this License applies to the Document are reproduced in all copies, and that you add no other conditions whatsoever to those of this License. You may not use technical measures to obstruct or control the reading or further copying of the copies you make or distribute. However, you may accept compensation in exchange for copies. If you distribute a large enough number of copies you must also follow the conditions in section 3.

You may also lend copies, under the same conditions stated above, and you may publicly display copies.

3. COPYING IN QUANTITY

If you publish printed copies (or copies in media that commonly have printed covers) of the Document, numbering more than 100, and the Document's license notice requires Cover Texts, you must enclose the copies in covers that carry, clearly and legibly, all these Cover Texts: Front-Cover Texts on the front cover, and Back-Cover Texts on the back cover. Both covers must also clearly and legibly identify you as the publisher of these copies. The front cover must present the full title with all words of the title equally prominent and visible. You may add other material on the covers in addition. Copying with changes limited to the covers, as long as they preserve the title of the Document and satisfy these conditions, can be treated as verbatim copying in other respects.

If the required texts for either cover are too voluminous to fit legibly, you should put the first ones listed (as many as fit reasonably) on the actual cover, and continue the rest onto adjacent pages.

If you publish or distribute Opaque copies of the Document numbering more than 100, you must either include a machine-readable Transparent copy along with each Opaque copy, or state in or with each Opaque copy a computer-network location from which the general network-using public has access to download using public-standard network protocols a complete Transparent copy of the Document, free of added material. If you use the latter option, you must take reasonably prudent steps, when you begin distribution of Opaque copies in quantity, to ensure that this Transparent copy will remain thus accessible at the stated location until at least one year after the last time you distribute an Opaque copy (directly or through your agents or retailers) of that edition to the public.

It is requested, but not required, that you contact the authors of the Document well before redistributing any large number of copies, to give them a chance to provide you with an updated version of the Document.

4. MODIFICATIONS

You may copy and distribute a Modified Version of the Document under the conditions of sections 2 and 3 above, provided that you release the Modified Version under precisely this

License, with the Modified Version filling the role of the Document, thus licensing distribution and modification of the Modified Version to whoever possesses a copy of it. In addition, you must do these things in the Modified Version:

A. Use in the Title Page (and on the covers, if any) a title distinct from that of the Document, and from those of previous versions (which should, if there were any, be listed in the History section of the Document). You may use the same title as a previous version if the original publisher of that version gives permission.

B. List on the Title Page, as authors, one or more persons or entities responsible for authorship of the modifications in the Modified Version, together with at least five of the principal authors of the Document (all of its principal authors, if it has fewer than five), unless they release you from this requirement.

C. State on the Title page the name of the publisher of the Modified Version, as the publisher.

D. Preserve all the copyright notices of the Document.

E. Add an appropriate copyright notice for your modifications adjacent to the other copyright notices.

F. Include, immediately after the copyright notices, a license notice giving the public permission to use the Modified Version under the terms of this License, in the form shown in the Addendum below.

G. Preserve in that license notice the full lists of Invariant Sections and required Cover Texts given in the Document's license notice.

H. Include an unaltered copy of this License.

I. Preserve the section Entitled "History", Preserve its Title, and add to it an item stating at least the title, year, new authors, and publisher of the Modified Version as given on the Title Page. If there is no section Entitled "History" in the Document, create one stating the title, year, authors, and publisher of the Document as given on its Title Page, then add an item describing the Modified Version as stated in the previous sentence.

J. Preserve the network location, if any, given in the Document for public access to a Transparent copy of the Document, and likewise the network locations given in the Document for previous versions it was based on. These may be placed in the "History" section. You may omit a network location for a work that was published at least four years before the Document itself, or if the original publisher of the version it refers to gives permission.

K. For any section Entitled "Acknowledgements" or "Dedications", Preserve the Title of the section, and preserve in the section all the substance and tone of each of the contributor acknowledgements and/or dedications given therein.

L. Preserve all the Invariant Sections of the Document, unaltered in their text and in their titles. Section numbers or the equivalent are not considered part of the section titles.

M. Delete any section Entitled "Endorsements". Such a section may not be included in the Modified Version.

N. Do not retitle any existing section to be Entitled "Endorsements" or to conflict in title with any Invariant Section.

O. Preserve any Warranty Disclaimers.

If the Modified Version includes new front-matter sections or appendices that qualify as Secondary Sections and contain no material copied from the Document, you may at your option designate some or all of these sections as invariant. To do this, add their titles to the list of Invariant Sections in the Modified Version's license notice. These titles must be distinct from any other section titles.

You may add a section Entitled "Endorsements", provided it contains nothing but endorsements of your Modified Version by various parties–for example, statements of peer review or that the text has been approved by an organization as the authoritative definition of a standard.

You may add a passage of up to five words as a Front-Cover Text, and a passage of up to 25 words as a Back-Cover Text, to the end of the list of Cover Texts in the Modified Version. Only one passage of Front-Cover Text and one of Back-Cover Text may be added by (or through arrangements made by) any one entity. If the Document already includes a cover text for the same cover, previously added by you or by arrangement made by the same entity you are acting on behalf of, you may not add another; but you may replace the old one, on explicit permission from the previous publisher that added the old one.

The author(s) and publisher(s) of the Document do not by this License give permission to use their names for publicity for or to assert or imply endorsement of any Modified Version.

5. COMBINING DOCUMENTS

You may combine the Document with other documents released under this License, under the terms defined in section 4 above for modified versions, provided that you include in the combination all of the Invariant Sections of all of the original documents, unmodified, and list them all as Invariant Sections of your combined work in its license notice, and that you preserve all their Warranty Disclaimers.

The combined work need only contain one copy of this License, and multiple identical Invariant Sections may be replaced with a single copy. If there are multiple Invariant Sections with the same name but different contents, make the title of each such section unique by adding at the end of it, in parentheses, the name of the original author or publisher of that section if known, or else a unique number. Make the same adjustment to the section titles in the list of Invariant Sections in the license notice of the combined work.

In the combination, you must combine any sections Entitled "History" in the various original documents, forming one section Entitled "History"; likewise combine any sections Entitled "Acknowledgements", and any sections Entitled "Dedications". You must delete all sections Entitled "Endorsements".

6. COLLECTIONS OF DOCUMENTS

You may make a collection consisting of the Document and other documents released under this License, and replace the individual copies of this License in the various documents with a single copy that is included in the collection, provided that you follow the rules of this License for verbatim copying of each of the documents in all other respects.

You may extract a single document from such a collection, and distribute it individually under this License, provided you insert a copy of this License into the extracted document, and follow this License in all other respects regarding verbatim copying of that document.

7. AGGREGATION WITH INDEPENDENT WORKS

A compilation of the Document or its derivatives with other separate and independent documents or works, in or on a volume of a storage or distribution medium, is called an "aggregate" if the copyright resulting from the compilation is not used to limit the legal rights of the compilation's users beyond what the individual works permit. When the Document is included in an aggregate, this License does not apply to the other works in the aggregate which are not themselves derivative works of the Document.

If the Cover Text requirement of section 3 is applicable to these copies of the Document, then if the Document is less than one half of the entire aggregate, the Document's Cover Texts may be placed on covers that bracket the Document within the aggregate, or the electronic equivalent of covers if the Document is in electronic form. Otherwise they must appear on printed covers that bracket the whole aggregate.

8. TRANSLATION

Translation is considered a kind of modification, so you may distribute translations of the Document under the terms of section 4. Replacing Invariant Sections with translations requires special permission from their copyright holders, but you may include translations of some or all Invariant Sections in addition to the original versions of these Invariant Sections. You may include a translation of this License, and all the license notices in the Document, and any Warranty Disclaimers, provided that you also include the original English version of this License and the original versions of those notices and disclaimers. In case of a disagreement between the translation and the original version of this License or a notice or disclaimer, the original version will prevail.

If a section in the Document is Entitled "Acknowledgements", "Dedications", or "History", the requirement (section 4) to Preserve its Title (section 1) will typically require changing the actual title.

9. TERMINATION

You may not copy, modify, sublicense, or distribute the Document except as expressly provided under this License. Any attempt otherwise to copy, modify, sublicense, or distribute it is void, and will automatically terminate your rights under this License.

However, if you cease all violation of this License, then your license from a particular copyright holder is reinstated (a) provisionally, unless and until the copyright holder explicitly and finally terminates your license, and (b) permanently, if the copyright holder fails to notify you of the violation by some reasonable means prior to 60 days after the cessation.

Moreover, your license from a particular copyright holder is reinstated permanently if the copyright holder notifies you of the violation by some reasonable means, this is the first time you have received notice of violation of this License (for any work) from that copyright holder, and you cure the violation prior to 30 days after your receipt of the notice.

Termination of your rights under this section does not terminate the licenses of parties who have received copies or rights from you under this License. If your rights have been terminated and not permanently reinstated, receipt of a copy of some or all of the same material does not give you any rights to use it.

10. FUTURE REVISIONS OF THIS LICENSE

The Free Software Foundation may publish new, revised versions of the GNU Free Documentation License from time to time. Such new versions will be similar in spirit to the present version, but may differ in detail to address new problems or concerns. See http://www.gnu.org/copyleft/.

Each version of the License is given a distinguishing version number. If the Document specifies that a particular numbered version of this License "or any later version" applies to it, you have the option of following the terms and conditions either of that specified version or of any later version that has been published (not as a draft) by the Free Software Foundation. If the Document does not specify a version number of this License, you may choose any version ever published (not as a draft) by the Free Software Foundation. If the Document specifies that a proxy can decide which future versions of this License can be used, that proxy's public statement of acceptance of a version permanently authorizes you to choose that version for the Document.

11. RELICENSING

"Massive Multiauthor Collaboration Site" (or "MMC Site") means any World Wide Web server that publishes copyrightable works and also provides prominent facilities for anybody to edit those works. A public wiki that anybody can edit is an example of such a server. A "Massive Multiauthor Collaboration" (or "MMC") contained in the site means any set of copyrightable works thus published on the MMC site.

"CC-BY-SA" means the Creative Commons Attribution-Share Alike 3.0 license published by Creative Commons Corporation, a not-for-profit corporation with a principal place of business in San Francisco, California, as well as future copyleft versions of that license published by that same organization.

"Incorporate" means to publish or republish a Document, in whole or in part, as part of another Document.

An MMC is "eligible for relicensing" if it is licensed under this License, and if all works that were first published under this License somewhere other than this MMC, and subsequently incorporated in whole or in part into the MMC, (1) had no cover texts or invariant sections, and (2) were thus incorporated prior to November 1, 2008.

The operator of an MMC Site may republish an MMC contained in the site under CC-BY-SA on the same site at any time before August 1, 2009, provided the MMC is eligible for relicensing.

ADDENDUM: How to use this License for your documents

To use this License in a document you have written, include a copy of the License in the document and put the following copyright and license notices just after the title page:

> Copyright (c) YEAR YOUR NAME. Permission is granted to copy, distribute and/or modify this document under the terms of the GNU Free Documentation License, Version 1.3 or any later version published by the Free Software Foundation; with no Invariant Sections, no Front-Cover Texts, and no Back-Cover Texts. A copy of the license is included in the section entitled "GNU Free Documentation License".

If you have Invariant Sections, Front-Cover Texts and Back-Cover Texts, replace the "with...Texts." line with this:

> with the Invariant Sections being LIST THEIR TITLES, with the Front-Cover Texts being LIST, and with the Back-Cover Texts being LIST.

If you have Invariant Sections without Cover Texts, or some other combination of the three, merge those two alternatives to suit the situation.

If your document contains nontrivial examples of program code, we recommend releasing these examples in parallel under your choice of free software license, such as the GNU General Public License, to permit their use in free software.

Appendix C

History

Title:	Introduction to Probability and Statistics Using R
Year:	2010
Authors:	G. Jay Kerns
Publisher:	G. Jay Kerns

Appendix D

Data

This appendix is a reference of sorts regarding some of the data structures a statistician is likely to encounter. We discuss their salient features and idiosyncrasies.

D.1 Data Structures

D.1.1 Vectors

See the "Vectors and Assignment" section of *An Introduction to R*. A vector is an ordered sequence of elements, such as numbers, characters, or logical values, and there may be NA's present. We usually make vectors with the assignment operator <-.

```
> x <- c(3, 5, 9)
```

Vectors are atomic in the sense that if you try to mix and match elements of different modes then all elements will be coerced to the most convenient common mode.

```
> y <- c(3, "5", TRUE)
```

In the example all elements were coerced to *character* mode. We can test whether a given object is a vector with `is.vector` and can coerce an object (if possible) to a vector with `as.vector`.

D.1.2 Matrices and Arrays

See the "Arrays and Matrices" section of *An Introduction to R*. Loosely speaking, a matrix is a vector that has been reshaped into rectangular form, and an array is a multidimensional matrix. Strictly speaking, it is the other way around: an array is a data vector with a dimension attribute (`dim`), and a matrix is the special case of an array with only two dimensions. We can construct a matrix with the `matrix` function.

```
> matrix(letters[1:6], nrow = 2, ncol = 3)

     [,1] [,2] [,3]
[1,] "a"  "c"  "e"
[2,] "b"  "d"  "f"
```

Notice the order of the matrix entries, which shows how the matrix is populated by default. We can change this with the `byrow` argument:

```
> matrix(letters[1:6], nrow = 2, ncol = 3, byrow = TRUE)

     [,1] [,2] [,3]
[1,] "a"  "b"  "c"
[2,] "d"  "e"  "f"
```

We can test whether a given object is a matrix with `is.matrix` and can coerce an object (if possible) to a matrix with `as.matrix`. As a final example watch what happens when we mix and match types in the first argument:

```
> matrix(c(1, "2", NA, FALSE), nrow = 2, ncol = 3)

     [,1] [,2]    [,3]
[1,] "1"  NA      "1"
[2,] "2"  "FALSE" "2"
```

Notice how all of the entries were coerced to character for the final result (except `NA`). Also notice how the four values were *recycled* to fill up the six entries of the matrix.

The standard arithmetic operations work element-wise with matrices.

```
> A <- matrix(1:6, 2, 3)
> B <- matrix(2:7, 2, 3)
> A + B

     [,1] [,2] [,3]
[1,]    3    7   11
[2,]    5    9   13

> A * B

     [,1] [,2] [,3]
[1,]    2   12   30
[2,]    6   20   42
```

If you want the standard definition of matrix multiplication then use the `%*%` function. If we were to try `A %*%B` we would get an error because the dimensions do not match correctly, but for fun, we could transpose `B` to get conformable matrices. The transpose function `t` only works for matrices (and data frames).

```
> try(A * B)       # an error

     [,1] [,2] [,3]
[1,]    2   12   30
[2,]    6   20   42

> A %*% t(B)       # this is alright

     [,1] [,2]
[1,]   44   53
[2,]   56   68
```

To get the ordinary matrix inverse use the solve function:

```
> solve(A %*% t(B))      # input matrix must be square
          [,1]      [,2]
[1,]  2.833333 -2.208333
[2,] -2.333333  1.833333
```

Arrays more general than matrices, and some functions (like transpose) do not work for the more general array. Here is what an array looks like:

```
> array(LETTERS[1:24], dim = c(3,4,2))
, , 1

     [,1] [,2] [,3] [,4]
[1,] "A"  "D"  "G"  "J"
[2,] "B"  "E"  "H"  "K"
[3,] "C"  "F"  "I"  "L"

, , 2

     [,1] [,2] [,3] [,4]
[1,] "M"  "P"  "S"  "V"
[2,] "N"  "Q"  "T"  "W"
[3,] "O"  "R"  "U"  "X"
```

We can test with is.array and may coerce with as.array.

D.1.3 Data Frames

A data frame is a rectangular array of information with a special status in R. It is used as the fundamental data structure by many of the modeling functions. It is like a matrix in that all of the columns must be the same length, but it is more general than a matrix in that columns are allowed to have different modes.

```
> x <- c(1.3, 5.2, 6)
> y <- letters[1:3]
> z <- c(TRUE, FALSE, TRUE)
> A <- data.frame(x, y, z)
> A
    x y     z
1 1.3 a  TRUE
2 5.2 b FALSE
3 6.0 c  TRUE
```

Notice the names on the columns of A. We can change those with the names function.

```
> names(A) <- c("Fred", "Mary", "Sue")
> A
```

```
  Fred Mary   Sue
1  1.3    a  TRUE
2  5.2    b FALSE
3  6.0    c  TRUE
```

Basic command is `data.frame`. You can test with `is.data.frame` and you can coerce with `as.data.frame`.

D.1.4 Lists

A list is more general than a data frame.

D.1.5 Tables

The word "table" has a special meaning in R. More precisely, a contingency table is an object of class "`table`" which is an array

Suppose you have a contingency table and would like to do descriptive or inferential statistics on it. The default form of the table is usually inconvenient to use unless we are working with a function specially tailored for tables. Here is how to transform your data to a more manageable form, namely, the raw data used to make the table.

First, we coerce the table to a data frame with :

```
> A <- as.data.frame(Titanic)
> head(A)
  Class    Sex   Age Survived Freq
1   1st   Male Child       No    0
2   2nd   Male Child       No    0
3   3rd   Male Child       No   35
4  Crew   Male Child       No    0
5   1st Female Child       No    0
6   2nd Female Child       No    0
```

Note that there are as many preliminary columns of `A` as there are dimensions to the table. The rows of `A` contain every possible combination of levels from each of the dimensions. There is also a `Freq` column, which shows how many observations there were at that particular combination of levels.

The form of `A` is often sufficient for our purposes, but more often we need to do more work: we would usually like to repeat each row of `A` exactly the number of times shown in the `Freq` column. The `reshape` package [89] has the function `untable` designed for that very purpose:

```
> library(reshape)
> B <- with(A, untable(A, Freq))
> head(B)
    Class  Sex   Age Survived Freq
3     3rd Male Child       No   35
3.1   3rd Male Child       No   35
3.2   3rd Male Child       No   35
3.3   3rd Male Child       No   35
3.4   3rd Male Child       No   35
3.5   3rd Male Child       No   35
```

Now, this is more like it. Note that we slipped in a call to the `with` function, which was done to make the call to `untable` more pretty; we could just as easily have done

```
untable(TitanicDF, A$Freq)
```

The only fly in the ointment is the lingering `Freq` column which has repeated values that do not have any meaning any more. We could just ignore it, but it would be better to get rid of the meaningless column so that it does not cause trouble later. While we are at it, we could clean up the `rownames`, too.

```
> C <- B[, -5]
> rownames(C) <- 1:dim(C)[1]
> head(C)
```

```
  Class  Sex   Age Survived
1   3rd Male Child       No
2   3rd Male Child       No
3   3rd Male Child       No
4   3rd Male Child       No
5   3rd Male Child       No
6   3rd Male Child       No
```

D.1.6 More about Tables

Suppose you want to make a table that looks like this:

There are at least two ways to do it.

- Using a matrix:

```
> tab <- matrix(1:6, nrow = 2, ncol = 3)
> rownames(tab) <- c("first", "second")
> colnames(tab) <- c("A", "B", "C")
> tab
```

```
       A B C
first  1 3 5
second 2 4 6
```

  - note that the columns are filled in consecutively by default. If you want to fill the data in by rows then do byrow = TRUE in the matrix command.
  - the object is a matrix

- Using a dataframe

```
> p <- c("milk", "tea")
> g <- c("milk", "tea")
> catgs <- expand.grid(poured = p, guessed = g)
> cnts <- c(3, 1, 1, 3)
> D <- cbind(catgs, count = cnts)
> xtabs(count ~ poured + guessed, data = D)
```

```
        guessed
poured milk tea
  milk    3   1
  tea     1   3
```

- again, the data are filled in column-wise.
- the object is a dataframe
- if you want to store it as a table then do A <- xtabs(count ~ poured + guessed, data = D)

D.2 Importing Data

Statistics is the study of data, so the statistician's first step is usually to obtain data from somewhere or another and read them into R. In this section we describe some of the most common sources of data and how to get data from those sources into a running R session.

For more information please refer to the R *Data Import/Export Manual*, [68] and *An Introduction to R*, [85].

D.2.1 Data in Packages

There are many data sets stored in the `datasets` package of base R. To see a list of them all issue the command `data(package = "datasets")`. The output is omitted here because the list is so long. The names of the data sets are listed in the left column. Any data set in that list is already on the search path by default, which means that a user can use it immediately without any additional work.

There are many other data sets available in the thousands of contributed packages. To see the data sets available in those packages that are currently loaded into memory issue the single command `data()`. If you would like to see all of the data sets that are available in all packages that are installed on your computer (but not necessarily loaded), issue the command

```
data(package = .packages(all.available = TRUE))
```

To load the data set `foo` in the contributed package `bar` issue the commands `library(bar)` followed by `data(foo)`, or just the single command

```
data(foo, package = "bar")
```

D.2.2 Text Files

Many sources of data are simple text files. The entries in the file are separated by delimeters such as TABS (tab-delimeted), commas (comma separated values, or `.csv`, for short) or even just white space (no special name). A lot of data on the Internet are stored with text files, and even if they are not, a person can copy-paste information from a web page to a text file, save it on the computer, and read it into R.

D.2.3 Other Software Files

Often the data set of interest is stored in some other, proprietary, format by third-party software such as Minitab, SAS, or SPSS. The foreign package supports import/conversion from many of these formats. Please note, however, that data sets from other software sometimes have properties with no direct analogue in R. In those cases the conversion process may lose some information which will need to be reentered manually from within R. See the *Data Import/Export Manual.*

As an example, suppose the data are stored in the SPSS file foo.sav which the user has copied to the working directory; it can be imported with the commands

```
> library(foreign)
> read.spss("foo.sav")
```

See ?read.spss for the available options to customize the file import. Note that the R Commander will import many of the common file types with a menu driven interface.

D.2.4 Importing a Data Frame

The basic command is read.table.

D.3 Creating New Data Sets

Using c

Using scan

Using the R Commander.

D.4 Editing Data

D.4.1 Editing Data Values

D.4.2 Inserting Rows and Columns

D.4.3 Deleting Rows and Columns

D.4.4 Sorting Data

We can sort a vector with the sort function. Normally we have a data frame of several columns (variables) and many, many rows (observations). The goal is to shuffle the rows so that they are ordered by the values of one or more columns. This is done with the order function.

For example, we may sort all of the rows of the Puromycin data (in ascending order) by the variable conc with the following:

```
> Tmp <- Puromycin[order(Puromycin$conc), ]
> head(Tmp)
```

```
   conc rate     state
1  0.02   76   treated
2  0.02   47   treated
13 0.02   67 untreated
14 0.02   51 untreated
3  0.06   97   treated
4  0.06  107   treated
```

We can accomplish the same thing with the command

```
> with(Puromycin, Puromycin[order(conc), ])
```

We can sort by more than one variable. To sort first by `state` and next by `conc` do

```
> with(Puromycin, Puromycin[order(state, conc), ])
```

If we would like to sort a numeric variable in descending order then we put a minus sign in front of it.

```
> Tmp <- with(Puromycin, Puromycin[order(-conc), ])
> head(Tmp)
```

```
   conc rate     state
11 1.10  207   treated
12 1.10  200   treated
23 1.10  160 untreated
9  0.56  191   treated
10 0.56  201   treated
21 0.56  144 untreated
```

If we would like to sort by a character (or factor) in decreasing order then we can use the `xtfrm` function which produces a numeric vector in the same order as the character vector.

```
> Tmp <- with(Puromycin, Puromycin[order(-xtfrm(state)), ])
> head(Tmp)
```

```
   conc rate     state
13 0.02   67 untreated
14 0.02   51 untreated
15 0.06   84 untreated
16 0.06   86 untreated
17 0.11   98 untreated
18 0.11  115 untreated
```

D.5 Exporting Data

The basic function is `write.table`. The `MASS` package also has a `write.matrix` function.

D.6 Reshaping Data

- Aggregation
- Convert Tables to data frames and back

`rbind`, `cbind`

```
ab[order(ab[,1]),]
complete.cases
aggregate
stack
```

Appendix E

Mathematical Machinery

This appendix houses many of the standard definitions and theorems that are used at some point during the narrative. It is targeted for someone reading the book who forgets the precise definition of something and would like a quick reminder of an exact statement. No proofs are given, and the interested reader should consult a good text on Calculus (say, Stewart [80] or Apostol [4, 5]), Linear Algebra (say, Strang [82] and Magnus [62]), Real Analysis (say, Folland [27], or Carothers [12]), or Measure Theory (Billingsley [8], Ash [6], Resnick [70]) for details.

E.1 Set Algebra

We denote sets by capital letters, A, B, C, *etc*. The letter S is reserved for the sample space, also known as the universe or universal set, the set which contains all possible elements. The symbol $\emptyset$ represents the empty set, the set with no elements.

Set Union, Intersection, and Difference

Given subsets A and B, we may manipulate them in an algebraic fashion. To this end, we have three set operations at our disposal: union, intersection, and difference. Below is a table summarizing the pertinent information about these operations.

Identities and Properties

1. $A \cup \emptyset = A, \quad A \cap \emptyset = \emptyset$
2. $A \cup S = S, \quad A \cap S = A$
3. $A \cup A^c = S, A \cap A^c = \emptyset$
4. $(A^c)^c = A$

Name	Denoted	Defined by elements	R syntax
Union	$A \cup B$	in A or B or both	`union(A, B)`
Intersection	$A \cap B$	in both A and B	`intersect(A, B)`
Difference	$A \backslash B$	in A but not in B	`setdiff(A, B)`
Complement	A^c	in S but not in A	`setdiff(S, A)`

Table E.1: Set operations

5. The Commutative Property:

$$A \cup B = B \cup A, \quad A \cap B = B \cap A \tag{E.1.1}$$

6. The Associative Property:

$$(A \cup B) \cup C = A \cup (B \cup C), \quad (A \cap B) \cap C = A \cap (B \cap C) \tag{E.1.2}$$

7. The Distributive Property:

$$A \cup (B \cap C) = (A \cup B) \cap (A \cup B), \quad A \cap (B \cup C) = (A \cap B) \cup (A \cap B) \tag{E.1.3}$$

8. DeMorgan's Laws

$$(A \cup B)^c = A^c \cap B^c \quad \text{and} \quad (A \cap B)^c = A^c \cup B^c, \tag{E.1.4}$$

or more generally,

$$\left(\bigcup_\alpha A_\alpha\right)^c = \bigcap_\alpha A_\alpha^c, \quad \text{and} \quad \left(\bigcap_\alpha A_\alpha\right)^c = \bigcup_\alpha A_\alpha^c \tag{E.1.5}$$

E.2 Differential and Integral Calculus

A function f of one variable is said to be one-to-one if no two distinct x values are mapped to the same $y = f(x)$ value. To show that a function is one-to-one we can either use the horizontal line test or we may start with the equation $f(x_1) = f(x_2)$ and use algebra to show that it implies $x_1 = x_2$.

Limits and Continuity

Definition E.1. Let f be a function defined on some open interval that contains the number a, except possibly at a itself. Then we say the *limit of $f(x)$ as x approaches a is L*, and we write

$$\lim_{x \to a} f(x) = L, \tag{E.2.1}$$

if for every $\epsilon > 0$ there exists a number $\delta > 0$ such that $0 < |x - a| < \delta$ implies $|f(x) - L| < \epsilon$.

Definition E.2. A function f is *continuous at a number a* if

$$\lim_{x \to a} f(x) = f(a). \tag{E.2.2}$$

The function f is *right-continuous at the number a* if $\lim_{x \to a^+} f(x) = f(a)$, and *left-continuous* at a if $\lim_{x \to a^-} f(x) = f(a)$. Finally, the function f is *continuous on an interval I* if it is continuous at every number in the interval.

Differentiation

Definition E.3. The *derivative of a function f at a number a*, denoted by $f'(a)$, is

$$f'(a) = \lim_{h \to 0} \frac{f(a+h) - f(a)}{h}, \tag{E.2.3}$$

provided this limit exists.

A function is *differentiable at a* if $f'(a)$ exists. It is *differentiable on an open interval (a, b)* if it is differentiable at every number in the interval.

Differentiation Rules

In the table that follows, f and g are differentiable functions and c is a constant.

$\frac{\mathrm{d}}{\mathrm{d}x}c = 0$	$\frac{\mathrm{d}}{\mathrm{d}x}x^n = nx^{n-1}$	$(cf)' = cf'$
$(f \pm g)' = f' \pm g'$	$(fg)' = f'g + fg'$	$\left(\frac{f}{g}\right)' = \frac{f'g - fg'}{g^2}$

Table E.2: Differentiation rules

Theorem E.4. *Chain Rule: If f and g are both differentiable and $F = f \circ g$ is the composite function defined by $F(x) = f[g(x)]$, then F is differentiable and $F'(x) = f'[g(x)] \cdot g'(x)$.*

Useful Derivatives

$\frac{\mathrm{d}}{\mathrm{d}x}\mathrm{e}^x = \mathrm{e}^x$	$\frac{\mathrm{d}}{\mathrm{d}x}\ln x = x^{-1}$	$\frac{\mathrm{d}}{\mathrm{d}x}\sin x = \cos x$
$\frac{\mathrm{d}}{\mathrm{d}x}\cos x = -\sin x$	$\frac{\mathrm{d}}{\mathrm{d}x}\tan x = \sec^2 x$	$\frac{\mathrm{d}}{\mathrm{d}x}\tan^{-1} x = (1 + x^2)^{-1}$

Table E.3: Some derivatives

Optimization

Definition E.5. A *critical number* of the function f is a value x^* for which $f'(x^*) = 0$ or for which $f'(x^*)$ does not exist.

Theorem E.6. *First Derivative Test. If f is differentiable and if x^* is a critical number of f and if $f'(x) \geq 0$ for $x \leq x^*$ and $f'(x) \leq 0$ for $x \geq x^*$, then x^* is a local maximum of f. If $f'(x) \leq 0$ for $x \leq x^*$ and $f'(x) \geq 0$ for $x \geq x^*$, then x^* is a local minimum of f.*

Theorem E.7. *Second Derivative Test. If f is twice differentiable and if x^* is a critical number of f, then x^* is a local maximum of f if $f''(x^*) < 0$ and x^* is a local minimum of f if $f''(x^*) > 0$.*

Integration

As it turns out, there are all sorts of things called "integrals", each defined in its own idiosyncratic way. There are *Riemann* integrals, *Lebesgue* integrals, variants of these called *Stieltjes* integrals, *Daniell* integrals, *Ito* integrals, and the list continues. Given that this is an introductory book, we will use the Riemannian integral with the caveat that the Riemann integral is *not* the integral that will be used in more advanced study.

Definition E.8. Let f be defined on $[a, b]$, a closed interval of the real line. For each n, divide $[a, b]$ into subintervals $[x_i, x_{i+1}]$, $i = 0, 1, \ldots, n-1$, of length $\Delta x_i = (b - a)/n$ where $x_0 = a$

and $x_n = b$, and let x_i^* be any points chosen from the respective subintervals. Then the *definite integral* of f from a to b is defined by

$$\int_a^b f(x)\,\mathrm{d}x = \lim_{n\to\infty} \sum_{i=0}^{n-1} f(x_i^*)\,\Delta x_i, \tag{E.2.4}$$

provided the limit exists, and in that case, we say that f is *integrable* from a to b.

Theorem E.9. *The Fundamental Theorem of Calculus. Suppose f is continuous on $[a, b]$. Then*

1. *the function g defined by $g(x) = \int_a^x f(t)\,\mathrm{d}t$, $a \le x \le b$, is continuous on $[a, b]$ and differentiable on (a, b) with $g'(x) = f(x)$.*
2. *$\int_a^b f(x)\,\mathrm{d}x = F(b) - F(a)$, where F is any* antiderivative *of f, that is, any function F satisfying $F' = f$.*

Change of Variables

Theorem E.10. *If g is a differentiable function whose range is the interval $[a, b]$ and if both f and g' are continuous on the range of $u = g(x)$, then*

$$\int_{g(a)}^{g(b)} f(u)\,\mathrm{d}u = \int_a^b f[g(x)]\,g'(x)\,\mathrm{d}x. \tag{E.2.5}$$

Useful Integrals

$\int x^n\,\mathrm{d}x = x^{n+1}/(n+1),\ n \neq -1$	$\int \mathrm{e}^x\,\mathrm{d}x = \mathrm{e}^x$	$\int x^{-1}\,\mathrm{d}x = \ln\lvert x\rvert$
$\int \tan x\,\mathrm{d}x = \ln\lvert\sec x\rvert$	$\int a^x\,\mathrm{d}x = a^x/\ln a$	$\int (x^2+1)^{-1}\,\mathrm{d}x = \tan^{-1} x$

Table E.4: Some integrals (constants of integration omitted)

Integration by Parts

$$\int u\,\mathrm{d}v = uv - \int v\,\mathrm{d}u \tag{E.2.6}$$

Theorem E.11. *L'Hôpital's Rule. Suppose f and g are differentiable and $g'(x) \neq 0$ near a, except possibly at a. Suppose that the limit*

$$\lim_{x\to a} \frac{f(x)}{g(x)} \tag{E.2.7}$$

is an indeterminate form of type $\frac{0}{0}$ or ∞/∞. Then

$$\lim_{x\to a} \frac{f(x)}{g(x)} = \lim_{x\to a} \frac{f'(x)}{g'(x)}, \tag{E.2.8}$$

provided the limit on the right-hand side exists or is infinite.

Improper Integrals

If $\int_a^t f(x)\mathrm{d}x$ exists for every number $t \geq a$, then we define

$$\int_a^{\infty} f(x)\,\mathrm{d}x = \lim_{t\to\infty} \int_a^t f(x)\,\mathrm{d}x, \tag{E.2.9}$$

provided this limit exists as a finite number, and in that case we say that $\int_a^{\infty} f(x)\,\mathrm{d}x$ is *convergent*. Otherwise, we say that the improper integral is *divergent*.

If $\int_t^b f(x)\,\mathrm{d}x$ exists for every number $t \leq b$, then we define

$$\int_{-\infty}^{b} f(x)\,\mathrm{d}x = \lim_{t\to-\infty} \int_t^b f(x)\,\mathrm{d}x, \tag{E.2.10}$$

provided this limit exists as a finite number, and in that case we say that $\int_{-\infty}^{b} f(x)\,\mathrm{d}x$ is *convergent*. Otherwise, we say that the improper integral is *divergent*.

If both $\int_a^{\infty} f(x)\,\mathrm{d}x$ and $\int_{-\infty}^{a} f(x)\,\mathrm{d}x$ are convergent, then we define

$$\int_{-\infty}^{\infty} f(x)\,\mathrm{d}x = \int_{-\infty}^{a} f(x)\,\mathrm{d}x + \int_a^{\infty} f(x)\mathrm{d}x, \tag{E.2.11}$$

and we say that $\int_{-\infty}^{\infty} f(x)\,\mathrm{d}x$ is *convergent*. Otherwise, we say that the improper integral is *divergent*.

E.3 Sequences and Series

A *sequence* is an ordered list of numbers, $a_1, a_2, a_3, \ldots, a_n = (a_k)_{k=1}^n$. A sequence may be finite or infinite. In the latter case we write $a_1, a_2, a_3, \ldots = (a_k)_{k=1}^{\infty}$. We say that *the infinite sequence $(a_k)_{k=1}^{\infty}$ converges to the finite limit L*, and we write

$$\lim_{k\to\infty} a_k = L, \tag{E.3.1}$$

if for every $\epsilon > 0$ there exists an integer $N \geq 1$ such that $|a_k - L| < \epsilon$ for all $k \geq N$. We say that *the infinite sequence $(a_k)_{k=1}^{\infty}$ diverges to* $+\infty$ (or $-\infty$) if for every $M \geq 0$ there exists an integer $N \geq 1$ such that $a_k \geq M$ for all $k \geq N$ (or $a_k \leq -M$ for all $k \geq N$).

Finite Series

$$\sum_{k=1}^{n} k = 1 + 2 + \cdots + n = \frac{n(n+1)}{2} \tag{E.3.2}$$

$$\sum_{k=1}^{n} k^2 = 1^2 + 2^2 + \cdots + n^2 = \frac{n(n+1)(2n+3)}{6} \tag{E.3.3}$$

The Binomial Series

$$\sum_{k=0}^{n} \binom{n}{k} a^{n-k} b^k = (a+b)^n \tag{E.3.4}$$

Infinite Series

Given an infinite sequence of numbers $a_1, a_2, a_3, \ldots = (a_k)_{k=1}^{\infty}$, let s_n denote the *partial sum* of the first n terms:

$$s_n = \sum_{k=1}^{n} a_k = a_1 + a_2 + \cdots + a_n. \tag{E.3.5}$$

If the sequence $(s_n)_{n=1}^{\infty}$ converges to a finite number S then we say that the infinite series $\sum_k a_k$ is *convergent* and write

$$\sum_{k=1}^{\infty} a_k = S. \tag{E.3.6}$$

Otherwise we say the infinite series is *divergent*.

Rules for Series

Let $(a_k)_{k=1}^{\infty}$ and $(b_k)_{k=1}^{\infty}$ be infinite sequences and let c be a constant.

$$\sum_{k=1}^{\infty} ca_k = c\sum_{k=1}^{\infty} a_k \tag{E.3.7}$$

$$\sum_{k=1}^{\infty}(a_k \pm b_k) = \sum_{k=1}^{\infty} a_k \pm \sum_{k=1}^{\infty} b_k \tag{E.3.8}$$

In both of the above the series on the left is convergent if the series on the right is (are) convergent.

The Geometric Series

$$\sum_{k=0}^{\infty} x^k = \frac{1}{1-x}, \quad |x| < 1. \tag{E.3.9}$$

The Exponential Series

$$\sum_{k=0}^{\infty} \frac{x^k}{k!} = \mathrm{e}^x, \quad -\infty < x < \infty. \tag{E.3.10}$$

Other Series

$$\sum_{k=0}^{\infty} \binom{m+k-1}{m-1} x^k = \frac{1}{(1-x)^m}, \quad |x| < 1. \tag{E.3.11}$$

$$-\sum_{k=1}^{\infty} \frac{x^n}{n} = \ln(1-x), \quad |x| < 1. \tag{E.3.12}$$

$$\sum_{k=0}^{\infty} \binom{n}{k} x^k = (1+x)^n, \quad |x| < 1.$$

Taylor Series

If the function f has a *power series* representation at the point a with radius of convergence $R > 0$, that is, if

$$f(x) = \sum_{k=0}^{\infty} c_k (x-a)^k, \quad |x-a| < R, \tag{E.3.14}$$

for some constants $(c_k)_{k=0}^{\infty}$, then c_k must be

$$c_k = \frac{f^{(k)}(a)}{k!}, \quad k = 0, 1, 2, \ldots \tag{E.3.15}$$

Furthermore, the function f is differentiable on the open interval $(a-R,\, a+R)$ with

$$f'(x) = \sum_{k=1}^{\infty} k c_k (x-a)^{k-1}, \quad |x-a| < R, \tag{E.3.16}$$

$$\int f(x)\,\mathrm{d}x = C + \sum_{k=0}^{\infty} c_k \frac{(x-a)^{k+1}}{k+1}, \quad |x-a| < R, \tag{E.3.17}$$

in which case both of the above series have radius of convergence R.

E.4 The Gamma Function

The *Gamma function* Γ will be defined in this book according to the formula

$$\Gamma(\alpha) = \int_0^{\infty} x^{\alpha-1} \mathrm{e}^{-x}\,\mathrm{d}x, \quad \text{for } \alpha > 0. \tag{E.4.1}$$

Fact E.12. *Properties of the Gamma Function:*

- $\Gamma(\alpha) = (\alpha-1)\Gamma(\alpha-1)$ *for any* $\alpha > 1$, *and so* $\Gamma(n) = (n-1)!$ *for any positive integer* n.
- $\Gamma(1/2) = \sqrt{\pi}$.

E.5 Linear Algebra

Matrices

A *matrix* is an ordered array of numbers or expressions; typically we write $\mathbf{A} = \left(a_{ij}\right)$ or $\mathbf{A} = \left[a_{ij}\right]$. If $\mathbf{A}$ has m rows and n columns then we write

$$\mathbf{A}_{\mathrm{m}\times\mathrm{n}} = \begin{bmatrix} a_{11} & a_{12} & \cdots & a_{1n} \\ a_{21} & a_{22} & \cdots & a_{2n} \\ \vdots & \vdots & \ddots & \vdots \\ a_{m1} & a_{m2} & \cdots & a_{mn} \end{bmatrix}. \tag{E.5.1}$$

The *identity matrix* $\mathbf{I}_{\mathrm{n}\times\mathrm{n}}$ is an $\mathrm{n}\times\mathrm{n}$ matrix with zeros everywhere except for 1's along the main diagonal:

$$\mathbf{I}_{\mathrm{n}\times\mathrm{n}} = \begin{bmatrix} 1 & 0 & \cdots & 0 \\ 0 & 1 & \cdots & 0 \\ \vdots & \vdots & \ddots & \vdots \\ 0 & 0 & \cdots & 1 \end{bmatrix}. \tag{E.5.2}$$

and the matrix with ones everywhere is denoted $\mathbf{J}_{n\times n}$:

$$\mathbf{J}_{n\times n} = \begin{bmatrix} 1 & 1 & \cdots & 1 \\ 1 & 1 & \cdots & 1 \\ \vdots & \vdots & \ddots & \vdots \\ 1 & 1 & \cdots & 1 \end{bmatrix}. \tag{E.5.3}$$

A *vector* is a matrix with one of the dimensions equal to one, such as $\mathbf{A}_{m\times 1}$ (a column vector) or $\mathbf{A}_{1\times n}$ (a row vector). The *zero vector* $\mathbf{0}_{n\times 1}$ is an $n \times 1$ matrix of zeros:

$$\mathbf{0}_{n\times 1} = \begin{bmatrix} 0 & 0 & \cdots & 0 \end{bmatrix}^{T}. \tag{E.5.4}$$

The *transpose* of a matrix $\mathbf{A} = (a_{ij})$ is the matrix $\mathbf{A}^{T} = (a_{ji})$, which is just like $\mathbf{A}$ except the rows are columns and the columns are rows. The matrix $\mathbf{A}$ is said to be *symmetric* if $\mathbf{A}^{T} = \mathbf{A}$. Note that $(\mathbf{AB})^{T} = \mathbf{B}^{T}\mathbf{A}^{T}$.

The *trace* of a square matrix $\mathbf{A}$ is the sum of its diagonal elements: $\mathrm{tr}(\mathbf{A}) = \sum_i a_{ii}$.

The *inverse* of a square matrix $\mathbf{A}_{n\times n}$ (when it exists) is the unique matrix denoted $\mathbf{A}^{-1}$ which satisfies $\mathbf{A}\mathbf{A}^{-1} = \mathbf{A}^{-1}\mathbf{A} = \mathbf{I}_{n\times n}$. If $\mathbf{A}^{-1}$ exists then we say $\mathbf{A}$ is *invertible*, or alternatively *nonsingular*. Note that $\left(\mathbf{A}^{T}\right)^{-1} = \left(\mathbf{A}^{-1}\right)^{T}$.

Fact E.13. *The inverse of the* 2×2 *matrix*

$$\mathbf{A} = \begin{bmatrix} a & b \\ c & d \end{bmatrix} \quad \textit{is} \quad \mathbf{A}^{-1} = \frac{1}{ad - bc}\begin{bmatrix} d & -b \\ -c & a \end{bmatrix}, \tag{E.5.5}$$

provided $ad - bc \neq 0$.

Determinants

Definition E.14. The *determinant* of a square matrix $\mathbf{A}_{n\times n}$ is denoted $\det(\mathbf{A})$ or $|\mathbf{A}|$ and is defined recursively by

$$\det(\mathbf{A}) = \sum_{i=1}^{n} (-1)^{i+j} a_{ij} \det(\mathbf{M}_{ij}), \tag{E.5.6}$$

where $\mathbf{M}_{ij}$ is the submatrix formed by deleting the ith row and j^{th} column of $\mathbf{A}$. We may choose any fixed $1 \leq j \leq n$ we wish to compute the determinant; the final result is independent of the j chosen.

Fact E.15. *The determinant of the* 2×2 *matrix*

$$\mathbf{A} = \begin{bmatrix} a & b \\ c & d \end{bmatrix} \quad \textit{is} \quad |\mathbf{A}| = ad - bc. \tag{E.5.7}$$

Fact E.16. *A square matrix* $\mathbf{A}$ *is nonsingular if and only if* $\det(\mathbf{A}) \neq 0$.

Positive (Semi)Definite

If the matrix $\mathbf{A}$ satisfies $\mathbf{x}^{T}\mathbf{A}\mathbf{x} \geq 0$ for all vectors $\mathbf{x} \neq \mathbf{0}$, then we say that $\mathbf{A}$ is *positive semidefinite*. If strict inequality holds for all $\mathbf{x} \neq \mathbf{0}$, then $\mathbf{A}$ is *positive definite*. The connection to statistics is that covariance matrices (see Chapter 7) are always positive semidefinite, and many of them are even positive definite.

E.6 Multivariable Calculus

Partial Derivatives

If f is a function of two variables, its *first-order partial derivatives* are defined by

$$\frac{\partial f}{\partial x} = \frac{\partial}{\partial x} f(x,y) = \lim_{h\to 0} \frac{f(x+h,\, y) - f(x,y)}{h} \tag{E.6.1}$$

and

$$\frac{\partial f}{\partial y} = \frac{\partial}{\partial y} f(x,y) = \lim_{h\to 0} \frac{f(x,\, y+h) - f(x,y)}{h}, \tag{E.6.2}$$

provided these limits exist. The *second-order partial derivatives* of f are defined by

$$\frac{\partial^2 f}{\partial x^2} = \frac{\partial}{\partial x}\left(\frac{\partial f}{\partial x}\right), \quad \frac{\partial^2 f}{\partial y^2} = \frac{\partial}{\partial y}\left(\frac{\partial f}{\partial y}\right), \quad \frac{\partial^2 f}{\partial x \partial y} = \frac{\partial}{\partial x}\left(\frac{\partial f}{\partial y}\right), \quad \frac{\partial^2 f}{\partial y \partial x} = \frac{\partial}{\partial y}\left(\frac{\partial f}{\partial x}\right). \tag{E.6.3}$$

In many cases (and for all cases in this book) it is true that

$$\frac{\partial^2 f}{\partial x \partial y} = \frac{\partial^2 f}{\partial y \partial x}. \tag{E.6.4}$$

Optimization

An function f of two variables has a *local maximum* at (a, b) if $f(x, y) \geq f(a, b)$ for all points (x, y) near (a, b), that is, for all points in an open disk centered at (a, b). The number $f(a, b)$ is then called a *local maximum value* of f. The function f has a *local minimum* if the same thing happens with the inequality reversed.

Suppose the point (a, b) is a *critical point* of f, that is, suppose (a, b) satisfies

$$\frac{\partial f}{\partial x}(a,b) = \frac{\partial f}{\partial y}(a,b) = 0. \tag{E.6.5}$$

Further suppose $\frac{\partial^2 f}{\partial x^2}$ and $\frac{\partial^2 f}{\partial y^2}$ are continuous near (a, b). Let the *Hessian matrix* H (not to be confused with the *hat matrix* $\mathbf{H}$ of Chapter 12) be defined by

$$H = \begin{bmatrix} \frac{\partial^2 f}{\partial x^2} & \frac{\partial^2 f}{\partial x \partial y} \\ \frac{\partial^2 f}{\partial y \partial x} & \frac{\partial^2 f}{\partial y^2} \end{bmatrix}. \tag{E.6.6}$$

We use the following rules to decide whether (a, b) is an *extremum* (that is, a local minimum or local maximum) of f.

- If $\det(H) > 0$ and $\frac{\partial^2 f}{\partial x^2}(a,b) > 0$, then (a, b) is a local minimum of f.
- If $\det(H) > 0$ and $\frac{\partial^2 f}{\partial x^2}(a,b) < 0$, then (a, b) is a local maximum of f.
- If $\det(H) < 0$, then (a, b) is a *saddle point* of f and so is not an extremum of f.
- If $\det(H) = 0$, then we do not know the status of (a, b); it might be an extremum or it might not be.

Double and Multiple Integrals

Let f be defined on a rectangle $R = [a, b]\times[c, d]$, and for each m and n divide $[a, b]$ (respectively $[c, d]$) into subintervals $[x_j, x_{j+1}]$, $i = 0, 1, \ldots, m-1$ (respectively $[y_i, y_{i+1}]$) of length $\Delta x_j = (b-a)/m$ (respectively $\Delta y_i = (d-c)/n$) where $x_0 = a$ and $x_m = b$ (and $y_0 = c$ and $y_n = d$), and let x_j^* (y_i^*) be any points chosen from their respective subintervals. Then the *double integral* of f over the rectangle R is

$$\iint\limits_R f(x,y)\,\mathrm{d}A = \int_c^d\!\!\int_a^b f(x,y)\,\mathrm{d}x\mathrm{d}y = \lim_{m,n\to\infty} \sum_{i=1}^{n}\sum_{j=1}^{m} f(x_j^*, y_i^*)\Delta x_j \Delta y_i, \tag{E.6.7}$$

provided this limit exists. Multiple integrals are defined in the same way just with more letters and sums.

Bivariate and Multivariate Change of Variables

Suppose we have a transformation[1] T that maps points (u, v) in a set A to points (x, y) in a set B. We typically write $x = x(u, v)$ and $y = y(u, v)$, and we assume that x and y have continuous first-order partial derivatives. We say that T is *one-to-one* if no two distinct (u, v) pairs get mapped to the same (x, y) pair; in this book, all of our multivariate transformations T are one-to-one.

The *Jacobian* (pronounced "yah-KOH-bee-uhn") of T is denoted by $\partial(x, y)/\partial(u, v)$ and is defined by the determinant of the following matrix of partial derivatives:

$$\frac{\partial(x,y)}{\partial(u,v)} = \begin{vmatrix} \frac{\partial x}{\partial u} & \frac{\partial x}{\partial v} \\ \frac{\partial y}{\partial u} & \frac{\partial y}{\partial v} \end{vmatrix} = \frac{\partial x}{\partial u}\frac{\partial y}{\partial v} - \frac{\partial x}{\partial v}\frac{\partial y}{\partial u}. \tag{E.6.8}$$

If the function f is continuous on A and if the Jacobian of T is nonzero except perhaps on the boundary of A, then

$$\iint_B f(x,y)\,\mathrm{d}x\,\mathrm{d}y = \iint_A f\left[x(u,v),\, y(u,v)\right] \left|\frac{\partial(x,y)}{\partial(u,v)}\right| \mathrm{d}u\,\mathrm{d}v. \tag{E.6.9}$$

A multivariate change of variables is defined in an analogous way: the one-to-one transformation T maps points $(u_1, u_2, \ldots, u_n)$ to points $(x_1, x_2, \ldots, x_n)$, the Jacobian is the determinant of the n × n matrix of first-order partial derivatives of T (lined up in the natural manner), and instead of a double integral we have a multiple integral over multidimensional sets A and B.

[1]For our purposes T is in fact the *inverse* of a one-to-one transformation that we are initially given. We usually start with functions that map $(x, y) \longmapsto (u, v)$, and one of our first tasks is to solve for the inverse transformation that maps $(u, v) \longmapsto (x, y)$. It is this inverse transformation which we are calling T.

Appendix F

Writing Reports with R

Perhaps the most important part of a statistician's job once the analysis is complete is to communicate the results to others. This is usually done with some type of report that is delivered to the client, manager, or administrator. Other situations that call for reports include term papers, final projects, thesis work, *etc.* This chapter is designed to pass along some tips about writing reports once the work is completed with R.

F.1 What to Write

It is possible to summarize this entire appendix with only one sentence: *the statistician's goal is to communicate with others.* To this end, there are some general guidelines that I give to students which are based on an outline originally written and shared with me by Dr. G. Andy Chang.

Basic Outline for a Statistical Report

1. Executive Summary (a one page description of the study and conclusion)
2. Introduction
   (a) What is the question, and why is it important?
   (b) Is the study observational or experimental?
   (c) What are the hypotheses of interest to the researcher?
   (d) What are the types of analyses employed? (one sample t-test, paired-sample t-test, ANOVA, chi-square test, regression, ...)
3. Data Collection
   (a) Describe how the data were collected in detail.
   (b) Identify all variable types: quantitative, qualitative, ordered or nominal (with levels), discrete, continuous.
   (c) Discuss any limitations of the data collection procedure. Look carefully for any sources of bias.
4. Summary Information

(a) Give numeric summaries of all variables of interest.

   i. Discrete: (relative) frequencies, contingency tables, odds ratios, *etc*.
   ii. Continuous: measures of center, spread, shape.

(b) Give visual summaries of all variables of interest.

   i. Side-by-side boxplots, scatterplots, histograms, *etc*.

(c) Discuss any unusual features of the data (outliers, clusters, granularity, *etc*.)

(d) Report any missing data and identify any potential problems or bias.

5. Analysis

   (a) State any hypotheses employed, and check the assumptions.
   (b) Report test statistics, p-values, and confidence intervals.
   (c) Interpret the results in the context of the study.
   (d) Attach (labeled) tables and/or graphs and make reference to them in the report as needed.

6. Conclusion

   (a) Summarize the results of the study. What did you learn?
   (b) Discuss any limitations of the study or inferences.
   (c) Discuss avenues of future research suggested by the study.

F.2 How to Write It with R

Once the decision has been made what to write, the next task is to typeset the information to be shared. To do this the author will need to select software to use to write the documents. There are many options available, and choosing one over another is sometimes a matter of taste. But not all software were created equal, and R plays better with some applications than it does with others.

In short, R does great with LaTeX and there are many resources available to make writing a document with R and LaTeX easier. But LaTeX is not for the beginner, and there are other word processors which may be acceptable depending on the circumstances.

F.2.1 Microsoft® Word

It is a fact of life that Microsoft® Windows is currently the most prevalent desktop operating system on the planet. Those who own Windows also typically own some version of Microsoft Office, thus Microsoft Word is the default word processor for many, many people.

The standard way to write an R report with Microsoft® Word is to generate material with R and then copy-paste the material at selected places in a Word document. An advantage to this approach is that Word is nicely designed to make it easy to copy-and-paste from RGui to the Word document.

A disadvantage to this approach is that the R input/output needs to be edited manually by the author to make it readable for others. Another disadvantage is that the approach does not work on all operating systems (not on Linux, in particular). Yet another disadvantage is that Microsoft® Word is proprietary, and as a result, R does not communicate with Microsoft® Word as well as it does with other software as we shall soon see.

Nevertheless, if you are going to write a report with Word there are some steps that you can take to make the report more amenable to the reader.

1. Copy and paste graphs into the document. You can do this by right clicking on the graph and selecting Copy as bitmap, or Copy as metafile, or one of the other options. Then move the cursor to the document where you want the picture, right-click, and select Paste.

2. Resize (most) pictures so that they take up no more than 1/2 page. You may want to put graphs side by side; do this by inserting a table and placing the graphs inside the cells.

3. Copy selected R input and output to the Word document. All code should be separated from the rest of the writing, except when specifically mentioning a function or object in a sentence.

4. The font of R input/output should be Courier New, or some other monowidth font (not Times New Roman or Calibri); the default font size of `12` is usually too big for R code and should be reduced to, for example, `10pt`.

It is also possible to communicate with R through OpenOffice.org, which can export to the proprietary (`.doc`) format.

F.2.2 OpenOffice.org and `odfWeave`

OpenOffice.org (OO.o) is an open source desktop productivity suite which mirrors Microsoft® Office. It is especially nice because it works on all operating systems. OO.o can read most document formats, and in particular, it will read `.doc` files. The standard OO.o file extension for documents is `.odt`, which stands for "open document text".

The `odfWeave` package [55] provides a way to generate an `.odt` file with R input and output code formatted correctly and inserted in the correct places, without any additional work. In this way, one does not need to worry about all of the trouble of typesetting R output. Another advantage of `odfWeave` is that it allows you to generate the report dynamically; if the data underlying the report change or are updated, then a few clicks (or commands) will generate a brand new report.

One disadvantage is that the source `.odt` file is not easy to read, because it is difficult to visually distinguish the noweb parts (where the R code is) from the non-noweb parts. This can be fixed by manually changing the font of the noweb sections to, for instance, Courier font, size `10pt`. But it is extra work. It would be nice if a program would discriminate between the two different sections and automatically typeset the respective parts in their correct fonts. This is one of the advantages to LyX.

Another advantage of OO.o is that even after you have generated the outfile, it is fully editable just like any other `.odt` document. If there are errors or formatting problems, they can be fixed at any time.

Here are the basic steps to typeset a statistical report with OO.o.

1. Write your report as an `.odt` document in OO.o just as you would any other document. Call this document `infile.odt`, and make sure that it is saved in your working directory.

2. At the places you would like to insert R code in the document, write the code chunks in the following format:

```
<<>>=
x <- rnorm(10)
mean(x)
@
```

   or write whatever code you want between the symbols <<>>= and @.

3. Open R and type the following:

```
> library(odfWeave)
> odfWeave(file = "infile.odt", dest = "outfile.odt")
```

4. The compiled (.odt) file, complete with all of the R output automatically inserted in the correct places, will now be the file outfile.odt located in the working directory. Open outfile.odt, examine it, modify it, and repeat if desired.

There are all sorts of extra things that can be done. For example, the R commands can be suppressed with the tag <<echo = FALSE>>=, and the R output may be hidden with <<results = hide>>=. See the odfWeave package documentation for details.

F.2.3 Sweave and LaTeX

This approach is nice because it works for all operating systems. One can quite literally typeset *anything* with LaTeX. All of this power comes at a price, however. The writer must learn the LaTeX language which is a nontrivial enterprise. Even given the language, if there is a single syntax error, or a single delimeter missing in the entire document, then the whole thing breaks.

LaTeX can do anything, but it is relatively difficult to learn and very grumpy about syntax errors and delimiter matching. there are however programs useful for formatting LaTeX.

A disadvantage is that you cannot see the mathematical formulas until you run the whole file with LaTeX.

A disadvantage is that figures and tables are relatively difficult.

There are programs to make the process easier AUCTeX

dev.copy2eps, also dev.copy2pdf

http://www.stat.uni-muenchen.de/~leisch/Sweave/

F.2.4 Sweave and LyX

This approach is nice because it works for all operating systems. It gives you everything from the last section and makes it easier to use LaTeX. That being said, it is better to know LaTeX already when migrating to LyX, because you understand all of the machinery going on under the hood.

Program Listings and the R language

This book was written with LyX.

http://gregor.gorjanc.googlepages.com/lyx-sweave

F.3 Formatting Tables

The prettyR package
the Hmisc package

```
> library(Hmisc)
> summary(cbind(Sepal.Length, Sepal.Width) ~ Species, data = iris)
```

```
cbind(Sepal.Length, Sepal.Width)    N=150

+-------+----------+---+------------+-----------+
|       |          |N  |Sepal.Length|Sepal.Width|
+-------+----------+---+------------+-----------+
|Species|setosa    | 50|5.006000    |3.428000   |
|       |versicolor| 50|5.936000    |2.770000   |
|       |virginica | 50|6.588000    |2.974000   |
+-------+----------+---+------------+-----------+
|Overall|          |150|5.843333    |3.057333   |
+-------+----------+---+------------+-----------+
```

There is a method argument to summary, which is set to `method = "response"` by default. There are two other methods for summarizing data: reverse and cross. See `?summary.formula` or the following document from Frank Harrell for more details `http://biostat.mc.vanderbilt.edu/tw`

F.4 Other Formats

HTML and prettyR
R2HTML

Appendix G

Instructions for Instructors

WARNING: THIS APPENDIX IS NOT APPLICABLE UNTIL THE EXERCISES HAVE BEEN WRITTEN.

Probably this *book* could more accurately be described as *software*. The reason is that the document is one big random variable, one observation realized out of millions. It is electronically distributed under the GNU FDL, and "free" in both senses: speech and beer.

There are four components to IPSUR: the Document, the Program used to generate it, the R package that holds the Program, and the Ancillaries that accompany it.

The majority of the data and exercises have been designed to be randomly generated. Different realizations of this book will have different graphs and exercises throughout. The advantage of this approach is that a teacher, say, can generate a unique version to be used in his/her class. Students can do the exercises and the teacher will have the answers to all of the problems in their own, unique solutions manual. Students may download a different solutions manual online somewhere else, but none of the answers will match the teacher's copy.

Then next semester, the teacher can generate a *new* book and the problems will be more or less identical, except the numbers will be changed. This means that students from different sections of the same class will not be able to copy from one another quite so easily. The same will be true for similar classes at different institutions. Indeed, as long as the instructor protects his/her *key* used to generate the book, it will be difficult for students to crack the code. And if they are industrious enough at this level to find a way to (a) download and decipher my version's source code, (b) hack the teacher's password somehow, and (c) generate the teacher's book with all of the answers, then they probably should be testing out of an "Introduction to Probability and Statistics" course, anyway.

The book that you are reading was created with a random seed which was set at the beginning. The original seed is 42. You can choose your own seed, and generate a new book with brand new data for the text and exercises, complete with updated manuals. A method I recommend for finding a seed is to look down at your watch at this very moment and record the 6 digit hour, minute, and second (say, 9:52:59am): choose that for a seed[1]. This method already provides for over 43,000 books, without taking military time into account. An alternative would be to go to R and type

```
> options(digits = 16)
> runif(1)
```

```
[1] 0.2170129411388189
```

[1]In fact, this is essentially the method used by R to select an initial random seed (see ?set.seed). However, the instructor should set the seed manually so that the book can be regenerated at a later time, if necessary.

Now choose 2170129411388188 as your secret seed... write it down in a safe place and do not share it with anyone. Next generate the book with your seed using LyX-Sweave or Sweave-LaTeX. You may wish to also generate Student and Instructor Solution Manuals. Guidance regarding this is given below in the How to Use This Document section.

G.1 Generating This Document

You will need three (3) things to generate this document for yourself, in addition to a current R distribution which at the time of this writing is `R version 2.11.1 (2010-05-31)`:

1. a LaTeX distribution,
2. Sweave (which comes with R automatically), and
3. LyX (optional, but recommended).

We will discuss each of these in turn.

LaTeX: The distribution used by the present author was TeX Live (`http://www.tug.org/texlive/`). There are plenty of other perfectly suitable LaTeX distributions depending on your operating system, one such alternative being MikTeX (`http://miktex.org/`) for Microsoft Windows.

Sweave: If you have R installed, then the required Sweave files are already on your system... somewhere. The only problems that you may have are likely associated with making sure that your LaTeX distribution knows where to find the `Sweave.sty` file. See the Sweave Homepage (`http://www.statistik.lmu.de/~leisch/Sweave/`) for guidance on how to get it working on your particular operating system.

LyX: Strictly speaking, LyX is not needed to generate this document. But this document was written stem to stern with LyX, taking full advantage of all of the bells and whistles that LyX has to offer over plain LaTeX editors. And it's free. See the LyX homepage (`http://www.lyx.org/`) for additional information.
If you decide to give LyX a try, then you will need to complete some extra steps to coordinate Sweave and LyX with each other. Luckily, Gregor Gorjanc has a website and an R News article [36] to help you do exactly that. See the LyX-Sweave homepage (`http://gregor.gorjanc.googlepages.com/lyx-sweave`) for details.

An attempt was made to not be extravagant with fonts or packages so that a person would not need the entire `CTAN` (or `CRAN`) installed on their personal computer to generate the book. Nevertheless, there are a few extra packages required. These packages are listed in the `preamble` of `IPSUR.Rnw`, `IPSUR.tex`, and `IPSUR.lyx`.

G.2 How to Use This Document

The easiest way to use this document is to install the `IPSUR` package from `CRAN` and be all done. This way would be acceptable if there is another, primary, text being used for the course and IPSUR is only meant to play a supplementary role.

If you plan for IPSUR to serve as the primary text for your course, then it would be wise to generate your own version of the document. You will need the source code for the Program which can be downloaded from CRAN or the IPSUR website. Once the source is obtained there are four (4) basic steps to generating your own copy.

1. Randomly select a secret "seed" of integers and replace my seed of 42 with your own seed.

2. Make sure that the **maintext** branch is turned ON and also make sure that both the **solutions** branch and the **answers** branch are turned OFF. Use LyX or your LaTeX editor with Sweave to generate your unique PDF copy of the book and distribute this copy to your students. (See the LyX User's Guide to learn more about branches; the ones referenced above can be found under Document ▹ Settings ▹ Branches.)

3. Turn the **maintext** branch[2] OFF and the **solutions** branch ON. Generate a "Student Solutions Manual" which has complete solutions to selected exercises and distribute the PDF to the students.

4. Leave the **solutions** branch ON and also turn the **answers** branch ON and generate an "Instructor Solutions and Answers Manual" with full solutions to some of the exercises and just answers to the remaining exercises. Do NOT distribute this to the students – unless of course you want them to have the answers to all of the problems.

To make it easier for those people who do not want to use LyX (or for whatever reason cannot get it working), I have included three (3) Sweave files corresponding to the main text, student solutions, and instructor answers, that are included in the IPSUR source package in the `/tex` subdirectory. In principle it is possible to change the seed and generate the three parts separately with only Sweave and LaTeX. This method is not recommended by me, but is perhaps desirable for some people.

Generating Quizzes and Exams

- you can copy paste selected exercises from the text, put them together, and you have a quiz. Since the numbers are randomly generated you do not need to worry about different semesters. And you will have answer keys already for all of your QUIZZES and EXAMS, too.

G.3 Ancillary Materials

In addition to the main text, student manual, and instructor manual, there are two other ancillaries. IPSUR.R, and IPSUR.RData.

G.4 Modifying This Document

Since this document is released under the GNU-FDL, you are free to modify this document however you wish (in accordance with the license – see Appendix B). The immediate benefit of this is that you can generate the book, with brand new problem sets, and distribute it to your students simply as a PDF (in an email, for instance). As long as you distribute less than 100

[2] You can leave the **maintext** branch ON when generating the solutions manuals, but (1) all of the page numbers will be different, and (2) the typeset solutions will generate and take up a lot of space between exercises.

such *Opaque* copies, you are not even required by the GNU-FDL to share your *Transparent* copy (the source code with the secret key) that you used to generate them. Next semester, choose a new key and generate a new copy to be distributed to the new class.

> But more generally, if you are not keen on the way I explained (or failed to explain) something, then you are free to rewrite it. If you would like to cover more (or less) material, then you are free to add (or delete) whatever Chapters/Sections/Paragraphs that you wish. And since you have the source code, you do not need to retype the wheel.

Some individuals will argue that the nature of a statistics textbook like this one, many of the exercises being randomly generated *by design*, does a disservice to the students because the exercises do not use real-world data. That is a valid criticism... but in my case the benefits outweighed the detriments and I moved forward to incorporate static data sets whenever it was feasible and effective. Frankly, and most humbly, the only response I have for those individuals is: "Please refer to the preceding paragraph."

Appendix H

`RcmdrTestDrive` Story

The goal of RcmdrTestDrive was to have a data set sufficiently rich in the types of data represented such that a person could load it into the R Commander and be able to explore all of Rcmdr's menu options at once. I decided early-on that an efficient way to do this would be to generate the data set randomly, and later add to the list of variables as more Rcmdr menu options became available. Generating the data was easy, but generating a *story* that related all of the respective variables proved to be less so.

In the Summer of 2006 I gave a version of the raw data and variable names to my STAT 3743 Probability and Statistics class and invited each of them to write a short story linking all of the variables together in a coherent narrative. No further direction was given.

The most colorful of those I received was written by Jeffery Cornfield, submitted July 12, 2006, and is included below with his permission. It was edited slightly by the present author and updated to respond dynamically to the random generation of RcmdrTestDrive; otherwise, the story has been unchanged.

Case File: ALU-179 "Murder Madness in Toon Town"

WARNING

> ***This file is not for the faint of heart, dear reader, because it is filled with horrible images that will haunt your nightmares. If you are weak of stomach, have irritable bowel syndrome, or are simply paranoid, DO NOT READ FURTHER! Otherwise, read at your own risk.***

One fine sunny day, Police Chief R. Runner called up the forensics department at Acme-Looney University. There had been 166 murders in the past 7 days, approximately one murder every hour, of many of the local Human workers, shop keepers, and residents of Toon Town. These alarming rates threatened to destroy the fragile balance of Toon and Human camaraderie that had developed in Toon Town.

Professor Twee T. Bird, a world-renowned forensics specialist and a Czechoslovakian native, received the call. "Professor, we need your expertise in this field to identify the pattern of the killer or killers," Chief Runner exclaimed. "We need to establish a link between these people to stop this massacre."

"Yes, Chief Runner, please give me the details of the case," Professor Bird declared with a heavy native accent, (though, for the sake of the case file, reader, I have decided to leave out the accent due to the fact that it would obviously drive you – if you will forgive the pun – looney!)

"All prints are wiped clean and there are no identifiable marks on the bodies of the victims. All we are able to come up with is the possibility that perhaps there is some kind of alternative method of which we are unaware. We have sent a secure e-mail with a listing of all of the victims' **races**, **genders**, locations of the bodies, and the sequential **order** in which they were killed. We have also included other information that might be helpful," said Chief Runner.

"Thank you very much. Perhaps I will contact my colleague in the Statistics Department here, Dr. Elmer Fudd-Einstein," exclaimed Professor Bird. "He might be able to identify a pattern of attack with mathematics and statistics."

"Good luck trying to find him, Professor. Last I heard, he had a bottle of scotch and was in the Hundred Acre Woods hunting rabbits," Chief Runner declared in a manner that questioned the beloved doctor's credibility.

"Perhaps I will take a drive to find him. The fresh air will do me good."

> ***I will skip ahead, dear reader, for much occurred during this time. Needless to say, after a fierce battle with a mountain cat that the Toon-ology Department tagged earlier in the year as "Sylvester," Professor Bird found Dr. Fudd-Einstein and brought him back, with much bribery of alcohol and the promise of the future slaying of those "wascally wabbits" (it would help to explain that Dr. Fudd-Einstein had a speech impediment which was only worsened during the consumption of alcohol.)***

Once our two heroes returned to the beautiful Acme-Looney University, and once Dr. Fudd-Einstein became sober and coherent, they set off to examine the case and begin solving these mysterious murders.

"First off," Dr. Fudd-Einstein explained, "these people all worked at the University at some point or another. Also, there also seems to be a trend in the fact that they all had a **salary** between $12 and $21 when they retired."

"That's not really a lot to live off of," explained Professor Bird.

"Yes, but you forget that the Looney Currency System works differently than the rest of the American Currency System. One Looney is equivalent to Ten American Dollars. Also, these faculty members are the ones who faced a cut in their salary, as denoted by '**reduction**'. Some of them dropped quite substantially when the University had to fix that little *faux pas* in the Chemistry Department. You remember: when Dr. D. Duck tried to create that 'Everlasting Elixir?' As a result, these faculty left the university. Speaking of which, when is his memorial service?" inquired Dr. Fudd-Einstein.

"This coming Monday. But if there were all of these killings, how in the world could one person do it? It just doesn't seem to be possible; stay up 7 days straight and be able to kill all of these people and have the energy to continue on," Professor Bird exclaimed, doubting the guilt of only one person.

"Perhaps then, it was a group of people, perhaps there was more than one killer placed throughout Toon Town to commit these crimes. If I feed in these variables, along with any others that might have a pattern, the Acme Computer will give us an accurate reading of suspects, with a scant probability of error. As you know, the Acme Computer was developed entirely in house here at Acme-Looney University," Dr. Fudd-Einstein said as he began feeding the numbers into the massive server.

"Hey, look at this," Professor Bird exclaimed, "What's with this **before/after** information?"

"Scroll down; it shows it as a note from the coroner's office. Apparently Toon Town Coroner Marvin – that strange fellow from Mars, Pennsylvania – feels, in his opinion, that given the fact that the cadavers were either **smoke**rs or non-smokers, and given their personal health, and family medical history, that this was their life expectancy before contact with cigarettes or second-hand smoke and after," Dr. Fudd-Einstein declared matter-of-factly.

"Well, would race or gender have something to do with it, Elmer?" inquired Professor Bird.

"Maybe, but I would bet my money on somebody was trying to quiet these faculty before they made a big ruckus about the secret money-laundering of Old Man Acme. You know, most people think that is how the University receives most of its funds, through the mob families out of Chicago. And I would be willing to bet that these faculty figured out the connection and were ready to tell the Looney Police." Dr. Fudd-Einstein spoke lower, fearing that somebody would overhear their conversation.

Dr. Fudd-Einstein then pressed Enter on the keyboard and waited for the results. The massive computer roared to life... and when I say roared, I mean it literally *roared*. All the hidden bells, whistles, and alarm clocks in its secret compartments came out and created such a loud racket that classes across the university had to come to a stand-still until it finished computing.

Once it was completed, the computer listed 4 names:

**********************SUSPECTS********************************

Yosemite Sam ("Looney" Insane Asylum)

Wile E. Coyote (deceased)

Foghorn Leghorn (whereabouts unknown)

Granny (1313 Mockingbird Lane, Toon Town USA)

Dr. Fudd-Einstein and Professor Bird looked on in silence. They could not believe their eyes. The greatest computer on the Gulf of Mexico seaboard just released the most obscure results imaginable.

"There seems to be a mistake. Perhaps something is off," Professor Bird asked, still unable to believe the results.

"Not possible; the Acme Computer takes into account every kind of connection available. It considers affiliations to groups, and affiliations those groups have to other groups. It checks the FBI, CIA, British intelligence, NAACP, AARP, NSA, JAG, TWA, EPA, FDA, USWA, R, MAPLE, SPSS, SAS, and Ben & Jerry's files to identify possible links, creating the most powerful computer in the world... with a tweak of Toon fanaticism," Dr. Fudd-Einstein proclaimed, being a proud co-founder of the Acme Computer Technology.

"Wait a minute, Ben & Jerry? What would eating ice cream have to do with anything?" Professor Bird inquired.

"It is in the works now, but a few of my fellow statistician colleagues are trying to find a mathematical model to link the type of ice cream consumed to the type of person they might become. Assassins always ate vanilla with chocolate sprinkles, a little known fact they would tell you about Oswald and Booth," Dr. Fudd-Einstein declared.

"I've heard about this. My forensics graduate students are trying to identify car thieves with either rocky road or mint chocolate chip... so far, the pattern is showing a clear trend with chocolate chip," Professor Bird declared.

"Well, what do we know about these suspects, Twee?" Dr. Fudd-Einstein asked.

"Yosemite Sam was locked up after trying to rob that bank in the West Borough. Apparently his guns were switched and he was sent the Acme Kids Joke Gun and they blew up in his face.

The containers of peroxide they contained turned all of his facial hair red. Some little child is running around Toon Town with a pair of .38's to this day.

"Wile E. Coyote was that psychopath working for the Yahtzee - the fanatics who believed that Toons were superior to Humans. He strapped sticks of Acme Dynamite to his chest to be a martyr for the cause, but before he got to the middle of Toon Town, this defective TNT blew him up. Not a single other person – Toon or Human – was even close.

"Foghorn Leghorn is the most infamous Dog Kidnapper of all times. He goes to the homes of prominent Dog citizens and holds one of their relatives for ransom. If they refuse to pay, he sends them to the pound. Either way, they're sure stuck in the dog house," Professor Bird laughed. Dr. Fudd-Einstein didn't seem amused, so Professor Bird continued.

"Granny is the most beloved alumnus of Acme-Looney University. She was in the first graduating class and gives graciously each year to the university. Without her continued financial support, we wouldn't have the jobs we do. She worked as a parking attendant at the University lots... wait a minute, take a look at this," Professor Bird said as he scrolled down in the police information. "Granny's signature is on each of these faculty members' **parking** tickets. Kind of odd, considering the Chief-of-Parking signed each personally. The deceased had from as few as 1 ticket to as many as 18. All tickets were unpaid.

"And look at this, Granny married Old Man Acme after graduation. He was a resident of Chicago and rumored to be a consigliere to one of the most prominent crime families in Chicago, the Chuck Jones/Warner Crime Family," Professor Bird read from the screen as a cold feeling of terror rose from the pit of his stomach.

"Say, don't you live at her house? Wow, you're living under the same roof as one of the greatest criminals/murderers of all time!" Dr. Fudd-Einstein said in awe and sarcasm.

"I would never have suspected her, but I guess it makes sense. She is older, so she doesn't need near the amount of sleep as a younger person. She has access to all of the vehicles so she can copy license plate numbers and follow them to their houses. She has the finances to pay for this kind of massive campaign on behalf of the Mob, and she hates anyone that even remotely smells like smoke," Professor Bird explained, wishing to have his hit of nicotine at this time.

"Well, I guess there is nothing left to do but to call Police Chief Runner and have him arrest her," Dr. Fudd-Einstein explained as he began dialing. "What I can't understand is how in the world the Police Chief sent me all of this information and somehow seemed to screw it up."

"What do you mean?" inquired Professor Bird.

"Well, look here. The data file from the Chief's email shows 168 murders, but there have only been 166. This doesn't make any sense. I'll have to straighten it out. Hey, wait a minute. Look at this, Person #167 and Person #168 seem to match our stats. But how can that be?"

It was at this moment that our two heroes were shot from behind and fell over the computer, dead. The killer hit Delete on the computer and walked out slowly (considering they had arthritis) and cackling loudly in the now quiet computer lab.

And so, I guess my question to you the reader is, did Granny murder 168 people, or did the murderer slip through the cracks of justice? You be the statistician and come to your own conclusion.

Detective Pyork E. Pig
End File

Bibliography

[1] Daniel Adler and Duncan Murdoch. *rgl: 3D visualization device system (OpenGL)*, 2009. R package version 0.87. Available from: `http://CRAN.R-project.org/package=rgl`. 5

[2] A. Agresti and B. A. Coull. Approximate is better than "exact" for interval estimation of binomial proportions. *The American Statistician*, 52:119–126, 1998.

[3] Alan Agresti. *Categorical Data Analysis*. Wiley, 2002. 211

[4] Tom M. Apostol. *Calculus*, volume II. Wiley, second edition, 1967. 339

[5] Tom M. Apostol. *Calculus*, volume I. Wiley, second edition, 1967. 339

[6] Robert B. Ash and Catherine Doleans-Dade. *Probability & Measure Theory*. Harcourt Academic Press, 2000. 339

[7] Peter J. Bickel and Kjell A. Doksum. *Mathematical Statistics*, volume I. Prentice Hall, 2001. 221

[8] Patrick Billingsley. *Probability and Measure*. Wiley Interscience, 1995. 118, 339

[9] Ben Bolker. *emdbook: Ecological models and data (book support)*, 2009. R package version 1.2. Available from: `http://CRAN.R-project.org/package=emdbook`. 172

[10] Bruce L. Bowerman, Richard O'Connell, and Anne Koehler. *Forecasting, Time Series, and Regression: An Applied Approach*. South-Western College Pub, 2004.

[11] P. J. Brockwell and R. A. Davis. *Time Series and Forecasting Methods*. Springer, second edition, 1991. 26

[12] Neal L. Carothers. *Real Analysis*. Cambridge University Press, 2000. 339

[13] George Casella and Roger L. Berger. *Statistical Inference*. Duxbury Press, 2002. vii, 168, 183, 198

[14] Scott Chasalow. *combinat: combinatorics utilities*, 2009. R package version 0.0-7. Available from: `http://CRAN.R-project.org/package=combinat`. 66

[15] Erhan Cinlar. *Introduction to Stochastic Processes*. Prentice Hall, 1975.

[16] William S. Cleveland. *The Elements of Graphing Data*. Hobart Press, 1994.

[17] Fortran code by Alan Genz and R code by Adelchi Azzalini. *mnormt: The multivariate normal and t distributions*, 2009. R package version 1.3-3. Available from: `http://CRAN.R-project.org/package=mnormt`. 172

[18] R core members, Saikat DebRoy, Roger Bivand, and others: see COPYRIGHTS file in the sources. *foreign: Read Data Stored by Minitab, S, SAS, SPSS, Stata, Systat, dBase, ...*, 2010. R package version 0.8-39. Available from: `http://CRAN.R-project.org/package=foreign`. 6

[19] Peter Dalgaard. *Introductory Statistics with R*. Springer, 2008. Available from: `http://staff.pubhealth.ku.dk/~pd/ISwR.html`. viii

[20] A. C. Davison and D. V. Hinkley. *Bootstrap Methods and Their Applications*. Cambridge University Press, 1997.

[21] Thomas J. DiCiccio and Bradley Efron. Bootstrap confidence intervals. *Statistical Science*, 11:189–228, 1996.

[22] Evgenia Dimitriadou, Kurt Hornik, Friedrich Leisch, David Meyer, and Andreas Weingessel. *e1071: Misc Functions of the Department of Statistics (e1071), TU Wien*, 2009. R package version 1.5-22. Available from: `http://CRAN.R-project.org/package=e1071`. 40

[23] Richard Durrett. *Probability: Theory and Examples*. Duxbury Press, 1996.

[24] Rick Durrett. *Essentials of Stochastic Processes*. Springer, 1999.

[25] Christophe Dutang, Vincent Goulet, and Mathieu Pigeon. actuar: An r package for actuarial science. *Journal of Statistical Software*, 2008. to appear. 154

[26] Brian Everitt. *An R and S-Plus Companion to Multivariate Analysis*. Springer, 2007.

[27] Gerald B. Folland. *Real Analysis: Modern Techniques and Their Applications*. Wiley, 1999. 339

[28] John Fox. *Applied Regression Analysis, Linear Models, and Related Methods*. Sage, 1997. 287

[29] John Fox. *An R and S Plus Companion to Applied Regression*. Sage, 2002. 294

[30] John Fox. *car: Companion to Applied Regression*, 2009. R package version 1.2-16. Available from: `http://CRAN.R-project.org/package=car`. 288

[31] John Fox, with contributions from Liviu Andronic, Michael Ash, Theophilius Boye, Stefano Calza, Andy Chang, Philippe Grosjean, Richard Heiberger, G. Jay Kerns, Renaud Lancelot, Matthieu Lesnoff, Uwe Ligges, Samir Messad, Martin Maechler, Robert Muenchen, Duncan Murdoch, Erich Neuwirth, Dan Putler, Brian Ripley, Miroslav Ristic, and Peter Wolf. *Rcmdr: R Commander*, 2009. R package version 1.5-4. Available from: `http://CRAN.R-project.org/package=Rcmdr`. 269

[32] Michael Friendly. *Visualizing Categorical Data*. SAS Publishing, 2000.

[33] Andrew Gelman, John B. Carlin, Hal S. Stern, and Donald B. Rubin. *Bayesian Data Analysis*. CRC Press, 2004. 167

[34] Alan Genz, Frank Bretz, Tetsuhisa Miwa, Xuefei Mi, Friedrich Leisch, Fabian Scheipl, and Torsten Hothorn. *mvtnorm: Multivariate Normal and t Distributions*, 2009. R package version 0.9-8. Available from: `http://CRAN.R-project.org/package=mvtnorm`. 172

[35] Rob Goedman, Gabor Grothendieck, Søren Højsgaard, and Ayal Pinkus. *Ryacas: R interface to the yacas computer algebra system*, 2008. R package version 0.2-9. Available from: `http://ryacas.googlecode.com`. 165

[36] Gregor Gorjanc. Using sweave with lyx. *R News*, 1:2–9, 2008. 356

[37] Charles M. Grinstead and J. Laurie Snell. *Introduction to Probability*. American Mathematical Society, 1997. Available from: `http://www.dartmouth.edu/~chance/`. viii

[38] Bettina Grün and Achim Zeileis. Automatic generation of exams in R. *Journal of Statistical Software*, 29(10):1–14, 2009. Available from: `http://www.jstatsoft.org/v29/i10/`. viii

[39] Frank E Harrell, Jr and with contributions from many other users. *Hmisc: Harrell Miscellaneous*, 2009. R package version 3.7-0. Available from: `http://CRAN.R-project.org/package=Hmisc`.

[40] Richard M. Heiberger. *HH: Statistical Analysis and Data Display: Heiberger and Holland*, 2009. R package version 2.1-32. Available from: `http://CRAN.R-project.org/package=HH`. 248

[41] Richard M. Heiberger and Burt Holland. *Statistical Analysis and Data Display: An Intermediate Course with Examples in S-Plus, R, and SAS*. Springer, 2004. Available from: `http://astro.temple.edu/~rmh/HH/`.

[42] Richard M. Heiberger and Erich Neuwirth. *R Through Excel: A Spreadsheet Interface for Statistics, Data Analysis, and Graphics*. Springer, 2009. Available from: `http://www.springer.com/statistics/computanional+statistics/book/978-1-4419-0`

[43] Robert V. Hogg, Joseph W. McKean, and Allen T. Craig. *Introduction to Mathematical Statistics*. Pearson Prentice Hall, 2005. 183

[44] Robert V. Hogg and Elliot A. Tanis. *Probability and Statistical Inference*. Pearson Prentice Hall, 2006. vii

[45] Torsten Hothorn and Kurt Hornik. *exactRankTests: Exact Distributions for Rank and Permutation Tests*, 2006. R package version 0.8-18.

[46] Torsten Hothorn, Kurt Hornik, Mark A. van-de Wiel, and Achim Zeileis. Implementing a class of permutation tests: The coin package. *Journal of Statistical Software*, 28:1–23, 2008.

[47] Norman L. Johnson, Samuel Kotz, and N. Balakrishnan. *Continuous Univariate Distributions*, volume 1. Wiley, second edition, 1994. 137

[48] Norman L. Johnson, Samuel Kotz, and N. Balakrishnan. *Continuous Univariate Distributions*, volume 2. Wiley, second edition, 1995. 137

[49] Norman L. Johnson, Samuel Kotz, and N. Balakrishnan. *Discrete Multivariate Distributions*. Wiley, 1997. 157

[50] Norman L. Johnson, Samuel Kotz, and Adrienne W. Kemp. *Univariate Discrete Distributions*. Wiley, second edition, 1993. 107

[51] Roger W. Johnson. How many fish are in the pond? Available from: `http://www.rsscse.org.uk/ts/gtb/johnson3.pdf`.

[52] G. Jay Kerns. *prob: Elementary Probability on Finite Sample Spaces*, 2009. R package version 0.9-2. Available from: `http://CRAN.R-project.org/package=prob`. 66

[53] G. Jay Kerns, with contributions by Theophilius Boye, Tyler Drombosky, and adapted from the work of John Fox et al. *RcmdrPlugin.IPSUR: An IPSUR Plugin for the R Commander*, 2009. R package version 0.1-6. Available from: `http://CRAN.R-project.org/package=RcmdrPlugin.IPSUR`.

[54] Samuel Kotz, N. Balakrishnan, and Norman L. Johnson. *Continuous Multivariate Distributions*, volume 1: Models and Applications. Wiley, second edition, 2000. 157, 170

[55] Max Kuhn and Steve Weaston. *odfWeave: Sweave processing of Open Document Format (ODF) files*, 2009. R package version 0.7.10. 351

[56] Michael Lavine. *Introduction to Statistical Thought*. Lavine, Michael, 2009. Available from: `http://www.math.umass.edu/~lavine/Book/book.html`. viii

[57] Peter M. Lee. *Bayesian Statistics: An Introduction*. Wiley, 1997. 167

[58] E. L. Lehmann. *Testing Statistical Hypotheses*. Springer-Verlag, 1986. vii

[59] E. L. Lehmann and George Casella. *Theory of Point Estimation*. Springer, 1998. vii

[60] Uwe Ligges. Accessing the sources. *R News*, 6:43–45, 2006. 12, 13

[61] Uwe Ligges and Martin Mächler. Scatterplot3d - an r package for visualizing multivariate data. *Journal of Statistical Software*, 8(11):1–20, 2003. Available from: `http://www.jstatsoft.org`. 179

[62] Jan R. Magnus and Heinz Neudecker. *Matrix Differential Calculus with Applications in Statistics and Econometrics*. Wiley, 1999. 339

[63] John Maindonald and John Braun. *Data Analysis and Graphics Using R*. Cambridge University Press, 2003.

[64] John Maindonald and W. John Braun. *DAAG: Data Analysis And Graphics data and functions*, 2009. R package version 1.01. Available from: `http://CRAN.R-project.org/package=DAAG`.

[65] Ben Mezrich. *Bringing Down the House: The Inside Story of Six M.I.T. Students Who Took Vegas for Millions*. Free Press, 2003. 77

[66] Jeff Miller. Earliest known uses of some of the words of mathematics. Available from: `http://jeff560.tripod.com/mathword.html`. 23

[67] John Neter, Michael H. Kutner, Christopher J. Nachtsheim, and William Wasserman. *Applied Linear Regression Models*. McGraw Hill, third edition, 1996. 209, 267, 287, 294

[68] R Development Core Team. *R: A Language and Environment for Statistical Computing*. R Foundation for Statistical Computing, Vienna, Austria, 2009. ISBN 3-900051-07-0. Available from: `http://www.R-project.org`. 334

[69] C. Radhakrishna Rao and Helge Toutenburg. *Linear Models: Least Squares and Alternatives*. Springer, 1999. 267, 271

[70] Sidney I. Resnick. *A Probability Path*. Birkhauser, 1999. 168, 339

[71] Maria L. Rizzo. *Statistical Computing with R*. Chapman & Hall/CRC, 2008. 297

[72] Christian P. Robert and George Casella. *Monte Carlo Statistical Methods*. Springer, 2004. 297

[73] Kenneth A. Ross. *Elementary Calculus: The Theory of Calculus*. Springer, 1980.

[74] P. Ruckdeschel, M. Kohl, T. Stabla, and F. Camphausen. S4 classes for distributions. *R News*, 6(2):2–6, May 2006. Available from: `http://www.uni-bayreuth.de/departments/math/org/mathe7/DISTR/distr.pdf`. 110, 114, 142, 186, 201

[75] Deepayan Sarkar. *lattice: Lattice Graphics*, 2009. R package version 0.17-26. Available from: `http://CRAN.R-project.org/package=lattice`. 268

[76] F. E. Satterthwaite. An approximate distribution of estimates of variance components. *Biometrics Bulletin*, 2:110–114, 1946. 209

[77] Luca Scrucca. qcc: an r package for quality control charting and statistical process control. *R News*, 4/1:11–17, 2004. Available from: `http://CRAN.R-project.org/doc/Rnews/`. 30

[78] Robert J. Serfling. *Approximation Theorems of Mathematical Statistics*. Wiley, 1980.

[79] Greg Snow. *TeachingDemos: Demonstrations for teaching and learning*, 2009. R package version 2.5. Available from: `http://CRAN.R-project.org/package=TeachingDemos`. 186

[80] James Stewart. *Calculus*. Thomson Brooks/Cole, 2008. 339

[81] Stephen M. Stigler. *The History of Statistics: The Measurement of Uncertainty before 1900*. Harvard University Press, 1986.

[82] Gilbert Strang. *Linear Algebra and Its Applications*. Harcourt, 1988. 339

[83] Barbara G. Tabachnick and Linda S. Fidell. *Using Multivariate Statistics*. Allyn and Bacon, 2006. 39, 40, 294

[84] W. N. Venables and B. D. Ripley. *Modern Applied Statistics with S*. Springer, New York, fourth edition, 2002. ISBN 0-387-95457-0. Available from: `http://www.stats.ox.ac.uk/pub/MASS4`. 212

[85] William N. Venables and David M. Smith. *An Introduction to R*, 2010. Available from: http://www.r-project.org/Manuals. 10, 13, 334

[86] John Verzani. *UsingR: Data sets for the text "Using R for Introductory Statistics"*. R package version 0.1-12. Available from: http://www.math.csi.cuny.edu/UsingR. 21

[87] John Verzani. *Using R for Introductory Statistics*. CRC Press, 2005. Available from: http://www.math.csi.cuny.edu/UsingR/. viii

[88] B. L. Welch. The generalization of "student's" problem when several different population variances are involved. *Biometrika*, 34:28–35, 1947. 209

[89] Hadley Wickham. Reshaping data with the reshape package. *Journal of Statistical Software*, 21(12), 2007. Available from: http://www.jstatsoft.org/v21/i12/paper. 332

[90] Hadley Wickham. *ggplot2: elegant graphics for data analysis*. Springer New York, 2009. Available from: http://had.co.nz/ggplot2/book. viii

[91] Graham Williams. *rattle: A graphical user interface for data mining in R using GTK*, 2009. R package version 2.5.12. Available from: http://CRAN.R-project.org/package=rattle. 8

[92] Peter Wolf and Uni Bielefeld. *aplpack: Another Plot PACKage: stem.leaf, bagplot, faces, spin3R, and some slider functions*, 2009. R package version 1.2.2. Available from: http://CRAN.R-project.org/package=aplpack. 25

[93] Achim Zeileis and Torsten Hothorn. Diagnostic checking in regression relationships. *R News*, 2(3):7–10, 2002. Available from: http://CRAN.R-project.org/doc/Rnews/. 256

Index